The White House and the World

A Global Development Agenda for the Next U.S. President

The White House and the World

A Global Development Agenda for the Next U.S. President

Nancy Birdsall, editor

Center for Global Development
Washington, D.C.

1776 Massachusetts Avenue, N.W.
Washington, D.C. 20036
www.cgdev.org

The White House and the World: A Global Development Agenda for the Next U.S. President may be ordered from:
BROOKINGS INSTITUTION PRESS
c/o HFS
P.O. Box 50370
Baltimore, MD 21211-4370
Tel.: 800/537-5487, 410/516-6956
Fax: 410/516-6998
Internet: www.brookings.edu

Library of Congress Cataloging-in-Publication Data

The White House and the world : a global development agenda
for the next U.S. president / Nancy Birdsall, editor.
p. cm.
ISBN-13: 978-1-933286-24-2 (alk. paper)
ISBN-10: 1-933286-24-5 (alk. paper)
1. United States—Foreign economic relations—Developing countries.
2. Developing countries—Foreign economic relations—United States.
3. Economic assistance, American—Developing countries.
I. Birdsall, Nancy. II. Title.
HF1456.5.D44W55 2008 2008012536
338.91'73—dc22

Editing and typesetting by Communications Development Incorporated, Washington, D.C.

Center for Global Development

The Center for Global Development is an independent, nonprofit policy research organization dedicated to reducing global poverty and inequality and to making globalization work for the poor. Through a combination of research and strategic outreach, the Center actively engages policymakers and the public to influence the policies of the United States, other rich countries, and such institutions as the World Bank, the International Monetary Fund, and the World Trade Organization to improve the economic and social development prospects in poor countries. The Center's Board of Directors bears overall responsibility for the Center and includes distinguished leaders of nongovernmental organizations, former officials, business executives, and some of the world's leading scholars of development. The Center receives advice on its research and policy programs from the Board and from an Advisory Committee that comprises respected development specialists and advocates. The Center's president works with the Board, the Advisory Committee, and the Center's senior staff in setting the research and program priorities and approves all formal publications. The Center is supported by an initial significant financial contribution from Edward W. Scott Jr. and by funding from philanthropic foundations and other organizations.

Contents

for all the world's citizens, Americans included—the next president should appoint a cabinet-level development official within the first weeks of taking office. The appointee should have responsibility for development, akin to that of the National Security Adviser for security, to bring a development perspective to the administration's policies on trade, aid, climate change, and other issues outlined in this book. In addition, the appointee should have a mandate to work with Congress and relevant federal agencies to create a cabinet-level Agency for Sustainable Global Development by the end of the president's (first) term.

Why global development matters for the United States

The next president will face a host of domestic and foreign policy challenges: the war in Iraq, domestic health care, energy and the environment, and Medicare and Social Security financing, among many others. Why make global development a priority?

The answer lies in an unusual convergence of values, politics, and national interests. Helping those in need is a moral imperative that Americans have long embraced. In the past decade, it has also become a bipartisan political opportunity, as when Jesse Helms and Jesse Jackson united in support of debt relief for the poorest countries. But development is also a national security necessity. Never before in U.S. history have so many threats to our prosperity risen within countries in which so many people are still so poor, from Afghanistan and Iraq to China, Nigeria, North Korea, Pakistan, and Venezuela. And perhaps except since the days of the Marshall Plan, never before has there been as great an opportunity for the United States to shore up its image and protect its interests abroad by helping build viable states and improving lives overseas.

Americans' sense of moral obligation to people far away has grown as the international movement of goods, information, and people has accelerated.[1] A surge in manufactured imports; tourism; the threat of terrorism in Bali, AIDS in Africa, child soldiers in Uganda, and the *janjaweed* in Sudan; a dramatic increase in overseas study among young Americans; even the long military entanglements in Afghanistan and Iraq have all increased Americans' awareness of the harsh realities of life for hundreds of millions of people in developing countries.

This new awareness can be seen in increased private and public support for development efforts. Americans may be weary of the traditional postwar burden of leadership in military security and Middle East problems, but they are increasingly attuned to the plight of the world's poor. Americans' charitable contributions for overseas humanitarian and development work have tripled since 1990.[2] And President Bush won bipartisan support for several foreign aid initiatives, including 100 percent debt relief for thirty of the world's poorest countries; a dramatic increase in foreign aid, from $12.6 billion in 2001 to $23 billion in 2006, the highest level in real terms since 1980 (even excluding the large amounts for Afghanistan and Iraq);[3] and two major new aid programs, the Millennium Challenge Account and the President's Emergency Plan for AIDS Relief.[4]

The rise of a multipolar global economy

As attitudes have shifted at home, economic power is spreading more widely abroad. The United States is no longer the world's hyper-power in economic terms. Although still the world's single largest economy, U.S. gross domestic product, currently about $12 trillion, accounts for a shrinking portion of the world economy, down from about 30 percent in 1960 to 20 percent today (using purchasing power parity exchange rates). By this measure, China's economy is second only to the U.S. economy.[5] And the combined gross domestic products of Brazil, China, India, and Russia, at about $11 trillion in purchasing power parity terms, will soon exceed that of the United States, given their faster growth rates.[6] Include Egypt, Indonesia, Mexico, Nigeria, South Africa, Vietnam, and other emerging market economies and an entirely new picture of the twenty-first century global economy emerges; by 2050, today's emerging economies may well be twice as big as the economies of the Group of Seven (G-7; figure 1).[7]

China and India loom large in the global economy because of their rapid economic growth—10 percent and 7 percent a year respectively in the past two decades—and their billion-plus populations. Americans and citizens of the other G-7 countries currently constitute about 12 percent of the world's population; by 2050, that share will have fallen to less than 9 percent (figure 2). Integrating China into the global economy effectively doubled the size of the global labor force.[8] China will become the largest consumer of energy in the world as early as 2010.[9] Three of the world's five largest companies by market capitalization are Chinese,[10] and India accounted for four of the top ten richest people in the world on Forbes' 2008 list. India's Tata Group and Mittal Steel are now buying European and U.S. firms.

Indeed, in a striking reversal of the textbook prediction that financial capital flows from rich to poor economies, the United States is a net importer of capital from China and other developing countries and in the past decade has become the world's largest sovereign debtor.[11]

Although the rise of a multipolar global economy brings new challenges, this state of affairs is in fact a triumph of successful U.S. policies and

Figure 1. By 2050 the seven big emerging market economies will dwarf the Group of Seven

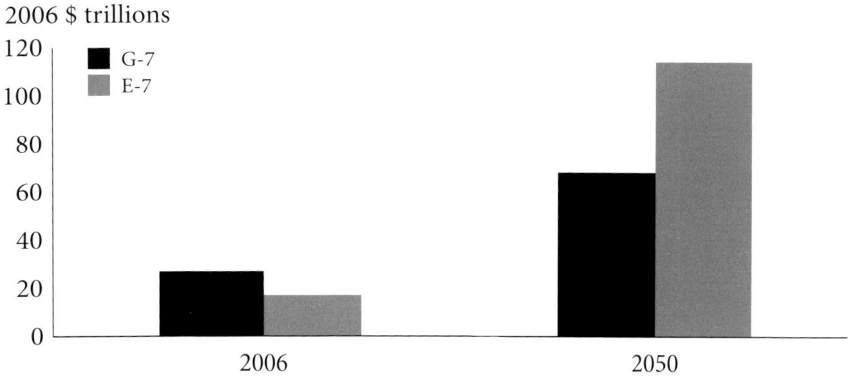

Note: G-7 comprises Canada, France, Germany, Italy, Japan, the United Kingdom, and the United States. E-7 comprises Brazil, China, India, Indonesia, Mexico, Russia, and Turkey.
Source: Hawksworth and Cookson 2008.

Figure 2. Of a projected world population of about 9 billion in 2050, more than 7 billion people will live in what are today developing countries

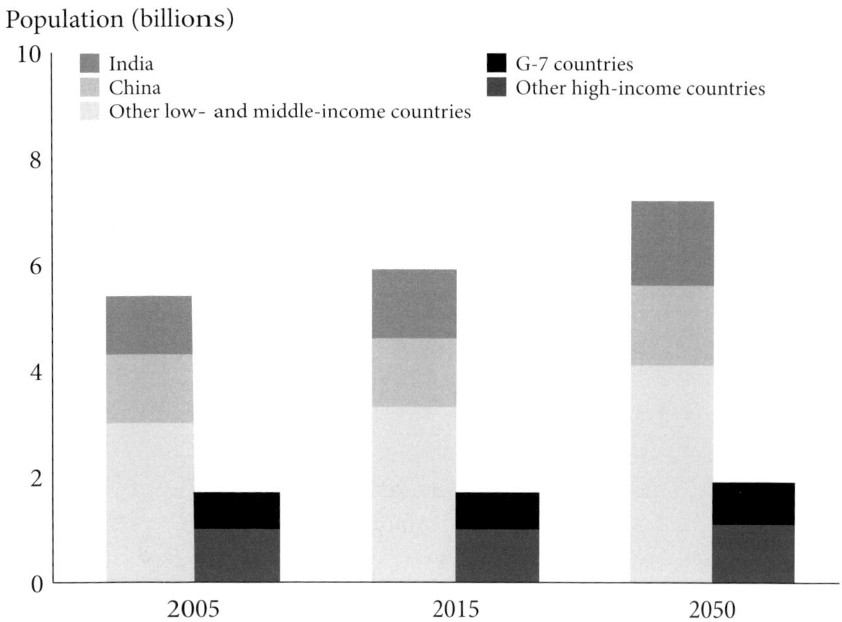

Note: G-7 comprises Canada, France, Germany, Italy, Japan, the United Kingdom, and the United States.
Source: United Nations 2007.

multilateral institution building in the second half of the twentieth century. Since the end of World War II, Democratic and Republican administrations alike have supported open and competitive markets in the interests of global prosperity and security. The emergence of China, India, and other middle-income countries is a sign of success for the U.S. model of economic development based on open markets, private sector–led growth, and rapid technological change. Much the same can be said for other gains in well-being throughout the world. Even in today's low-income countries (with gross domestic product per capita below about $800 a year), life expectancy, literacy, and school enrollment are far higher than they were decades ago, thanks to the diffusion of technologies such as vaccines and antibiotics, of norms such as the value of education and the rights of girls and women, and of democratic systems for holding leaders accountable.

With this success has come interdependence and opportunity. More than 45 percent of U.S. exports go to developing countries, up from 39 percent two decades ago.[12] An estimated 10 percent of U.S. jobs—about 12 million—depend directly on exports. These jobs typically pay 13–18 percent more than the average U.S. wage.[13] Rapid growth in middle-income countries has meant a dramatic globalization of opportunities for U.S. investors, producers, and entrepreneurs. For one thing, an emerging developing-country middle class (with per capita incomes of $4,000 and above, excluding the richest) will soon exceed the total population of the United States (figure 3).[14]

Yet many emerging economies, while geopolitically ascendant, still contend with widespread poverty and weak domestic management and governance. In China and India, an estimated 1.5 billion people still live on less than $2 a day. In India, approximately 2 million children die before age five, and 21 million children of primary school age are not in school.[15] In Mexico and South Africa, high inequality is associated with U.S.-style globalization, complicating democratic politics. In Egypt and Pakistan, ethnic and religious tensions are fueled by the lack of political rights, which are associated with U.S. support for the current regimes. In oil-rich Nigeria and Venezuela, corruption plagues public services. In many developing countries, including ones with responsible leadership, management and capacity constraints deeply undermine the good intentions of willing but weak governments in their efforts to reduce poverty.

The risks for Americans

These problems create risks for Americans. One is familiar: anti-Americanism.

Four other risks are newer and more challenging: weak and failing states, climate change, emerging infectious disease, and the growing irrelevance and dysfunction of international financial and development

Figure 3. The growing developing-country middle class will soon exceed the total population of the United States

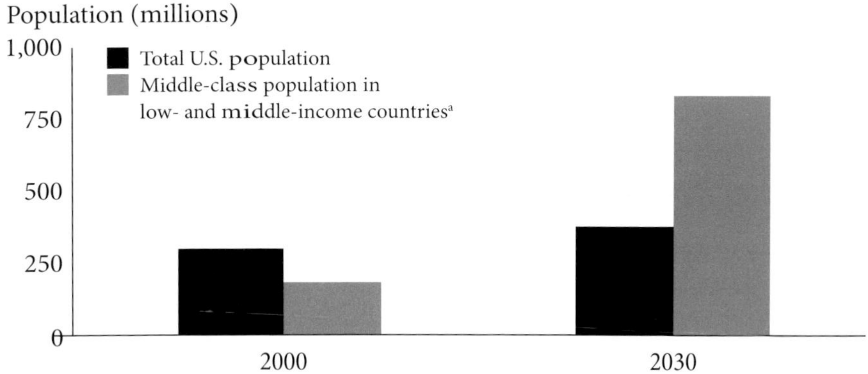

a. Defined as households with per capita income between $4,000 and $17,000 in 2000 international dollars—that is, people who are not rich but who nonetheless have significant consumer purchasing power.
Source: World Bank 2006; United Nations 2007.

institutions.[16] For the most part, none of these has yet elicited a coherent and effective response from U.S. policymakers, despite their combination of risks and opportunities.

Anti-Americanism. Globalization is associated with U.S. corporate and financial interests and U.S. culture, and the insecurity and inequality that are its companions in many parts of the world are easily blamed on the United States. Where democracy is weak and the benefits of globalization are not broadly shared, a backlash by the excluded can easily morph into anger at the United States and opposition to U.S. values, institutions, investment, and trade. When anti-Americanism runs deep, diplomacy is disarmed and defense becomes a poor substitute for development options forgone. The result is increased risks to U.S. security and commercial interests—not only in the Middle East but also in Bolivia and Ecuador in our own hemisphere. This is especially dangerous when the United States is seen to be pursuing a unilateral agenda.

Weak and failing states. More than fifty of the world's poorest, least-developed countries are fragile or failing states with one or more of the following characteristics: they are unable to control their own territory, they cannot meet the basic needs of their people, or they lack a minimum amount of legitimacy among their citizens. These countries are weak links in the chain of global security and well-being, increasing risks from the rapid spread of infectious diseases, illegal narcotics trafficking, terrorism, and even unsecured nuclear weapons. Among these states are not only Afghanistan, Iraq, and North Korea but also the Democratic Republic of Congo, Myanmar, Nepal, Pakistan, Somalia, and Sudan.[17] Even countries such as Colombia, Kenya, Mexico, and the Philippines struggle with drug trafficking, local insurgencies, and volatile ethnic factionalism that create risks and costs for the United States and other countries. Finding ways for the United States to support development in these countries constitutes an investment in a safer world in which security relies less on military interventions and more on capable partners.

Climate change. Global warming will quickly reach a catastrophic tipping point unless both developing countries and developed countries cut greenhouse gas emissions.[18] But rapidly growing developing countries with high levels of poverty will not switch to low-carbon-emissions electricity and other sustainable technologies without technical and financial transfers from the United States and other rich countries. This is a new type of problem in which development success, a good thing, will generate negative spillovers of immense concern to the United States and the rest of the world—unless there is an effective international agreement to create and share new energy technologies. The challenge is most evident in large middle-income and emerging market economies—such as Brazil, China, India, Mexico, and South Africa—but it also extends to small, low-income countries as well, where rapid deforestation and growing demand for electricity contribute to rising greenhouse gas emissions. To deal with this global challenge effectively requires not only multilateral engagement with governments in the post-Kyoto negotiating process led by the United Nations (where the virtual absence of the United States for the past eight years has been so costly to our image and to the planet) but also engagement with the business groups and with civil society and environmental activists in developing countries. That requires a deep understanding of the political imperative of rapid growth and development in those countries and a willingness to collaborate on investments and provide support that will maximize income growth in a way that does not push the planet over the tipping point to disastrous climate change.

Emerging infectious disease. SARS (severe acute respiratory syndrome) was contained, but its example illustrates the risk of the rapid spread of a pandemic flu around the world. Infectious disease flourishes where resources are limited and public health infrastructure inadequate—including in China, much of Africa, and many other developing countries. The U.S. response so far has been to invest in preparedness at home.[19] But the primary prevention needed, to protect Americans and citizens everywhere, is in developing countries.

Growing irrelevance and dysfunction of the international financial and development institutions. The United States was the leading architect of the multilateral institutions meant to support sustainable development around the world: the United Nations and many of its agencies, the International Monetary Fund, the World Bank, and the regional development banks. These institutions were set up in a world with concentrated economic power, with a shortage of savings and underdeveloped local capital markets in developing countries, and with high barriers to cross-border trade and investment. Power and influence were naturally concentrated with the economies that mattered most for global stability and growth: the United States and the other trans-Atlantic powers. But the world has changed. It is no longer possible to define a small oligarchy and assign it global leadership or to predict which economies are the stabilizers and engines of growth and which are the sources of heightened risk, as the U.S. role at the epicenter of the turmoil in global financial markets in 2008 amply demonstrated. Yet the United States and its traditional Western allies have yet to meaningfully ease their firm grip on positions, power, and decisionmaking in these institutions. Without the incentives for full engagement that responsibility and influence would bring, China, India, and other large emerging market economies no longer regard these institutions as responsive to their own needs or as valuable forums for collective action. The legitimacy and effectiveness of these institutions are thus at risk at the very moment when, in an increasingly interdependent system, the traditional powers need them most.[20]

Learning to contend with new risks. How can the United States more effectively address these and other problems of global interdependence? Just as in the post–World War II era, when we invested heavily in the prosperity and security of our European allies in our own interest, we must now make a comparable investment in understanding and helping solve the problems of the more than 100 low- and middle-income countries. The challenge is not solely about "country relations" in the traditional foreign policy sense; it also includes learning to contend with the risks of powerful forces outside the traditional foreign policy realm that threaten prosperity and security everywhere.

In sum, the twenty-first century is bringing tectonic shifts in the political and economic landscape. Developing countries are no longer part of a marginal "third" world. The good news is that a coherent U.S. strategy to help improve the lives of billions of people beyond our shores is not only a political and security imperative, it is also fully consistent with the values Americans have long promoted for the larger world.

What to do: leadership in the fullest sense

What exactly should the next president do? The chapters in this volume offer a wealth of practical suggestions for ways to make the United States a true leader in an increasingly interdependent world. They fall into four categories: deploying U.S. technological and business prowess; ensuring that U.S. trade, migration, and investment policies are development-friendly; modernizing U.S. foreign aid; and leading fundamental reform of the international development institutions to give more power to developing countries.

The net cost of the proposals highlighted is surprisingly low in budgetary terms. Including an estimated $45 billion from annual auctions of emissions rights, total net costs amount to just $7 billion a year (table 1), or about 19 days of "Iraq time" in 2007.[21] Indeed some proposals, such as doubling investment in renewable energy technologies, could easily generate net gains in jobs and economic growth for the U.S. economy. The proposals pose more of a political leadership challenge than a fiscal one. Take trade, where Americans have become unduly pessimistic about our own competitiveness. Overall, compared with defense and even diplomacy, the "D" of development is a bargain for the United States and the world.

1. Put U.S. technological and business prowess to work for the world's poor: health, climate change, and agriculture

In a world awash in capital, what is the U.S. comparative advantage in addressing global poverty and social dysfunction? The answer involves the depth of its world-class public and private scientific research and post-graduate educational institutions, its near-monopoly of venture capital, and the U.S. entrepreneurial acumen and knack for innovation. There is tremendous promise, for example, in new scientific developments where U.S. labs are at the forefront, such as the rapid sequencing of the genomes of pathogens that will yield new life-saving medicines.[22] At the same time, the United States is also the world's leader in taking science from the lab to the market in the form of commercially viable new technologies, and it leads the world in such key twenty-first-century fields as information technology, pharmaceuticals, and graduate technical education. Here is a domain where the U.S. president can confidently assert U.S. leadership.

Ruth Levine (chapter 1) and David Wheeler (chapter 2) discuss practical proposals for U.S. research and technological contributions in two key areas: health and climate change. In both of these areas as well as in agriculture,

Table 1. Net annual budget cost of the recommendations in *The White House and the World* is about $7 billion

	Average annual budget cost (2008 $ millions)[a]	Significant political cost	Significant bureaucratic cost
1. Put U.S. technological and business prowess to work for the world's poor: global health, climate change, and tropical agriculture			
Health			
Refocus priorities at National Institutes of Health to include diseases that disproportionately affect developing countries	2,300		✔
Work with developing countries to create an international clinical trials system	500		
Pass legislation creating a framework to fund advance market commitments	1,000[b]	✔	
Establish a global health corps	85		
Climate change			
Establish a carbon charge or cap and trade system to limit emissions	(Revenue) 45,000	✔	
Commit more public funds to energy research and development	10,000		
Cooperate in creating a multilateral clean energy program that accelerates the switch to renewable energy sources everywhere	12,500	✔	
Contribute to multilateral Climate Change Adaptation Fund and Forest Carbon Partnership Facility	17,500		
Agriculture			
Double the 2006 financial commitment to the Consultative Group on International Agricultural Research	120		
Sponsor an advance market commitment to encourage private sector research on dryland and tropical agriculture	1,000[c]		

(continued)

Table 1. Net annual budget cost of the recommendations in *The White House and the World* is about $7 billion (continued)

	Average annual budget cost (2008 $ millions)[a]	Significant political cost	Significant bureaucratic cost
2. Share prosperity: trade, migration, and investment policies			
Development-friendly trade policies			
Send Congress legislation providing duty-free, quota free access for the world's poorest countries and most countries of Sub-Saharan Africa	(Lost tarriff revenue) 1,000	✔	
Simplify and make permanent existing preference arrangements such as the African Growth and Opportunity Act	None	✔	
Call for a bipartisan review of U.S. farm policy	None		
Support transfers to developing countries for safety nets to protect those who lose from trade in the short-term	500[d]		
Desist from enforcing intellectual property rules that exceed WTO standards	None		
Work constructively to help the poorest countries' importation of lower cost medicines under current TRIP rules	None		
Development-friendly migration policies			
Raise the number of visas granted to highly skilled workers to levels comparable to those of our international competitors	None		
Work toward bilateral agreements with sending countries with respect to expanding the number of low-skilled workers, ensuring that sending countries will take responsibility for bringing workers home	None	✔	

	Average annual budget cost (2008 $ millions)[a]	Significant political cost	Significant bureaucratic cost
Development-friendly investment policies			
For Africa, use the Overseas Private Investment Corporation and the Export-Import Bank to encourage the development of a continental road and power system	None		
Propose a new regional investment agreement in the Western Hemisphere to boost investment through a collective effort to set standards for key determinants of the investment climate	50		
Close loopholes regarding corrupt payments in the Foreign Corrupt Practices Act	None	✔	
3. Modernize outmoded foreign assistance programs			
Work with Congress to overhaul U.S. development assistance, including new legislation and creation of a new organizational structure with the U.S. Agency for International Development (USAID), the Millennium Challenge Corporation, and the President's Emergency Plan for AIDS Relief (PEPFAR) under a single cabinet-level agency	None	✔	
Commit to contributing 25 percent of any increase in the proportion of foreign aid to multilateral channels	None		
Take leadership on truly independent evaluation of U.S. and multilateral aid programs, including by joining the new International Initiative for Impact Evaluation	1.5		
Shift funding and responsibility for development programs in Afghanistan, Iraq, and other insecure settings now concentrated in the Pentagon to USAID	None		✔

(continued)

Table 1. Net annual budget cost of the recommendations in *The White House and the World* is about $7 billion (continued)

	Average annual budget cost (2008 $ millions)[a]	Significant political cost	Significant bureaucratic cost
Establish a large well-funded contingency fund for unforeseen disaster events	100[e]	✔	
Create a civilian "expeditionary" capacity within the State Department and USAID that can be deployed to crisis countries	250	✔	
Strengthen substantially the prevention component of PEPFAR	1,000	✔	
Allocate new AIDS treatment funding to multilateral programs to help manage the AIDS treatment entitlement	None		✔
4. Reform international development institutions to give greater influence and power to developing countries			
Work with other members of the World Bank to establish a credible selection process for the next Bank president.	None	✔	✔
Ensure full engagement of developing countries in the financing and management of the global "goods" stressed throughout this essay	None		✔

a. Estimated costs are taken from costs indicated in the chapters of this volume except where indicated. In most cases they refer to direct costs and exclude minor administrative costs and the costs of domestic programs that are referred to in this introduction and in some chapters.

b. One-time cost. Were the framework created, the U.S. commitment (given a successful malaria product) could be on the order of $1 billion (see Barder and others 2005).

c. One-time cost. Given a framework (see above under health), the U.S. commitment (given a successful product) could be on the order of $1 billion.

d. Annual spending on domestic Trade Adjustment Assistance programs is about $1 billion. U.S. spending on foreign aid in 2007 was about $25 billion.

e. See the Commission on Weak States and U.S. National Security 2004.

whatever resources are deployed will likely yield multiple returns for Americans and the world's poor.

Health. Few issues can compete with health to attract the interest and sympathy of Americans for poor people living far away. The bipartisan support for the Bush administration's initiative to massively fund and energetically implement the President's Emergency Plan for AIDS Relief (PEPFAR) is an obvious example. The next president should take advantage of the enthusiasm for supporting improved health worldwide by exploiting more fully and more visibly the U.S. potential contribution through its impressive research and development capabilities.

The U.S. government is the world's single biggest funder of biomedical research (on the order of $28 billion a year). But it could much better deploy this strength to improve health in poor countries while reducing health risks here and around the world. The next president should:

- Ask the National Institutes of Health to define priorities for additional research on vaccines and drugs that would benefit people in poor countries.
- Encourage the National Institutes of Health, in cooperation with the Food and Drug Administration, to work with international partners in creating an international clinical trial system that fully engages developing countries' own regulatory and ethical review agencies.
- Include the outcome in the subsequent Budget Message of the President.[23]

Still, public resources pale in comparison with what the profit-making private sector could bring to the table. The next president should also:

- Develop and send to Congress legislation to create a framework for funding of advance market commitments—guaranteed purchases of socially desirable new products that meet prespecified criteria, designed to create incentives for private firms to develop products that otherwise have limited market appeal, often because their potential consumers are poor. The lack of a framework was one factor constraining U.S. participation in a current advance market commitment initiative to jump-start production of a pneumococcal vaccine suited to the needs of low-income countries. With a framework in place, the United States could be a serious player in developing an advance market commitment for malaria drugs and an AIDS vaccine.

  A significant and growing number of well-educated young Americans are both passionately interested in global health and eager for an opportunity to serve overseas.[24] To reinforce this trend the next president should:

- Establish a Global Health Corps as a kind of "public health Peace Corps" to support U.S. health professionals for two-year periods of service in poor countries.

Climate change. The responsibility of the United States to exploit and export its technical know-how is especially urgent in the case of global warming. In rich countries, the impact of climate change over the next few decades will be counted largely in higher economic costs—of seawalls along the coasts and increased insurance protection against more volatile weather. The impact of climate change in Bangladesh and other low-lying areas will be much harsher, potentially displacing hundreds of millions of poor people due to rising sea levels. In much of the tropical belt, climate change will be counted in sharply reduced agricultural productivity due to drought and in the expanded range of malaria and other diseases.[25]

To contribute to an international effort to bring climate change under control, the next president should:

- Take the lead—even unilaterally—in setting federal emissions limits on greenhouse gasses and enforcing them through effective market mechanisms (carbon charges or cap-and-trade) at home. Such measures are key to increasing incentives for private U.S. investment in low-carbon renewable energy, thus accelerating innovation in this crucial area.[26]
- Commit far more public resources to energy research and development (even doubling spending relative to nominal GDP would bring resources back to the 1988 level of just 0.04 percent of gross domestic product).[27]
- Undo the current subsidies for ethanol and other biofuels that are diverting grains and other commodities from food to energy markets and raising world food prices, with significant environmental costs at home and no clear benefit to the climate.[28]
- Make the United States a leader in financing a multilateral clean energy program that strategically invests in private research and development, buys finished products in volume to accelerate the achievement of scale economies, and subsidizes the costs of energy production in developing countries using solar and other renewable technologies.[29]

Agriculture. Sharply rising global food prices in spring 2008 illustrated the terrible consequences to the world's poor when food demand suddenly appears to outrun supply. Will supply catch up as it has always done in the past? Or do rising food prices signal the onset of a new kind of era in which elevated food prices are a long-term reality? Three key changes suggest that the second view may have more credence today than in the past: rising demand for more and more energy-intensive food in fast-growing Asia; the competition that new biofuels are posing for land; and the effect of climate-change-induced drought on global agricultural supplies. If these factors do herald a new, higher-cost food world, they would underscore the need to increase agricultural production and productivity in the many low-income countries with a comparative advantage in agriculture. Beyond what the World Bank and other international donors are doing,[30] the United States also has a critical role in raising agricultural potential and rural incomes in these poor countries by tapping the full potential of its large and sophisticated private and public research and development network to create and test products and methods applicable in tropical agriculture.

The United States can:

- Reverse the precipitous decline in its contributions to the Consultative Group on International Agricultural Research, the international network of agricultural research institutions that gave birth in the 1970s to the first Green Revolution.[31] The next U.S. president should not ignore the evidence that agricultural research has yielded among the highest single economic rates of return of any investment anytime anywhere.[32]
- Complement increased funding for agricultural research with an advance market commitment to encourage research on dryland and tropical agriculture by the impressive private and university agricultural science system in the United States. In 2006, Monsanto and Syngenta spent a total of $1.5 billion on research and development, while total spending by the international public agricultural research institutes amounted to only about $400 million.[33] As with health, an advance market commitment would create the market-like incentive needed to stimulate private investment in new plant strains and technologies that could generate a new Green Revolution in Africa and other low-income settings.

2. Share prosperity: trade, migration, and investment policies

The next president will need to convince Americans that globalization is not going away and that its benefits exceed its costs.[34] Though gains in jobs and income exceed losses in the aggregate, there are some losers. They deserve much more attention by the next president, who should work with Congress to strengthen domestic policies to cushion the effects, including universal health insurance and much greater investments in job retraining and wage insurance, to allow for job mobility, reduce costs that burden export competitiveness, and eliminate a deep source of anxiety for U.S. families.[35]

Along with supporting domestic policies and programs to protect vulnerable Americans and discourage protectionism, the president should emphasize the relationship between policy choices and poverty reduction in developing countries. Development-friendly globalization is especially cheap in budgetary terms—but especially demanding of political leadership.

Development-friendly trade policies. U.S. markets are generally open, and U.S. performance on trade policy is better than that of many other rich countries. But our trade regime still discriminates against developing countries, including some of the poorest (box 1). Barriers to imports of sugar, dairy, and clothing and subsidies to U.S. producers of cotton and other agricultural commodities deprive poor countries of export revenues, jobs, and wages in the sectors where they are most competitive. Moreover, the United States must share blame with Europe and Japan if the Doha Round of trade talks fails; it is foundering in large part (and, ironically, given high food prices as this book goes to press) because of rich-country agricultural protection. Taxpayer-financed subsidies to U.S. cotton producers earning on average more than $200,000 a year have been a particular embarrassment. These subsidies depress world cotton prices, undercutting the market for the sole cash crop of desperately poor households in West Africa.

U.S. tariffs hit poor countries hardest. The United States collects as much on imports from Bangladesh as from the United Kingdom, though imports from the United Kingdom are twelve times as great in dollar terms.[36] And in addition to reducing poor countries' access to our rich consumer market, U.S. tariff revenue on those countries' imports often exceeds our aid to those countries! In 2006, the duties the United States collected on Bangladeshi and Cambodian imports (approximately $850 million) dwarfed the $120 million in U.S. aid they received.[37] Tariffs on imports from India, Indonesia, Sri Lanka, and Thailand bring more than $1 billion into the U.S. treasury every six months—more than the entire U.S. aid package for those tsunami-hit countries in 2005.

When trade barriers are removed—for example, under the African Growth and Opportunity Act, which provides preferential access to such countries as Kenya and Lesotho—the result is the creation of jobs, especially in textiles and apparel, sectors that tend to employ women with little education.[38]

To get serious about development-friendly trade policies, the next president must tackle powerful vested interests: the farm, textile, and pharmaceutical lobbies. Despite record high prices, the farm lobby continues to push

Box 1. The Commitment to Development Index

First published in 2003, the annual Commitment to Development Index rates and ranks nearly two dozen rich industrial countries on how much their policies help or hurt developing countries. Countries are scored in seven policy domains, and the average of their scores is the overall Commitment to Development Index score (table 1). Scores are scaled so that 5 means "average." The scoring is designed to measure how well countries live up to their potential to help, which allows small countries such as Denmark and the Netherlands to score high while the United States, though it is the world's largest donor and its largest market for exports, ranks two-thirds of the way down at 14. On the index, the United States is not a development leader (table 2).

The index offers a useful diagnostic for U.S. development policy. Despite the Bush administration's substantial aid increases and U.S. tax deductibility of private giving by individuals and foundations, the United States is still weak on aid. Its public giving, at $21.5 billion in 2006, amounted to 0.16 percent of gross domestic product, or 20 cents per person per day. Private giving of $9.0 billion, equal to another 0.7 percent of gross domestic product or 8 cents per person per day, still left the country at the bottom of aid quantity rankings. And nearly a quarter of the government aid went to Iraq; this the index discounts at 90 percent because of the high corruption and weak rule of law there.

The United States is stronger on opening its markets for goods from developing countries. And it scores high for positioning naval fleets to secure sea lanes for this trade—a measure that is meant to proxy for the country's long-standing role as a hegemonic protector of the international economic order.

The United States is surprisingly middling, however, when it comes to allowing people from developing countries to enter its labor markets—a reminder that Europe too is now a major destination for migrants. And it is among the weakest of all countries on environmental policy. After Australia, it is the largest per capita emitter of greenhouse gases among the rated countries and levies the lowest gasoline taxes.

Table 1. Country rankings in the 2007 Commitment to Development Index

Rank	Country	Aid	Trade	Investment	Migration	Environment	Security	Technology	Overall (Average)
1	Netherlands	10.7	5.7	8.0	4.6	7.2	5.4	5.2	6.7
2	Denmark	12.0	5.3	5.8	5.3	5.8	5.9	5.4	6.5
2	Sweden	11.6	5.4	6.9	6.2	5.9	4.3	5.3	6.5
4	Norway	10.5	0.3	7.5	5.4	8.0	7.0	5.6	6.3
5	Canada	4.1	6.8	8.0	5.3	4.3	4.3	6.7	5.6
5	Finland	4.9	5.5	6.5	3.1	7.5	5.7	6.2	5.6
5	New Zealand	3.6	7.2	3.4	6.4	6.8	6.5	5.0	5.6

(continued)

Rank	Country	Aid	Trade	Investment	Migration	Environment	Security	Technology	Overall (Average)
8	United Kingdom	4.8	5.4	8.1	3.1	7.4	5.1	4.3	5.5
9	Austria	2.9	5.3	3.9	11.5	6.1	3.8	4.4	5.4
10	Australia	3.1	7.0	7.6	4.0	4.3	6.7	4.6	5.3
10	Ireland	6.9	5.2	3.4	6.3	7.7	4.8	3.1	5.3
12	Germany	2.6	5.3	8.0	6.2	6.4	3.7	4.3	5.2
13	France	4.0	5.4	6.5	2.9	6.4	3.4	6.9	5.1
13	United States	2.2	6.8	7.0	5.4	2.9	6.3	4.9	5.1
15	Spain	2.9	5.5	7.1	7.3	3.3	2.8	6.0	5.0
16	Belgium	5.7	5.3	6.2	3.5	6.9	2.4	4.5	4.9
17	Portugal	2.4	5.5	6.5	2.3	5.9	5.6	5.2	4.8
18	Italy	2.7	5.6	6.1	2.7	4.7	3.8	5.0	4.4
19	Switzerland	4.5	0.2	6.7	5.5	4.6	3.3	4.9	4.2
20	Greece	2.0	5.4	4.9	2.0	5.2	5.1	3.0	3.9
21	Japan	1.2	1.7	5.9	2.1	4.6	1.8	6.3	3.4

Source: CGD 2007.

Table 2. U.S. development policy strengths and weaknesses in the Commitment to Development Index

Policy	Strengths	Weaknesses
Aid	Large amount of private charitable giving attributable to tax policy.	Low net aid volume as a share of the economy. Large share of tied or partially tied aid. Selectivity: large share of aid to less poor and relatively undemocratic governments.
Trade	Low tariffs on agricultural products. Low agricultural subsidies.	High barriers against textiles. High barriers against apparel.
Investment	Employs foreign tax credits to prevent double taxation of corporate profits earned abroad. Active in the Extractive Industries Transparency Initiative and in the G-8 Anti-Corruption and Transparency Action Plan.	Limits insurance against political risk to domestically owned firms. Employs inappropriate home-country national economic tests for eligibility of projects—a project is formally ineligible if it would cost even one U.S. job. Negligent in identifying bribery and corrupt practices on the part of home-country firms abroad.

Policy	Strengths	Weaknesses
Migration	Large increase during the 1990s in the number of unskilled immigrants from developing countries living in the (rank by share of population: 5). Large share of foreign students from developing countries (79 percent; rank: 7).	Bears small share of the burden of refugees during humanitarian crises (rank: 17).
Environment		High greenhouse gas emissions rate per capita Low gas taxes Has not ratified the Kyoto Protocol on climate change
Security	Has the most military ships in the world stationed in sea lanes important to international trade	High arms exports to poor and undemocratic governments Small financial and personnel contributions to internationally sanctioned peacekeeping and humanitarian interventions over last decade.
Technology	High government expenditure on research and development.	Large share of government research and development expenditure on defense. Low tax subsidy rate for business research and development. Allows patents on plant and animal varieties. Allows patents on software programs Pushes to incorporate into bilateral free trade agreements "TRIPS-plus" measures that restrict the flow of innovations to developing countries.

Source: CGD 2007.

—*David Roodman*

for production-distorting subsidies that are bad for U.S. taxpayers, harm the environment, and, in the case of nonfood crops, hurt the world's poor farmers by depressing global prices.[39] The textile industry continues to fight tariff reductions in the Doha Round and to block extension of preferential access to Bangladesh, Cambodia, and other non-African least-developed countries. The pharmaceutical lobby, after years of pushing for stringent protection of patent rights on life-saving medicines, has finally yielded to a compromise at the World Trade Organization that clarifies the rights of low-income countries to produce and import low-cost generic medicines. And under pressure from international nongovernment organizations, the industry has provided donations and price cuts in the case of patented AIDS drugs. But overall the industry continues to resist the price competition, including from generics, which in a competitive market might well result in broader distribution and access in low-income countries.

Kimberly Elliott (chapter 7) and Carsten Fink and Kimberly Elliott (chapter 8) provide compelling background for the following recommendations on trade and intellectual property issues. The next U.S. president should:

- Work with Congress to pass legislation providing the world's poorest countries and most countries of Sub-Saharan Africa permanent duty-free, quota-free access to the U.S. market,[40] without exceptions, for such protected sectors as sugar and apparel.
- Simplify existing preference arrangements such as the African Growth and Opportunity Act and make them permanent to encourage domestic and foreign investment in potential export sectors.
- Call for a bipartisan review of U.S. farm policy to ensure that future legislation is more consistent with relieving poverty and hunger at home and abroad at a lower cost to U.S. taxpayers.
- Ensure in any new trade negotiations that the United States takes the lead in supporting transfers to help developing countries develop their own safety nets to protect those who lose in the short term.[41]

In the difficult area of intellectual property rights, the next president should build on the initial steps taken last spring to shift U.S. policy from distinctly unfriendly to friendly to development needs and to:

- Desist from enforcing intellectual property rules negotiated in existing bilateral trade agreements that exceed World Trade Organization standards.
- Work constructively to ensure that developing countries are able to import adequate supplies of affordable medicines under current rules in the Trade-Related Intellectual Property Rights Agreement. (Among other benefits, this will help ensure that U.S. money spent to maintain AIDS treatment overseas will be spent cost-effectively.)

Development-friendly migration policies. Although we are a country of immigrants, from a purely development perspective our policies toward people in developing countries who want to come here and work are currently no better than those in Europe (see box 1). Moreover, the United States is losing its traditional dominance as the most desirable destination for high-skilled migrants, partly because other rich countries are aggressively competing to attract them[42] and perhaps because post-9/11 security and bureaucratic obstacles are discouraging interest in coming to work and study here. The biggest obstacle is the current tiny visa quota for high-skilled workers: the annual allotment of 65,000 was exhausted last year in the first three hours of the first day that they were available.

This is silly from the narrow point of view of U.S. interests. Bill Gates has made that point in congressional testimony, arguing that the United States is at grave risk of losing its competitive position in high-technology sectors; indeed, Microsoft has moved some of its operations across the border to Canada so that it can hire more skilled talent from overseas.[43] It is also silly because new evidence increasingly demonstrates the tremendous benefits to the sending countries of having talented citizens abroad. India's software and information technology services have been fueled in part by Indian-Americans' investments in their home country—investments of money but more critically of know-how.

Immigration of less-skilled workers is even more of a political minefield, as the Bush administration discovered in seeking even modest reforms that would have included an expanded guest worker program. That is unfortunate since even modest increases in legal temporary worker immigration to the United States have ended poverty for millions of households in Mexico and other poorer countries—both directly for the emigrants and indirectly through their remittances, their return investments, and the increased demand for schooling that the potential to emigrate provides to young people in poor households.[44]

Like globalization, the cross-border movement of people is bound to increase in this century, despite any country's efforts to confine them—it is an "irresistible force," as one analyst has put it.[45] The attraction the U.S. holds for people everywhere as a land of opportunity and freedom is best treated as an opportunity and a soft power asset. Well managed, it can capture gains for Americans, for migrants themselves, and for their families and communities in developing countries.

Its advantages notwithstanding, successful reform of U.S. immigration policy during the next administration will require outstanding presidential leadership and considerable political finesse. But with those ingredients there is potential to improve Americans' understanding of the issues and generate new, sensible legislation.

Michael Clemens and Sami Bazzi (chapter 9) argue that the next president should:

- Make the case to Americans that, with reasonable border security in place, legal immigration of talented workers from abroad should be considerably expanded because such immigration will keep the United States at the global frontier in new technology and science fields.

- Introduce legislation that would raise the number of visas granted to high-skilled workers to levels at least comparable with those of our international competitors, which is to say from the current number of less than 100,000 to between half a million and one million per year.[46]
- Work toward bilateral agreements with key countries that send large numbers of less-skilled workers, including Mexico, under which the sending country would take responsibility for ensuring that temporary workers return home.[47] A reasonable proposal would be to increase the number of legal and temporary guest workers from the current 100,000 to about 500,000 annually. Close to 500,000 now enter illegally each year, so the real change would be ensuring a fair process for choosing those able to enter, greater respect for the rights of those who are here, and a shared understanding of the benefits and costs of temporary stays.

Development-friendly investment policies. The United States does well on development-friendly investment policy, but as with trade we are in a position to do much better (see box 1). Vijaya Ramachandran (chapter 3), Theodore Moran (chapter 4), Dennis de Tray and Theodore Moran (chapter 5), and Nancy Lee (chapter 6) provide the background and motivation for the next president to seize three major opportunities to make a difference. All three combine U.S. private investment and business acumen with effective public policy to help jump-start private sector–led growth in poor regions:

- First, for Africa, the next president should champion the development of a unified regulatory and financial framework to underpin a continental road and power system. The United States could make this a priority at both the World Bank and the African Development Bank, and it could use its own mechanisms, including the Overseas Private Investment Corporation and the Export-Import Bank, to jump-start the participation of U.S. investment groups in the necessary public-private partnerships. In particular, the tremendous potential for solar thermal power in Africa is an opportunity private investors should not miss.[48]
- Second, in this hemisphere, the next president should propose a new regional agreement to boost investment through a collective effort to set standards for key determinants of the investment climate. A standards-based approach covering business startup rules, licensing, border controls, taxes, access to credit and infrastructure,

environmental and labor protection, and even some aspects of macroeconomic policy would address some of the most important constraints on growth and help spread its gains to those now outside the formal economy.[49]

- Third, on corruption and money laundering, the next president should work to close loopholes regarding corrupt payments in the Foreign Corrupt Practices Act, further strengthen programs to combat money laundering, and expand U.S. engagement with current transparency initiatives such as the U.K.-led Extractive Industry Transparency Initiative on both the local and international levels.[50]

3. Modernize outmoded U.S. foreign assistance programs

Foreign assistance is a central tool of foreign policy and perhaps the most immediate vehicle for restoring America's reputation abroad.[51] But the United States has been far from "smart" in its approach to foreign aid over the past several decades.[52] In fact, there is broad agreement across the political spectrum—in Congress, the current administration, advocacy and service-provision nongovernmental organizations, and independent development policy experts, that U.S. foreign assistance is badly out of date and in need of modernization.[53] The law that shapes U.S. foreign aid policy, the 1961 Foreign Assistance Act, is rapidly approaching its fiftieth anniversary. With amendments and congressional directives responsive to special interests, both for-profit and nonprofit, the act is 500 pages long and has accumulated, like barnacles, a complex set of rules, regulations, and objectives. These have left the U.S. Agency for International Development, the principal agency responsible for delivering aid, foundering and weakened by dramatic losses of experienced staff.

Worse, the U.S. system is incredibly fragmented, with three major aid agencies, increasing Pentagon involvement (confusing ends and means and creating security risks for U.S. aid workers and nongovernmental organizations), and at least fifteen other federal players, making the "whole of government" approach much less than the sum of its parts.

Another problem, tying U.S. aid to U.S. contractors in response to special interests, has long resulted in poor value for U.S. taxpayer money. The problem has been most visible in Afghanistan, where tied aid combined with excessive conservatism on funding local recurrent and other costs means that as much as 40 percent of the U.S. aid spent there may have gone to foreign consultant salaries or corporate profits.[54] By contrast, using more local resources—to build schools, for example—would have created jobs, encouraged entrepreneurial initiatives, and cost less.

In addition, the United States is hobbled in the pursuit of its own interests in multilateral development institutions, including the World Bank, regional development banks, and UN development agencies, because officials at the U.S. Agency for International Development, the Millennium Challenge Corporation, PEPFAR, and the Treasury and State Departments have few incentives to collaborate with each other on a sustained coherent approach to multilateral aid programs.

Overhauling the current system is daunting politically, but from a practical point of view the steps the next administration should take are clear: work with Congress on an agreed vision and strategy for new foreign assistance legislation and bring together existing fragmented programs under one roof.[55]

Sheila Herrling and Steven Radelet (chapter 10), Mead Over (chapter 11), Stewart Patrick (chapter 12), and Kate Vyborny and I (chapter 13) provide a rich menu of ideas for practical reforms—Herrling and Radelet on overall U.S. foreign assistance reform, Patrick on our approach to fragile states, Over on more emphasis on prevention in the large and impressive PEPFAR, and Vyborny and Birdsall on paying for results in our aid for education. The next president should:

- Launch a complete overhaul of the U.S. approach to development assistance, including a new strategy and new legislation with Congress, a commitment that at least 25 percent of any increase in foreign aid will go through multilateral channels, and a new organizational structure with the U.S. Agency for International Development, the Millennium Challenge Corporation, and PEPFAR under a single cabinet-level agency (see below).[56]
- Continue support for the Millennium Challenge Account program in countries where aid is most likely to work; take a leadership role on truly independent evaluation of U.S. and multilateral aid programs, including by joining the new International Initiative for Independent Evaluation;[57] and ask the U.S. Agency for International Development and the Millennium Challenge Corporation to develop innovative aid delivery mechanisms that build in a results-driven approach in U.S. programs in support of countries' progress toward the Millennium Development Goals, especially for health and education;[58]
- Adopt a balanced and forward-looking strategy toward fragile states by increasing aid allocations for democracy building and for meeting people's needs and creating jobs, as strategic "prevention" of the security and other costs of political breakdowns; shifting funding and responsibility for development programs in Afghanistan, Iraq, and other insecure settings now concentrated in the Pentagon to

the U.S. Agency for International Development; establishing a large well-funded contingency fund ($1 billion[59]) to assist governments in the wake of conflict or political transition; and creating a civilian "expeditionary" capacity within the State Department and the U.S. Agency for International Development that can be deployed to crisis countries.[60]

- Strengthen substantially PEPFAR's prevention component, setting as an objective the reduction of new infections in the 15 PEPFAR countries to 140,000 a year by 2016, targeting prevention efforts to high-risk groups, removing the current constraint (favoring abstinence) on countries' choice of prevention programs, and allocating any increased funding for AIDS treatment to multilateral programs as part of a strategy to encourage financial sustainability of the existing treatment "entitlement" of more than 1 million AIDS patients in developing countries.[61]

4. Reform international development institutions to give greater influence and power to developing countries

In the aftermath of World War II, the United States was the unquestioned global leader and the major force in shaping the multilateral system: the United Nations, the open trading system (the General Agreement on Tariffs and Trade, the precursor to the World Trade Organization), and the international financial institutions (the International Monetary Fund, the World Bank, and the regional development banks). At the financial institutions in particular, Washington became accustomed to having its way, using a combination of de facto economic leverage and de jure voting power. Moreover, the United States could usually count on its European allies to follow its lead, given the congruence of values and interests.

Today the United States cannot rely on a newly united Europe to consistently follow its lead as interests on some issues diverge.[62] And both the United States and Europe must work to share global leadership more broadly. The next president will want to replace what is widely seen as failed and discredited unilateralism with a new approach to global leadership that emphasizes collaboration and cooperation. But just as democracy is about more than talking with others, multilateralism is about more than collaborating with others. As those constructing the post-war multilateral system understood, true multilateralism involves support for international institutions—not just for ad hoc coalitions of the willing on specific issues but for organizations that bind the United States as well as other countries to shared norms and agreed rules of the game, while providing the United States with "standing capacity" to act over time.[63]

Developing countries, especially those in Asia that no longer need the international financial institutions for access to capital (or even for access to expertise), will increasingly ignore those institutions unless they genuinely have a say in how they are run. Only by helping to shape and comply with fair rules now and by sharing with developing countries appropriate power and influence can the United States increase the likelihood that others will share the U.S. agenda and comply with commonly agreed rules in the future. Perhaps ironically, it is through sharing power at the global economic institutions that the United States can best secure the engagement of developing countries in a global agenda reflecting our own values and objectives.

Properly strengthened and reformed, multilateral institutions can provide a setting where Brazil, China, India, and Russia can be engaged as partners in addressing their own and global development problems, rather than as recipients of Western largesse. For example, China has become a donor to and investor in Africa, particularly in resource-rich economies, and it is through and at the World Bank that agreement is being forged now on standards of transparency for China and other donors in donor and investor relations.[64]

In a hyper-connected world in which collective action is difficult and the proportional weight of the United States in the global economy is declining, shared institutions matter more, and a better approach to organizing those institutions can have high returns for the goals and interests of the United States. The challenge is to use America's still substantial influence to reform international institutions into effective organizations for truly collaborative problem solving. A president who places priority on development—in the interests of security and prosperity worldwide—will start with leadership in reform at the World Bank, where the United States still has considerable influence.

The next president should:

- Work with other members of the World Bank to establish a credible, open, merit-based selection process for choosing the next head of the bank, of any nationality, and commission an independent, high-level expert assessment, to be made public, of voting shares, board representation, and other indicators of influence on the bank's operations and policies, including options for changes.[65]
- Support changes in World Bank financing and management of the global "goods" stressed throughout this introduction that ensure more engagement of developing country members: new health and solar technologies, reduction of international corruption and money laundering, more coherent programs to deal with fragile states, and with increasing economic interdependence, cross-border transfers

for training and education to minimize the human costs of job and income losses of poor households in low-income countries.

Making the case and getting organized for success

The next U.S. president has a rare opportunity to restore respect for the United States in the world and a sense of pride in the contributions the United States has made and can make to a stable, prosperous, and more democratic world. The margin for success in doing so is enormous in development. Righting the lopsided stool—strengthening the "D" of development so that it effectively complements and supports our investments in defense and diplomacy—is both compelling and widely endorsed. The challenges are considerable, and they are as much about political leadership as fiscal resources.

This introduction and the chapters that follow offer many concrete suggestions on what to do: lead with our strong suit, technology, in global health, agriculture, and climate change; ensure that our trade, migration, and investment policies are explicitly development-friendly; modernize our foreign assistance programs; and leverage our influence in international institutions by giving developing countries greater voice and power.

This is a huge agenda. How should the next president proceed to implement it while taking into account the many other competing domestic and foreign policy demands?

First he or she should resolve to be the constant spokesperson and champion for development as a crucial "soft power" foreign policy tool of the United States, representing U.S. values, the national interests, and our natural strengths as a country contributing to a better world. Second, to provide the constant and intelligent high-level support required if he or she is to take on that role effectively, the next president should appoint a development official quickly on assuming office and ask that appointee to work with Congress and the relevant federal agencies toward the creation of a Cabinet-level agency for development that should take its rightful place alongside the existing cabinet agencies for defense and diplomacy.

Champion global development from the bully pulpit

Surveys find tremendous support among Americans for improving economic opportunities and raising living standards around the world, if credible ways can be found to do it.[66] Yet the same surveys also reflect an odd paradox: on the one hand, nervousness and uncertainty about our role in the world; on the other, an assumption that our actions and approach overseas are somehow beyond reproach.[67]

The White House provides an unparalleled bully pulpit for rebuilding confidence among Americans about our ability to make a positive difference and for translating that confidence into real gains for Americans and people everywhere.

Why should this be the job of the president? As a foreign policy tool, development as much (and sometimes more) than defense and diplomacy requires a readiness to take the long view. In the U.S. political system, it is the president who bears responsibility for the long-term legacy. Without effective presidential leadership, it is in the nature of politics that the longer-term goals of development are often eclipsed by short-term needs and problems—which naturally tend to dominate in Congress, in the press, and in the minds of Americans. As this volume goes to press, for example, the United States Treasury is struggling with the fallout from the subprime mortgage crisis, the State and Defense Departments with military and diplomatic strategies in Afghanistan and Iraq, and the United States Trade Representative with the Democratic Congress' suspension of the "fast track" negotiating authority. At the top policy level, engaging with China on its activities in Africa and with the United Nations and Europe on a long-term strategy to cope with elevated global food prices ends up taking a back seat.

The experience of the United States in Pakistan provides a telling example. Over the past twenty years, the United States provided about $11 billion in military aid—to build a professional army, to encourage the army to contain extremist elements along the border with Afghanistan, and, for the past seven years, to support President Musharraf in the interests of stability, if not democracy. All these were sensible objectives, though in retrospect the amounts spent seem too great given the results. By contrast, relatively little went for child health, democracy assistance, and other development aid that would have improved well-being and generated greater sympathy for antiterrorist efforts. In 2006, for example, less than a third of the $1 billion in economic and military support was spent on development programs. Of course there is no guarantee that more resources and attention to education and democracy building would have forestalled today's problems in Pakistan. But at least the United States would not have created the impression among Pakistani moderates that Americans will willingly trade democracy and social progress for a short-term and possibly misguided view of our own security interests.

Similarly, if the United States had provided greater access to its market for apparel producers in Botswana, or agricultural producers in South Africa, or insisted on early and rigorous evaluation of the impact of alternative approaches to AIDS prevention, Africans and Americans would both be better off today. If the United States had been as concerned with rural development and land reform as with coca eradication in Bolivia, the Bolivian leadership might not have abandoned U.S.-supported economic reforms and entered into a new round of potentially destructive populism, or become dependent on the increasingly U.S.-baiting President Chavez for financial support.

In making the case to Americans, the emphasis should not be only or mostly on foreign aid but on U.S. interests, values, and responsibilities as a leader, whether by investing in technological solutions to problems of developing countries, setting an example at home on climate change, or governing international institutions in ways that bring new powers into the fold. That is the stance that will help redress America's global image problem, make the country a less-easy target for hatred, and prevent fissures in the international order.

Create a Cabinet-level agency for global development

While the president must lead on the development agenda, he or she will need help. That help should come in the form of creating a new Cabinet-level position with full responsibility for development policy writ large. The first responsibility of the person named to this new position would be the critical task of building the political consensus for a new agency in Congress and among the myriad of federal players whose responsibilities include aspects of development. Before the end of the (first) presidential term, the next president should have options and recommendations for the mission and mandate of the new agency.

Reform of U.S. development assistance alone will require considerable political and bureaucratic finesse, but that is just the start. The president will also have to take on the larger cause of systematically incorporating a development perspective into decision-making on trade, energy and climate change, immigration, and more. That job that cannot be done without a visible and effective appointee at his or her side, someone who keeps the focus on addressing the antecedents of instability in poverty, who is a voice for the potential benefits of preventive investments in people and democracy, who pushes for rapid policy responses to risks and opportunities in weak and fragile states in the pursuit of our national security objectives, and who brings a development lens to U.S. engagement with Brazil, China, India, and other powerful but often still poor emerging market economies.

But perhaps most important, a Cabinet-level development official is needed to restore the United States to a position of leadership on global development issues with our traditional allies, with important rising powers, and with low-income countries whose policies affect our own security.

The issue of a cabinet-level agency for development is more difficult—and cannot be resolved overnight. The fact is, however, that since September 11, 2001, there have been increasing calls for the United States to take such a step from a string of distinguished high-level commissions concerned with fragile states and foundering U.S. foreign aid programs.[68]

There are counterarguments. One is that control of U.S. aid programs outside the State Department would mean that aid would not be adequately aligned with foreign policy goals. Another is that the most recent experience of creating a new cabinet-level agency, the Department of Homeland Security, has not been a happy one. Sheila Herrling and Steve Radelet discuss and dispose convincingly of these concerns in chapter 10.

In any case, against reasonable doubts must be put the positive gains for a more vital and effective U.S. foreign policy in a changing world. The reality is that more effective development strategies and foreign assistance programs are key to restoring U.S. global leadership—and require the kind of strategic coordination and interaction with the defense and diplomacy arms of foreign policy that have simply not worked in the past. It may be that restoring U.S. leadership relies at least in part on development, the third "D," finally being placed on an equal footing with the powerful Cabinet positions representing defense and diplomacy.

Concluding note: a new opportunity for a new president

The next president is likely to enter office at a difficult moment—when many Americans are unhappy with their own economic circumstances, uncomfortable with the apparent pressures of globalization, frustrated with the high costs and limited returns to the Iraq intervention, and generally pessimistic about U.S. ability to do good in the world. But at the same time they are yearning for the United States to regain a position of leadership and respect in the world.[69] The situation represents an opportunity as well as a responsibility for the next president: to restore to Americans a sense of pride in the contributions the United States makes to a stable and prosperous world, while restoring respect for the United States abroad.[70]

I have argued above that the single best arena for doing so may well be global development. Why? First, because working to improve people's lives everywhere so singularly reflects traditional U.S. values. And second, because global development represents, in this century as never before, clear and urgent U.S. interests.[71] In an increasingly multipolar and interdependent world, economic growth, improved well-being, and good political relations with developing countries, where five of six people in the world live, are fundamental to sustaining and increasing the economic opportunities ordinary Americans enjoy and to reducing the threats they face—in a manner not heretofore seen in U.S. history.[72]

The chapters in this book set out an agenda for how the president and the next administration and Congress should proceed to put global development to work for the United States and the world. The agenda includes a call not only for a major overhaul of foreign aid but also for a more practical and more development-friendly perspective in U.S. trade, immigration, climate change, and other policies. The proposals start from a position of optimism—about U.S. technological and entrepreneurial prowess, can-do spirit, knack for innovation, and generosity. My colleagues and I hope this book will help to motivate our next president to develop and hew to a clear and visible strategy in which development takes its full place alongside defense and diplomacy in the foreign policy tool kit of the United States.

References

Albright, Madeleine. 2008. "Confidence in America: The Best Change the Next President Can Make." *Washington Post*, January 7. [www.washingtonpost.com/wp-dyn/content/article/2008/01/06/AR2008010601827.html].

Armitage, Richard L., and Joseph S. Nye, Jr. 2007. *A Smarter More Secure America. Report of the CSIS Commission on Smart Power*. November. Washington D.C.: Center for Strategic and International Studies.

Barder, Owen, Michael Kremer, and Ruth Levine. 2005. *Making Markets for Vaccines: Ideas to Action*. A Report of the Center for Global Development Advance Market Commitment Working Group, Ruth Levine, Michael Kremer, and Alice Albright, co-chars. Washington, D.C.: Center for Global Development.

Belasco, Amy. 2008. "The Cost of Iraq, Afghanistan, and Other Global War on Terror Operations Since 9/11." CRS Report for Congress. Congressional Research Service, The Library of Congress, Washington, D.C.

Bradford, Scott C., Paul L.E. Grieco, and Gary C. Hufbauer. 2005. "The Payoff to America from Global Integration." In Fred. C. Bergsten, ed., *The United States and the World Economy: Foreign Economic Policy for the Next Decade*. Washington, D.C.: Institute for International Economics.

Birdsall, Nancy. 2003. "Why It Matters Who Runs the IMF and the World Bank." Working Paper 22. Center for Global Development, Washington.

———. 2006. "The World Bank: Toward a Global Club." In Colin I. Bradford Jr. and Johannes F. Linn, eds., *Global Governance Reform: Breaking the Stalemate*. Washington, D.C.: Brookings Institution.

Birdsall, Nancy, and Owen Barder. 2006. "Payments for Progress: A Hands-Off Approach to Foreign Aid." Working Paper 102. Center for Global Development, Washington, D.C.

Birdsall, Nancy, and Peter Hakim. 2007. "Poverty and Inequality in Latin America: How the U.S. Can Really Help." Center for Global Development and The Inter-American Dialogue Policy Brief. Center for Global Development, Washington, D.C.

Birdsall, Nancy, and Arvind Subramanian. 2007. "From World Bank to World Development Cooperative." CGD Essay. Center for Global Development, Washington, D.C.

Center for Global Prosperity. 2006. *The Index of Global Philanthropy*. Washington, D.C.: The Hudson Institute.

CGD (Center for Global Development). 2005. *The Hardest Job in the World: Five Crucial Tasks for the New President of the World Bank*. A CGD Working Group Report, Nancy Birdsall and Devesh Kapur, co-chairs. Washington, D.C.: Center for Global Development.

———. 2006. *When Will We Ever Learn? Improving Lives Through Impact Evaluation*. A Report of the Evaluation Gap Working Group, William D. Savedoff, Ruth Levine, and Nancy Birdsall, co-chairs. Washington, D.C.: Center for Global Development.

———. 2007. "Commitment to Development Index." Washington, D.C. [www.cgdev.org/section/initiatives/_active/cdi].

CGIAR (Consultative Group on International Agricultural Research). 2006. *Annual Report*. Washington, D.C.

Chicago Council on Global Affairs and WorldPublicOpinion.org. 2007. "World Publics Reject U.S. Role as the World Leader: Majorities Still Want U.S. to Do Its Share in Multilateral Efforts, Not Withdraw from International Affairs." April 17. Program on International Policy Attitudes, Washington D.C. [www.worldpublicopinion.org/pipa/articles/views_on_countriesregions_bt/345.php?lb=btvoc&pnt=345&nid=&id=].

Clemens, Michael, and Lant Pritchett. 2008. "Income per Natural: Measuring Development as If People Mattered More than Places." CGD Working Paper 143. Center for Global Development, Washington, D.C.

Cline, William. 2005. *The United States as Debtor Nation*. Washington, D.C.: Center for Global Development and the Peterson Institute for International Economics.

———. 2007. "Global Warming and Agriculture: Impact Estimates by Country." Center for Global Development, Washington D.C.

Commission on Weak States and U.S. National Security. 2004. *On the Brink: Weak States and US National Security*. Washington, D.C.: Center for Global Development.

Elliott, Kimberly. 2006. *Delivering on Doha: Farm Trade and the Poor*. Washington, D.C.: Center for Global Development and the Peterson Institute for International Economics.

———. 2007. "A Trade Policy for Development: Reforming U.S. Trade Preferences." CGD Brief. Center for Global Development, Washington D.C.

Freeman, Richard. 2005. "What Really Ails Europe (and America): The Doubling of the Global Workforce." June 3. *The Globalist*. [www.theglobalist.com/StoryId.aspx?StoryId=4542].

Gates, William. 2007. "Written Testimony of William H. Gates, Chairman, Microsoft Corporation, before the Senate Committee on Health, Education, Labor, and Pensions." March 7. [http://help.senate.gov/Hearings/2007_03_07/Gates.pdf].

Goldstein, Markus P., and Todd J. Moss. 2003. "The Surprise Party: An Analysis of US ODA Flows to Africa." Working Paper 30. Center for Global Development, Washington, D.C.

Haass, Richard. 2007. "The Atlantic Becomes a Little Wider." *Financial Times*, December 18. [http://us.ft.com/ftgateway/superpage.ft?news_id=fto121820071354429028].

Hawksworth, John, and Gordon Cookson. 2008. "The World in 2050: Beyond the BRICs: A Broader Look at Emerging Market Growth Prospects." Pricewaterhouse-Coopers LLP, London.

HELP Commission (U.S. Commission on Helping to Enhance the Livelihood of People around the Globe). 2007. *Beyond Assistance: The HELP Commission Report on Foreign Assistance Reform*. Washington, D.C. [www.helpcommission.gov/].

IEA (International Energy Agency). 2007a. *China and India Insights*. World Energy Outlook. Paris.

———. 2007b. Energy R&D Statistics Database. Paris.

IMF (International Monetary Fund). 2007. "Picture This: Globalization of Labor." *Finance and Development* 44 (2).

IPCC (Intergovernmental Panel on Climate Change). 2007. "Summary for Policy-makers." In M.L. Parry, O.F. Canziani, J.P. Palutikof, P.J. van der Linden, and C.E. Hanson, eds., *Climate Change 2007: Impacts, Adaptation and Vulnerability. Contribution of Working Group II to the Fourth Assessment Report of the Intergovernmental Panel on Climate Change*. Cambridge, U.K.: Cambridge University Press. [www.ipcc.ch/pdf/assessment-report/ar4/wg2/ar4-wg2-spm.pdf].

Kapur, Devesh, and John McHale. 2005. *Give Us Your Best and Brightest: The Global Hunt for Talent and Its Impact on the Development World*. Washington, D.C.: Center for Global Development.

Kohut, Andrew, and Bruce Stokes. 2006. *America against the World: How We Are Different and Why We Are Disliked*. Washington, D.C.: The Pew Research Center.

Kuhlmann, Katrin. 2007. "U.S. Trade Preference Programs: How Well Do They Work?" Written Testimony by Katrin Kuhlmann, Senior Vice President, Global Trade Program, Women's Edge Coalition, before the U.S. Senate Finance Committee. May 16. Washington, D.C.

Lawrence, Robert. 2008. *Blue-Collar Blues: Is Trade to Blame for Rising US Income Inequality?* Washington, D.C.: Peterson Institute for International Economics.

McGregor, Richard. 2007. "World Bank to Work with China in Africa." *Financial Times*, December 18.

McPherson, Peter. 2008. "Written Testimony of Peter McPherson, President, National Association of State Universities and Land-Grant Colleges, before the Senate Foreign Relations Committee." May 14. Washington, D.C. [www.senate.gov/~foreign/testimony/2008/McPhersonTestimony080514a.pdf].

Mosanto. 2007. *Annual Report*. St. Louis, Mo.

OECD–DAC (Organisation for Economic Co-operation and Development–Development Assistance Committee). 2007. Development Database on Aid from DAC Members.

Over, Mead. 2008. "Prevention Failure: The Ballooning Entitlement Burden of U.S. Global AIDS Treatment Spending and What to Do About It." CGD Working Paper 144. Center for Global Development, Washington, D.C.

Pritchett, Lant. 2006. *Let Their People Come: Breaking the Gridlock on Global Labor Mobility*. Washington D.C.: Center for Global Development.

———. 2007. "Bilateral Guest Worker Agreements: A Win-Win Solution for Rich Countries and Poor People in the Developing World." CGD Brief. Center for Global Development, Washington, D.C.

Rachman, Gideon. 2007. "America Loses Faith in Imperialism." *Financial Times*, November 20. [www.ft.com/cms/s/0/f84deb1a-96b2-11dc-b2da-0000779fd2ac.html?nclick_check=1].
Salaam-Blyther, Tiaji. 2006. "U.S. and International Responses to the Global Spread of Avian Flu: Issues for Congress." CRS Report for Congress. Congressional Research Service, The Library of Congress, Washington D.C.
Stiglitz, Joseph E., and Linda Bilmes. 2008. *The Three Trillion Dollar War: The True Cost of the Iraq Conflict*. New York: W.W. Norton & Company.
Syngenta Global. 2007. *Annual Report*. Washington, D.C.
UNCTAD (United Nations Conference on Trade and Development). 2006. *Handbook of Statistics 2006–2007*. Geneva.
UNDP (United Nations Development Programme). 2007. *Human Development Report 2007/2008: Fighting Climate Change: Human Solidarity in a Divided World*. New York.
United Nations. 2007. *World Population Prospects: The 2006 Revision Database*. New York.
USTR (United States Trade Representative). 2007. "Fact Sheet: Trade Promotion Authority Delivers Jobs, Growth, Prosperity and Security at Home." Office of the United States Trade Representative, Washington, D.C. [www.ustr.gov/Document_Library/Fact_Sheets/2007/Trade_Promotion_Authority_Delivers_Jobs,_Growth_Prosperity_Security_at_Home.html].
Waldman, Matthew. 2008. "Afghanistan: Development and Humanitarian Priorities." Oxfam America Briefing Paper. Oxfam America, Washington, D.C.
Wheeler, David. 2007. "Another Inconvenient Truth: A Carbon-Intensive South Faces Environmental Disaster, No Matter What the North Does." CGD Working Paper 134. Center for Global Development, Washington D.C.
Wilson, Dominic, and Roopa Purushothaman. 2003. "Dreaming With BRICs: The Path to 2050." GS Global Economics Paper 99. Goldman Sachs, New York. [http://www2.goldmansachs.com/ideas/brics/book/99-dreaming.pdf].
World Bank. 2006. *Global Economic Prospects 2007: Managing the Next Wave of Globalization*. Washington, D.C.
———. 2007a. *World Development Indicators*. Washington, D.C.
———. 2007b. *World Development Report 2008: Agriculture and Development*.
———. 2008. "2005 International Comparison Program." Washington, D.C.
Zoellick, Robert. 2008. "A Challenge for Economic Statecraft." Speech delivered at the Center for Global Development, April 2, Washington, D.C. [www.cgdev.org/content/calendar/detail/15699/].

Notes

1. In surveys, Americans indicate a willingness to see far more spent on foreign assistance by the government than is actually spent. See box 1 in chapter 10 by Herrling and Radelet.
2. Individual giving plus U.S. grants from private and family foundations increased from an estimated $2.5 billion in 1990 to an estimated $8.6 billion in

2005 (OECD–DAC 2007). Another source measures U.S. private giving more expansively, placing it at more than $33 billion in 2006 (excluding remittances of $61.7 billion, which are included but better treated as intrafamilial transfers than as giving; Center for Global Prosperity 2006).

3. These figures are for total gross U.S. official development assistance. Excluding assistance to Afghanistan and Iraq, U.S. foreign aid in 2005 would be reduced from $25.3 billion to $13.1 billion (OECD–DAC 2007). See also figure 1 in chapter 10 by Herrling and Radelet.
4. Of course, it helped that until 2006 the Republican Party held the majority in both houses of Congress. Goldstein and Moss (2003) show that U.S. aid to Africa has been higher when the presidency and both houses of Congress are controlled by the same party.
5. China's gross domestic product is about $2.2 trillion using current market exchange rates and an estimated $5.3 trillion based on purchasing power parity measures (World Bank 2008).
6. The European Union is now bigger than the United States in economic terms, although it is economically less powerful because it is less politically cohesive.
7. Hawksworth and Cookson 2008; Wilson and Purushothaman 2003.
8. IMF 2007.
9. IEA 2007a.
10. Rachman 2007.
11. Cline 2005.
12. UNCTAD 2006.
13. USTR 2007.
14. Excluding the very richest households, an estimated 400 million people in developing countries have annual incomes per person above $4,000. By 2030, this group is projected to surpass 1 billion (World Bank 2006). In India alone, there are an estimated 50 million people at this income level—able to buy the $2,000 Model T car now being manufactured for this market.
15. World Bank 2007a.
16. Addressing the second and third risks involves various forms of what economists call global public goods (or bads), a set of goods that no single country has sufficient incentive to produce (or limit) in optimal amounts but which have great benefits (or costs) for all countries.
17. Commission on Weak States and US National Security 2004. See also chapter 12 by Patrick.
18. See chapter 2 by Wheeler and Wheeler 2007.
19. In 2005, President Bush requested $7.1 billion to fund the National Strategy for Pandemic Influenza, of which just $500 million was requested for internationally related activities (Salaam-Blyther 2006).
20. Birdsall 2003, 2006.

21. In chapter 2 Wheeler assumes that auction revenue could be used to offset annual costs of other programs (see footnote 26). Work done by the Congressional Research Service estimates that in 2007, the war in Iraq cost approximately $133.6 billion (Belasco 2008). Operating costs are projected to exceed $12.5 billion a month (Stiglitz and Bilmes 2008).
22. See chapter 1 by Levine. She notes that each year the United States spends more than $28 billion on biomedical research, primarily at the National Institutes of Health and through its grants to academic institutions.
23. See chapter 1 by Levine. Additionally, the next president should extend the mandate of the National Science Foundation to include support of global health research in such new areas as identifying managerial and behavioral barriers to large-scale deliver of new technologies—the so-called field of "implementation science," improving surveillance, and tracking the emergence of drug-resistant strains and policing the sale of counterfeit drugs. For example, with respect to tracking drug-resistant strains, operations research could test the effectiveness of disease surveillance by paying people to use their cell phones to report certain types of information directly; statistical principles would be applied to extract signal from noise generated by false opportunistic reporting (for these ideas, correspondence with Mead Over, March 2008).
24. Undergraduate and graduate courses in international health are oversubscribed and even medical students, sometimes criticized for eschewing family medicine or work in underserved communities for high-income specialties, are increasingly choosing to postpone the day when they can pay off their student loans in order to pursue opportunities to heal the sick or shore up the health care systems of poor countries.
25. In Africa, by 2020, between 75 million and 250 million people are projected to be exposed to increased water stress due to climate change. Agricultural production, especially rainfed agriculture, is projected to be reduced by up to 50 percent by 2020. Endemic morbidity and mortality due to diarrheal disease primarily associated with floods and droughts are expected to rise in South and Southeast Asia due to projected changes associated with global warming (IPCC 2007). For more, see Cline 2007 and UNDP 2007.
26. Wheeler in chapter 2 estimates auctions of emissions rights under a cap and trade system could generate $45 billion annually. The resulting costs would be passed on to consumers, inducing carbon-saving behavior. Alternatively, a cap-and-trade system, or carbon taxes, could be made revenue-neutral by reducing other taxes. Table 1 assumes that auction revenue would offset the costs of increased public financing of research and development and increased funding for adaptation costs in developing countries. For example, the revenue from a tax on gasoline to encourage more fuel-efficient cars and gradual changes in residence decisions could be returned to taxpayers.

27. U.S. public spending in energy research and development was about 0.02 percent of GDP in 2006, or less than $4 billion (IEA 2007b). Doubling this amount would be about $8 billion; In chapter 2 Wheeler proposes $10 billion.
28. A revenue-neutral tax on gasoline (returned to taxpayers through some reduction in other taxes) would make eminent sense as well.
29. The Bush administration took the first step in this direction in late 2007 with a commitment of $2 billion for a Clean Energy Fund at the World Bank.
30. World Bank 2007b; Zoellick 2008.
31. While there was a limited increase is U.S. Agency for International Development (USAID) funding to the Consultative Group on International Agricultural Research (CGIAR) in the early years of the Bush Administration, the last 15 years or so have shown a substantial decrease in USAID funding to CGIAR. Between 1982 and 1991, average annual USAID funding to CGIAR was about $44 million in nominal terms, falling to about $39 million in nominal terms between 1992 and 2001, implying a substantial decline from the 1980s (CGIAR 2006). In testimony before the Senate Foreign Relations Committee, McPherson (2008) highlights the alarming point of no allocation for core funding for the CGIAR in the 2008 allocation for USAID.
32. According to *World Development Report 2008*, which focused on agriculture for development, agriculture research and development investments in developing countries have an average rate of return of 43 percent (World Bank 2007b).
33. Mosanto 2007; Syngenta Global 2007; World Bank 2007b.
34. One credible estimate suggests that Americans are an estimated $1 trillion a year richer (more than 10 percent richer) than they would be due to increased trade with the rest of the world since 1945 (Bradford, Grieco, and Hufbauer 2005).
35. See chapter 7 by Elliott.
36. Elliott 2007.
37. Elliot 2007; HELP Commission 2007.
38. The African Growth and Opportunity Act has generated thousands of jobs in Sub-Saharan Africa: 26,000 in Lesotho, 30,000 in Kenya, and 45,000 in Swaziland. Approximately 75 percent of these jobs have gone to poor women (Kuhlmann 2007).
39. Suppressing global food prices because of rich-country subsidies may also have discouraged the increased production in developing countries that is, with the sudden price hikes in 2008, now even more desirable.
40. The proposal would apply to all least-developed countries in the World Trade Organization system and to most countries of Sub-Saharan Africa—excluding only those currently under legislatively determined sanctions (such as Sudan). See chapter 7 by Elliott for additional detail.

41. Birdsall and Hakim (2007) make this proposal for U.S. free trade agreements with Latin America; the U.S. could take this approach (cross-border trade adjustment assistance) in bilateral agreements and—better—could take leadership in proposing a multilateral fund for trade adjustment assistance.
42. Kapur and McHale 2005.
43. Gates 2007.
44. Clemens and Pritchett (2008) note that two of five Mexicans and four of five Haitians escaped poverty by leaving their respective countries. See also chapter 9 by Clemens and Bazzi for discussion and evidence on other benefits to migrants themselves and their countries of origin.
45. Pritchett 2007.
46. See chapter 9 by Clemens and Bazzi.
47. Pritchett 2006
48. See chapter 3 by Ramachandran.
49. See chapter 6 by Lee.
50. The president could also ask Congress to fix an unfortunate constraint on the use of U.S. programs to insure overseas investments in difficult environments—investments that would create jobs in poor countries as well as at home. A project is currently ineligible if it would "cost" one existing American job (for example, in low-wage office work) even were it simultaneously to create many new jobs (for example, in high-end research or marketing). See chapter 4 by Moran.
51. Surveys indicate a substantial decline in America's reputation almost everywhere in the world in the past decade—including in Europe, but most dramatically in the Middle East and, interestingly, less so in Africa. The Bush administration's substantial efforts to deal with the AIDS pandemic and the Millennium Challenge Corporation aid program, for which many African countries are eligible, have probably helped sustain that favorable rating.
52. Several recent reports focus on the neglected "smart power" foreign policy tools, especially diplomacy and development including foreign aid. For a recent report, see Armitage and Nye 2007.
53. HELP Commission 2007; Armitage and Nye 2007; see also chapter 10 by Herrling and Radelet.
54. Waldman 2008.
55. HELP Commission 2007; Armitage and Nye 2007; and others on the legislation and need for a new organizational setup.
56. Chapter 10 by Herrling and Radelet explains and elaborates on this agenda.
57. For more information on the International Initiative for Impact Evaluation refer to the Evaluation Gap Working Group Report (CGD 2006) or www.3ieimpact.org/.
58. In chapter 5 De Tray and Moran in this volume emphasize the logic of such "results-based" aid for fragile states. See Birdsall and Barder 2006; Vyborny

and Birdsall in chapter 13; and the discussion of cash-on-delivery aid on the Center for Global Development's Web site (www.cgdev.org/section/initiatives/_active/pbaedu).

59. In 2004, the Commission on Weak States and U.S. National Security, convened by the Center for Global Development, recommended maintaining a $1 billion permanent country-in-transition fund. It could be used to finance a range of activities including efforts to mitigate conflict, respond to instability that threatens regional or international security, support post conflict reconstruction and peace and humanitarian operations, and provide assistance to countries in transition.
60. In chapter 12 Stewart explains and elaborates on this agenda.
61. In a background paper, Over (2008) points out that a target of averted infections opens the possibility that a given person's infection can be averted multiple times, which depends upon hypothetical calculations, exaggerates the number of people helped, and obscures any lack of progress in achieving the actual goal of reduced infections. His chapter proposes specific prevention interventions as candidates for increased support, including male circumcision and assuring access to family planning services for HIV positive women. In chapter 1 Levine refers to the potential for greater use of tested interventions, asserting there is little link between research results produced by the National Institutes of Health and the Center for Disease Control and implementation of programs under PEPFAR.
62. The United States and Europe have had trouble agreeing on the appropriate response of donors to corruption in developing countries and to conditionality in lending, as well as, of course, on foreign policy issues such as Iraq. Russia, as well as China, is a new factor, especially for Western Europe, given its proximity (and its dependence on Russian-supplied oil and gas). Haass (2007) makes the additional point that lack of predictable threats and obligations will loosen traditional strong ties among allies.
63. In the terminology of the outstanding report of the CSIS Commission on Smart Power (Armitage and Nye 2007), the distinction is between consensus-based internationalism, sometimes useful to handle short-term challenges, and norms-based internationalism in the form of treaties and multilateral organizations that provide the United States with "standing capacity" to act over time with other countries on current and future challenges.
64. McGregor (2007) quotes World Bank President Robert Zoellick, upon return from his trip to China, as saying, "From statistics I have seen, China has paid attention to debt sustainability, and there is certainly a willingness to discuss that issue because they want to get paid back, too."
65. A package in which the United States gave up its automatic right to the World Bank presidency and the Europeans gave up some of their seats on the board in favor of more African seats, would be a step in the direction of greater

legitimacy. For other intermediate steps, including a governance structure for a Global Public Good Trust Fund in which Brazil, China, India and other large emerging economies could have more influence, see CGD 2005.

66. Chicago Council on Global Affairs and WorldPublicOpinion.org 2007.
67. Albright (2008) referred to a "dangerous lack of self-awareness" on the part of Americans. See also Kohut and Stokes 2006.
68. Commission on Weak States and U.S. National Security 2004; Armitage and Nye 2007.
69. More than two-thirds of Americans surveyed in 2004 felt that respect for the United States had declined, and four in ten considered the decline in respect to be a major foreign policy problem. The portrait of the United States that emerges from those and other subsequent surveys is that of a confused and beleaguered superpower, with Americans firmly rejecting isolationism but ambivalent about internationalism and world-weary about the burden of global leadership. Kohut and Stokes (2006), pp. 22–28 and table 2.1, p. 27.
70. Since the end of the Cold War and especially since the 2003 intervention in Iraq, U.S. power has been increasingly resented and even feared. Surveys of attitudes in 2002–05 in fifty countries reveal high and rising levels of suspicion of U.S. power. The share of respondents with a favorable opinion of the United States in 2005 was only 55 percent in the United Kingdom and 43 percent in Germany. It was lower still in most majority Muslim countries—38 percent in Indonesia (down from 75 percent in 1999–2000) and 23 percent in Pakistan. The surveys also indicate that Americans are aware of that resentment (Kohut and Stokes 2006, pp. 22–28 and table 2.1, p. 27).
71. Virtually all U.S. presidents have responded to humanitarian emergencies in developing countries with full support from Americans. But since the days of the Marshall Plan, with the possible exception of John F. Kennedy's Alliance for Progress, visible and energetic support for expanding economic opportunities for people overseas has not been a high priority for U.S. presidents—certainly not compared with such twentieth-century foreign policy concerns as peace in the Middle East, trade and military relations with our traditional allies in Europe, or nuclear nonproliferation.
72. In the fall of 2007, as this introduction was being written, the three top candidates for the Democratic Party's nomination (Clinton, Edwards, and Obama) all issued statements on global development objectives and priorities. In March 2008, presumed Republican presidential nominee John McCain delivered a foreign policy speech at the World Affairs Council in Los Angeles, California, which included global development solutions.

1 Healthy Foreign Policy: Bringing Coherence to the Global Health Agenda

Ruth Levine

Starting on January 20, 2009, the president of the United States can reshape the role of this country in fostering a healthier, more just world. The president can—through executive orders, the agendas of federal agencies, and messages to Congress about priorities within the budget—champion a long-term, coherent strategy that marshals the technical, financial, and political instruments of the United States to improve global health. In doing this, the president can build on the impressive record of the past thirty years of U.S. engagement in international health and improve on past performance by alignment of research, development assistance, regulatory, domestic health care, and other policies to create an unmatched legacy in saved lives and improved livelihoods around the world.

Along with the emerging priority of combating climate change, global health deserves a special status in the engagement of the United States with low- and middle-income countries, as well as with other industrialized countries. There are several reasons for this. First, the health sector has defined and measurable global dimensions, which require close coordination and interaction among countries: infectious diseases spread across borders as quickly as planes fly—and the health and economic consequences of major outbreaks can be immense. Estimates of the cost

---

Ruth Levine is the vice president for programs and operations and a senior fellow at the Center for Global Development. She is grateful for the input of Stephen Blount, Nils Daulaire, Roger Glass, Kent Hill, and Philip Musgrove.

of an outbreak in the United States based on economic losses reach as high as $100–$200 billion; when extrapolated to other high-income countries, the losses reach $550 billion.[1]

Pharmaceutical products are traded internationally, and because of their life-saving potential and the differential market "pulls" of rich and poor countries, access to affordable drugs serves as a lighting rod in debates about economic justice and global inequality. Physicians and nurses are the most migratory skilled workers, meriting special immigration status and licensing regimes. As a global citizen, and particularly one with a massive and growing domestic health sector, the United States both affects and is affected by all other countries in the area of human health.

Second, the United States has a long record of technical and funding leadership through support to international health efforts such as smallpox eradication and funding for oral rehydration therapy programs (box 1.1). Other donor countries and international organizations, such as the World Health Organization, the United Nations Children's Fund, and the Global

Box 1.1. The U.S. role in global health successes

The U.S. Agency for International Development (USAID) is spearheading U.S. efforts to provide mass integrated treatment of tropical neglected diseases, including trachoma and onchocerciasis in East and West Africa, to be under way in 2007 in cooperation with drug donations from pharmaceutical companies.

USAID provided support for a Hib vaccine trial in the Gambia, involving more than 40,000 infants. The trial's dramatic results led to the introduction of the vaccine to the national immunization program in 1997 and the virtual elimination of Hib disease from the country.

USAID has provided financial assistance to the Bangladesh family planning program. Fertility decreased from more than six children per woman in 1975 to about three in 2004—a decline that exceeded the pace of change in most other countries at Bangladesh's economic level.

USAID has provided technical support and $26 million in financial assistance to Egypt's National Control of Diarrheal Disease Project. Infant diarrheal deaths were reduced 82 percent between 1982 and 1987, and the program contributed to the prevention of 300,000 child diarrheal deaths between 1982 and 1989.

The Centers for Disease Control (CDC) led the global movement to eradicate guinea worm with a decade-long advocacy campaign begun in 1981. In collaboration with the Carter Center and twelve other countries, USAID provided financial support for the guinea worm eradication programs in Africa and Asia. Since the start of the campaign in 1986, the prevalence of the disease has dropped 99 percent, and the number of cases has fallen from 3.5 million to less than 35,000.

Through its participation in the Inter-Agency Coordinating Committee, USAID contributed financial support to the regional initiative that eliminated polio in Latin America in 1991.

USAID was the largest donor in the twenty-eight-year Onchocerciasis Control Program in West Africa. USAID contributed $75 million to the successful program, which virtually eliminated the disease as a public health threat in West Africa and made 25 million hectares of arable land—enough to feed an additional 17 million people—safe for resettlement.

The CDC played a central role in the global smallpox eradication effort, providing technical and financial support, and offering crucial momentum and support when the program was revived in the mid-1960s. Under the leadership of Dr. D.A. Henderson, the CDC contributed staff, equipment, and technical expertise to programs in Central and West Africa. Between 1967 and 1979 the United States contributed just under $25 million, or approximately 40 percent of total donor contributions. The majority of U.S. assistance went toward eradicating smallpox in Central and West Africa. Smallpox was eradicated in 1977.

The CDC provided funding for the measles vaccination initiatives in Southern Africa, to supplement the resources provided by the region's ministries of health. The number of measles cases was reduced from 60,000 in 1996 to just 117 four years later; the number of measles deaths fell from 166 to zero.

Source: Levine 2007.

Fund to Fight AIDS, Tuberculosis, and Malaria, count on and have been shaped by expertise and dollars from the United States. Maintaining and strengthening that leadership are required, even as the demands increase and the technical challenges intensify. Failing to do so would send a signal to the international community that the United States is unwilling to live up to implied obligations and is no longer able or willing to contribute to meeting humanitarian needs.

Third, energetic, visible, and effective international health endeavors, which are among the international activities most favored by U.S. taxpayers, can help to reestablish a positive relationship with many global partners—both in the industrialized world and in developing countries—after a period in which military actions and unilateralism have weakened those bonds. According to a poll conducted in 2006 by *Research!America,* health is among Americans' top priorities for development assistance.

The rationale for deploying U.S. policies and programs to benefit global health are unambiguous, but decisions about what to do are not as clear cut. The track record over the past ten years or so, which has largely shaped the situation facing the incoming administration in 2009, demonstrates the complexity with both signature contributions and serious shortcomings. On the positive side, the amount of U.S. resources to development assistance for health has increased significantly. By helping to establish the Global Fund to Fight AIDS, Tuberculosis, and Malaria and the Global Alliance for Vaccines and Immunization, the United States has contributed through novel multilateral mechanisms, as well as through its growing bilateral effort. The National Institutes of Health, which is the dominant funder of scientific research in the world, has expanded its engagement on global health concerns, particularly but not solely in AIDS vaccine research. And the Bush administration has featured the global health priorities of HIV/AIDS and malaria as prominent parts of a "soft power" agenda that is otherwise quite limited—witness the dominance in foreign aid discussions of the U.S. President's Emergency Plan for AIDS Relief (PEPFAR) and the President's Malaria Initiative (PMI). In surprising ways, the global health agenda of the Bush administration has been a meeting ground for interest groups that otherwise are at odds, from gay rights advocates on the left to evangelical conservatives on the right.

The accomplishments are significant but so are the weaknesses that now need to be redressed. The vast majority of new global health spending has been dedicated to one disease—HIV/AIDS—and spent in a way that may constrain the availability of funding over the foreseeable future for HIV prevention and other health (and broader development) priorities. The AIDS and family planning programs have been shaped by domestic political agendas, and the AIDS program in particular, although awe-inspiring in size, has been subject to critique for its orientation to a limited set of output targets, its failure to work in coordination with either the national governments or the multilateral AIDS efforts in the same countries, and its distortional effects on public health infrastructure and delivery of care. Moreover, preparatory activities for an avian influenza pandemic have reflected a serious lack of understanding of global interconnectedness, with only a small fraction of the total resources going to strengthen the ability to respond to initial outbreaks where they are most likely—East Asia and Africa.

So while there is much to build upon, the United States has clear opportunities to do better in the future. The president's main leadership challenge is to cut through bureaucratic barriers to form a coherent set of government activities—including and beyond aid—that support global health goals. The priorities manifested through the development assistance allocations, which are the most visible part of the U.S. global health agenda, should be part of a broader picture that includes the way resources are devoted to the government research budget, to tax credits for pharmaceutical and other commercial players, to trade and agriculture policy, and—at least in a limited way—to domestic health care policy itself. This does not mean a slavish adherence to promoting one or two disease areas across all government actions, but it suggests that—at a minimum—the development assistance budget should not be used simply as a positive offset for the negative impacts on global health of defense, agriculture, trade, or Medicare reimbursement policies. In creating a coherent agenda, the president would be well placed to adhere to a set of "rules of engagement" that favor realism and reliability over ideology and political games (box 1.2).

Box 1.2. Core rules of engagement in global health

Place priority on multilateral cooperation. In recognition of the importance of coordinating and making the most of limited resources, the United States should emphasize multilateral efforts and minimize the extent to which U.S.-only approaches are taken. This can be done both through contributions to multilateral mechanisms, such as U.N. agencies, development banks, and global health funds, and through explicit coordination of the bilateral development assistance program with other partners. Moreover, it can be done by ensuring that global health support reflects genuine needs and opportunities in developing countries and is developed in close collaboration with national authorities and other stakeholders, rather than serving the commercial aims of the pharmaceutical industry or adhering to particular perspectives about the role of the private sector.

Focus on health impact. Support to global health programs has multiple aims, including advancing a positive image of the United States, but priorities should be established in light of potential for health impact over a ten- to fifteen-year period as the metric by which competing claims on limited resources are judged. This would affect the geographic allocation of resources, so that funds would be focused on countries and populations with the health conditions subject to the greatest improvement, and it would affect the types of programs supported, with the likely outcome of greater emphasis on preventive and broad public health measures for both infectious and noncommunicable diseases, including investments outside the health sector (for example, on education and water and sanitation as a complement to direct health services). Employing an explicit health impact metric for the purpose of setting priorities would also stimulate careful measurement of the health impact of programs, moving beyond a simple accounting of dollars spent, drugs delivered, and health workers trained.

Be reliable. In global health, as in other domains of development-related policy, the United States should be seen as an actor that lives up to its commitments—consistently and wholeheartedly. This is a particularly trenchant priority in global health—a field that is littered with populist promises that are incompletely realized and where good results depend heavily on the predictability of resources. Fulfilling commitments already made for AIDS programs is the primary challenge, but smaller scale commitments have also been made and should be fulfilled in malaria prevention and treatment and in child health.

Base decisions on scientific evidence. U.S. policies should be based on the best available scientific and technical evidence, combined with the findings from rigorous evaluations of program implementation. It should be insulated to the maximum degree possible from politics. The international health activities of the United States should not be the battleground for domestic political agendas on abortion, sex between unmarried people, illegal drugs, and other contentious issues.

Making the most of U.S. assets in global health

Interagency coordination as a top priority

The president has the unique ability and responsibility to look across agencies and instruments of government to maximize impact. To do this in global health, where a broad range of agencies have some role to play, requires focused investments across the administration within a well-articulated and strategic framework. A new interagency task force on global health within the U.S. government is needed to bring a more coherent and coordinated strategy among the multiple federal agencies that are involved in global health. This mechanism, which was recommended a decade ago,[2] would foster a closer working alliance among the Department of Health and Human Services, the U.S. Agency for International Development (USAID), the Department of Defense, and other technical agencies. This coordination mechanism is especially important where there is a strong connection between science and implementation.

To take just three examples of what an interagency task force could work on:

- *Deploying and testing multiple HIV prevention strategies based on successfully tested interventions.* Currently, there is a significant disconnect between the research undertaken on HIV prevention approaches by either the National Institutes of Health or the Centers for Diseases Control and Prevention (CDC), and the implementation of programs under PEPFAR. Tremendous improvements could be realized simply by linking up the knowledge-generating and knowledge-utilizing parts of the government.
- *Global disease surveillance and creation, and mobilization of scientific capabilities to identify new patterns of disease and modes of transmission,* including the establishment of sentinel sites where the potential of emerging infectious disease is greatest. Again, the potential for multiagency efforts, involving the National Institutes of Health, the CDC, USAID, and the Department of Defense are vast—and largely untapped to date.
- *Building clinical trial and regulatory capacities.* One of the most positive developments in global health this decade has been the renewed pipeline for neglected diseases, thanks in large part to public private partnerships such as the Medicines for Malaria Venture and the Global Alliance for TB Drug Development, enabled by the support of the Bill & Melinda Gates Foundation. Notably, these types of partnerships now manage three-quarters of all identified neglected drug development projects and offer stable and innovative product

development pathways for academic research centers. However, with more than 300 products for neglected disease in development globally, even with expected attrition rates, the trial capacity does not exist to support the current pipeline. In many disease-endemic countries, limited local regulatory capacities further constrain the opportunities for trials. Addressing this problem will require an integrated, international clinical trial system engaging local investigators, communities, ethical review committees, and regulatory bodies in low- and middle-income countries. Bridging these structural gaps will require scientific and regulatory leadership as well as significant new investments at strategic sites. For this, there will be no substitute for coordination across the National Institutes of Health, the Food and Drug Administration, and other agencies involved in the protection of human subjects and related issues.

Setting up an interagency task force should be an early priority for the new administration but should not preempt a close look at how particular parts of the executive branch can do a better job, regardless of coordination with other agencies. That close look should focus, in order of priority, on aid, biomedical research, participation in global health institutions, and the military.

A broader vision for development assistance

The agencies involved in development assistance and their respective budget allocations are the most visible instruments through which the U.S. role in global health is played out. The PEPFAR program and, more recently, PMI, focus unprecedented new resources on specific diseases in particular countries.

In the case of PEPFAR, $15 billion will be spent over the plan's first five years. The dollars have been tightly earmarked: Within the AIDS programs, Congress has required that 55 percent of the resources be dedicated to treatment (with 75 percent of these resources going directly to the provision of antiretroviral therapy), 15 percent to palliative care (broadly defined), 20 percent to prevention, and 10 percent to care of those with HIV and AIDS orphans and vulnerable children. In the case of PMI, a total of $1.5 billion has been committed over five years, with efforts focused on fifteen high-burden countries in Africa. PEPFAR is on track be reauthorized at an even higher annual spending level, with many (albeit not all) of the restrictions in place and a continuing focus on the provision of AIDS medicines to those affected by the disease.

In addition to the disease-specific spending in Africa, Afghanistan has been seen as a priority. In 2005 alone, some $82 million were committed to the health program in Afghanistan, which primarily involves the delivery of services through contracted nongovernmental organizations.[3] Importantly, there are hopeful signs from that work: Although Afghanistan has the dubious distinction of having the second highest maternal mortality ratio in the world (surpassed only by Sierra Leone), new strategies by projects such as the Rural Expansion of Afghan Community-Based Health Care have successfully improved access to health care in Afghanistan as shown in key indicators such as an increased number of births attended by skilled attendants and increased rates of immunization for rural children.[4]

Where there are winners, there have also been losers. International family planning, traditionally an area of leadership for the United States, has taken a hard hit, with many observers claiming that the "budget hydraulics" have drawn down the family planning funding as a partial offset to the increase for HIV/AIDS (figure 1.1). Similarly, maternal and child health

Figure 1.1. U.S. government funding trends in global health

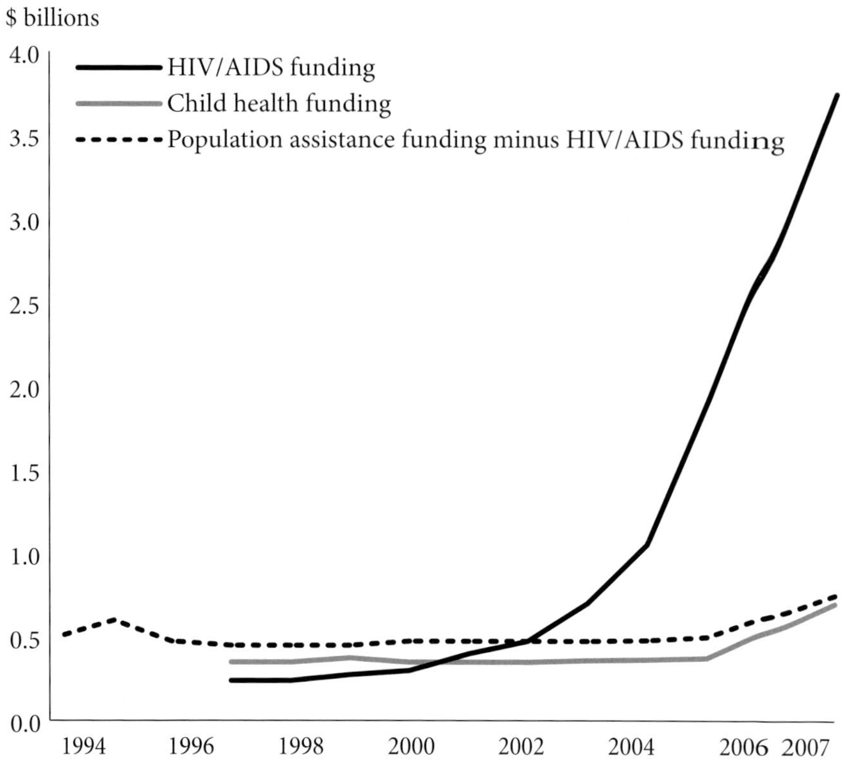

Source: Global Health Council 2007.

programs have grown very little. Although USAID has distributed $2.5 billion to child survival programs since 1990, this has not kept pace with either inflation or population growth. For example, the appropriation for fiscal year 2007 represented a 20 percent decline in funding from 1997.[5]

The large overall increase in global health funding must be taken as good news, but reasonable doubts exist about whether the best evidence has been marshaled—or is now being generated—to ensure that the dollars are being used as effectively as possible. Debates about the U.S. AIDS program and the earmarked allocation for "abstinence before marriage" programs have been the most headline-grabbing. A 2007 congressionally mandated evaluation of PEPFAR by the Institute of Medicine, for example, notes that the budget allocations for abstinence before marriage in the Leadership Act hamper prevention efforts; more data need to be accumulated on the precise nature of the epidemic in each country, and the prevention program needs to be tailored to meet those specific needs. To date, operating very much in "emergency mode," PEPFAR has rapidly expanded services and access to drugs but not sustainable programs or adequate monitoring and evaluation.[6]

If we assume that the total envelope for development assistance during the next administration is kept at current levels, we can see quite clearly the net effect of recent spending dynamics—and the implications for the future: First, the development budget is now allocated differently than it would have been without the need for post-conflict reconstruction and aid in Afghanistan; this foretells future demands during the eventual aftermath of the Iraq war. Second, AIDS programs are the major vehicle through which U.S. bilateral development assistance for health is provided, and the focus on expanding the number of infected persons taking relatively expensive medicines has dramatic implications for the future. Donors are now in essence "locked in" to both maintaining the complex and changing treatment needs of those already receiving life-saving medication as well as serving the expanding numbers of patients who will require treatment in the future (see chapter 11 by Over). Thus, between the post-conflict aid for health and the recurrent cost burden of the scaled-up AIDS treatment programs, the room for discretionary increases in the broader health budget is limited without expansion of the overall funding envelope.

Given recent history and the likely constraints on much higher levels of spending in the future, four main tasks should be highest on the agenda for the next administration's development assistance in health.

1. *Laying the groundwork for health-related support to Iraq.* The president should initiate the diplomatic and technical groundwork to provide health-related support to Iraq, working across U.S. agencies but as much as possible through multilateral channels, including the

World Health Organization, the World Bank, and U.N. agencies, and with international nongovernmental organizations that are able to work in Iraq. The political and humanitarian imperative is acute, and the U.S. administration should be fully prepared, working hand-in-hand with others, to ensure that the health-related challenges can be taken up systematically and on a technically sound footing, rather than in a piecemeal, emergency manner that is likely to be far less effective. The central aim of that work should be to recover the dramatic losses to child welfare experienced in Iraq over the past decade and to increase the capacity of the Iraqi government and civil society—rather than U.S. contractors—to respond to citizens' needs in a positive and effective way.

2. *Reevaluating U.S. spending on HIV/AIDS.* A fresh and future-oriented look is needed at how the United States is spending HIV/AIDS. Because of its importance, this is covered in-depth in chapter 11 by Over, but the key points are reiterated here. The United States should:
   - Maximize the success of ongoing treatment in PEPFAR-supported countries through strategies that include effective supervision and assured salaries to AIDS treatment personnel, and reductions in the unit costs of treatments through donor and other agency collaborations.
   - Minimize the need for treatment through strengthened prevention, a course of action that would lead to a reduced projected burden of treatment costs and, more importantly, AIDS-related mortality in these countries.
   - Ensure that the AIDS transition occurs, a move that would include seeing the number of people on treatment exceed the number of people newly infected with HIV and helping to shift HIV and AIDS away from being an acute disease and toward chronic disease management models.
3. *Working with multilateral partners to improve health of the poor.* It is important that the United States work with multilateral partners, including the World Health Organization and the World Bank, to provide financial and technical support to low-income countries that have a demonstrated commitment to improving the health of people living in poverty. This work may mean identifying countries that have well-formulated poverty reduction strategies and associated plans that prioritize public health measures, nutrition support, and health services that would benefit poor communities and households, within a ten-year framework to enhance the government's ability to implement the plans. The types of support provided should be based on national

requirements, rather than on a set of globally established, disease-specific priorities. It could include both funding for focused programs—for example, for the reduction in undernutrition among children and pregnant women through micronutrient supplementation—and for programs that have systemwide benefits, such as enhancing the capacity to contract for health service delivery with private providers.

4. *Establishing exchanges for training, research, and practice.* The fourth main task is to develop, finance, and implement a set of professional exchanges between low- and middle-income countries and U.S. institutions involved in health service training, research, and practice. These professional exchanges could include, for example, single- or multiple-year international residencies by U.S. medical students, in addition to their conventional residencies, or shorter term training assignments by U.S. medical and public health school faculty in counterpart schools in Africa, Asia, and Latin America. They could also include expansion of a global network of epidemiologists trained by the CDC. Moreover, the professional exchanges could encompass short- and long-term training and research opportunities in the United States for health professionals in health ministries and universities, in both biomedical and management disciplines. Such exchanges already exist to some extent, but they are piecemeal and generally poorly funded. Building up such exchange programs would both contribute to the diplomatic mission of health aid and help to build capacity to plan, manage, and deliver health services. It would create and strengthen connections between health professionals in the United States and overseas that would provide the basis of trust and mutual understanding that is essential to address global challenges such as outbreaks of infectious disease. One example of how professional exchanges could work is shown in box 1.3.

Genuine partnership in global health institutions

The United States exerts significant influence over leading global health institutions, largely by virtue of its financial contributions. Since 2005, the United States has contributed approximately $100 million annually to the World Health Organization's budget, with the president's request for fiscal year 2009 $106.5 million.[7] The United States is the majority contributor to UNICEF and, by tradition, nominates the director of the official child health agency; it has in the past been a significant donor to United Nations Population Fund, the United Nation's population and reproductive health agency; and it is an active participant in all discussions at the World Trade Organization on issues related to intellectual property, including and perhaps particularly within the

Box 1.3. Global Health Corps

As part of its push to restructure international health assistance and to symbolize the generous spirit of the new administration's foreign policy, we recommend that the president propose the creation of a Global Health Corps. Like the Peace Corps, which President Kennedy created on March 1, 1961, only 39 days after his inauguration, the Global Health Corps would be a tangible demonstration of the U.S. commitment to world peace and development.

Just as the Peace Corps built upon the experience of existing private overseas volunteer programs such as the American Friends Service Corps, the Global Health Corps will complement, learn from, and expand upon an array of government and private programs that have been working for years to give enthusiastic young doctors and other health workers the opportunity to serve the poor of developing countries. A 2005 Institute of Medicine study, which first proposed the creation of a Global Health Corps as a part of the U.S. response to the international AIDS epidemic, cited eight U.S. government programs and six private programs that could serve as models. Although the idea of a Global Health Corps was not incorporated into the PEPFAR enabling legislation, several similar initiatives have been launched by universities using private funding. Some examples include Baylor University's International Pediatric AIDS Initiative, Duke University's Center for Global Health, the University of Northern Iowa's Global Health Corps, and Operation Smile. All of these innovative programs offer recently graduated doctors and other health care personnel a structured opportunity to receive training in the health problems and health care systems in developing countries and then to apply their skills for a year or more in a specific developing-country health care system. We propose that the new president launch a national Global Health Corps to expand this service opportunity to more Americans and to improve health care and strengthen health systems for more poor people in developing countries. In the United States as well as abroad, Peace Corps volunteers spread the idea that the ultimate objective of U.S. foreign policy in the poor countries is economic and human development. By sending out Global Health Corps volunteers, the new president will renew and enhance this message by committing the United States to improving people's health.

Key features of the Global Health Corps

The proposed Global Health Corps would start by recruiting 200 individuals in the first year of its enactment, half of whom would be medical doctors who recently finished their training and half would be other health care professionals. Among the criteria for admission to the Global Health Corps would be coursework or other accredited training in tropical disease problems and development health care systems. The rate of recruitment would increase over time, attaining a total recruitment of some 700 individuals per year by 2012 and leveling off at 2,500 per year by 2,016, with medical doctors accounting for one-third of recruits. The other health professionals would include not only nurses and intermediate personnel, such as physicians' assistants and nurse midwives, but also epidemiologists and public health specialists. As with the Peace Corps today, recruitment would be to specific country programs and matched to the needs of those individual countries. While some countries might request doctors to assist with AIDS treatment, others might have more pressing needs such as the delivery of maternal and child health care in rural health centers or the provision of care in trauma centers. Most recruits would be recent graduates of health training programs, but positions would also be available for senior medical personnel who would like to take time off from their busy careers to serve in a developing country. The typical period of service would be two years but could be less for senior medical personnel. Global Health Corps recruits would be mentored on site by senior local health personnel in their field. These mentors would be nominated by national health ministries and confirmed by Global Health Corps staff. Compensation would include a modest stipend during service plus forgiveness of a portion of the recruit's student loans. Eligibility would be open to any graduate of an U.S. health care training program regardless of nationality, with some slots allocated preferentially to Americans and non-Americans whose ancestry is linked with a specific host country.

Estimated costs

Because of the student loans most health care workers accumulate during their training, the compensation package necessary to enable them to serve in the Global Health Corps must be larger than that offered to Peace Corps volunteers. However, we expect the impact and benefit for both participants and recipients to be proportionate. The annual salary would be paired with loan forgiveness, which would be budgeted as an average amount but made available on a sliding scale. Assuming two years of service for each professional, medical doctors would receive an annual salary of $44,000, and other health professionals would receive $30,000, plus an average loan forgiveness of $25,000 and $17,000 respectively. We also account for indirect costs, which double the total annual direct costs.

The cost of local infrastructure is more difficult to estimate. Most of the model programs that facilitate volunteer health work in poor countries, including the Peace Corps, the programs cited by the Institute of Medicine, the university programs cited here, and Doctors Without Boarders, maintain local offices in each host country. The costs of such local offices must include not only the salaries of the U.S. and local staff and the cost of the building and infrastructure but also the cost of stipends offered to local counterparts and mentors. Based on the published budget breakdowns of Doctors Without Borders, our preliminary estimate is that the total expense for all the offices and infrastructure of the Global Health Corps would cost about the same as the direct personnel costs of the organization.

At this scale of operation, the budget requirement would be $341 million for the first four years of the new presidency, increasing to approximately $1.233 billion for the second four years (2013–2016).

—*Mead Over*

Source: Institute of Medicine 2005; Jolly 2004; Sarfaty and Arnold 2005.

pharmaceutical sector. In each of those roles, the United States uses its financial power, political muscle, and technical strength to influence the direction of policies and practices that affect virtually every country on the planet. To date, in large measure because of the political nature of the debates in each of those institutions and among the domestic constituencies that pay attention to actions on the global stage, the U.S. positions have not all been aligned under a set of coherent global health aims.

Take AIDS alone, for example, as the global health challenge with the highest visibility. And take the importance for the effectiveness of AIDS programs of attending to the special needs and vulnerabilities of adolescent girls, who are without question bearing the highest cost of the uncontrolled epidemic; they are at the greatest risk, with the least power to protect themselves, and they are suffering under the greatest weight of the burden of caring for those who are sick and the children left behind.

The signals about U.S. support for programs that seek to protect adolescent girls from HIV infection are mixed: On the one hand, the Global Fund, which benefited from a $300 million[8] contribution from the United States in fiscal year 2007, explicitly invites proposals that focus on prevention and treatment of AIDS among adolescents and stipulates that gender issues be specifically taken into consideration in the development of country-level programs. On the other hand, the United Nations Population Fund, which works to foster the sexual and reproductive health of adolescent girls, as well as older women, has received no public U.S. funding for several years,[9] after an initial "defunding" in 2002 of about 12 percent of its budget ($34 million) due to U.S. backlash against perceived support by the fund for safe abortions.

There will be many opportunities over the coming years to do better in global leadership. At the end of the incoming president's first term, in 2012, the United States will hold the G-8 chair. By that target date, the United States should aim to have at least 50 percent of development assistance for health channeled through multilateral institutions; and it should be an active, constructive and up-to-date dues-paying supporter of all the U.N. agencies with a significant role in global health (including, for example, the World Health Organization, UNICEF, and the United Nations Population Fund). The support to multilateral institutions should be the centerpiece in the U.S. support to global public goods such as international disease surveillance efforts and the implementation of strategies to reduce the spread of drug resistance.

Tapping into biomedical research and technical capacity in public health

Each year, the U.S. government spends more than $28 billion on biomedical research, primarily through the National Institutes of Health. Research is undertaken both through intramural programs and through competitively awarded grants to academic institutions. For progress in global health, and particularly for reducing the burden of tropical and parasitic diseases, there is tremendous promise in new scientific developments, and the National Institutes of Health is clearly at the forefront of these developments. These include, for example, the rapid sequencing of the genomes of pathogens that will yield new immunogens and drug targets and the development of new assays that enable scientists to measure biological changes at the genetic and molecular levels.

At the National Institutes of Health, the Fogarty International Center, with a budget so small that it barely appears on a graph comparing the different institutes' resources, is a focal point for important training and scientific exchange programs, and other institutes have research programs that operate—through clinical trials and other research endeavors—in developing countries. The National Institute of Allergy and Infectious Diseases has a particularly active global health program, with major investments in HIV/AIDS, malaria and, tuberculosis research. The AIDS vaccine trials are among the most visible examples of this, and the National Institutes of Health has a major stake in testing AIDS vaccine candidates in developing countries.

Given its unparalleled strength in biomedical research, the United States has the opportunity to do much, much more to realize the potential for global health aims—both those in which the United States has a clear self-interest (such as avian influenza) and those that are part of a broader development-related agenda, such as many tropical diseases. To put priority on global health across government, in a coherent way, the Fogarty International Center should be charged by the president with preparing an analysis of global health investments across the National Institutes of Health. The analysis should document the current levels and types of spending on programs that have international research or training components or both, or that are directed at biomedical problems that have particular salience in developing countries, including both diseases and means of using drugs, vaccines, and diagnostics (such as heat-stable insulin or vaccines). Moreover, it should identify a clear set of priorities for additional spending, with priorities driven by a combination of importance, probable lack of private sector involvement, and potential for significant advances within a five- to ten-year period. A particular emphasis should be given to establishing and strengthening institutional partnerships with universities and other research organizations in low- and middle-income countries, to permit capacity building and transfer of technology. These should be included in the president's budget message.

As an addition to the direct support provided for research on diseases that disproportionately affect developing countries, the president should promote and encourage Congress to fund an advance market commitment for a future vaccine product that would benefit developing countries. The advance market commitment concept is built around an understanding that commercial pharmaceutical firms are unlikely to invest in research and development or manufacturing capacity that would benefit low-income countries unless they can achieve a commercially viable return on investment.[10] Intended to make the development and manufacture of vaccines for developing countries more desirable, the advance market commitment provides a guaranteed and relatively high price to manufacturers if and when they license a product that meets specifications set out in advance and the products are in demand by developing countries. The new administration should work with Congress to provide U.S. support to an advance market commitment for a future vaccine product.

The current role of the CDC, and its potential for increased contributions in the future, is more complicated. With its tremendous concentration of technical expertise in public health, the CDC has been a key source of technical input and support to a range of multilateral organizations, including the World Health Organization and the World Bank, and has had an important in-country presence during the design, implementation, and evaluation of many successful health programs. Often without fanfare or attribution to the United States, CDC personnel have worked tirelessly to contain disease outbreaks; to transfer technical skills in epidemiology, surveillance, and health promotion to counterparts in developing countries; and to establish evidence-based technical norms and standards that have international applications. In recent years, the orientation of the CDC's global health program has changed, as it has become a key part of the PEPFAR effort and as new AIDS-focused dollars have flowed to and through the agency. In 2006, some $123 million were allocated to the program,[11] representing about one-third of all of the agency's international spending.[12]

Beyond the more traditional areas of assisting with the development of technical strategies and undertaking capacity development, CDC's global AIDS efforts are primarily devoted to on-the-ground implementation. CDC personnel in the fifteen PEPFAR focus countries are managing and staffing programs to provide treatment for AIDS, tuberculosis, and other infections that affect immuno-suppressed populations, as well as care and prevention services.

Given the recent transformation of the CDC's role in global health, the incoming administration will have to take a hard look at whether the "emergency response" to AIDS has had the unintended consequence of undermining (or at least hampering the development of) other important global health contributions that the agency could and should be making. The president should convene an independent high-level, expert commission to examine the CDC's global health work in the past decade, with particular attention to the activities under PEPFAR. The commission should produce specific recommendations about how to most effectively and appropriately deploy CDC's technical assets in the arena of global health, and establish the ground rules for CDC's engagement in implementation of development assistance programs. These ground rules should be respected in the execution of the second phase of PEPFAR.

Counting the casualties

Wars are bad for health, plain and simple. And not just the health of combatants but the health of the general public in affected countries as a result of internal displacement, exposure to increased environmental risks, breakdown in supply chains, and other factors. In most conflict situations, the majority of health impacts are indirect: Although a subject of debate, the ratio of indirect to direct deaths due to conflict has been reported to be as high as 9:1.[13] No definitive and agreed-upon estimates exist of the health toll of the Iraq war, for example, but it is widely accepted that between 2002 and 2006 more than 100,000 Iraqi civilians[14] lost their lives as a direct or indirect result of military action. Children have been hard hit by both the pre-invasion sanctions and the military conflict. In 2005, one in eight Iraqi children died of disease or violence before age five. Strikingly, a review conducted by Save the Children in 2007 showed that the death rate for children under age five increased in Iraq over a decade by 150 percent—the greatest increase among all sixty countries included in the study.[15]

Decisions about military actions are not and will never be predicated on the potential health effects. However, the civilian health effects of war should be measured, along with the other costs. At a minimum, the new president should issue an executive order requiring that relevant federal agencies, under the guidance of an independent expert panel, cooperate to apply standard epidemiologic methods to measure and publicly report on population-based health indicators in conflict-affected areas.

An opportunity to shine on the world stage, building on fundamental strengths

The incoming president will have many domestic and international challenges to face, and the natural inclination will be to put on the back burner the programs that are reasonably well funded and generally uncontroversial. This could well happen with the U.S. engagement in global health: keep it bubbling along, keep on spending an increasing number of dollars on life-extending medicines for people with AIDS, and make no major effort to set a straighter and more productive course that would take advantage of the many strengths of the U.S. government and U.S. citizens.

That would be a mistake.

If there is one part of the broad development agenda that is of interest to the U.S. public, it is health. We want our government to be part of the solution—to help provide the best that the United States has to alleviate the most apparent and immediate types of human suffering. American voters will hold the president accountable for taking actions that will save lives, foster the basis for prosperity, and help to restore America's damaged reputation.

But responding with compassion and urgency alone will never create the platform for the best outcomes over the long term, nor will it permit the full range of U.S. assets to be deployed. What the new president needs—and can create through a specific set of actions, within a coherent framework—is a clear, ambitious, and practical agenda across all agencies to achieve broad development goals.

Notes

1. World Bank 2005.
2. Institute of Medicine 1997.
3. OECD–DAC 2007.
4. Wilson Center 2006.
5. Global Health Council 2007.
6. Institute of Medicine 2007.
7. Global Health Council n.d.
8. Friends of the Global Fight against AIDS, Tuberculosis, and Malaria 2006.
9. UNAUSA 2006.
10. Levine, Kremer, and Albright 2005.
11. PEPFAR n.d.
12. CDC 2007.
13. Murray and others 2002.
14. IBC 2008.
15. Save the Children 2007.

References

CDC (Centers for Disease Control and Prevention). 2007. "FY2008 President's Budget: Detail Table." Atlanta, Ga. [www.cdc.gov/fmo/PDFs/FY_2008_Presidents_Budget_Detail_Table.pdf].

Friends of the Global Fight against AIDS, Tuberculosis, and Malaria. 2006. "White House Announces FY07 Budget Request for Global Fund to Fight AIDS, Tuberculosis and Malaria." [http://theglobalfight.org/downloads/Releases/Release_FY07Budget_06Feb06.pdf].

Global Health Council. 2007. *Global Health Opportunities Report: 2007 Update on Priorities and US Investments*. Washington, D.C. [www.globalhealth.org/view_top .php3?id=568].

———. n.d. "Global Health Funding." [www.globalhealth.org/public_policy/ funding/].

IBC (Iraq Body Count). 2008. [www.iraqbodycount.org/].

Institute of Medicine. 1997. *America's Vital Interest in Global Health: Protecting Our People, Enhancing Our Economy, and Advancing Our International Interests.* Washington, D.C.: National Academies Press.

———. 2005. *Healers Abroad: Americans Responding to the Human Resource Crisis in HIV/AIDS*. Washington, D.C.: National Academies Press.

———. 2007. *PEPFAR Implementation: Progress and Promise*. Washington, D.C.: National Academies Press.

Jolly, P. 2004. "Medical School Tuition and Young Physician Indebtedness." Association of American Medical Colleges, Washington, D.C. [https://services.aamc.org/ Publications/showfile.cfm?file=version21.pdf&prd_id=102&prv_id=113&pdf_id=21].

Levine, Ruth. 2007. *Case Studies in Global Health: Millions Saved*. Boston, Mass.: Jones and Bartlett Publishers.

Levine, R., M. Kremer, and A. Albright. 2005. *Making Markets for Vaccines: Ideas to Action*. Washington, D.C.: Center for Global Development.

Murray, C.J.L., G. King, A.D. Lopez, N. Tomijima, and E.G. Krug. 2002. "Armed Conflict as a Public Health Problem." *British Medical Journal* 324: 346–49.

NIH (National Institutes of Health). "Funding Strategy: Fiscal Year 2008." John E. Fogarty International Center, Washington, D.C. [www.fic.nih.gov/funding/ 2008funding.htm#budget].

OECD–DAC (Organisation for Economic Co-operation and Development–Development Assistance Committee). 2007. "International Development Statistics." Creditor Reporting System, Paris. [www.oecd.org/document/0/0,2340,en_2649_ 34447_37679488_1_1_1_1,00.html].

PEPFAR (President's Emergency Plan for AIDS Relief). n.d. "Sources of Funding FY 2004–FY 2006." [www.pepfar.gov/about/77649.htm].

Research!America. 2006. *Investing in Health Can Change the World*. Alexandria, Va. [www.researchamerica.org/uploads/poll2006ghr.pdf]

Sarfaty, S., and L.K. Arnold. 2005. "Preparing for International Medical Service." *Emergency Medicine Clinics of North America* 23: 149–75.

Save the Children. 2007. *State of the World's Mothers 2007: Saving the Lives of Children under 5*. Westport, Conn. [www.savethechildren.org/campaigns/state-of-the-worlds -mothers-report/2007/].

UNAUSA (United Nations Association of the United States of America). 2006. "United Nations Funding." New York. [www.unausa.org/site/pp.asp?c=fvKRI8MPJpF&b= 667579].

Wilson Center (Woodrow Wilson International Center for Scholars). 2006. "Mechanisms for Health Systems Management: Reflections on the World Bank and USAID Experiences." Conference, October 24. [www.wilsoncenter.org/index.cfm ?fuseaction=events.event_summary&event_id=208176].

World Bank. 2005. *East Asia Update: Countering Global Shocks*. Washington, D.C.

2

Global Warming: An Opportunity for Greatness

David Wheeler

The next president can secure a place in history by mobilizing America to confront climate change, while starting a clean energy revolution that will strengthen American security and create the next wave of economic growth. The president should seize this opportunity because climate change presents a mortal threat: If left unchecked, global warming will undermine the hard-won achievements of developing countries, inflict severe damage on the United States and other rich countries, and destabilize so many societies that the international system will be threatened.

Reducing carbon emissions will also involve both developed and developing countries because each side is emitting enough to create an environmental disaster The next president will confront this challenge immediately on taking office. Only eleven months after Inauguration Day, the international community will meet in Copenhagen to negotiate the successor to the Kyoto Protocol. The Copenhagen compact promises to be a milestone in world history that will commit both developed and developing countries to a low-carbon future. To prevent environmental disaster, the compact will have to limit carbon emissions and promote clean energy sources. But to be sustainable, it will also have to enlist the support of developing countries by aligning itself with the struggle against poverty. This struggle cannot succeed without more energy, and for that reason the compact

---

David Wheeler is a senior fellow at the Center for Global Development.

will have to finance the costly switch from fossil fuels to clean power in developing countries. It will also have to finance adaptation to climate change so that past development gains will not be lost. This is fair, because poor countries that have contributed the least to global warming will suffer its harshest impacts. It is also politically necessary, because China, India, and other developing countries will not participate without adaptation assistance.

Negotiating such a broad arrangement will be daunting for the next president, and it will be futile if the U.S. Senate refuses to ratify the compact. Fortunately, the president will be able to ride the surge of support for the needed measures that has accompanied greater public understanding of the problem. During the past year, bipartisan legislation for efficient regulation of U.S. greenhouse gas emissions reached the Senate floor; the European Union proposed new emissions regulations that can easily be harmonized with U.S. legislation; China and India acknowledged the need for emissions limits at the U.N. Bali conference; the Bush administration accepted the principle of emissions limits; and the administration began supporting new multilateral programs to finance clean technology investment, forest conservation, and adaptation to global warming in poor countries.

With these elements in place, the next president can rapidly develop a negotiating package for Copenhagen that commands strong bipartisan support. The president can also make a powerful argument that the compact will promote American economic and security interests. It will increase prosperity by exploiting America's comparative advantage in clean energy, which is based on the most plentiful and most diverse renewable energy resources in the world. By reducing the dependence of the United States and its allies on Middle Eastern oil, the compact will broaden the options for U.S. foreign policy. Equally important, leadership at Copenhagen and strong promotion of the international transition to clean energy will revive confidence in the U.S.'s commitment to responsible global governance.

The critical role of developing countries

Developing countries are critical to U.S. engagement at Copenhagen and beyond for two major reasons: First, they will be hardest hit by global warming because so many are in the tropical belt that will bear the brunt of climate change. If global warming is not halted, its impact will undermine the global war on poverty by impoverishing millions, expanding the range of dangerous communicable diseases, and creating major instability in areas that are critical to U.S. security interests. U.S. development efforts of the last eight years—the Africa initiative and the campaigns against malaria and HIV/AIDS—will also be set back enormously. Second, the well-being of Americans themselves depends on limiting greenhouse emissions from developing countries. These are rising so rapidly that they will soon create a level of global warming that is dangerous for the United States, even if the United States and other rich countries eliminate their carbon emissions entirely. In short, global warming has bound the fate of the United States to the fate of all developing countries. We either prosper sustainably together, or not at all.

Impacts of global warming on developing countries

Global warming is well under way, and its consequences are already visible in many developing countries. Severe drought lurks behind the Darfur conflict,[1] a rising sea level is already driving thousands of people off islands in the Sundarbans of Bangladesh and India,[2] and a report issued by the World Meteorological Organization in August 2007 links global warming to unprecedented rainfall and flooding in China and South Asia.[3] The poorest countries are least capable of adapting to such impacts, and the poorest people in those countries will be hardest hit.

Map 2.1, which is based on research at the Center for Global Development, displays the projected impact of temperature and rainfall changes on agriculture if global warming is not halted. A dark swath, signifying agricultural productivity losses greater than 25 percent, covers many developing regions: Central America, northern South America, and much of Africa, the Middle East, and South Asia. A billion of the world's poorest people live in these areas, many of them dependent on agriculture for their livelihood. Losses of the projected magnitude—more than 40 percent in many parts of India, for example—will be unprecedented (box 2.1).

While some areas will bake in the rising heat, others will drown. A warmer world will also be a wetter world, as greater evaporation leads to

Map 2.1. Projected global agricultural productivity losses

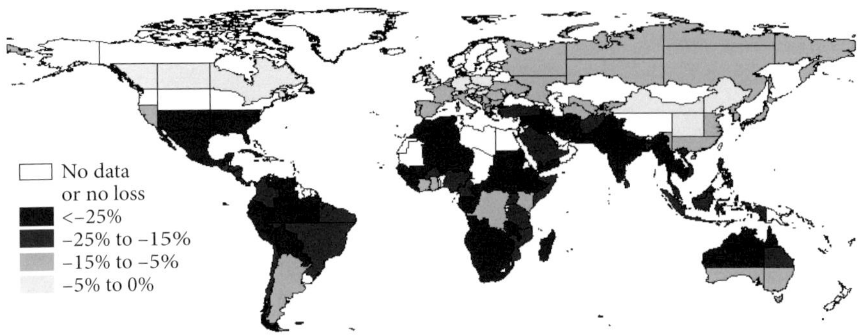

Source: Cline 2007.

Box 2.1. The threat of global warming to world agriculture

Among the most serious risks of global warming is the threat to world agriculture. Especially near the equator, temperatures are already near crop-tolerance levels. The loss of water through evaporation from the soil and through transpiration will increase rapidly as temperatures rise, outstripping any increases in rainfall in many major agricultural areas. Incidence of severe drought, like that of the 1930s dust bowl or more recently in Australia, would likely increase.

Cline (2007) combines the averaged projections of six leading climate models with models from agricultural economics to project the effects of global warming on world agriculture by the 2080s. Only such a long-term view can begin to show the extent of damages from severe global warming. The impact models incorporate results from experimental evidence relating agricultural yields to temperature, rainfall, and soil quality with results from statistical models relating differences in the value of farmland to differences in climate. Applying these models requires estimating how much yields might increase from the uncertain effect of "carbon fertilization" in a more carbon-rich atmosphere, because photosynthesis uses carbon dioxide as an input, along with water and sunlight, to create plant material.

The calculations indicate that, by the 2080s, unarrested global warming would reduce world agricultural potential 5–15 percent from the levels that it would otherwise reach, depending on whether carbon fertilization is included. This range is most likely an understatement because it omits damage from severe drought and increased insect pests and because it does not consider the effects of even more severe global warming subsequent to the period examined.

Furthermore, the estimated damages fall disproportionately on developing countries, which tend to be closer to the equator. By the 2080s, reductions in productivity would be severe in India (losses of 30–40 percent), Africa (20–30 percent), and Latin America (15–25 percent). For both China and the United States the overall average would be plus or minus about 7 percent, depending on carbon fertilization, but with large regional variations.

The southern half of the United States would suffer losses of 15–25 percent, while the northern half would see gains of 15–30 percent. In China there would be similar disparities. Losses in Mexico would reach 25–35 percent and likely put pressure on immigration to the United States.

The study finds that technological change is no panacea for this problem. The green revolution has slowed as annual global yield increases in grains have fallen from about 2.8 percent in the 1960s and 1970s to 1.6 percent in the last quarter century. Population growth and rising incomes are likely to multiply the demand for food threefold by the 2080s, but the diversion of land to biofuels could reduce by a third the area of land otherwise available for food crops. The race between growth in supply and growth in demand will be close even if the pace of technological change does not slow any further—the agricultural losses due to global warming could be very painful indeed, especially in developing countries.

—William Cline

more moisture and much heavier rainfall and severe flooding in some areas. Warmer seas and greater atmospheric moisture will also increase the power of hurricanes, magnifying their destructive coastal impacts in the Caribbean, Central America, East Asia, and South Asia.[4] As part of this trend, 2007 witnessed the first major hurricane landfalls in Brazil and the Arabian Peninsula.[5]

Coastal storm surges from hurricane-force winds are increased by sea-level rise, which will be accelerated by icecap melting. The Fourth Assessment of the Intergovernmental Panel on Climate Change does not take a clear position on this problem, but recently published extrapolations from new data on icecap melting in Greenland and West Antarctica indicate that the sea level could rise as much as ten feet in this century.[6] Recent work by researchers at the Center for Global Development and the World Bank shows the stark consequences for developing countries if this occurs: Major food-producing delta areas in countries such as Bangladesh, Egypt, and Vietnam will be lost to the sea, and more than 200 million people in developing countries will become refugees from coastal flooding.[7]

To summarize, unchecked global warming will have an enormous impact on developing countries. Many will be afflicted by droughts, wildfires, floods, coastal storms and inundation, massive population displacements, and enormous financial losses. The impact will be most catastrophic for the poorest, who are most vulnerable. The current international order seems unlikely to remain stable in the face of such shocks. And, in fact, the U.S. military has already begun thinking about the consequences for national security. In a recent report, several retired American generals have highlighted the severity of potential threats from global warming.[8]

Developing countries as sources of global warming

Recent research has overturned the notion that developed countries caused global warming, so developed countries will have to solve it. In this outmoded view, developing countries have contributed only marginally to the problem, and in any case they must focus on overcoming poverty before they can worry about reducing carbon emissions. Unfortunately, as figures 2.1 and 2.2 show, this view is wrong, dangerous for developing countries themselves, and potentially catastrophic for global society.[9] Figure 2.1 summarizes the most recent evidence on cumulative carbon dioxide emissions from developed and developing countries since 1965, with a projection to 2035 from the Intergovernmental Panel on Climate Change. It shows, contrary to the conventional wisdom, that the two groups are already close to parity as sources of global warming and that developing countries will become the dominant source within 20 years.

Figure 2.1. Cumulative CO_2 emissions from developed and developing countries, actual and projected

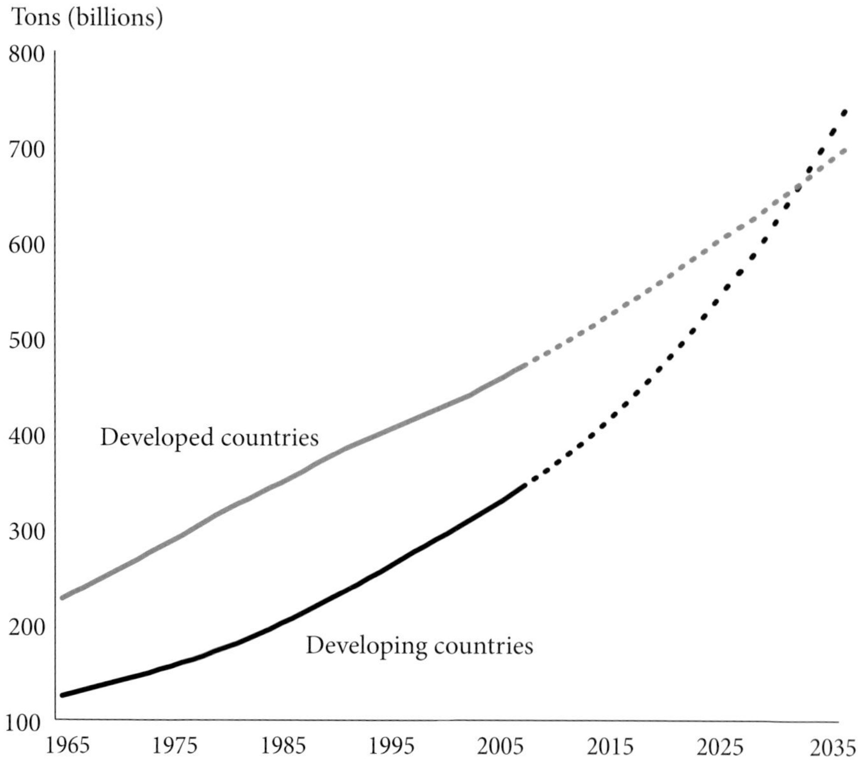

Source: Wheeler and Ummel 2007.

Three powerful forces are behind this trend: The first is economic growth along the carbon-intensive path that rich countries followed. The second is rapid deforestation, which is releasing enormous volumes of carbon into the atmosphere. The third is population growth—developing countries are far more populous than developed countries, and for that reason their total emissions will reach crisis levels at much lower levels of income (and emissions) per capita.

Figure 2.2 translates the cumulative emissions in figure 2.1 into historical atmospheric carbon dioxide concentrations for the entire world, as well as the part that is attributable to developing countries. Its implication is stark: By 2025, developing countries alone will match the global situation in 1986—when the scientific community's sense of impending climate crisis catalyzed U.S. support for the 1992 U.N. Conference on Environment and Development in Rio de Janeiro.

Figure 2.2. Comparative atmospheric CO_2 concentrations: world and developing countries, actual and projected

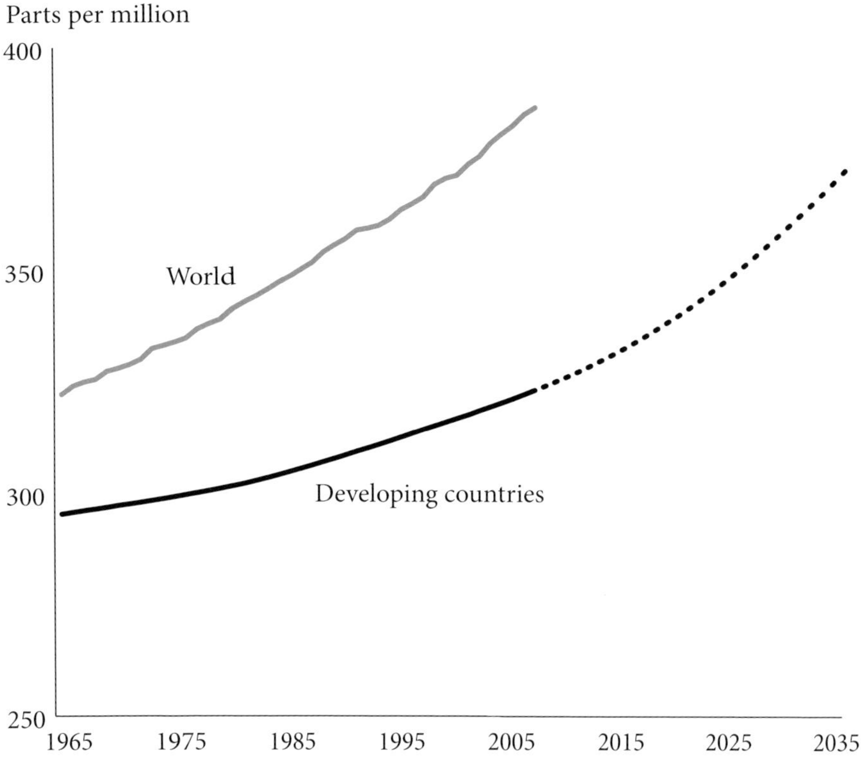

Source: Wheeler and Ummel 2007.

For the next president, this sobering reality defines a critical message: Carbon emissions from either developed or developing countries alone are sufficient to set off a climate crisis in this generation. Neither side has a hope of vanquishing global warming without the other, and for that reason the president cannot avoid developing countries in mapping a path to Copenhagen and beyond. As concerned global citizens, Americans cannot be indifferent to the potentially ruinous impact of climate change on many of the world's poorest people. And self-interest also mandates a focus on developing countries, for two reasons: First, U.S. security will be threatened if global warming creates mass instability and millions of environmental refugees in developing countries. Second, and even more fundamentally, climate change from developing-country emissions will ultimately devastate the United States if they remain unchecked.

Recent policy developments: setting the stage for Copenhagen

In preparing for Copenhagen, the next president can draw on a legacy of strong U.S. leadership. Twenty years ago, Ronald Reagan demonstrated that a U.S. president can lead rapid, decisive international action to prevent catastrophic global damage from polluting emissions. Faced with the threat of atmospheric ozone depletion and massive exposure to ultraviolet radiation, the United States led the international community in negotiating and implementing the Montreal Protocol to phase out ozone-depleting chemicals.[10] The negotiating issues in Montreal closely resembled the issues to be addressed at the Copenhagen conference: multiple emitted substances that pose long-term risks of serious but uncertain magnitude, the need to set ambitious targets for emissions reduction by individual countries; uncertainties about the path of clean technology development and associated costs, the threat of rapid emissions expansion from developing countries, and the need to sanction noncompliance. The Montreal Protocol incorporated all these elements, was ratified by the U.S. Senate and ultimately by more than 190 countries, and proved largely successful in phasing out ozone-depleting chemicals at significantly lower cost than originally estimated.

Led by the United States, the global community coalesced rapidly around the Montreal Protocol because of two factors that also characterize the current crisis: First, the international community could act rapidly on ozone-depleting substances because substitutes were commercially available, albeit at higher cost. The same is true for many carbon-emitting activities: Low-carbon alternatives are commercially available at higher costs, which will decline as expanding use promotes scale economies and movement down learning curves. Second, the scientific community had convincingly demonstrated that ozone depletion was extremely dangerous. Now the *Fourth Assessment Report of the Intergovernmental Panel on Climate Change* has demonstrated the same thing for greenhouse gas emissions.[11] The next president should respond by following President Reagan's example and leading the United States into a comprehensive accord at Copenhagen. This will require rapid action after Inauguration Day, but the necessary elements are already falling into place.

Efficient regulation of greenhouse emissions

To be efficient, regulation of U.S. greenhouse gas emissions requires a commitment to emissions limits, implementation via a market-based regulatory instrument (cap-and-trade or carbon charges), and full transparency to ensure credibility. Fortunately for the next president, all three elements are now in place. The first element is a change in the U.S. position on emissions limits. At the U.N. December 2007 climate change conference in Bali, Indonesia, the Bush administration dropped its previous categorical rejection of binding greenhouse emissions limits. The U.S. position changed for two essential reasons: increased popular support for carbon emissions control at home and a decision by China and India to accept the principle that reduction of their emissions could be part of a future agreement.

The concession made by China and India is important because the exclusion of developing countries from emissions limits has consistently been cited as the main reason for U.S. refusal to limit its own emissions. In July 1997, the U.S. Senate preemptively voted 95–0 to reject the Kyoto Protocol if it contained a developing-country exclusion, and Democratic Senator John Kerry reiterated the same principle at the Bali conference.[12] It seems nearly certain that the Senate will refuse to ratify any global compact that excludes developing countries from emissions limits.

The second element is rapid movement toward domestic regulation of emissions via market-based instruments. Regional programs to reduce carbon dioxide emissions through cap-and-trade programs now include half of the U.S. states, and more than 700 U.S. cities have launched low-carbon initiatives under the Mayors Climate Protection Agreement. Rising public concern has also led members of the Senate and House to introduce many proposals for carbon emissions regulation—nine focused on cap-and-trade and three on carbon taxes.[13] The furthest-advanced measure is the bipartisan America's Climate Security Act, a cap-and-trade measure sponsored by Independent Senator Joseph Lieberman and Republican Senator John Warner. The act was approved by the Senate Committee on Environment and Public Works in December 2007.

The third element is transparency, which is well advanced in the United States. The U.S. Environmental Protection Agency's Toxics Release Inventory, established under the Emergency Planning and Community Right-to-Know Act of 1986, requires public reports from all large toxic polluters in the United States. This program is widely credited with achieving major reductions in toxic chemical emissions. The agency's Emissions and Generation Resource Integrated Database publicly reports carbon dioxide emissions from thousands of power plants. Thirty-nine states and the District of Columbia have joined the Climate Registry, which publicly reports emissions from business firms and municipalities, and Congress has considered several mandates for public disclosure of carbon emissions in the United States. These include a provision in the Senate's appropriations bill for the Interior Department for fiscal year 2008, the Greenhouse Gas Accountability Act of 2007, and America's Climate Security Act.

Harmonization with EU greenhouse emissions regulation

The European Union and the United States are moving toward similar cap-and-trade systems for carbon emissions regulation, which could be linked at Copenhagen to form the core of an expanding global system. In January 2008, the European Union announced plans for revised carbon regulations that closely resemble the provisions of America's Climate Security Act. The previous EU cap-and-trade system generated windfall profits by distributing emissions permits to polluters, and it did little to reduce overall emissions. Like America's Climate Security Act, the new EU plan sets tough emissions reduction goals, auctions a significant percentage of emissions permits, and covers a large percentage of emitters. It also includes a mandatory increase in the use of biofuels that parallels a provision of the U.S. Energy Independence and Security Act, signed by President Bush in December 2007.[14]

Promotion of clean technology

The United States has numerous programs that subsidize the development of clean energy technologies.[15] The U.S. Department of Energy currently spends about $3 billion a year on clean energy development, mostly through grants and contracts awarded to U.S. national research laboratories, universities, and private firms. Smaller-scale efforts, generally focused on more basic scientific research, are funded by the National Science Foundation. The clean-energy research and development complex in the United States—including national labs, private labs, and universities—is so large that it could easily absorb a major increase in funding. The government also promotes clean technology indirectly, through mandated standards. An important recent example is the Energy Independence and Security Act, which will reduce the intensity of carbon emissions from motor vehicles by raising fuel economy standards and extending them to more vehicle classes.

Incentives for clean technology adoption in developing countries

Until recently, U.S. international assistance policy has focused on relatively small clean technology promotion measures such as the Asia-Pacific Partnership on Clean Development and Climate, the Global Village Energy Partnership, the Global Partnership for Clean Fuels and Vehicles, and the Renewable Energy Policy Network. This modest posture changed abruptly in January 2008, when President Bush launched an international Clean Technology Fund, committed $2 billion for its first three years, and invited other donors to participate. The initial fund will be administered by the World Bank and will be open to proposals from a large number of multilateral and bilateral aid agencies.[16]

Incentives for forest conservation in developing countries

U.S. development assistance has long included programs for tropical forest conservation, which is important to limit the enormous volume of emissions from forest-clearing. An appropriate multilateral fund for this purpose, the Forest Carbon Partnership Facility, was launched by the World Bank and nine donor countries in conjunction with the Bali conference in December 2007. The fund is focused on payment for forest conservation in developing countries. It has nine initial donors and an initial subscription of $160 million.[17] The United States has not yet subscribed to the facility, but it seems quite likely to do so in the near future.

Adaptation assistance

Traditional U.S. development assistance has many elements that are relevant for adaptation to climate change, including improved weather forecasting, development of drought-resistant crops, and flood control. However, the United States is now focusing on multilateral support through the Adaptation Fund, which was launched at the U.N. Nairobi conference in 2006. This fund will be financed by a 2 percent tax on transactions through the Clean Development Mechanism, under which rich countries receive carbon credits for investing in carbon-saving projects in developing countries. Management of the Adaptation Fund was assigned to the Global Environment Facility at the Bali conference in December 2007.

To summarize, recent policy developments have created all the basic elements for an integrated U.S. climate policy position at Copenhagen. The challenge for the next president will be to assemble these elements into a policy package, scale the proposed funding to the requisite levels, and sell the program to the American people.

Leading the clean energy revolution

Keeping greenhouse emissions within safe limits will require a rapid, massive shift to clean energy sources. Fortunately, U.S. scientists, engineers, and leading venture capitalists are convinced that the next president can launch this clean energy revolution without further delay. For example, Vinod Khosla, called the best venture capitalist in the world by *Forbes* magazine, is promoting large-scale investment in solar thermal power.[18] It is not hard to see why: The sun annually supplies the earth with over 80,000 terawatts of energy, while current human power consumption is about 15 terawatts. Current solar technology could power the whole United States from a small portion of Nevada (map 2.2).

In January 2008, *Scientific American* extended Khosla's vision by presenting a Solar Grand Plan to provide 69 percent of U.S. electricity and 35 percent of its total energy from solar power by 2050.[19] The program would require federal support of about $400 billion spread over 40 years (for

Map 2.2. Nevada: area required to power the entire U.S. with solar energy

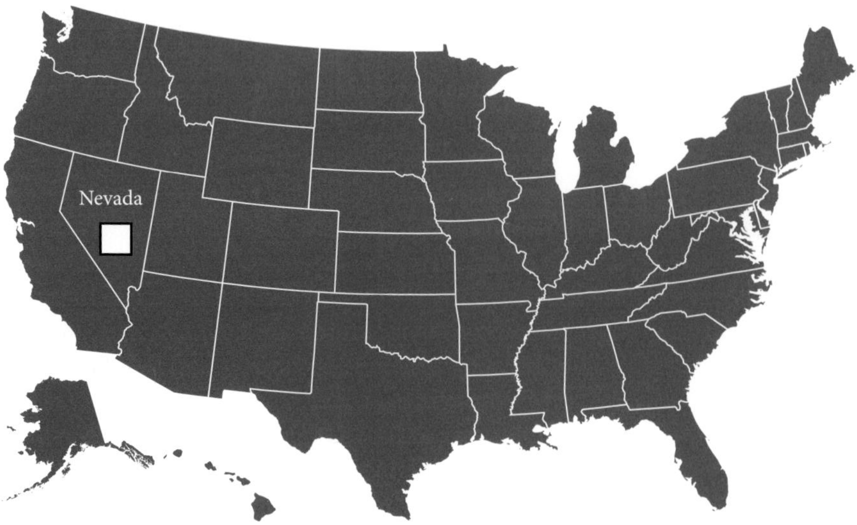

Source: Reprinted with permission from Turner 1999.

comparison, the Iraq war has cost more than $500 billion in only five years). The program's authors estimate that the system would deliver electricity to consumers for about 5 cents per kilowatt-hour—the same as today's average rate. Parallel development of biofuel, wind, and geothermal resources would provide 100 percent of the nation's electricity and 90 percent of its energy by 2100. The proposed system would eliminate almost all oil imports, relieve the balance of payments, reduce total U.S. carbon emissions by 62 percent, and eliminate a huge source of domestic air pollution. Once installed, it would tap an infinite, free source of power. Installing and operating the system would also catalyze an economic boom, generating millions of new jobs.

It is important to stress that programs like the Solar Grand Plan are not science fiction—all the needed technologies exist today. Such large-scale federal programs have driven U.S. technological and economic development for many years. Examples include nuclear energy, the interstate highway system, the moon landing, digital computing and communications, and the Internet.

What is true for the United States is also true for the world. With existing technologies, solar and other renewable energy sources can power most countries with room to spare. Recently, researchers at the Center for Global

Development and the World Bank quantified renewable energy potentials for 200 countries, basing their calculations on technologies that can be implemented now. Their results show that renewable energy potential meets or exceeds total energy demand in almost every country in the world's developing regions, including giants such as Brazil, China, and India.[20]

Policies for promoting a low-carbon economy

To succeed, the Copenhagen negotiations will have to link developed and developing countries in a compact that simultaneously raises the price of carbon emissions, lowers the price of clean energy, finances a rapid transition to clean energy in developing countries, and assists them with adaptation to the warming that is already inevitable. The Copenhagen compact will replace the Kyoto Protocol, which has set emissions reduction targets for only 36 of its 174 signatory countries. Despite its limitations, the protocol has established useful precedents by setting targets, implementing a market-based mechanism (cap-and-trade) for reaching them, and establishing a Clean Development Mechanism that enables developed countries to finance carbon emissions reduction projects in developing countries. However, the Copenhagen compact must go well beyond the Kyoto Protocol to insure against dangerous global warming. It will have to set emissions reduction targets for many more countries, while holding overall emissions within scientifically determined safe limits. For success at Copenhagen, the next president should pursue the following objectives.

1. Public disclosure of global carbon emissions

The Kyoto Protocol has already created a global consensus in favor of carbon pricing via market-based regulation of emissions sources. This consensus has immediate significance for policy because carbon charges and cap-and-trade require the same information for credible monitoring and enforcement. In the run-up to Copenhagen, the next president should immediately promote an audited global inventory of all significant carbon emissions sources that will provide the common database for market-based regulation. The program should be vested in a U.N.-affiliated institution that has the resources, technical skills, and global reach to sustain the inventory permanently. The World Bank appears best qualified to assume this role.

Setting up the inventory will be a major challenge, requiring common measurement standards, reporting protocols for emissions sources, and technical assistance to firms that will be charged with reporting emissions. An independent system for auditing emissions reports also has to be established. These tasks will take some time to complete, and for that reason the work should begin immediately.

The next step toward efficient global regulation is also straightforward. Once the global inventory is established, it should report emissions from all sources to the public. This is important for several reasons: First, it provides an entry point for countries that accept the principle of global regulation, without imposing formal sanctions on polluters. Second, disclosure is a necessary prelude to efficient carbon regulation. For market-based regulation to work credibly in the global arena, it will have to operate in a transparent, audited information environment. Starting disclosure now will work out the kinks in the information system, establish the principle of transparency, and develop generally-accepted emissions benchmarks for formal regulation. Third, extensive experience in developed and developing countries indicates that disclosure itself will reduce emissions by empowering stakeholders (such as consumers, investors, and community organizations) to pressure polluters.[21]

2. A higher price for carbon

Promoting a rapid shift to clean energy requires raising the price of carbon. This can be done directly, by limiting the supply of fossil fuels, or indirectly, by restricting or charging for carbon emissions. Extensive regulatory experience shows that a market-based approach—carbon charges, cap-and-trade, or a hybrid system—is the most economically efficient. Both carbon charges and cap-and-trade have their strengths and weaknesses, and each system has strong partisans.[22]

Carbon charges are administratively convenient because they do not require any new institutions, and they can be made fiscally neutral by cutting other taxes or fees. But economies are complex, and the ultimate impact of a particular charge rate on carbon emissions cannot be predicted with any accuracy. For that reason, a politically acceptable program with emissions reduction targets will undoubtedly include rules for adjusting the charge as the emissions response is revealed.[23]

A cap-and-trade system, in contrast, requires a new institution to allocate emissions permits. It provides an element of certainty by enforcing an overall emissions reduction target for the economy, but the resulting permit price cannot be predicted with any accuracy. Accordingly, a politically acceptable cap-and-trade program will undoubtedly include rules for adjusting the supply of permits as the price response is revealed.[24] Cap-and-trade also confronts the problem of initial permit allocation, by auction or distribution to existing polluters. Although the latter is politically easier, it generates no public revenue and rewards polluters with free permits that will have high market value as the overall carbon emissions limit tightens.

Experience shows that either carbon charges or cap-and-trade can work, and for that reason the next president's position at Copenhagen should emphasize fast action rather than a uniform global regulatory program that is unlikely to work anyway. Recent policy developments indicate that Australia, Canada, the European Union, and the United States will almost certainly prefer cap-and-trade. But many European countries also have carbon taxes, and Japan continues to debate the issue. Many developing countries may be unwilling or unable to implement cap-and-trade because they have neither the institutional capacity nor the requisite policy experience.[25] Some may prefer cruder measures that are much easier to monitor and enforce, such as restricting fossil fuel supplies by phasing out domestic extraction. Some developing countries may opt for source-based carbon charges, which offer administrative simplicity and potential fiscal neutrality. Such charges are levied on the carbon content of fossil fuels at the relatively few points where they are mined or imported, thereby raising their relative price in local energy markets and encouraging substitution toward cleaner alternatives. Fiscal neutrality can be ensured by reducing other taxes as carbon revenues increase.

Different approaches will be appropriate for different circumstances, and for that reason the Copenhagen negotiators should not attempt to impose one global regulatory system. Rather, the Copenhagen compact should emulate the successful Montreal Protocol by focusing on country-specific emissions targets, flexibility to adjust targets as science and economics evolve, and transparent reporting and accountability for commitments. The compact should leave individual countries considerable latitude in the choice of measures to fulfill their commitments.

The global emissions disclosure program operated for the United Nations by the World Bank will provide consistent tracking of countries' compliance with the Copenhagen compact. This program should publish yearly audits by country and emissions source, easily accessible on the Internet. Compliance incentives should focus on collaborative resolution of disputed cases and relentless public pressure from multilateral organizations, political leaders, and nongovernmental organizations. The Montreal Protocol experience suggests that these measures should suffice. In the last resort, explicit sanctions could be invoked. These should be avoided initially, however, because they can easily degenerate into protectionist invocation of trade sanctions.

3. A lower price for clean energy

The critical measures to lower the price are clean-energy research and development and subsidies for large start-up investments to achieve scale economies and movement down learning curves. In the United States and other developed economies, the necessary financing can be generated by earmarking revenues from emissions charges or auctioned emissions permits. The next president should promote international collaboration to minimize redundancy in national programs, ensure timely publication of results, and manage patenting to ensure rapid, competitive development of promising technologies. Common resources could also be devoted to very large public awards for development of clean technologies that meet prespecified criteria.

Ample precedents exist for these measures. Recently, coordinated mass purchases of vaccines that benefit the poor have been recommended to the Group of Eight.[26] The World Trade Organization's compulsory licensing provision is also a useful precedent. It allows for relaxation of patent laws to ensure local supplies of essential drugs at affordable prices in developing countries.[27] Since the Intergovernmental Panel on Climate Change has declared global warming to be a planetary crisis, a similar principle could be invoked. The primary challenge will be to design intellectual property policies that promote rapid diffusion of clean technologies without unduly discouraging clean-energy research and development by the private sector.

4. Low-carbon development in poor countries

Moving poor countries onto the low-carbon development path will require large-scale financial and technical assistance, as well as incentives from higher carbon prices and lower clean technology prices. The three most critical tasks are the transition to renewable energy, greater efficiency in energy use, and the end of large-scale forest-burning.

Energy-related assistance should be delivered in two parallel, multilateral tracks that have complementary roles. On one track, a clean technology fund should support large-scale development of renewable energy systems to replace fossil-fuel systems as rapidly as possible. The fund should finance the cost gap between renewable and fossil power, concentrating its resources to close this gap as rapidly as possible through production scale economies and learning curves. On the other track, a reformed version of the Kyoto Protocol's Clean Development Mechanism would use more decentralized incentives to finance a broader spectrum of clean technologies and energy-efficiency improvements.

A Clean Technology Fund. In January 2008, the United States proposed a Clean Technology Fund that will be multilateral, potentially large (the initial U.S. contribution is $2 billion for three years), administered by one agency (initially the World Bank), and open to proposals from diverse international aid institutions. To realize its potential, however, the fund will have to meet several additional criteria.

First, it will have to operate at an appropriate scale. The International Energy Administration has estimated that closing the cost gap between conventional and clean energy technologies will require about $30 billion annually for many years. One prominent study, *The Economics of Climate Change: The Stern Review*, estimates the annual gap at around $20 billion.[28] Obviously, the Clean Technology Fund's initial U.S. contribution of $2 billion over three years should be viewed only as a down payment.

Second, the fund will have to focus multilateral resources on common objectives, with allocations based on project evaluation rather than political criteria. A recent development shows that this is far from guaranteed. Simultaneously with the U.S. proposal for a Clean Technology Fund, Japan announced a Cool Earth Partnership that will have $10 billion in funding for five years. At Copenhagen, the next president should urge Japan and other donors to coordinate their contributions, while preserving a healthy measure of competition in the provision and allocation of funds.

Third, the Clean Technology Fund should focus on renewable energy, not "clean coal" and other incremental improvements that will barely slow the growth of global carbon emissions. To ensure this focus, the fund should consider only those energy project proposals that treat a renewable energy source as the default option, and it should require rigorous justification for any carbon-emitting option that is recommended. Justification should include explicit carbon accounting, using a carbon emissions charge that is compatible with the international emissions reduction target of the Copenhagen compact. The Stern Review has proposed an appropriate charge of about $80 per ton for carbon dioxide emissions.[29, 30] The new EU climate action plan envisions a charge of around $50 per ton for its proposed emissions regulation system.[31] According to a recent study at the Center for Global Development, either charge would make renewable energy the preferred option for many projects.[32] In an illustration for Botswana, the study shows that both solar thermal power and carbon capture and storage are less costly than conventionally "efficient" supercritical coal combustion at a carbon dioxide emissions charge of about $35 per ton.

Fourth, the Clean Technology Fund should promote innovative investor guarantees to encourage rapid adoption of renewable technologies. Because the fund will initially be administered by the World Bank, the simplest reform might be an extension of risk insurance services offered by the Bank Group's Multilateral Investment Guarantee Agency. Initially, private investors in developing countries may assign high risks to renewable technologies whose local viability has not been demonstrated. This may be particularly true for large baseload power facilities, whose failure to deliver contracted power could incur serious financial liability. To accelerate adoption of renewable energy, the Clean Technology Fund should provide financial backing for an appropriate insurance service from the Multilateral Investment Guarantee Agency or another institution.

Finally, the Clean Technology Fund should not be monolithic about its project portfolio because countries have very different renewable resources. Recent work by Center for Global Development and World Bank researchers has quantified renewable energy resources that can be exploited with existing technologies in more than 200 countries. To illustrate, renewable energy potentials are very high by world standards in solar energy for Egypt (64 percent of total renewable resources) and Peru (61 percent); in biofuels for Mongolia (87 percent) and Uganda (83 percent); in hydro for Nepal (53 percent) and Papua New Guinea (28 percent); in wind for Cape Verde (71 percent) and China (21 percent); and in geothermal for Turkmenistan (11 percent) and Indonesia (6 percent).[33]

A reformed Clean Development Mechanism. The Kyoto Protocol established the Clean Development Mechanism, which allows rich countries with emissions reduction commitments to invest in developing-country projects for emissions reduction that are less costly than home-country projects. These investments yield carbon credits that are counted against emissions reduction commitments. The key criterion is that the developing-country carbon reduction would not have occurred without the incentive provided by the mechanism, which was established, largely at U.S. insistence, to acquaint developing countries with a surrogate emissions trading system and pave the way for an eventual global cap-and-trade system. By November 2007, more than 800 projects registered by the mechanism's executive board represented transactions worth billions of dollars.

In principle, the Clean Development Mechanism has useful roles to play. The first is its "surrogate training" feature, although developing countries have yet to display official interest in a global cap-and-trade system. Second, its establishment of a carbon credit market, with an exchange-based carbon price, gives entrepreneurs a profit incentive to search for projects accreditable under the mechanism that are less costly than their market values at the going carbon price. This decentralized system has the potential for identifying valuable projects that could be missed by large-scale programming in the Clean Technology Fund.

In practice, the Clean Development Mechanism has suffered from serious institutional, measurement, and moral hazard problems. Stern (2008) has noted the cumbersome micro-focus of the current approval process, which prevents the scaling-up that will be essential in the future. The use of disputed "counterfactual" baselines to estimate carbon savings has led to charges that actual carbon savings have been minimal; highly carbon-intensive projects have been rationalized using dubious counterfactuals; and many projects would have been funded by the private sector anyway. To illustrate, the mechanism's board has stirred controversy by awarding credits to coal-fired plants in developing countries that employ high-efficiency combustion technologies. Although coal-fired plants using these technologies reduce carbon emissions intensity (emissions/power produced) by 10–20 percent, they remain extremely dirty. For example, a coal-fired power project in India, approved under the Clean Development Mechanism, will receive subsidized multilateral financing, despite the project's own estimate that the plant will emit more than 24 million tons of carbon dioxide per year and more than 700 million tons during its working lifetime.[34] This will rank the plant in the top 150 polluters among 25,000-plus carbon-emitting power facilities in the world.[35]

Such practices will obviously not propel developing countries onto the low-carbon path. Despite the Clean Development Mechanism's attractive features—"surrogate training" for emissions trading and decentralized, incentive-based operation—criticism of the mechanism's failings is so severe that it seems unlikely to survive at Copenhagen without major reform. To be sustainable, the Clean Development Mechanism should adopt the proposed Clean Technology Fund policy of making renewables the default choice for energy project proposals. This would be more costly, of course, but many renewable energy projects under the mechanism should be profitable once stricter cap-and-trade systems in the European Union and the United States raise the market price of carbon credits.

Payments for forest conservation. Poor countries have limited resources and regulatory capacity, as well as a focus on poverty alleviation, and for those reasons forest conservation will be weakly supported as long as forested land has a higher market value in other uses. The solution lies in direct payments for forest conservation that match the market opportunity cost of the forested land. This is the principle underlying the Forest Carbon Partnership Facility, launched by the World Bank in December 2007. The next president should support this fund as the multilateral vehicle for forest conservation payments, with an emphasis on transparency, accountability, and respect for evidence, not political criteria, in the allocation of project funds.

Supporting adaptation to global warming

A multilateral approach to adaptation assistance was established at the U.N. Nairobi conference in 2006 and amended by the Bali conference in 2007. The

Adaptation Fund will be financed by a 2 percent tax on Clean Development Mechanism transactions, managed by the Global Environment Facility, and open to tenders from a variety of development institutions and national governments. This structure provides the right basic vehicle for adaptation assistance, but several caveats apply.

Evidence-based allocations will be critical; conventional approaches based on standard per capita allocations or political criteria would be extremely wasteful because countries (and regions within countries) face very different conditions. For example, recent work by researchers at the Center for Global Development indicates that agricultural productivity losses from global warming in Africa will vary from over 50 percent in Senegal and Sudan to around 5 percent in Kenya. In Latin America, they will vary from over 35 percent in Mexico to 11 percent in Argentina. A recent analysis of inundation from sea-level rise shows even more skewed patterns among coastal countries: nearly half the population displaced in some, very few people in others.[36]

For efficient allocation, the Adaptation Fund should tailor the scale and focus of country programs to local conditions. For example, adaptive infrastructure and urbanization programs will be appropriate for Egypt, Suriname, and Vietnam, where inundation from sea-level rise will be massive.[37] Adaptive agriculture and urban relocation should be the focus of assistance in countries facing huge agricultural productivity losses, such as India, Mexico, Senegal, and Sudan.[38] Broader micro-insurance coverage for the poor should also be part of these programs. Programs combining adaptive infrastructure and micro-insurance should be the focus for countries facing high flood-disaster risks, such as Bangladesh, Benin, Cambodia, Jamaica, Honduras, and Mozambique.[39]

Political strategy

Immediately after Inauguration Day, the next president should focus on laying the groundwork for U.S. participation at Copenhagen in December 2009. The first two years in office will be absorbed by assembling the policy package, negotiating the global compact at Copenhagen, winning Senate ratification, and implementing the domestic program to promote the clean energy revolution. The next two years should focus on effective implementation of the domestic and global programs.

The next president's first concrete task will be rallying the American people behind the climate change agenda. The president's inaugural address should communicate four key messages:

- Climate change is potentially fatal for the United States and for the world.

- We're all in this together; both developed and developing countries are sources and victims of the problem.
- The scale of this problem is unprecedented, and nothing less than full international mobilization will solve it.
- The problem can be solved; we have the skills and resources to mount a successful assault on global warming.

Legislative measures

The president's second task will be a legislative initiative that builds domestic support and global credibility. Five specific legislative measures should be included:

1. *Mandatory public reporting of carbon emissions by all significant emitters in the United States.* This is essential for credibility and monitoring of outcomes, both domestically and internationally. It will also provide public and private interest groups with additional levers to influence emitters' behavior. The program can be rapidly implemented by combining and expanding two current programs: the U.S. Environmental Protection Agency's Emissions and Generation Resource Integrated Database (eGRID), which publicly reports carbon emissions from thousands of power plants in the United States, and the Climate Registry, a national voluntary program that collects and publicly reports greenhouse gas emissions data from business firms and municipalities.
2. *A mandatory national program that will achieve emissions reductions consistent with the U.S. share of an ambitious international effort.* Because there will only be eleven months until Copenhagen, the emphasis should be on rapid adoption of a program that has already been vetted by Congress. The most likely candidate at present is the Warner-Lieberman America's Climate Security Act, a cap-and-trade program that was cleared with strong bipartisan support by the Senate Committee on Environment and Public Works in December 2007. Because rapid action is needed to prevent dangerous climate change, the enacted legislation should minimize start-up delays and maximize the percentage of emitters covered, the percentage of emissions permits auctioned, and the emissions reduction required by 2020. Revenues from auctions of emissions permits should be earmarked for three purposes: adjustment assistance for severely affected U.S. workers and businesses in sectors tied to fossil fuels (particularly coal); support for the U.S. clean energy program; and multilateral financing for clean technology adoption, forest conservation, and climate-change adaptation in developing countries.

Under the conservative assumption that the initial emissions permit auction price will be $15 per ton of carbon dioxide, a program with America's Climate Security Act's emitter coverage and auctioned permit percentage will generate about $45 billion annually, which can be allocated to finance the measures detailed below, with adjustments if the auction price is greater or less than $15 per ton.

3. *Adjustment assistance for U.S. workers and businesses.* Adjustment assistance will be funded at $5 billion initially.
4. *A coordinated, large-scale program to promote clean technologies.* The previously described Solar Grand Plan has proposed $10 billion a year as an appropriate figure for federal support.[40] The program to promote clean technologies should focus on developing the national clean energy infrastructure, along with support for energy-efficient designs for buildings and vehicles. In addition to targeted, federally sponsored research and development, the program could guarantee financial rewards for private clean technology developers who deliver proven, replicable, scalable designs.
5. *A major increase in U.S. support for the Clean Technology Fund, the Forest Carbon Partnership Facility, and the Adaptation Fund.* The International Energy Agency estimates that $30 billion annually will be required to close the incremental cost gap between clean and conventional energy investments. The United Nations Framework Convention on Climate Change estimates total forest conservation payments at $12 billion annually.[41] The annual funding requirement for adaptation assistance has been estimated at $50 billion by Oxfam International[42] and at $28 million to $67 billion by the U.N. framework convention.[43] For the present purpose, I will conservatively estimate the cost to be $30 billion a year.

In light of these estimates, the remaining permit auction funds ($30 billion) would be allocated as follows: 40 percent to the Clean Technology Fund ($12 billion), 40 percent to the Adaptation Fund ($12 billion), and 20 percent to the Forest Carbon Partnership Facility ($6 billion). Of these contributions, $18 billion would initially be administered by the World Bank (through the Clean Technology Fund and the Forest Carbon Partnership Facility) and $12 billion by the Global Environment Facility (through the Adaptation Fund). With matching funds from other donors, these two institutions will become responsible for much larger grant funds than they have ever administered. This will work only if they operate at the highest standards of transparency, efficiency, and accountability. If they fail, it may be necessary to establish a new institution to administer the funds. The same principles apply to the Clean Development Mechanism, which should be renewed at Copenhagen only if clean technologies become the default choices for energy project proposals. Any departure from renewable options would have to be rigorously defended case by case.

Preparation for Copenhagen

Once passage of federal emissions control legislation has established U.S. credibility, the president should initiate talks with major emitters in developed and developing countries about the design and scope of the Copenhagen compact for global emissions limitation. On the successful model of the Montreal Protocol, the president should advocate a compact with three principal features: full transparency, with global public reporting of all significant emissions sources along the lines of the proposed U.S. model; country-specific emissions targets, with flexibility to adjust the targets as the science and economics evolve; and accountability for commitments, supported by mechanisms for dispute resolution and public disclosure of noncompliance. Formal sanctions should be contemplated only if repeated violations of the compact occur. Appropriate technical assistance should also be offered to countries that want to initiate domestic carbon-charge or cap-and-trade programs to provide incentives for emissions reduction.

After Copenhagen

The next president's first State of the Union address in January 2010 should report successful negotiation of the Copenhagen compact; describe major provisions of the compact and their compatibility with U.S. interests; present the compact to the U.S. Senate for ratification; and summarize progress in implementing U.S. programs to regulate carbon emissions, assist severely impacted workers and businesses, expand research and development for clean technology development, and expand clean energy infrastructure. Implementing the full domestic and international program will absorb a great deal of time, energy, and resources during the remainder of the president's first term.

An opportunity for greatness

The United States and the world are now poised for rapid action to limit dangerous carbon emissions. In the United States, recent policy developments have created the foundations for progress toward a low-carbon economy. Internationally, the United States has begun integrating itself into a global movement to promote country-specific emissions limits, clean technology adoption, and adaptation assistance for developing countries. We are at a watershed moment, and the next president has a genuine opportunity for greatness at Copenhagen. Strong, visionary leadership will produce a rapid recovery of America's global stature, greater energy independence, and a powerful catalyst for prosperity in the clean energy revolution.

Notes

1. Faris 2007.
2. Sengupta 2007.
3. WMO 2007.
4. Emmanuel 2005; Webster and others 2006.
5. WMO 2007.
6. Hanna and others 2005; Lowe and others 2006; NSIDC 2007; Rahmstorf 2007; Rignot and others 2008.
7. Dasgupta and others 2007.
8. CNA Corporation 2007.
9. Wheeler and Ummel 2007.
10. For a detailed history and policy discussion, see Benedick 1998.
11. See IPCC 2007.
12. Spotts 2007.
13. For a detailed discussion, see Arimura and others 2007.
14. *Washington Post* 2008.
15. For a detailed discussion of U.S. programs, see Newell 2007.
16. McCormick 2008.
17. World Bank 2008.
18. Pontin 2007.
19. Zweibel 2008.
20. Buys and others 2007.
21. For a detailed discussion of public pollution disclosure, see Dasgupta and others 2006.
22. Cogent support for charges can be found in Mankiw 2007 and Nordhaus 2007. For useful assessments of the EU cap-and-trade system for carbon emissions, see Ellerman and Buchner 2007; Convery and Redmond 2007; Kruger and others 2007.
23. For elaboration of this approach as applied to conventional pollutants, see Baumol and Oates 1971.
24. For discussion, see Olmstead and Stavins 2006; McKibbin and Wilcoxen 2002; Pizer 2002.
25. For further discussion, see Stern 2008.
26. Levine and others 2005.
27. For discussion, see Lanjouw and Jack 2003.
28. Stern 2007.
29. Stern 2007.
30. Stern 2007. For further discussion, see Weitzman 2007 and Stern 2008.

31. See EC 2008.
32. See Wheeler 2008a.
33. Buys and others 2007.
34. See Wheeler 2008b.
35. The ranking was established by Carbon Monitoring for Action (www.carma.org).
36. Dasgupta and others 2007.
37. Dasgupta and others 2007.
38. Cline 2007.
39. Buys and others 2007.
40. Zweibel and others 2008.
41. UNFCCC 2008.
42. Oxfam International 2008.
43. UNFCCC 2008.

References

Arimura, Toshi, Dallas Burtraw, Alan Krupnick, and Karen Palmer. 2007. "U.S. Climate Policy Developments." Discussion Paper RFF DP 07-45. Resources for the Future, Washington, D.C.

Baumol, William, and Wallace Oates. 1971. "The Use of Standards and Prices for Protection of the Environment." *The Swedish Journal of Economics* 73 (1): 42–54.

Benedick, Richard. 1998. *Ozone Diplomacy: New Directions in Safeguarding the Planet*. Cambridge, Mass.: Harvard University Press.

Buys, Piet, Uwe Deichmann, Craig Meisner, Thao Ton That, and David Wheeler. 2007. "Country Stakes in Climate Change Negotiations: Two Dimensions of Vulnerability." Policy Research Working Paper 4300. World Bank, Washington, D.C.

Cline, William. 2007. *Global Warming and Agriculture: Impact Estimates by Country*. Washington, D.C.: Center for Global Development and Peterson Institute for International Economics.

CNA Corporation. 2007. "National Security and the Threat of Climate Change." [http://securityandclimate.cna.org/].

Convery, Frank, and Luke Redmond. 2007. "Market and Price Developments in the European Union Emissions Trading Scheme." *Review of Environmental Economics and Policy* 1: 88–111.

Dasgupta, Susmita, Hua Wang, and David Wheeler. 2006. "Disclosure Strategies for Pollution Control." In T. Tietenberg and H. Folmer, eds., *The International Yearbook of Environmental and Resource Economics 2006/2007: A Survey of Current Issues*. Cheltenham, U.K.: Edward Elgar Publishing, Ltd.

Dasgupta, Susmita, Benoit Laplante, Craig Meisner, David Wheeler, and Jianping Yan. 2007. "The Impact of Sea Level Rise on Developing Countries: A Comparative Analysis." Policy Research Working Paper 4136. World Bank, Washington, D.C.

EC (Commission of the European Communities). 2008. "Impact Assessment: Package of Implementation Measures for the EU's Objectives on Climate Change and Renewable Energy for 2020." Commission Staff Working Document. SEC (2008) 85/3. January. Brussels.

Ellerman, A. Denny, and Barbara Buchner. 2007. "The European Union Emissions Trading Scheme: Origins, Allocation, and Early Results." *Review of Environmental Economics and Policy* 1:66–87.

Emmanuel, Kerry. 2005. "Increasing Destructiveness of Tropical Cyclones over the Past 30 Years." *Nature* 436 (4): 686–88.

Faris, Stephan. 2007. "The Real Roots of Darfur." *Atlantic Monthly*. April.

Hanna, E., P. Huybrechts, I. Janssens, J. Cappelen, K. Steffen, and A. Stephens. 2005. "Runoff and Mass Balance of the Greenland Ice Sheet: 1958–2003." *Journal of Geophysical Research* 110, D13108, doi:10.1029/2004JD005641.

IPCC (Intergovernmental Panel on Climate Change). 2007. *Fourth Assessment Report of the Intergovernmental Panel on Climate Change*. 4 vols. [www.ipcc.ch/].

Kruger, Joseph, Wallace Oates, and William Pizer. 2007. "Decentralization in the EU Emissions Trading Scheme and Lessons for Global Policy." *Review of Environmental Economics and Policy* 1: 112–33.

Lanjouw, Jean, and William Jack. 2003. "Financing Pharmaceutical Innovation: How Much Should Poor Countries Contribute?" Working Paper 28. Center for Global Development, Washington, D.C.

Levine, Ruth, Michael Kremer, and Alice Albright. 2005. *Making Markets for Vaccines: Ideas to Action*. Washington, D.C.: Center for Global Development.

Lowe, J., J. Gregory, J. Ridley, P. Huybrechts, R. Nicholls, and M. Collins. 2006. "The Role of Sea-Level Rise and the Greenland Ice Sheet in Dangerous Climate Change: Implications for the Stabilization of Climate." In H. Schellnhuber, W. Cramer, N. Nakicenovic, T. Wigley, and G. Yohe, eds., *Avoiding Dangerous Climate Change*. Cambridge, U.K.: Cambridge University Press.

Mankiw, N. Gregory. 2007. "One Answer to Global Warming: A New Tax." *New York Times*. September 17.

McCormick, David. 2008. "Remarks by Treasury Under Secretary David H. McCormick on China's Journey to Environmentally Sustainable Growth at the West Coast Leadership Dialogue." Press Release. January 14. [www.ustreas.gov/press/releases/hp761.htm].

McKibbin, Warwick, and Peter Wilcoxen. 2002. "The Role of Economics in Climate Change Policy." *Journal of Economic Perspectives* 16 (2): 107–29.

Newell, Richard. 2007. "Climate Technology Research, Development, and Demonstration: Funding Sources, Institutions, and Instruments." Backgrounder. September. Resources for the Future, Washington, D.C.

Nordhaus, William. 2007. "To Tax or Not to Tax: Alternative Approaches to Slowing Global Warming." *Review of Environmental Economics and Policy* 1:26–44.

NSIDC (U.S. National Snow and Ice Data Center). 2007. "Overview of Current Sea Ice Conditions." September 20. [nsidc.org/news/press/2007_seaiceminimum/20070810_index.html].

Olmstead, Sheila, and Robert Stavins. 2006. "An International Policy Architecture for the Post-Kyoto Era." *American Economic Review Papers and Proceedings* 96 (2): 35–38.

Oxfam International. 2008. "Financing Adaptation: Why the UN's Bali Climate Conference Must Mandate the Search for New Funds." [www.oxfam.org/en/policy/briefingnotes/bn_bali_financiing_adaptation_0712].

Pizer, William. 2002. "Combining Price and Quantity Controls to Mitigate Global Climate Change." *Journal of Public Economics* 85 (3): 409–34.

Pontin, Jason. 2007. "Vinod Khosla: A Veteran Venture Capitalist's New Energy." *MIT Technology Review*. March/April.

Rahmstorf, Stefan. 2007. "A Semi-Empirical Approach to Projecting Future Sea-Level Rise." *Science* 315 (5810): 368–70.

Rignot, Eric, Jonathan Bamber, Michiel van den Broeke, Curt Davis, Yonghong Li, Willem Jan van de Berg, and Erik van Meijgaard. 2008. "Recent Antarctic Ice Mass Loss from Radar Interferometry and Regional Climate Modeling." *Nature Geoscience* 1 (January 13): 106–10.

Sengupta, Somini. 2007. "Sea's Rise in India Buries Islands and a Way of Life." *New York Times*. April 11.

Spotts, Peter. 2007. "In Bali Talks, U.S. Balks at European Emission Targets." *Christian Science Monitor*. December 12.

Stern, Nicholas. 2007. *The Economics of Climate Change: The Stern Review*. London: Cambridge University Press.

Stern, Nicholas. 2008. "Economics of Climate Change." Richard T. Ely Lecture. American Economic Association Meetings, New Orleans, January 4th (forthcoming, *American Economic Review*, May 2008).

Turner, John A. 1999. "A Realizable Renewable Energy Future." *Science* 285: 687–89.

UNFCCC (United Nations Framework Convention on Climate Change). 2007. "Report on the Analysis of Existing and Potential Investment and Financial Flows Relevant to the Development of an Effective and Appropriate International Response to Climate Change." Dialogue Working Paper 8. August. Vienna.

Washington Post. 2008. A European Climate Plan: An Intriguing Approach that Meshes Well with Bills on Capitol Hill." January 28. [www.washingtonpost.com/wp-dyn/content/article/2008/01/27/AR2008012701591.html].

Webster, Peter, G. Holland, J. Curry, and H. Chang. 2006. "Frequency, Duration and Intensity of Tropical Cyclonic Storms in a Warming Environment." Eighty-sixth Annual American Meteorological Society Meeting, Eighteenth Conference on Climate Variability and Change. Atlanta, Georgia, January 28–February 3.

Weitzman, Martin. 2007. "A Review of the Stern Review on the Economics of Climate Change." *Journal of Economic Literature*. 45(3): 703–24.

Wheeler, David. 2008a. "Crossroads at Mmamabula: Will the World Bank Choose the Clean Energy Path?" Working Paper. Center for Global Development, Washington, D.C.

———. 2008b. "CARMA Watch: Red Light for The World Bank Group on Coal-Fired Power." January. Center for Global Development, Washington, D.C. [http://blogs.cgdev.org/globaldevelopment/2008/01/carma_watch_red_light_for_the.php].

Wheeler, David, and Kevin Ummel. 2007. "Another Inconvenient Truth: A Carbon-Intensive South Faces Environmental Disaster, No Matter What the North Does." Working Paper 134. December. Center for Global Development, Washington, D.C.

WMO (World Meteorological Organization). 2007. "Report on Extreme Weather and Climate Events." August 7. [www.wmo.ch/pages/mediacentre/press_releases/pr_791_e.html].

World Bank. 2008. "Forest Carbon Partnership Facility Launched at Bali Climate Meeting." Press Release 2008/142/SDN. Washington, D.C. [http://web.worldbank.org/WBSITE/EXTERNAL/NEWS/0,,contentMDK:21582088~pagePK:34370~piPK:34424~theSitePK:4607,00.html].

Zweibel, Ken, James Mason, and Vasilis Fthenakis. 2008. "A Solar Grand Plan: By 2050 Solar Power Could End U.S. Dependence on Foreign Oil and Slash Greenhouse Gas Emissions." *Scientific American*. January.

3

Power and Roads for Africa: What the United States Can Do

Vijaya Ramachandran

The past decade has witnessed a rapid increase in aid to Sub-Saharan Africa. In the first four years of the Bush administration, aid levels reached over $4 billion a year, accounting for almost 20 percent of the total aid budget and representing a fourfold increase from the year 2000. Two ambitious new initiatives—the President's Emergency Plan for AIDS Relief and the Millennium Challenge Corporation—were launched, in part to address the continent's health and development needs. In 2001, the African Growth and Opportunity Act was implemented to provide African businesses with better access to the U.S. market (see chapter 7 by Elliott). Along with other such initiatives, media interest in Africa has also grown, and the public has expressed its support for Africa's economic and social development through consumer campaigns such as Product Red and public events.

Why does promoting economic growth in Africa matter to the United States? For two simple reasons: It's the right thing to do and the smart thing to do. There is increasing public interest in the United States as well as bipartisan support for helping Africa, as recently witnessed by renewed

---

Vijaya Ramachandran is a senior fellow at the Center for Global Development. Parts of this chapter are excerpted from a forthcoming publication on Africa's private sector, to be published by the Center for Global Development. She is grateful to Manju Kedia Shah, Robin Kraft, and Sarah Rose for their contributions, and to Nancy Birdsall, Lawrence MacDonald, Dennis de Tray, Kim Elliott, Michael Clemens, David Wheeler, and Joshua Lozman for helpful comments and suggestions.

funding for the President's Emergency Plan for AIDS Relief. Furthermore, there are several new opportunities for U.S. firms to compete, particularly in the area of renewable energy.

A perceptible increase in gross domestic product per capita growth in Sub-Saharan Africa since 2003 has relieved some of the Afro-pessimism so prevalent in debates about Africa's prospects. Some countries that are not resource-rich are doing very well: Benin, Burkina Faso, Ethiopia, Ghana, Mali, Mauritania, Mozambique, Rwanda, Senegal, Tanzania, and Uganda are growing at over 5 percent a year.[1] Another group of countries is growing at even higher rates, albeit with the help of oil and other resource commodities. Most of the increase in exports of countries eligible for assistance under the African Growth and Opportunity Act comes from oil-related products (figure 3.1). But not all countries have done well, and there is uncertainty about whether even the successful economies will be able to sustain their gains, given their possible dependence on special factors, such as aid or temporary terms-of-trade windfalls. Meanwhile,

Figure 3.1. Exports under the African Growth and Opportunity Act

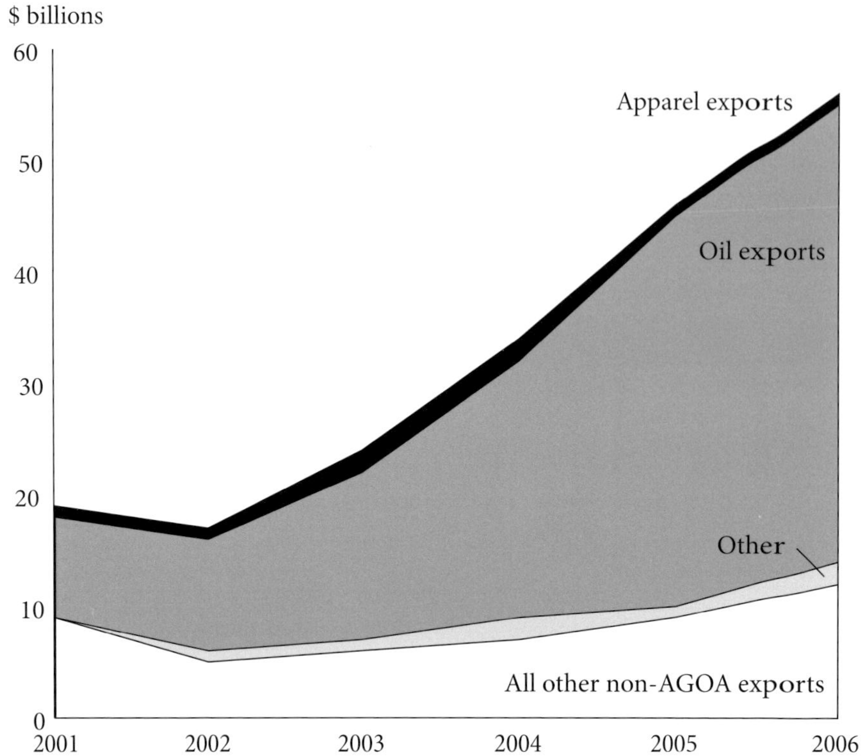

Source: Elliott 2007.

the larger issue of boosting long-term growth in Africa to levels that would close the income gap with other regions remains a concern.

Central to the issue of growth is the development of the private sector. Without the creation of jobs and businesses, there is no real chance for many Africans to raise their standard of living. Extensive surveys of private sector businesses carried out over the past decade show that the poor performance of the private sector can be attributed mostly to the high costs of the business environment. This chapter looks at solutions to the problem of low growth in Africa, focusing on two key constraints identified by these surveys: the lack of power and roads. There is an urgent need for the United States to support a Clean Infrastructure Initiative to provide modern energy through a variety of renewable energy sources and facilitate the construction of roads. Moreover, this will be beneficial to both the United States and to Africa. To this end, the United States should take the following three steps:

1. Support a $1 billion Clean Energy Fund for Africa, facilitated by the Overseas Private Investment Corporation, to transfer clean technology, including renewable energy, from the United States to Africa.[2]
2. Encourage the African Development Bank to focus on regional clean infrastructure projects only, in return for which the United States should increase its capital contribution to the organization by 25 percent a year for each of the next four years.
3. Ensure that the World Bank increases its allocation toward *regional* infrastructure projects in Africa, making this a central mission of the International Development Association, the World Bank's soft loan window for the poorest countries. At least 50 percent of the International Development Association's allocation for Africa should be spent on regional infrastructure projects, with a strong emphasis on clean technology.

"No electricity presently available"

In the summer of 2007, the government of Kenya made an unusual appeal to the Kenya Association of Manufacturers, urgently requiring them to move their production schedule from their regular hours to a nighttime schedule of 11:00 p.m. to 5:00 a.m. Unable to provide power for more than a few hours a day, the government called for massive load-shedding to protect the power system from being overwhelmed. The manufacturers were in turn faced with the problem of getting workers to and from work in the dark, with vastly increased logistical and security costs over the roughly 4 percent of sales they were already paying to keep their workers and equipment safe.[3] Such infrastructure problems are not uncommon in Sub-Saharan Africa.

With a sixth of the world's population, Africa generates only about 4 percent of the world's electricity, three-quarters of which is used by South Africa and northern Africa. The need for electricity is both enormous and unmet, with many cities and towns experiencing blackouts several times a day.[4] Indeed, the *Independent* reports that the popularity of the U.N. War Crimes Court has more to do with its restoration of power in parts of Freetown, Sierra Leone, than to its justice-related activities.[5] In Conakry, Guinea, young men go to the airport every evening to study because it is one of the only places with reliable lighting. And in almost every major city, the constant roar of backup generators can be heard in the wealthier neighborhoods.

According to World Bank data, about 500 million Africans (75 percent of all households or two-thirds of the total population) are without "modern energy." The World Bank reports that about $17 billion is spent by the "energy-poor" in Africa on fuel-based lighting systems, such as kerosene lamps, that are expensive, provide poor lighting, and create indoor air pollution.[6] Biomass (mostly firewood) constitutes about 56 percent of all energy use in Sub-Saharan Africa, which is home to seventeen of the top twenty biomass users in the world.[7] Such fuels also accelerate deforestation; the World Bank estimates that 45,000 square kilometers of forest were lost between 1990 and 2005 across all low-income countries.[8]

A better understanding of business conditions has emerged through a comprehensive set of enterprise surveys conducted by the World Bank. The data in these surveys are derived from face-to-face interviews with managers and owners of several thousand enterprises of all sizes. This chapter is based on surveys of about 11,000 businesses in twenty-seven African countries.[9] To ensure comparability across countries, only manufacturing sector data in four traditional subsectors—food processing, wood products, metal working, and textiles and apparel—are discussed here. The data illustrate how seriously the lack of infrastructure is constraining growth in this region.

Perhaps no country in Africa is worse affected than Nigeria. Data from a 2001 survey and from other sources show that almost 40 percent of electricity is privately provided by generators, which costs three times as much as electricity from the public grid.[10] Almost all businesses own generators of varying quality and vintage to compensate for the extraordinarily unreliable supply provided by the Nigerian Electric Power Authority (often referred to by the citizenry as "No Electricity Presently Available"). At the same time, fuel is sometimes hard to find in this oil-exporting country, and maintenance of generator equipment imposes further costs on businesses.[11]

Figure 3.2 shows the number of days that a power outage occurred each year in the countries surveyed. The worst cases are the Democratic Republic of Congo, Gambia, and Guinea (each with more than 170 days of outages), while Rwanda, Tanzania, and Uganda come next with 120 outages. Most of the remaining countries experience outages on more than 50 days in the year. However, six countries—Guinea-Bissau, Lesotho, Mali, Senegal, Swaziland, and Zambia—fare better, reporting outages on between 10 and 50 days. Only a handful of countries—Botswana, Mauritius, Namibia, and South Africa—report outages on less than 10 days a year. Almost 50 percent of all businesses surveyed cite power as a major or severe constraint; the share rises to 60 percent when only low-income countries are considered. Comparable data for China show that the burden of power outages is far smaller for businesses there. Finally, outages are not just frequent but also unpredictable and long. The average length of a power outage in Africa is five hours; outages can sometimes stretch to more than twelve hours.

Figure 3.2. The magnitude of power outages, by country

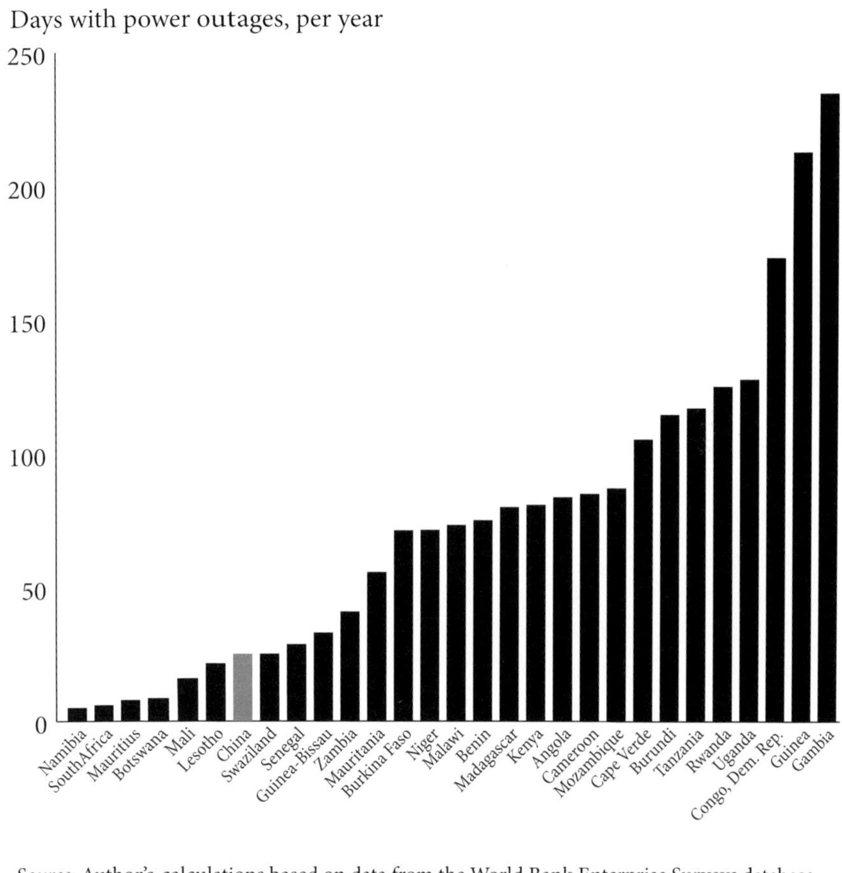

Source: Author's calculations based on data from the World Bank Enterprise Surveys database.

How do businesses cope? In Angola, Cameroon, Gambia, Guinea, Guinea-Bissau, Rwanda, and Senegal, over 50 percent of businesses resort to acquiring generators to offset the erratic supply and load-shedding of the public grid. Kenya tops the list with 70 percent of businesses owning generators; electricity is now rated an even greater constraint than corruption, a long-standing complaint of Kenyan businesses. Even in very low-income countries such as Benin, Madagascar, Mauritania, and Niger, 20–30 percent of businesses own generators.

The ability to offset power fluctuations varies greatly by enterprise size. Large businesses with 100 or more employees are much more likely to own a generator than a small or medium-size enterprise is—twenty times

Figure 3.3. Share of businesses that own generators, by business size and country

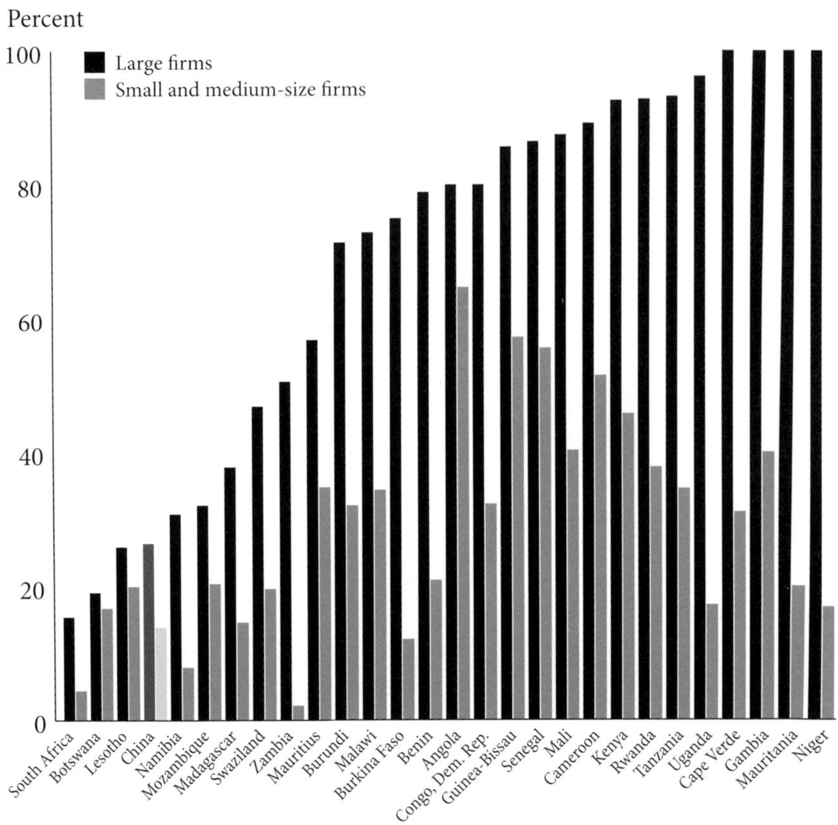

Source: Author's calculations based on data from the World Bank Enterprise Surveys database.

more likely in Zambia, and two to five times more likely in Cape Verde, Gambia, Mauritania, and Niger, where all large businesses own generators (figure 3.3).

Energy, as a share of total cost, is very high in Africa's manufacturing sector (figure 3.4). In China, the cost of energy is 3 percent of total cost for businesses in the same sector. Only one country in Africa—South Africa—shows a comparable share, and even that is changing as many cities experience rolling blackouts. Even more troublesome is the fact that this situation will likely deteriorate further before it improves. The *New York Times* quotes Lawrence Musaba, manager of the Southern Africa Power Pool, as saying, "We've had no significant capital injection into generation and transmission, from either the private or public sectors, for fifteen, maybe twenty, years."[12]

Figure 3.4. Energy as a share of total cost, by country

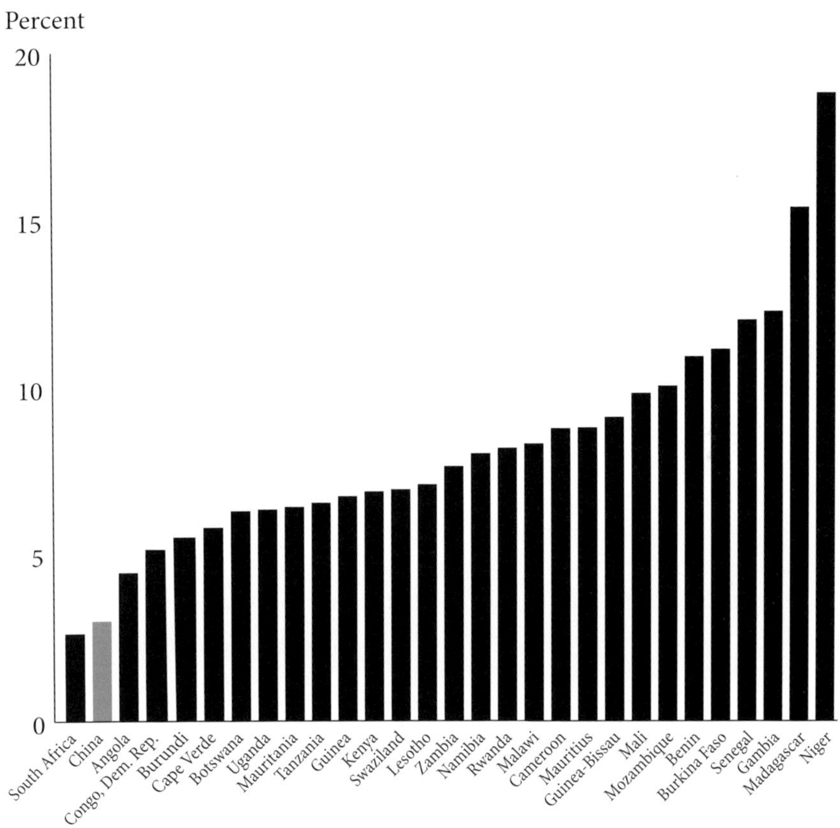

Source: Author's calculations based on data from the World Bank Enterprise Surveys database.

Roads that are almost as bad

In addition to power, the limited availability of physical infrastructure—including roads and railways—also seriously hampers private sector competitiveness. The low-income economies of Sub-Saharan Africa lag far behind every other region in the world in paved-road mileage and modern freight- and passenger-transportation systems. This lack of adequate transportation impacts the level of business activity by lowering productivity and limiting the entry of new enterprises. Businesses in Africa either supply only to fragmented regional markets or restrict themselves to market opportunities with profits large enough to cover high transportation costs. These effects are difficult to reverse because, unlike the power supply, which can improve or deteriorate rapidly, transportation bottlenecks are typically long-term—bad roads and limited transnational links have kept markets and businesses highly segmented for decades in Africa.

We can see the importance of transportation bottlenecks to existing businesses in the data evaluated in the enterprise surveys database. Large differences in the performance of firms across countries are clearly correlated with the overall level of economic development and infrastructure facilities. In middle-income countries such as Botswana, Mauritius, Namibia, South Africa, and Swaziland, less than 20 percent of firms complain about transportation problems, whereas in Kenya 53 percent of firms consider transportation a major obstacle. In the poorest countries, most businesses sell their goods only in local markets and do not even consider selling anywhere else.

Figure 3.5 illustrates that transportation is a very real constraint for larger businesses. In East and Southern Africa, large businesses are much more likely to complain about transportation than smaller firms are. These businesses account for a large share of manufacturing jobs and most of industrial value added, and they are most likely to expand beyond the local market. Yet, in all but the richest countries in the sample, less than half of inputs are delivered by road. Some businesses even rely on costly air shipments to meet their needs; one investor discussed how he had on occasion airlifted cement between countries because the roads are so poor.

Finally, businesses were asked about losses due to transportation failures, measured as the percentage of consignment value lost due to theft, spoilage, or breakage in transit. Figure 3.6 shows that businesses in the low-income economies of Sub-Saharan Africa suffer the most, with the larger businesses suffering greater losses than smaller ones. Such losses are much higher than in China, where the average loss is only about 1.25 percent of consignment value.

Figure 3.5. Share of businesses ranking transport as a major or severe obstacle to doing business, by country

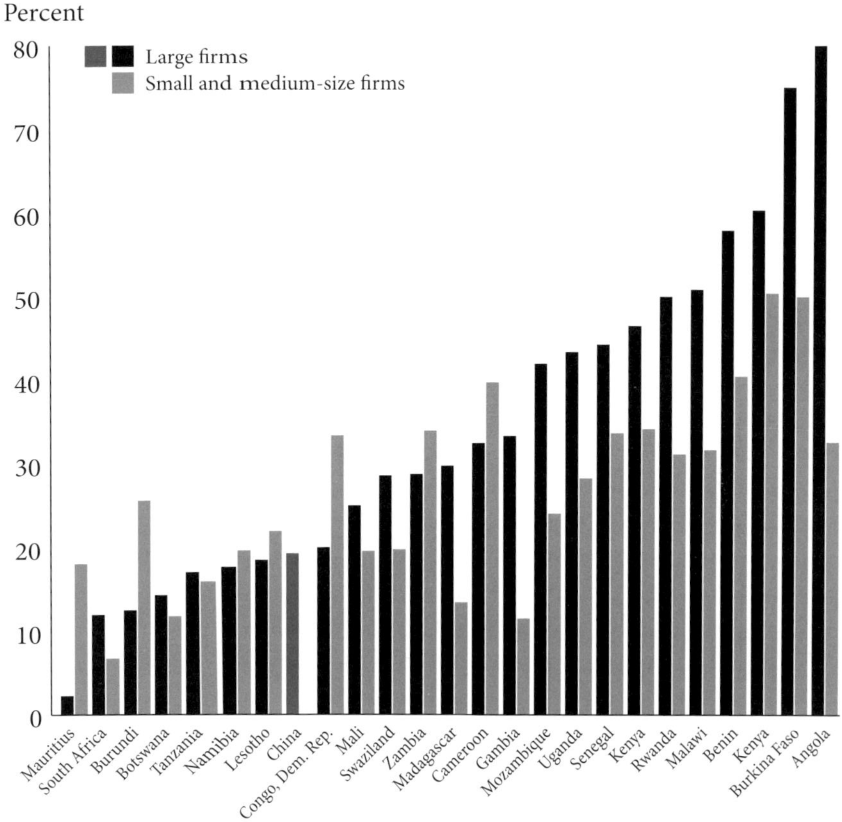

Source: Author's calculations based on data from the World Bank Enterprise Surveys database.

Overall, business losses caused by poor infrastructure are staggering, imposing high cost burdens on African businesses. The result is that, compared with Chinese businesses, the productivity of African businesses is 10–20 percent less on average when indirect costs, such as electricity and transportation, are subtracted from value added.[13] It is important to keep in mind that these losses do not include the impact of the various bottlenecks on the entry of businesses into the private sector. Finally, the lack of roads and power affects not just manufacturing but agriculture as well. The lack of infrastructure has meant that farmers are often unable to increase the value added through processing or to transport their goods overland to domestic markets or international ports.[14]

Figure 3.6. Estimated losses from theft and delays in transportation as a share of consignment value, by country

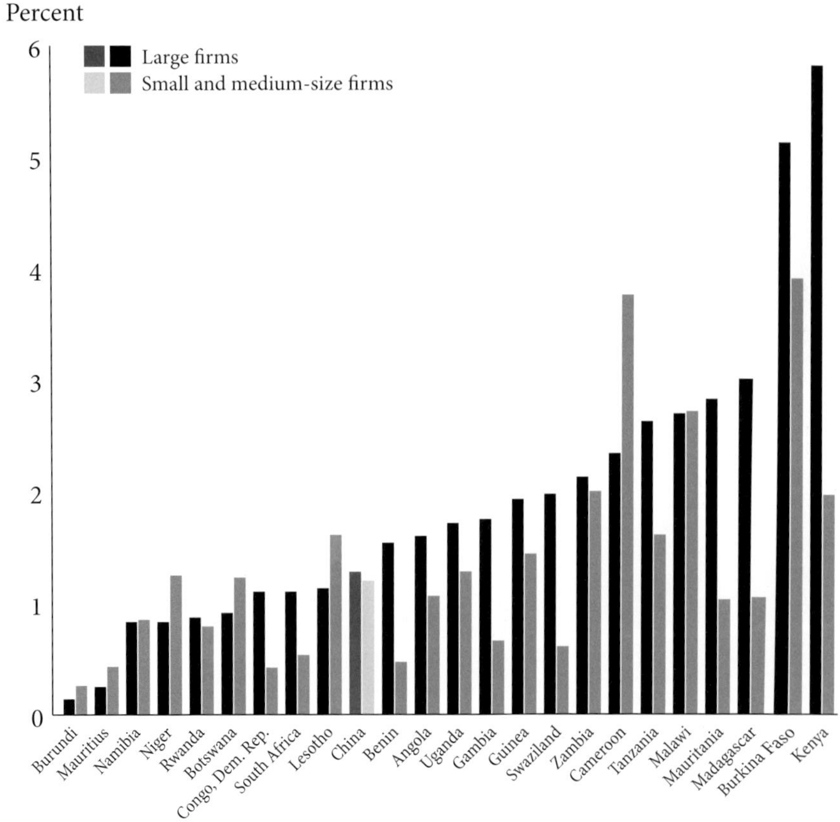

Source: Author's calculations based on data from the World Bank Enterprise Surveys database.

What should the United States do to help Africa?

The evidence points overwhelmingly to the need to invest in infrastructure, particularly a sustainable supply of electric power and a good network of roads that will enable businesses to buy inputs and sell their goods. From the data, it is clear that investing in infrastructure will reduce the cost of doing business for *all* businesses, large and small. Small and medium-size enterprises, which are less able to cope with power shortages, will likely benefit to a greater extent from these investments. Without major new investments in infrastructure, it will be impossible for businesses in Sub-Saharan Africa to substantially increase their level of efficiency or expand their markets.

There is enormous potential for the United States to contribute solutions to this problem. U.S. businesses have the technology and the know-how and must be given the opportunity to compete on bids to develop Africa's power and roads. The expertise of power companies—both large and small—can be harnessed to address the shortage of electricity in Africa. And construction companies can help to build roads, using the best of U.S. technology and human resources. These efforts will benefit the African people as well as the companies and employees who provide infrastructure services. U.S. investment in African infrastructure can also lead to more business partnerships between the two regions, which can be profitable to both in the long run.

All investments in energy must be in newer, cleaner forms, notably hydroelectric and solar power. Africa has a unique opportunity to lead the way for the rest of the world in becoming a producer (and even an exporter) of energy with zero net emissions of greenhouse gases. It can avoid the predicament that some rapidly growing countries find themselves in, where rising incomes are accompanied by a high incidence of ill health and respiratory disease caused by air and water pollution. It can also avoid the problems that come with dependence on coal, ranging from environmental degradation to high carbon emissions.

Africa has tremendous potential for the production of various kinds of renewable energy.[15] According to Buys and others (2007), African countries have annual solar, wind, hydro, and biofuel generation potential that greatly exceeds annual consumption. Table 3.1 groups by region the top thirty-three countries in the world for solar, wind, hydro, and geothermal energy. Overall,

Table 3.1. Location of top 33 developing country producers of solar, wind, hydroelectric, and geothermal energy, by region

Region	Total	Solar	Wind	Hydro	Geothermal
Sub-Saharan Africa	17	21	6	11	7
Latin America and the Caribbean	7	5	8	9	3
East Asia and Pacific	4	5	3	6	4
Europe and Central Asia	3	0	6	5	14
Middle East and North Africa	2	3	3	0	2
South Asia	0	0	1	1	0

Source: Buys and others 2007.

seventeen countries in Sub-Saharan Africa are in the top thirty-three with combined reserves of solar, wind, hydro, and geothermal energy. Among these thirty-three countries, Sub-Saharan Africa has twenty-one countries for solar energy, six countries for wind, eleven countries for hydro, and seven countries for geothermal. Individual country estimates show reserves greatly in excess of annual energy consumption.

Much of Sub-Saharan Africa receives solar radiation of the order of 6–8 kilowatt-hours per square meter per day—among the highest amounts of solar radiation in the world. Map 3.1 shows Africa's solar radiation potential. For businesses using low-quality, unreliable electricity, small-scale installation of solar panels would reduce their reliance on poorly maintained grids, thereby lowering costs and enabling them to compete more effectively in the global market. Solar energy generated by rooftop solar panels is also less likely to run into the regulatory and management problems that have plagued delivery of grid-based energy by public utilities. *The Economist* argues that solar energy will become cost effective in Africa if costs are lowered by 30 percent.[16]

There is enormous potential to address the transportation bottleneck as well. In 2006, researchers Buys, Deichmann, and Wheeler made a compelling argument for the creation of a major road network in Sub-Saharan Africa. They argue that a network of roads connecting all Sub-Saharan capitals and other cities with populations over 500,000 would result in an expansion of overland trade of about $250 billion over fifteen years, with both direct and indirect benefits for Africa's rural poor. They estimate an upfront cost of $20 billion and $1 billion in yearly maintenance to build this network. They point out that overland shipments between South Africa and Nigeria—the two largest economies in Africa—are almost nonexistent because of the poor quality of roads in between. Map 3.2 shows the transnational road network proposed by Buys, Deichmann, and Wheeler, along with the transcontinental corridors proposed by the African Development Bank.

The technology for road construction is fairly mature, and U.S. construction companies have considerable expertise in building roads in a variety of topographical and climatic conditions. Furthermore, road construction is labor intensive and would generate much needed jobs across several African countries. Finally, Buys, Deichmann, and Wheeler argue that an emphasis on the preservation of biodiversity and wildlife habitat can lead to more environmentally sensitive construction of roads in Africa—there does not have to be as much of a tradeoff as in the past.

What about the maintenance of road and power projects? This is often cited as a bigger challenge than building infrastructure is, but there are two reasons to be optimistic: the existence of best-practice models for road

Map 3.1. Annual average solar radiation in Africa

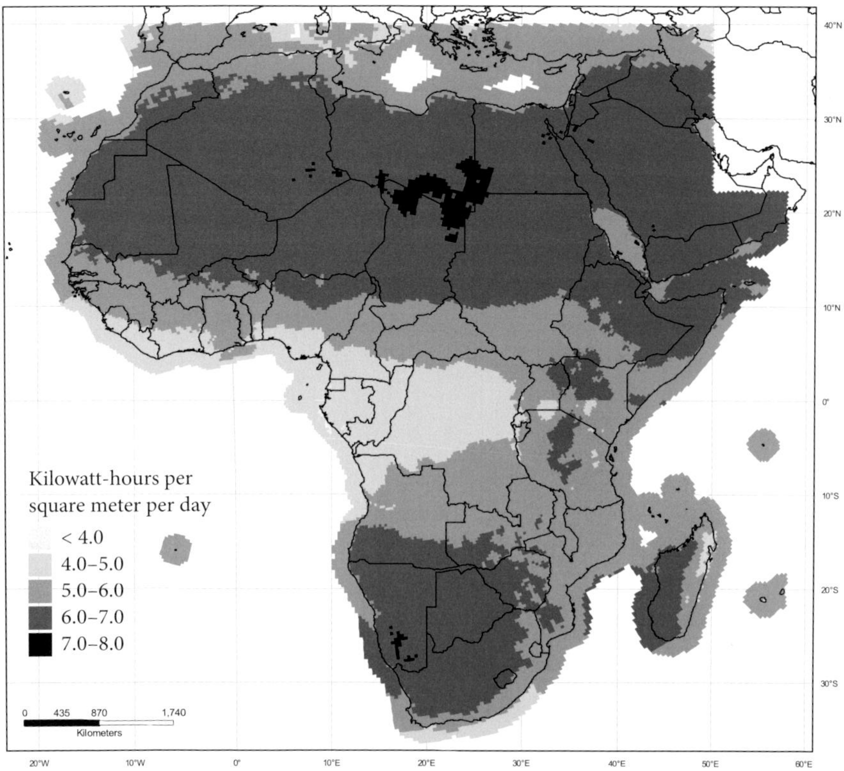

Model estimates of monthly average daily total radiation using inputs derived from satellite and surface observations of cloud cover, aerosol optical depth, precipitable water vapor, albedo, atmospheric pressure, and ozone sampled at a 40km resolution.

Note: Solar radiation can be measured by "latitude tilt," the total radiation (sun plus sky and clouds) falling on a flat plate that is angled from the ground toward the sun at an angle equal to the latitude. In this way, the sun is closer to being perpendicular to the plate during parts of the year, and the overall solar resource is somewhat higher than the "global horizontal" value. This is usually the way in which photovoltaic panels and solar water-heating systems are oriented. Because photovoltaic and solar water-heating systems are likely to be the dominant solar technologies to be used in Africa in the near future, the "latitude tilt" map is probably the most relevant. The author is grateful to Dr. David Renne at the National Renewable Energy Laboratory in Golden, Colorado, who provided this explanation.
Source: SWERA 2006.

construction and maintenance, and the rise of a technocratic class in many African countries. It is beyond the scope of this essay to go into detail on the various ways in which roads can be maintained, but it is worth mentioning that maintenance can be included in construction contracts, outsourced to independent providers, or contracted in other ways based on competitive

Map 3.2. Proposed transnational road network in Sub-Saharan Africa

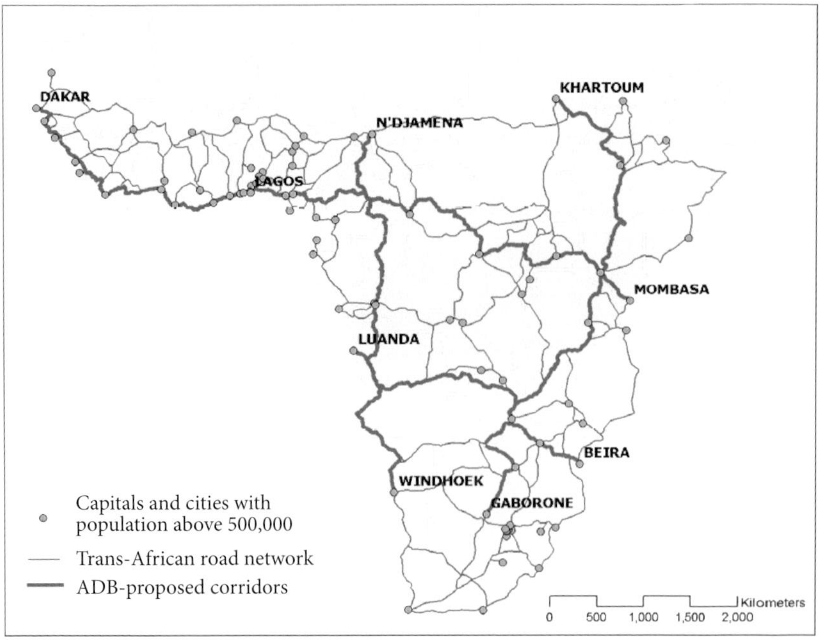

Source: Buys, Deichmann, and Wheeler 2006.

bidding. User charges can also play a role in funding maintenance costs.[17] Funding for infrastructure projects, no matter what the source, must include mechanisms by which maintenance costs can be met, with these costs acknowledged upfront and provided for when the infrastructure contract is signed. Most likely, the best way to ensure competitive bidding is for maintenance projects to be bundled regionally, thereby providing enough scale to interest a large number of bidders.

The rising technocratic class in Sub-Saharan Africa is well aware of the challenges of infrastructure investments and maintenance. This is not the Africa of the 1970s when many infrastructure projects failed because of poor design and lack of maintenance. Many countries in Africa have undergone macroeconomic reforms and succeeded in checking inflation. As mentioned earlier, several non-resource-rich countries are enjoying high growth rates.[18] Many of Africa's central banks are run by competent, highly trained individuals—some of the best finance minds in the world. In several countries, democratically elected leaders have searched the world to bring the best talent back to their countries to run their ministries. As a middle class emerges across the continent, there will be even greater demand for the maintenance of infrastructure. Designing, constructing, and maintaining infrastructure have a greater promise of success than ever before.

A Clean Infrastructure Initiative for Africa

The next president should announce a Clean Infrastructure Initiative to end Africa's power and transportation problems. This initiative should have two main objectives:

- Harnessing innovations in clean energy for Africa
- Financing the construction and maintenance of infrastructure through multilateral institutions

Harnessing innovations in clean energy. Links must be facilitated between U.S. businesses engaged in cost-reducing innovations in renewable energy and African businesses and governments interested in using these technologies. This could include carefully designed financing mechanisms to fund the transfer of clean technology, such as private equity funds that would invest in these technologies in Africa. The United States can also consider advance market commitments—such as those currently being used to develop vaccines and other health products—to spur the development of renewable energy sources that are clean and safe alternatives to biomass fuels.[19]

U.S. businesses, funded by venture capitalists and others, are engaged in the production of an array of new, cleaner power technologies, many of which can be transferred to Africa. The United States can play a role by monitoring new developments in solar, wind, and hydropower, and funding start-up or other costs that would bring these technologies to the region. Similarly, exciting new developments are being reported in micro-hydro, wind power, and biofuels, such as oil from the jatropha plant. Micro-hydro projects in Kenya and elsewhere in Africa are now providing electricity for several hundred households each, bringing modern energy to far-flung areas. The community-owned Tungu-Kabiri Micro Hydro project has 200 shareholders, each of whom bought $50 shares in the enterprise.[20] The project supplies 18 kilowatts of mechanical power. On an even smaller scale, pico-hydro schemes, which typically supply power up to 5 kilowatts, are also proving to be good value. In two towns in the Kirinyaga District in Kenya, pico-hydro units are providing power to about sixty households each, while substantially reducing the use of kerosene and biomass fuels.[21] These technological options are extremely relevant for a continent where traditional grid-based electricity will likely never be cheap, reliable, or far-reaching.

Dozens of energy firms in the United States, many funded by venture capital, are engaged in research and development to bring down the cost of renewable energy. Venture capital activity in solar energy has increased almost fourfold from $59 million in 2004 to $308 million in 2006.[22] Rich-country governments' interest in the development of alternative energies, in addition to legislated emissions reductions, are creating demand that investors see as a major incentive for investments in renewable energy sources. Currently, twenty-five states and the District of Columbia have binding clean energy standards, and California's recent greenhouse gas law requires the state to reduce its overall emissions by 25 percent by 2020. Solar efficiency has increased dramatically since the 1970s, accompanied by declines in cost. The U.S. Department of Energy's goal is to make solar power cost-competitive with the grid by 2015, and many in the field think this is a conservative target.[23] Some companies are trying to build large-scale plants that will store and supply base-load power around the clock at competitive prices.

Most recently, Google, one of the world's most visible technology companies, launched a $500 million effort to develop electricity from renewable energy sources that will be cheaper than electricity generated by burning coal.[24] Like some other companies, Google is taking bold steps in this area, focusing on such renewables as solar thermal and high-altitude wind energy. Table 3.2 lists some of the venture-capital-funded efforts in the United States and in other rich countries that are focused on lowering the costs of solar energy.

The United States can use incentives such as tax credits to lower the risks of technological development and speed up the production of clean technologies, and facilitate connections between U.S. businesses and relevant partners in Africa. The Overseas Private Investment Corporation, which has a strong tradition of providing support to the private sector, can play a key role. In 2007, the organization launched a program to support investments that are focused on energy efficiency and clean technology. It also announced the creation of a Catalyst Private Equity Fund, with a target capitalization of $100 million, to invest in water and clean energy projects in the Middle East and North Africa. This type of market-based mechanism could potentially be scaled up to meet the needs of Sub-Saharan Africa. The Overseas Private Investment Corporation could set up a fund (or funds) similar to the Catalyst Fund that would provide guarantees to investors and facilitate the transfer of clean energy technologies. A $1 billion Clean Energy Fund for Africa would be a great way to get started.

Many of the renewable energies discussed thus far can be provided on a small scale. This is very important for a continent where the population is sparsely distributed. But large-scale power is also necessary, especially for metropolitan areas that will require more electricity as they grow. Of the various types of large-scale projects, hydropower has great potential to meet a significant share of Africa's power needs. Several hydro projects are currently

Table 3.2. Development of solar energy

Privately held and venture-capital-funded companies

Firm	Location	Contribution to solar market	Investors (or past investors)
U.S. firms			
Advent Solar	Albuquerque, NM	Manufactures thin-film wafers that use less silicon; simplified assembly, higher energy production to drive down costs; locates all electrical content on back of solar cell to free up top surface for more sunlight absorption	ZBI Ventures; Sun Mountain Capital; Globespan Capital Partners; Battery Ventures; EnerTech; Firelank Capital; @Ventures; New Mexico Co-Investment Partners
Akeena Solar	Los Gatos, CA	Provider of solar energy systems	Kleiner Perkins Caufield & Byers
BrightSource Energy	Oakland, CA	Utility-scale solar thermal power plant that uses mirrors to focus solar rays on water to convert it to steam and drive turbines	VantagePoint Venture Partners
Energy Innovation	Pasadena, CA	Solar chip manufacturer; Sunflower product tracks sunbeams and produces both photovoltaic power and hot water	Mohr, Davidow Ventures; Idealab Holdings LLC
HelioVolt	Austin, TX	Uses copper, indium, gallium, diselenide (CIGS) technology; claims it can achieve efficiencies near those of silicon cells but with 1/100th of the material; reusable template capable of mass producing material	Paladin Capital Group; Masdar Clean Tech Fund; New Enterprise Associates; Solúcar Energías; Morgan Stanley Principal Investments; Sunton United Energy; Yellowstone Capital
INFINIA Corp.	Kennewick, WA	High-efficiency heat and power systems; solar generators	Khosla Ventures; Vulcan Capital; EQUUS Total Return, Inc.; Idealab; Power Play Energy, LLC
Konarka	Lowell, MA	Leading the arena of organic solar cells; technology relies on a dye to absorb solar energy; could be incorporated into flexible panels or fabrics	Draper Fisher Jurvetson; ChevronTexaco; New Enterprise Associates

(continued)

Table 3.2. Development of solar energy (continued)

Privately held and venture-capital-funded companies

Firm	Location	Contribution to solar market	Investors (or past investors)
Miasole	San Jose, CA	Makes thin-film solar cells with less semiconductor material than traditional silicon-based cells (less than 1 percent of the silicon of traditional cells); designing a continuous manufacturing process (more automation, faster) that should help reduce cost; pursuing CIGS technology which is higher efficiency	VantagePoint Venture Partners; Kleiner Perkins Caufield & Byers
Nanosolar	Palo Alto, CA	Thin-film solar panels and continuous manufacturing process to reduce costs; copper thin-film panels will cost five to ten times less than silicon panels; pursuing CIGS technology and is looking at solutions to efficiency loss of CIGS over large areas; designing cells to be more flexible and attractive than other solar panels, perhaps included in building materials; company claims it will achieve grid parity this year; building world's largest solar cell fabrication lab near San Francisco; building panel fabrication facility in Berlin	Larry Page & Sergey Brin; Mohr, Davidow Ventures; US Venture Partners; OnPoint Technologies; Benchmark Capital; Capricorn Management LLC; SAC Capital Advisors LLC; GLG Partners LP; Grazia Equity GmbH; Beck Energy GmbH; Klaus Tschira; Dietmar Hopp; Christian Reitberger; Jeff Skoll
Petra Solar	Green Brook, NJ	Creating a portfolio of semiconductor patents and a variety of products to boost efficiency and power management capabilities of solar power	DFJ Element; Blue Run Ventures; National Technology Enterprises Co.
Practical Instruments Inc.	Pasadena, CA	Uses optical technology to try to reduce the cost of rooftop solar panels; uses less photovoltaic material per panel	Nth Power; RockPort Capital Partners; Trinity Ventures; Rincon Venture Partners

Privately held and venture-capital-funded companies

Firm	Location	Contribution to solar market	Investors (or past investors)
Silicon Valley Solar Inc.	Santa Clara, CA	Acquired NuEdison Inc., a maker of photovoltaic modules; designs modules that concentrate energy in flat panels; uses an advanced internal concentrator; sells to large solar integrators	Bessemer Venture Partners
Solaicx	Santa Clara, CA	Dedicated to cutting costs of single crystalline wafers for the solar industry; aims to cut 75 percent of cost of solar cell manufacturing	Applied Materials; DE Shaw Group; Mitsui Ventures; Applied Ventures LLC; Firsthand Capital Management Inc.; Big Sky Ventures; Greenhouse Capital Partners
Solaria	Fremont, CA	Developing a way to make solar panels more efficient and cheaper to manufacture	Sigma Partners; NGEN
SolFocus	Palo Alto, CA	Uses lenses and mirrors to concentrate sunlight onto high-efficiency solar cells to reduce cost per watt; increases efficiency of cells	New Enterprise Associates; NGEN
SoloPower Inc.	Milpitas, CA	Manufactures CIGS technology thin-film; can be made in large batches, which can help reduce costs	Convexa Capital; Scatec AS; Spencer Energy AS; Crosslink Capital; Firsthand Capital Management
Stion Corp. (formerly nStructures)	Menlo Park, CA	Developing thin-films that lower the cost of manufacturing models; improving efficiency of crystalline silicon materials	Lightspeed Venture Partners; General Catalyst Partners; Khosla Ventures; Braemar Energy Ventures; Moser Baer Photovoltaic
Tioga Energy Inc.	San Mateo, CA	Provides solar systems to customers; guarantees predictable costs	NGEN; Draper Fisher Jurvetson; RockPort Capital; DFJ Frontier; Kirlan Ventures

(continued)

Table 3.2. Development of solar energy (continued)

Privately held and venture-capital-funded companies

Firm	Location	Contribution to solar market	Investors (or past investors)
Non-U.S. firms			
6N Silicon Inc.	Mississauga, ON, Canada	Produces solar-grade silicon tailored specifically to the solar industry	Ventures West; Yaletown Venture Partners
CSG Solar AG	Thalheim, Germany	Manufactures thin-film on glass modules that use less silicon, involve fewer production steps	Apax Partners; Good Energies Inc.; Renewable Energy Corp.; IBG Beteiligungsgesellschaft Sachsen-Anhalt mbH
Day4 Energy	Vancouver, BC, Canada	Produces flat panel modules with an electrode that reduces the resistance of a traditional photovoltaic cell; produces sun concentrators	Chrysalix Energy; British Columbia Discovery Fund
EnerWorks	London, ON, Canada	Manufactures solar thermal products, including solar power water heaters; its goal is to reduce water-heating energy costs	Chrysalix; Investeco Capital
G24 Innovations (G24i)	Cardiff, Wales	Manufactures non-silicon-based cells; cells based on colored dye and titanium oxide crystals, which are used to copy photosynthesis; estimated at 1/5 price of silicon cells; working with mobile phone companies to test whether cells could be used to charge handsets in rural Africa; plans to sell inexpensive devices (for light bulb or cell phone charging) in poor regions of India and Africa to jump-start sales	Renewable Capital
Hydrogen Solar	UK	Uses sunlight to generate hydrogen fuel	E-Synergy
Jiamgsu Shunda Group	China	Makes 6- and 8-inch monocrystalline silicon ingots used in solar power cells	Actis; JOLMO Capital Management; Waichun

Privately held and venture-capital-funded companies

Firm	Location	Contribution to solar market	Investors (or past investors)
Orionsolar	Jerusalem, Israel	Uses dye cell nanotechnology, which does not use silicon; trying to build a low-cost energy panel	21 Ventures LLC
Solarcentury Holdings Ltd.	London, UK	Designs and installs solar modules	VantagePoint Venture Partners

Formerly privately held or venture-capital-funded companies that have gone public

Firm (year of IPO)	Location	Contribution to solar market	Investors (or past investors)
U.S. firms			
Evergreen Solar (2000)	Marlboro, MA	Manufactures rooftop panels; uses conventional silicon but in a new, more frugal fashion that uses 30 percent less	Nth Power; RockPort; Arete Corp.; SAM Private Equity; Zero Stage Capital Co.; Rockefeller & Co. Inc.; Perseus LLC; CDP Capital Technology Ventures; Massachusetts Renewable Energy Trust; Impax Asset Management
First Solar (2006)	Phoenix, AZ	Cadmium telluride-based solar panels (efficiency lower than silicon models, but manufacturing cost is much lower, so price per watt is lower); ground-based, large commercial systems; hopes to be grid competitive by 2010	
SunPower Corp. (2005)	Sunnyvale and San Jose, CA	Manufactures silicon solar cells on a large scale	Associated Venture Investors; Technology Funding Inc.; Nipsco Development Co.; Honda Motor Co., Ltd.; Cypress Semiconductor Corp. bought it in 2002

(continued)

Table 3.2. Development of solar energy (continued)

Formerly privately held or venture-capital-funded companies that have gone public

Firm (year of IPO)	Location	Contribution to solar market	Investors (or past investors)
Non-U.S. firms			
PV Crystalox Solar (2007)	Oxford, UK; Germany	Manufactures silicon components for solar electricity industry	Ventizz
Q-Cells AG (2005)	Thalheim, Germany	One of the world's largest solar manufacturers	Apax Partners; Good Energies Inc. (Apax made largest gain by a venture capital group since the collapse of the dotcom bubble.)
SunTech Power (2005)	Wuxi, China	Large-scale solar cell manufacturer	Actis; Goldman Sachs; Dragon Tech Ventures

under consideration or at early stages of development in countries such as Ethiopia and Uganda. The most ambitious of all is Grand Inga, which seeks to vastly expand Africa's power generation capacity by harnessing the Inga Falls on the Congo River. Inga sends 42.5 million liters of water pouring into the Atlantic Ocean every second—a flow volume second only to that of the Amazon. Grand Inga is estimated to cost upward of $40 billion and generate up to 39,000 megawatts of electric power, supplying the needs of most of the African continent. This project is of enormous scale, and its cost is estimated to be over three times the total amount of investment in infrastructure in Africa since 1985. Several other hydropower projects in various stages of development also have the potential to address Africa's energy crisis.

Hydropower projects continue to generate controversy because of environmental concerns, but there are new, best-practice models that can be relied upon to mitigate negative effects. There are also concerns about increasing dependence on hydropower during an era of climate-change-induced drought and unreliable rainfall. But it is important to note that water storage capacity is underexploited and is currently at about 5 percent of potential storage levels. If this capacity can be increased, there is considerable potential for hydropower even in areas of variable rainfall. Other concerns—about resettlement of large numbers of people, the destruction of waterfalls, and the loss of habitat for wildlife—are serious, but they can be addressed by consultative processes, involvement of community organizations at every stage of design and construction, and external monitoring by relevant agencies. The Nam Theun 2 hydroelectric project in Laos serves as an excellent example of getting the process right.[25] This 1,070-megawatt hydropower project has various environmental and social safeguards to protect the people affected by the project and to preserve the biodiversity in the area.[26]

Governance concerns also loom large (see chapter 5 by de Tray and Moran). Several issues will need to be carefully managed, including the tendering and procurement processes, setting and collecting user fees, and contracting for maintenance. Despite considerable pessimism about the ability of African governments to cope with these issues, governments and investors have new best-practice models to use (including Nam Theun 2), as well as a vast reserve of technical capacity, especially within multilateral institutions such as the World Bank and the African Development Bank. New arrangements may also be needed to address governance issues in the context of specific regions in Africa, especially if projects are very large.

Regional investment projects with substantial amounts of international funding can lead to perceptions of a loss of sovereignty in decisionmaking at the national level. But international investors and multilateral funding partners will bring with them layers of safeguards, including requirements pertaining to procurement, distribution, and the pricing of services. Policymakers must keep in mind that the ultimate result of major regional investments will be a reliable supply of electricity and transportation services that will drive growth.

One example of excellent cooperation is the West African Power Pool, in which collaborating governments have successfully given up some decision-making power in order to maximize the supply of electricity on a regional basis.[27] Under the umbrella of the Economic Community of West African States, heads of state meet periodically to set the terms of the regional electricity generation and distribution system. In many ways, this type of large-scale infrastructure investment is more likely to succeed than smaller efforts that come with less money, less international attention, and fewer safeguards. Unfortunately, most investments in infrastructure in Africa have been financed at the national level, resulting in small, poorly functioning projects that have generated more Afro-pessimism than electricity. Big projects at the regional level that visibly improve infrastructure can motivate governments to do more and do better, while providing adequate budgets for supervision and transparent procedures.

Supporting construction and maintenance through multilateral initiatives. To support the development of clean, large-scale power and road projects, the United States must work through the multilateral process, especially by providing support to the African Development Bank. Despite the enormous demand, donor financing and the support of infrastructure projects have fallen sharply in recent times (figure 3.7). In 2006, a working group convened by the Center for Global Development made a strong case for the African Development Bank to focus exclusively on infrastructure over the next three to five years (AfDB Working Group 2006). The report argues that this focus makes sense for four reasons: The bank has substantial experience in infrastructure (which currently accounts for about 40 percent of its approved projects); infrastructure investment and related expertise is in strong demand among the bank's clients; the bank already has a mandate for infrastructure development; and infrastructure is central to growth, and governance of infrastructure is an important part of the wider agenda of governance.

Figure 3.7. Social and infrastructure aid to Sub-Saharan Africa as a share of total aid

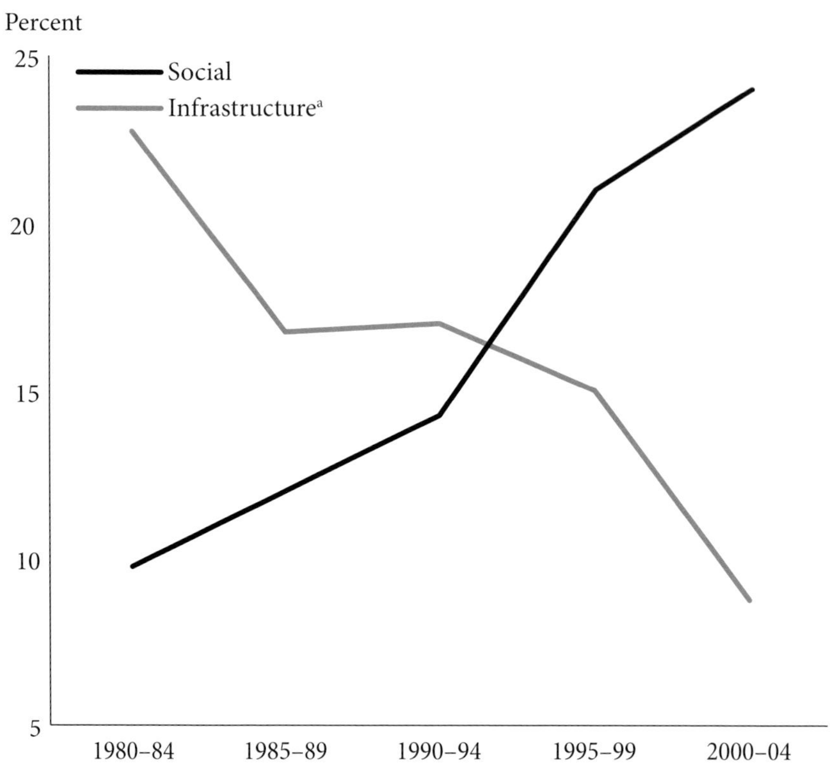

a. Includes transport, water, and energy.
Source: AfDB Working Group 2006.

The African Development Bank should also provide support for tendering, procurement, and ongoing maintenance of infrastructure facilities. Currently, the bank's portfolio is very fragmented, resulting in a small average project size of \$20–\$40 million, within an overall lending program of \$2–\$3 billion. About 40 percent of this amount goes toward infrastructure. This is a tiny share of Africa's infrastructure needs, estimated by various sources (such as the Blair Commission for Africa) to be anywhere from \$10 billion to \$30 billion per year. The United States, as the second largest nonregional shareholder, should emphasize the need for larger projects focused on clean infrastructure, such as hydropower and other renewable energy. It should also encourage the African Development Bank to build up its professional capacity in the area of infrastructure, particularly in facilitating public-private partnerships for financing, construction, and maintenance. If the bank can deliver on this objective, the United States should consider increasing its capital contribution to the organization by up to 25 percent a year for the next four years.

Another key player on the continent, the New Partnership for Africa's Development, has effectively partnered with the African Development Bank in an arrangement in which the bank has the main responsibility for infrastructure investments. In 2006, the New Partnership for Africa's Development launched its Infrastructure Investment Facility to raise financing for the construction of infrastructure projects. This facility is an outcome of discussions of the African Business Roundtable, a private sector forum that is well aware of the burden of Africa's deteriorating roads and unreliable power supply. The United States can provide support to the New Partnership for Africa's Development and the African Development Bank on the financing of clean infrastructure projects, as well as technical assistance on the maintenance, regulation, and pricing of services.

The World Bank, with its human resources and accompanying technical capacity, is also well positioned to play a role in infrastructure provision, both directly and by assisting the African Development Bank in its efforts. The solution to Africa's roads and power crisis is much more regional than national, and the World Bank's soft loan facility—the International Development Association—has a regional project component that can address these needs.[28] Clean energy and transportation projects are ideal candidates for this new funding window, as are road maintenance projects that comprise roads linking several countries.

But none of these multilateral efforts will be easy, and not just because of the scale of the projects. The World Bank Group, the African Development Bank, and other multilateral institutions are largely geared toward working at the level of individual countries. Getting managers to work across country lines and collaboratively is difficult in this setup. For staff, it means reporting to multiple managers and a greatly increased administrative burden; there are currently few incentives for staff to take on regional projects. Disbursement rates on commitments to regional projects are often low, in part because of these bureaucratic hurdles. Fixing the incentive structure within multilateral institutions is a crucial part of the solution to delivering regional public goods to Africa, and the United States—as a major shareholder of these institutions—is uniquely positioned to get this done.

Conclusion

Africa's road and power crisis can be solved with resources, technological know-how, and support from the U.S. government and from the U.S. private sector. Africa has a unique opportunity to build its infrastructure by using new and clean technology. It has the opportunity to avoid many of the environmental problems that have plagued the rest of the world. Using technology that is low-carbon or carbon-free is not good just for the African people but for the whole world. The United States has an unprecedented opportunity to help Africa in its search for a high and sustainable rate of growth.

Notes

1. Gelb and Turner 2007.
2. The United Kingdom and the United States have clean energy initiatives to help developing countries finance the development and use of renewable energy. The plan outlined in this chapter is specific to Africa, and it emphasizes the need to link technology development in the United States with businesses and governments in Sub-Saharan Africa.
3. Mbogo 2007.
4. *The Economist* 2007a.
5. Soares 2007.
6. World Bank 2007c.
7. World Bank 2007b.
8. World Bank 2007a.
9. As surveys vary slightly from country to country, not all twenty-seven countries are represented in every figure. For more information on the Enterprise Surveys, see www.enterprisesurveys.org.
10. Adenikinju 2005.
11. World Bank 2002.
12. Wines 2007.
13. Eifert and others 2005.

14. There is a large literature that looks at the returns to investment in infrastructure. Of particular relevance is Limao and Venables (2001), which looks at losses arising from the lack of investment in infrastructure in Africa. Canning and Pedroni (1999) and Munnell (1992) look at the returns to infrastructure investment in a broader context.
15. OECD 2004; Buys and others 2007.
16. *The Economist* 2007a.
17. Heggie and Fon 1991.
18. Gelb and Turner 2007.
19. See Barder 2005, and chapter 2 by Wheeler in this book.
20. ITDG/Practical Action 2007.
21. Television Trust for the Environment 2002.
22. *The Economist* 2007b.
23. *The Economist* 2007b.
24. Google.org 2007.
25. For more details, see www.namtheun2.com.
26. ADB 2007. Many of the locations that would be ideal for road or power projects in Africa are also of great importance from a conservation point of view. But we now have detailed information that can substantially mitigate the effects of new construction. A database compiled by the Global Environment Facility, the World Bank's Development Research Group, and the World Conservation Union contains information about habitats and other data relating to 5,329 amphibians, 4,612 mammals, and 1,098 endangered birds. These data enable the overlay of biodiversity maps with potential road networks to identify sensitive zones (Buys, Deichmann, and Wheeler 2006). More generally, the United States can tap into the considerable expertise on biodiversity that exists within its scientific community to make sure that conservation planning is a mandatory component of infrastructure projects in Africa.
27. For more information about the West African Power Pool, see www.ecowapp.org.
28. World Bank 2007d.

References

Adenikinju, Adeola F. 2005. "African Imperatives in the New World Trade Order: Country Case Study of the Manufacturing Sector in Nigeria." In E. Ogunkola O, and A. Bankole, eds., *Nigeria's Imperatives in the New World Trade Order*. Nairobi and Ibadan, Nigeria: Africa Economic Research Consortium and the Trade Policy Research and Training Programme.

ADB (Asian Development Bank). 2007. "Nam Theun 2 Maintains Momentum." Press release. June 6. Manila. [www.adb.org/media/Articles/2007/11923-laos-hydroelectrics-projects/].

AfDB (African Development Bank) Working Group. 2006. "Building Africa's Development Banks: Six Recommendations for the AfDB and Its Shareholders." Working Group Report. Center for Global Development, Washington, D.C. [www.cgdev.org/files/10033_file_AfDB_ENG.pdf]

Barder, Owen. 2005. "Making Markets for Vaccines—Ideas to Action." Brief. Center for Global Development, Washington, D.C. [www.cgdev.org/content/publications/detail/2792/].

Buys, Piet, Uwe Deichmann, and David Wheeler. 2006. "Road Network Upgrading and Overland Trade Expansion in Sub-Saharan Africa." Policy Research Working Paper 4097. World Bank, Washington, D.C.

Buys, Piet, Uwe Deichmann, Craig Meisner, Thao Ton-That, and David Wheeler. 2007. "Country Stakes in Climate Change Negotiations: Two Dimensions of Vulnerability." Policy Research Working Paper 4300. World Bank, Washington, D.C.

Canning, David, and P. Pedroni. 1999. "Infrastructure and Long Run Economic Growth." Computer printout. Econometric Society Summer Meeting, Madison, Wisc.

The Economist. 2007a. "The Dark Continent." August 16. [www.economist.com/research/articlesBySubject/displaystory.cfm?subjectid=8780295&story_id=9660077].

———. 2007b. "Bright Prospects." March 8. [www.economist.com/search/displaystory.cfm?story_id=8766045].

Eifert, Benn, Alan Gelb, and Vijaya Ramachandran. 2005. "Business Environment and Comparative Advantage in Africa: Evidence from the Investment Climate Data." Working Paper 56. Center for Global Development, Washington, D.C.

Elliott, Kimberly. 2007. "Trade Policy for Development." Brief. Center for Global Development, Washington, D.C. [www.cgdev.org/files/14348_file_CGD_brief_TradePolicy_web.pdf].

Gelb, Alan, and Ginger Turner. 2007. "Policy, Aid and Performance in Africa: The G11 and Other Country Groups." World Bank, Washington, D.C.

Google.org. 2007. "Google's Goal: Renewable Energy Cheaper than Coal." Press release. November 27. [www.google.com/intl/en/press/pressrel/20071127_green.html].

Heggie, Ian, and Vincent Fon. 1991. "Optimal User Charges and Cost Recovery for Roads in Developing Countries." Policy Research Working Paper 780. World Bank, Washington, D.C.

ITDG (Intermediate Technology Development Group)/Practical Action. 2007. "Microhydro." [www.itdg.org/?id=micro_hydro].

Limao, Nuno, and Anthony Venables. 2001. "Infrastructure, Geographical Disadvantage, Transport Costs, and Trade." *World Bank Economic Review* 15 (3): 451–79.

Mbogo, Steve. 2007. "Big Companies Demand Higher Rebates in Energy Saving Plan." *Business Daily Africa*. July 26.

Munnell, Alicia H. 1992. "Policy Watch: Infrastructure Investment and Economic Growth." *Journal of Economic Perspectives* 6 (4): 189–98.

OECD (Organization for Economic Co-operation and Development). 2004. *African Economic Outlook 2003/2004*. Paris: African Development Bank/OECD Publishing.

Soares, Claire. 2007. "Lighting Up Africa: Why Today's Residents Are Still Making Do with Wax and Wicks." *The Independent*. August 28.

SWERA (Solar and Wind Energy Resource Assessment). 2006. Africa Flat Plate Tilted at Latitude, Annual Average. Map. [http://swera.unep.net/typo3conf/ext/metadata_tool/archive/download/africatilt_R1_218.pdf.]

Television Trust for the Environment. 2002. "Stream Line Kenya." ITDG East Africa and Nottingham Trent University, Pico Hydro Unit. [www.tve.org/ho/doc.cfm?aid=871].

Wines, Michael. 2007. "Toiling in the Dark: Africa's Power Crisis." *New York Times*. July 29. [www.nytimes.com/2007/07/29/world/africa/29power.html].

World Bank. 2002. *An Investment Climate Assessment for Nigeria*. Washington, D.C.: World Bank. [http://siteresources.worldbank.org/EXTAFRSUMAFTPS/Resources/ICA005.pdf]

———. 2007a. "*Little Green Data Book 2007*: Carbon Dioxide Emissions on the Rise, Warns World Bank Publication." Press release. May 8. World Bank, Washington, D.C. [http://go.worldbank.org/9IOTC591C0].

———. 2007b. *The Little Green Data Book*. World Bank.

———. 2007c. "World Bank Group Launches New Initiative to 'Light Africa.'" Press release. September 5. [http://go.worldbank.org/OMNIAW9RA1].

———. 2007d. *Clean Energy for Development Investment Framework: The World Bank Group Action Plan*. March 28. [http://siteresources.worldbank.org/DEVCOMMINT/Documentation/21289621/DC2007-0002(E)-CleanEnergy.pdf].

4

Foreign Direct Investment and Development

Theodore Moran

In the heyday of the Washington Consensus, there was unqualified enthusiasm for the spread of foreign direct investment (FDI)—the more the better—throughout developing countries. This uncritical support for the supposed benefits of multinational investment has now been replaced by widespread popular skepticism. Multinational corporate investment in extractive industries can turn rich resource endowments into a curse, with oil and "blood diamonds" fortifying corrupt elites or financing civil wars and regional instability. Multinational corporate manufacturing investment in protected host-country markets may distort the economy and retard growth. Multinational corporate investment in labor-intensive assembly may result in violations of labor standards and in sweatshop abuses.

What policies should the next U.S. president adopt to maximize the contribution FDI can make to development?

Under the right conditions, FDI can play an important, and in some ways unique, role in promoting broad-based economic and social development. The challenge for the next administration is to endorse policies that promote the benefits of FDI and to pursue them with vigor, while leading an international effort to reform policies that allow FDI to cause harm.

FDI in extractive industries exemplifies this challenge. FDI in oil and mining has the capacity to generate

Theodore Moran is a nonresident fellow at the Center for Global Development.

extraordinary revenues that can be used to strengthen the host economy and alleviate domestic poverty, as cases presented below illustrate. But FDI in extractive industries will not do this unless the United States takes the lead in closing loopholes in anticorruption laws, supporting transparency in investor payments, enforcing environmental standards, and helping to fund monitoring and surveillance among local nongovernmental organizations and watchdog groups.

FDI in manufacturing and assembly of least-skill-intensive products offers an entry point for poorer countries to start on the path upward into international markets, as some of the countries described below have done, with doable guidelines that others can follow. But this requires the United States to ensure that international investors observe core labor standards, and then, when they do, the next president must remove the obstacles—and sometimes the explicit prohibitions—faced by the Overseas Private Investment Corporation (OPIC), the United States Agency for International Development, and the Millennium Challenge Corporation to enable them to help with investment promotion and export-led growth. Here it may be surprising to note that U.S. policy to promote development through FDI has not grown more supportive over time, has not even stood still, but rather has grown increasingly restrictive.

FDI in middle-skill-intensive goods and services, when meshed with strong education and vocational training programs in host countries, allows poorer, developing countries to move toward the ranks of more advanced developing countries. Here FDI becomes the instrument of dynamic comparative advantage, transforming the production possibilities within the host economy well beyond the apparent limitations of the country's natural factor endowments. For this reason, the next president's approach to trade and investment liberalization around the globe could critically affect the potential contribution from FDI.

But does the globalization of industry through FDI come at the expense of good jobs here in the United States? This chapter argues that the evidence offers a pleasant surprise: Outward investment by U.S. firms is not a zero-sum phenomenon that damages the U.S. economy. Instead, outward investment enhances the competitiveness of U.S. firms at home and increases demand for (and wages paid to) skilled workers in both developed and developing countries.

Thus, under reasonably competitive conditions, with safeguards against corrupt payments, environmental violations, and abuses of labor standards, FDI can be a powerful force for development. But the United States today is seriously deficient in helping FDI play this positive role, restraining and sometimes weakening core U.S. agencies that could help, while turning a blind eye to loopholes in the Foreign Corrupt Practices Act. The next U.S. president can turn this around, simultaneously supporting FDI as a vehicle to propel developing countries toward prosperity, as sketched out below, while curtailing the possibilities for FDI to do harm.

Foreign direct investment in extractive industries: avoiding the "resource curse"

In any contemporary textbook on development, the chapter on natural resources is the most marked up, crossed out, and scribbled over. Long considered an advantage for a poor country, a rich natural resource base is now viewed as a dangerous liability. Diamond mines financed civil wars in West Africa for more than a decade, while oil revenues sustained both sides of the civil war in Angola. Upwards of $1 billion a year in Nigerian oil receipts have, until recently, gone unaccounted for. Africa is not alone in the misuse of extractive industry revenues. Across Central Asia, Southeast Asia, and Latin America, Transparency International's 2006 Bribe Payers Index continues to rank extractive industries near the top of those sectors where corrupt payments figure prominently.

But this need not be the outcome. Well-managed natural resource endowments can promote broad and sustained growth. The keys are transparency and institutions for good governance (box 4.1).

Botswana and Chile are not alone in avoiding the resource curse. Last year, foreign investors in the extractive sector generated 50 percent of all exports from Peru, 40 percent of all exports from Tanzania, and 34 percent of all exports from Ghana. A positive record of FDI in oil and minerals in Argentina, Indonesia, Malaysia, and Tunisia could be added to the list.

At the same time, however, FDI in the extractive sector in Equatorial Guinea and the Republic of Congo—including international investors from Europe and the United States—helped leaders siphon off revenues for their own personal use, hidden from the eyes of their citizens. The preferred vehicle for corrupt payments has been a partnership formed between the multinational resource company and the relatives or business associates of the leadership, designed in a fashion that exploits loopholes in the Foreign Corrupt Practices Act and the Organisation for Economic Co-operation and Development (OECD) Anti-Bribery Convention (see chapter 5 by de Tray and Moran).[1]

The next president should change the Foreign Corrupt Practices Act to prohibit such payments to friends and relatives of developing-country leaders unless these payments can be shown to be for services rendered other than securing concessions and favorable treatment, and take the lead in pressing OECD members to do the same. The new administration should also expand the scope of the Extractive Industries Transparency Initiative to cover infrastructure, while making sure the initiative's process begins to function effectively (see chapter 5 by de Tray and Moran). Some of the most egregious instances of corrupt partnerships have occurred in infrastructure investments, a finding all the more serious given the importance of efficient power and

Box 4.1. Avoiding the "resource curse" in Botswana and Chile

Flying in the face of numerous studies where natural resources constitute a "curse" are the experiences of Botswana and Chile.

Diamonds and minerals in Botswana

When Botswana became independent in 1966, the landlocked, tropical country was the third poorest nation in the world. The new leaders presided over an economy whose principal activity was cattle ranching. The entire country boasted no more than twenty-two college graduates, plus a mere 100 with a diploma from high school, and twelve kilometers of paved roads. FDI diamond exports began in the early 1970s, and within ten years, Botswana was one of the top three diamond producers in the world. Two decades after independence, the FDI mining sector supplied 82 percent of the country's exports and 55 percent of the government's revenues. In the 1990s, foreign investment in copper and nickel came on stream. Between 2002 and 2006, FDI mineral exports grew from $2 billion to $3.4 billion per year, with government mining tax revenues climbing from $1.1 billion to $4.6 billion (accounting in 2006 for 89 percent of all exports and 71 percent of all government revenues).

For three decades, Botswana has enjoyed an average GDP growth rate above 7 percent. To be sure, natural resource wealth has by no means been a panacea. The economy has not been able to diversify very broadly. The rate of unemployment has remained high, especially for migrant workers from rural areas. The incidence of HIV/AIDS is devastating, affecting perhaps 25–30 percent of the adult population. But FDI in the extractive sector has given—and continues to provide—the base for public expenditures, sometimes reaching 40 percent of GDP, well above the average for Africa. Besides the provision of infrastructure and other general economic services, and payments to the country's well-respected professional civil service, the largest single public expenditure has consistently been for education, a preeminence that is now being replaced by outlays for health.

Copper in Chile

The Chilean experience with copper offers a second case of natural resources providing a base for broad economic and social development, without becoming a curse. With a population of 15.8 million people and a per capita income above $5,000 a year—the highest in South America—Chile has a much larger and more diversified economy than Botswana. The country has become the largest copper producer in the world, accounting for almost 40 percent of global output. Copper exports earned more than $32 billion in 2006, 56 percent of all Chilean exports.

The role of FDI in Chile's extractive sector has changed over time, first dominating early copper mining operations, then being nationalized, and now leading a resurgence of mining expansion alongside government-owned copper companies with sound professional credentials. Revenues from mining taxes amounted to some $10.9 billion between 1991 and 2003, and then climbed abruptly, from $592 million in 2003, to $2.9 billion in 2004, $4.4 billion in 2005, and $8.3 billion in 2006. Both investor payments and government expenditures consistently have a high degree of transparency.

Since 1990 (the end of the Pinochet regime) annual gross domestic product growth in Chile has averaged 5.4 percent, real wages have increased by 2.4 percent a year, and the number of people living in poverty has decreased by nearly 50 percent. Infant mortality, life expectancy, and literacy rates show that Chile has outperformed both its regional and income comparators over this period. On the Human Development Index, Chile has achieved one of the highest rankings in Latin America and the Caribbean.

* * *

For both Botswana and Chile, good governance, reliable institutions, reasonable transparency, and low levels of corruption have been vital to turning mineral resources into an asset instead of a curse. In 2006, Botswana received a score of 48 on the World Bank's Doing Business index, placing the country in a relatively investment-friendly category that only three of forty-six other African countries achieved. In the Transparency International Global Corruption Perceptions Index, Botswana achieved a mark of 5.6 in 2006, the highest in all of Africa. Since World Bank governance indicators began to be collected in 1996, Chile has been a leader in Latin America, with particularly high scores in regulatory quality, control of corruption, rule of law, and government effectiveness. On the World Bank's Doing Business index, Chile received a 28 in 2006, ranking first in South America. In the Transparency International Global Corruption Perceptions Index, Chile received a score of 7.3 in 2006, placing the country not just in first place for Latin America but also scoring on a par with the United States.

Sources: For information on Botswana's economy: Acemoglu, Johnson, and Robinson 2003; Criscuolo 2007; Good 1992. For Botswana's mineral exports: EIU 2007a and earlier editions. For Chile's experience with copper: ICMM 2007. For Chile's revenues from mining taxes: EIU 2007b and earlier editions.

other infrastructure services to development (see chapter 3 by Ramachandran). As the Extractive Industries Transparency Initiative becomes more effective, the United States can help fund the training of local parliamentarians and civil society actors to monitor the transactions between international investors and public authorities in their own countries.

In short, a rich natural resource base need not be a curse, and the next president will want the United States to support FDI in natural resources in a manner that promotes, rather than undermines, good governance and the strengthening of host-country institutions.

Helping poor countries get started with foreign direct investment in manufacturing and assembly

The list of impediments to FDI in manufacturing and assembly in least-developed countries is long, and the stories of failed efforts to attract FDI are many. Yet the lessons from initially poor states that have succeeded in attracting foreign investment in low-skill, labor-intensive sectors are straightforward and replicable for today's least-developed countries in Africa, Asia, and Central and South America. And the role of external rich-country support—often in relatively small amounts—has proven critical. The puzzle is why the United States does not do a consistently better, and more coherently executed, job of helping poorer countries launch themselves on a path of FDI-led growth. The next president has the opportunity to turn this around, based on an understanding of a now well-established literature on what has and has not worked for countries seeking to attract FDI.

Mauritius was one of the most remote tropical African countries when it began to harness FDI for exports. Foreign investors fueled a growth record that ranked Mauritius seventh among the fifteen most successful exporters of manufactured products in the world, with exports reaching more than $1.2 billion in 2006 (39 percent of all exports) and sustaining more than 68,000 jobs. The Dominican Republic had a per capita gross domestic product only two-thirds as high as that of Mauritius when the government started to lure FDI into manufacturing and assembly. By 2006, total zone investment exceeded $1 billion, total zone employment was 197,000, and total zone exports reached $4.5 billion (81 percent of all exports).

Explicitly trying to emulate Mauritius, Madagascar achieved an even more rapid pace of success in attracting foreign investors, with 120 firms setting up operations in the first five years, compared with 100 firms in the first ten years for Mauritius. By 2006, Madagascar's FDI exports reached $547 million (54 percent of all exports), providing jobs to 107,000 workers. Elsewhere in Africa, Lesotho attracted fifty-five foreign export-oriented manufacturing firms between 1996 and 2005, with thirty-eight producing clothing, three producing footwear, four producing electronics, four involved in food processing, and the rest producing assorted products such as umbrellas and plastic goods, for a total of more than $700 million in exports, generating 43,000 jobs.

Typically, countries establish export processing zones (EPZs) where operating conditions, infrastructure services, and freedom from trade restrictions allow foreign investors to operate competitively. Success in attracting FDI then has required an investment promotion agency (IPA) with a mission of providing up-to-date information, lowering the cost and difficulty of search and comparison for foreign investors, and creating a one-stop shop to help companies obtain permits and other documents. EPZ management can often be turned over to private international developers, who then have a self-interest to use their home-country networks (in countries such as India, Japan, the Republic of Korea, Taiwan, and the United States, and countries in Europe) to find new investors to become their tenants. In success stories, the EPZs provide a demonstration effect for broader liberalization throughout the host economy, and not a substitute for broader liberalization, while the IPA becomes an advocate for improvement of the investment climate more generally, not merely a pleader for special treatment of foreign firms.

Investment promotion has a cumulative dynamic: it takes a well-staffed, efficient agency to attract the early investors; the presence of the early investors lures private EPZ developers; the interaction of already established investors and aggressive developers provides comfort and credibility to follow-on investors in established sectors and to pioneer investors in novel sectors.

For countries unable to launch an effective EPZ-IPA strategy, this virtuous cycle never gets started. In Africa, twenty-five countries have signed their so-called IPAs up as members of the World Association of Investment Promotion Agencies, but their Web sites do not exhibit up-to-date economic or legal information, nor do they provide direct access to key ministries or links to satisfied investors. EPZs and industrial parks are supervised by understaffed and underpaid government regulators, and often dominated by bureaucracies trained for heavy-handed, case-by-case screening of FDI applications.

Support to help poorer countries attract FDI clearly qualifies as a prime candidate for external assistance and capacity building on the part of developed countries. For example, the Lesotho National Development Corporation, now a central player in the country's dynamic FDI-led export drive, was launched with an equity stake from the German Finance Company for Investments in Developing Countries.

The U.S. record in this endeavor is on balance quite disappointing. The U.S. Agency for International Development has from time to time demonstrated considerable capability in helping to renovate IPAs (as in Costa Rica), but the effort has not been consistent or sustained. The Millennium Challenge Corporation has not defined its responsibilities in this arena, and should be instructed during the next administration to emphasize investment promotion in the design of its compacts. The Millennium Challenge Corporation occupies a special niche in facilitating international investment among those developing countries that are accelerating their internal reform process. Whereas the U.S. Agency for International Development works via the Global Development Alliance with U.S. multinationals to focus the charitable and corporate social responsibility efforts of member firms, Millennium Challenge Corporation has uniquely powerful potential (as yet unexploited) to use its compact grants—which have been as much as $700 million—to foster mainline international investment activities (not just corporate social responsibility projects) that are crucial to host-country growth. The next president should direct the Millennium Challenge Corporation to design compacts with the goal of eliminating bottlenecks and facilitating both international and local private sector investment.

The record of OPIC in helping poor developing countries get started along the path of FDI-led growth is, to craft a precise characterization, distressingly poor. OPIC was originally launched with an explicit development mission, but its posture has grown cautious and restrictive over the past decade and a half. OPIC is prohibited from providing political risk insurance or financial guarantees to labor-intensive "sensitive sector" investments of the kind where most developing countries have a comparative advantage. OPIC is precluded from supporting textile or garment projects, or agricultural processing projects if the crops involved are "in surplus" in the United States. Concern about sensitive sectors has kept OPIC from offering insurance to U.S. investors interested in setting up EPZs, effectively precluding U.S. companies from playing the investor-developer role that has proved such a powerful force in poor-country investment promotion.

The next president will not want U.S. agencies to reinvent the wheel by duplicating what other international and multilateral institutions are already doing. Recognizing the high payoff of effective investment promotion, the Inter-American Development Bank and the Asian Development Bank, like the Foreign Investment Advisory Service of the World Bank Group, sometimes provide assistance for IPAs and training for IPA staff. So do a handful of aid agencies in developed countries. The Multilateral Investment Guarantee Agency offers a Web-based interactive system that, for countries that keep their country sites up-to-date, has dramatically reduced the search time, effort, and expense for investors to evaluate countries, compare legislation, and link up with established investors on a real-time basis. The new administration will want to build upon these efforts by first removing the impediments that keep U.S. agencies from actively promoting investment in poor countries, and then integrating the liberated capabilities of the U.S. government with other international and multilateral programs.

From low- to middle-income development: the role of trade and investment liberalization

Conventional wisdom often portrays FDI in manufacturing and assembly as flowing primarily into lowest-skill activities, such as production of garments, footwear, toys, and soccer balls. The reality is quite at odds with this image and has major implications for the next president's approach to trade and investment liberalization.

The surprise of recent decades has been the expansion of FDI into increasingly sophisticated manufacturing and service activities. By far the largest proportion of FDI flows from developed countries into medium-skill industrial sectors, such as electrical equipment, electronics, semiconductors, auto parts, industrial machinery, chemicals, medical equipment, and pharmaceuticals in developing countries. Indeed, the flow of FDI into more advanced industrial sectors is more than ten times larger each year than the flow to low-skill, labor-intensive operations, and is rising over time.[2] The cumulative stock of FDI is ten times greater in advanced industrial sectors than in low-skill, labor-intensive sectors, and building up more rapidly every year.

Foreign investors with operations in these more sophisticated manufacturing and assembly operations pay their production workers two to three times—and their technical and supervisory personnel perhaps ten times—what workers in lower-skill FDI plants earn. Sometimes initially motivated by corporate social responsibility, they nonetheless find that it is in their economic self-interest to provide higher wages and benefits in order to attract and keep workers upon whose productivity they depend to keep their plants competitive. Independent survey data show that they offer better working conditions and canteen and medical facilities, provide more job-related and after-hours training, promote more consistently on the basis of merit, and have more women in supervisory positions than comparable host-country firms. This has important implications for the value of ongoing trade and investment liberalization.

How important can FDI be to the transition from poorer to middle-income countries in Africa, Asia, and Latin America? Traditional models to calculate the value of FDI to development relied upon conventional trade analytics of comparative advantage: multinational firms provide capital to put the host economy's abundant resource, low-skilled labor, to work, allowing the country to do what its natural endowment allowed more efficiently. But this conceptualization now proves to be far too static. When multinational corporations build plants that are integrated into their global competitive strategies, they bring a package of management, technology, and quality-control procedures that places the host country at the cutting edge of best practices around the globe. To enhance their own position in global markets, multinational corporations upgrade the capabilities of these plants continuously to keep them at the frontier in the international industry.

As a consequence, the globalization of industry through international investment means that comparative advantage is not fixed, immutable, or given by nature. Instead, through FDI, host countries that build up semi-skilled workforces and reasonable infrastructure can transform their own development trajectory to incorporate steadily more advanced manufacturing sectors. This revolutionizes the calculation of how important FDI in manufacturing and services can be to the process of development: the returns to trade and investment liberalization in a setting of dynamic comparative advantage are orders of magnitude greater (two to twenty times greater) than conventional static calculations.[3]

Within one generation in Costa Rica, there has been a paradigm shift from static to dynamic comparative advantage through FDI. Thirty years ago, Costa Rica's natural endowment consigned the country to a production base of coffee and bananas. Fifteen years later, with the beginnings of FDI, Costa Rica's production base had come to include garments and footwear. Today, combining more sophisticated FDI with good infrastructure and medium-skilled workers, Costa Rica's production base includes semiconductors and other electronics, medical products, industrial equipment, pharmaceuticals, call centers, and financial and management services. In 2006, multinational corporation–based exports exceeded $5 billion.

The globalization of industry through the liberalization of trade and investment, with complementary policies for education and infrastructure, provides a strong—and unusually rapid, in generational terms—path upward

Box 4.2. Foreign direct investment builds plants with middle-skilled workers in Malaysia, Mexico, and Thailand

Conventional economic theory predicted that foreign direct investment would enter countries such as Malaysia, Mexico, and Thailand to exploit their most abundant resource, which is least-skilled labor. Although some FDI has entered all three countries to produce garments, footwear, toys, and other least-skill, lowest-wage products, the principal thrust of FDI has been to turn Mexico into a powerhouse producer of autos and auto parts (exports of $42 billion in 2006), and Thailand and Malaysia into large producers of semiconductors and computers (exports of $51 billion and $83 billion, respectively, in 2006), and other electronic products.

In Mexico, the predominant impact of a growing multinational presence has been to raise the demand for semi-skilled workers, resulting in premium wage levels for those with higher levels of education or on-the-job experience. As part of this process, the returns to basic education for Mexicans—for example, completion of ninth grade—have grown. Indeed, the average skill intensity of production has risen on both sides of the border, increasing demand for trained workers in the United States as well as Mexico.

In Malaysia and Thailand international disk-drive companies such as Seagate and Read-Rite bring three or four dozen local engineers, managers, and line operators to work with product developers and manufacturing specialists in the United States two months before the introduction of each new model. Then the entire "new product transfer team," including U.S. counterparts, returns to Southeast Asia to launch the latest model. The competitive position of thousands of U.S. workers and executives, as well as Asian workers and executives, depends upon this seamless supply chain of mostly middle- and high-skilled employees.

Sources: For information on Mexico: Hanson 2004. For information on Malaysia and Thailand: McKendrick, Donner, and Haggard 2000.

for developing host countries (box 4.2). Costa Rica can now aim for the ranks of Ireland or Portugal. Costa Rica's status, meanwhile, is within range of countries such as the Dominican Republic and Mauritius. Less-developed countries such as El Salvador and Lesotho can replicate the progress that trade and FDI have brought to the Dominican Republic and Mauritius.

This provides dramatic reinforcement on how the next president should approach trade (see chapter 7 by Elliott). Indeed, while debate continues about whether trade reforms alone promote growth, the evidence shows that trade and investment liberalization raise the growth rate in developing countries that undertake the reforms simultaneously.[4] Trade and FDI together constitute "trade on steroids," in a nonpejorative use of that phrase.

But the next president's commitment to global trade liberalization must be backed with a corresponding dedication to investment liberalization. Here the past administration has been surprisingly deficient.

Not all FDI in manufacturing and assembly is good for development. Host countries that try to use FDI for import substitution find themselves with subscale plants and inefficient production techniques that hinder their infant industries from growing to competitive maturity. Manufacturing FDI that takes place in protected developing-country markets actually subtracts from host-country welfare, and retards or prevents host-country development.

The imposition of performance requirements upon foreign firms—such as mandatory domestic content and joint venture regulations—has a particularly negative effect. Developing countries that require multinational investors to take on a local partner or produce a given amount of output using local sources prevent international companies from integrating affiliates into their global supply chains. The evidence shows—somewhat counterintuitively—that developing countries achieve more value added and receive newer technology when they do not impose such requirements.

From this perspective, it is startling to discover that the United States and other developed countries acquiesced in a process of weakening the Trade-Related Investment Measures Agreement in the World Trade Organization Ministerial in Hong Kong in 2005, permitting developing countries to impose performance requirements upon multinational investors until 2020. This represents a dramatic step backward in helping developed countries to harness FDI to the task of development, because the evidence on the impact of domestic content mandates is consistently negative. There are indeed some areas under the World Trade Organization umbrella where developing countries would benefit from more "policy space" than is currently permitted (the Agreement on Trade-Related Intellectual Property Rights may be one example), but the ability to impose domestic content requirements on foreign investors is not among them.

It is equally alarming to find that OPIC provides political risk insurance to FDI projects that rely upon trade protection to be successful, agreeing to compensate them if the host liberalizes its domestic market. One U.S. investor with OPIC insurance recently objected when the host government lowered trade barriers and opened its market to competition despite assurances given to the investor that its position would be protected, and presented a claim for host-country breach of contract to OPIC. OPIC paid the claim.

As part of the administration's development agenda, the next president should redouble efforts to advance trade liberalization around the world, reaffirm the Trade-Related Investment Measures Agreement within the World Trade Organization, and instruct OPIC to refuse coverage to investors who want U.S. taxpayers to pay if hosts break their promise to keep them protected.

But the dynamic contribution that the globalization of industry brings to developing countries generates anxiety among rich nations—not least the United States—that outward investment may undermine the strength and vitality of the home economy. Is such anxiety justified?

Outward foreign direct investment and its impact on U.S. home country firms, workers, and communities

The ability of investment to create dynamic supply chains across developed–developing country borders provides a powerful force for development in poorer countries, but does this process pose a threat to the U.S. economy, where the investment originates? Popular opinion throughout developed countries tends to view outward investment as a zero-sum phenomenon, in which multinational firms either invest at home or invest abroad; either build plants at home or build plants abroad; either export from the home country or substitute for exports by moving plants overseas.

But the data repeatedly show that U.S. firms that invest abroad are more competitive at home—they export more from the home base—than similar U.S. firms that do not invest abroad.[5] Outward investment establishes their presence internationally, allowing them to penetrate wider markets from the United States. The stay-at-home U.S. firms do less well, and their workers and communities suffer in comparison.

U.S. firms that invest abroad also invest more at home—again, in comparison with similar kinds of U.S. firms that do not build plants and other facilities overseas.[6] Thus, deployment of capital is not an either-or process; U.S. firms that raise more capital to use abroad also raise more capital for use at home.

Finally, U.S. firms that engage in outward investment are more likely to use cutting-edge technologies, management, and quality-control techniques at home than are firms that do not.[7] As a consequence, they suffer fewer bankruptcies, have more productive workers, and pay them higher wages and benefits.[8]

In short, outward investment strengthens the firms, workers, and communities associated with that investment. If outward FDI were hindered, or prevented, home-country firms, workers, and communities would be worse, not better, off. To be sure, not every industry in which outward investment takes place is expanding on a net basis. Some are growing, some contracting, some simply changing the composition of activities that are present in

Box 4.3. Adjusting to globalization in North Carolina

Between 2002 and 2006, North Carolina lost 72,000 manufacturing jobs, of which three-fourths were in textiles, furniture construction, and electronics. At the same time, however, the state upgraded its economic activities in new manufacturing sectors such as biotechnology, pharmaceuticals, and—surprise!—textiles.

To prepare for the challenges of globalization, North Carolina worked with newly arriving businesses to design courses in the community college network that would meet their worker needs. Not all of the workers laid off can be, or have been, retrained. But a state recruitment director identifies Regina Whitaker as a model of those that have. Ten years ago, fresh from high school, she took a job at the same yarn texturing plant where her mother had worked for three decades. As the company opened plants in Brazil and China, it laid off workers in the Piedmont region.

In 2003, Whitaker enrolled in biotechnology classes at Forsyth Technical Community College and was hired as a lab technician at Targacept, a biotech firm in Winston-Salem, when she graduated eighteen months later. She reports that her salary today is "significantly more" than the $13.40 an hour she received at the yarn factory.

The number of workers in biosciences has grown from 20,000 to 47,000 in ten years, with entry-level salaries ranging from $27,000 to $35,000 a year. But alongside biomanufacturing companies, there has been an upgrading of some textile plants as well. Losing in the struggle to produce nylon pantyhose, the Glen Raven Company shifted to producing the high-grade industrial yarn used in upholstery. This more capital-intensive plant downsized from 225 workers to 156, paying $10.50 to $22 per hour. The company's exports to China saw a fivefold expansion between 2003 and 2006, to $52 million. Although Glen Raven has not yet invested abroad (other high-end textile firms have), the company's story illustrates the more general finding that even in declining industries, there may be international opportunities that provide benefits to firms, workers, and communities.

Sources: For the number of job losses and the upgrading of economic activities in North Carolina: Keltzer, Levinsohn, and Richardson 2007. For Regina Whitaker's story: Goodman 2007.

the home economy (box 4.3). But in all these situations, those firms that are "globally engaged"—through imports, exports, and FDI—show better performance at home than do counterpart firms that do not engage in outward investment.

Overall, the spread of multinational manufacturing investment around the world has raised the demand for skilled workers wherever the investment is located. This increases the premium earned by those with education and training, and justifies policies to provide greater access to education and training in both developed and developing countries.

Conclusions and implications for the next administration

This evidence from a review of the relationship between FDI and development is a far cry from the simplistic Washington Consensus view that all foreign investment flows are good, and the larger the better. FDI in natural resources can promote broad-based economic and social development, or it can be a source of corruption and chaos. FDI in manufacturing and assembly can provide the dynamic underpinning for increasingly sophisticated industrial activities, complete with positive spillovers and backward linkages into the host economy, or become a protected location for inefficient plants and noncompetitive operations. The next president must ensure that U.S. policies—and U.S. support for multilateral policies—promote the positive outcomes, and stifle or prevent negative results.

The agenda for foreign direct investment in extractive industries and infrastructure

In natural resource investments and infrastructure, the next president must lead the reform of developed-country legislation to combat corrupt payments, beginning with the Foreign Corrupt Practices Act and the OECD Anti-Bribery Convention (see chapter 5 by de Tray and Moran). This must be backed with endorsement of the evolution of international arbitration to refuse to enforce contracts obtained by corrupt means, including contracts of Chinese, Russian, and other non-OECD investors. To enhance transparency, the new administration should expand the Extractive Industries Transparency Initiative to include other industries, establish credible timetables for compliance, and fund the capacity building of monitors.

Accomplishing this agenda will take time and effort. But beginning on day one, the next president should instruct OPIC and the U.S. Export-Import (Ex-Im) Bank to stop providing capital, insurance, or guarantees to projects that do not pass the "smell test" of anticorrupt propriety.

The agenda for foreign direct investment in manufacturing and assembly
As multinational corporations expand their supplier networks around the world, it is heartening to discover that the positive contributions FDI can offer to developing countries do not come at the expense of economic well-being in the home countries where the investors are headquartered. Instead, there is a win-win dynamic that benefits workers as well as companies in both developed and developing countries. Multinational corporations that engage in outward investment in the developing world export more goods and services, offer more "good jobs" with higher wages and benefits, suffer fewer bankruptcies, and hence provide more stability for the communities where they are headquartered than counterpart firms that stay at home.

The next president need not therefore be hesitant or defensive about the globalization of industry under reasonably competitive conditions. Quite the contrary, a more vigorous and proactive approach to integrating global supply networks will serve the interests of American firms, workers, and communities. The liberalization of trade and investment, undertaken simultaneously, would bring a particularly potent dynamic to the development relationship between developed and developing countries.

However, before providing official support for outward investment, such as offering government-sponsored political risk insurance, the next president will have a legitimate interest in assessing the impact of any particular investment project on the home economy. The appropriate test for support should be what would transpire at home if the investment did not go forward. In the great majority of cases, the rigorous answer is that economic activity would be less dynamic, job composition less favorable, and the competitive position of the home economy weaker. But the U.S. agency that provides guarantees and insurance for U.S. investors abroad, OPIC, does not currently perform any appraisal along these lines. Instead, OPIC refuses to support all outward investment projects if there will be any single job lost even if net job creation within the United States falls clearly in the plus-column. The next president needs to instruct OPIC to replace its current "U.S. effects" calculation with a commonsense application of the test of whether the home economy will be better off.

The new administration also needs to play a much more proactive role in promoting those investment projects that most benefit developing-country economies. Today, U.S. government agencies (such as OPIC, as indicated earlier) are prevented from providing support to many of the most promising projects. High on the next president's development agenda should be to rededicate OPIC to its original mission, which was to promote development! The potential of the Millennium Challenge Corporation, meanwhile, should be directed toward overcoming bottlenecks to investment in countries undergoing rapid reform, and helping authorities design and fulfill compacts that facilitate both local and multinational private sector activity. Similarly, the Foreign Commercial Service, working with the Ex-Im Bank, the Department of Commerce, and the Small Business Administration, has much underutilized (indeed, unutilized) potential to help facilitate FDI in developing countries.

The Foreign Commercial Service does help U.S. firms identify export opportunities, and the U.S. Foreign Service assists U.S. firms on bidding on some developing-country contracts, but neither has been trained to identify potential foreign investment projects. This is a major missed opportunity, since the typical sequence is for an international company first to export to a target market, and then consider investing in a distribution or assembly facility.

What is needed is not some new bureaucracy, but rather simply to introduce investor support services into the already functioning export-assistance infrastructure. The Foreign Commercial Service provides export counseling services to U.S. firms through a network of offices in forty-seven states and has officers in the U.S. embassies of eighty-four countries. The Ex-Im Bank is represented in six of these domestic centers in the United States. Department of Commerce specialists located domestically and overseas offer "Gold Key" custom-tailored service for U.S. exporters planning to visit a country, a service that includes briefings, industry reports, interpreters, and introductions to potential partners. Many states and municipalities have special export support offices. There are nineteen U.S. Export Assistance Centers, dedicated to providing export promotion services that combine the Department of Commerce, the Ex-Im Bank, the Small Business Administration, and other export-related federal and state agencies.[9]

By providing FDI training to these export promotion officers and helping to build a one-stop shop for exporting and investing, the United States can mobilize those already involved in export promotion to search out those U.S. companies that are ready to undertake FDI to complement their penetration of external markets. Upgrading the U.S. Foreign Commercial Service should be an essential component of the next president's developmental to-do list.

The lesson that not all FDI in manufacturing and assembly is "good" for development—that FDI in protected markets and burdened with performance requirements subtracts from host welfare and hinders host growth—has important implications for the next president's approach to trade and investment liberalization. It is important not only to push forward on global trade negotiations, but also to reaffirm multilateral commitment to the

Trade-Related Investment Measures Agreement within the World Trade Organization (see chapter 7 by Elliott).

Given the harmful effect that FDI in protected markets can have on host-country welfare, it is a scandal to discover that eighteen out of nineteen OECD countries with official political risk guarantee agencies—plus their multilateral counterparts such as the International Finance Corporation and the Multilateral Investment Guarantee Agency of the World Bank Group—offer political risk insurance to foreign investment projects that depend on trade restrictions to survive, often providing coverage against the loss of protection.[10] The political risk insurance agencies of Canada, France, Germany, Italy, Japan, and the United Kingdom—and, not least, the United States—ask only whether applicant investors are likely to earn a profit, not whether applicant investors are structured to make a net positive contribution to the host country's welfare. Because boutique plants, offering highly specialized services or products, are often highly profitable in protected markets, they are allowed to qualify for official political risk insurance coverage. In the case of the United States, the next president should see that this practice ceases: Instead of merely calculating whether a given project will make money for the investor, OPIC should make itself into a model for other developed-country and multilateral guarantee agencies by favoring projects that can stand up to international competition and by refusing to protect projects that cannot.

For all the positive benefits that FDI can bring when it takes place under reasonably competitive conditions, the globalization of trade and investment creates losers as well as winners in both developed and developing countries. The challenge of the coming decades, therefore, is to strengthen training, retraining, and adjustment mechanisms to cushion the burdens of globalization in rich and poor countries alike. Trying to retard or prevent change—when the direction is positive—is both fruitless and counterproductive. The common interest of citizens in both developed and developing countries is served by helping them take advantage of globalization, not by locking companies and their employees in inefficient and uncompetitive economic activities.

Notes

1. U.S. Senate 2004. See also the Approved Judgement of the Honourable Mr. Justice Cooke between Kensington International and the Republic of Congo in the High Court of Justice, Queens Bench Division, Commercial Court, Royal Court of Justice, Strand, London. November 28, 2005.
2. UNCTAD 2006. These are the most recent multinational enterprise investment statistics by industry sector.

3. Paul Romer 1992 and 1994; Grossman and Helpman 1991; Aghion and Howitt 1998; and Markusen 2005.
4. Melitz 2005.
5. Lipsey and Weiss 1981; Blomstrom, Lipsey, and Kulchyck 1988; Lipsey, Ramstetter, and Blomstrom 2000; and Markusen and Maskus 2003.
6. Desai, Foley, and Hines 2005.
7. Bernard, Jensen, and Schott 2005.
8. Richardson 2005.
9. U.S. Export Assistance Centers are located in Atlanta, Baltimore, Boston, Charlotte, Chicago, Cleveland, Dallas, Denver, Detroit, Long Beach, Miami, Minneapolis, New Orleans, New York, Philadelphia, Portland, San Jose, St. Louis, and Seattle.
10. CGD 2007.

References

Acemoglu, Daron, Simon Johnson, and James A. Robinson. 2003. "An African Success Story: Botswana." In Dani Rodrik, ed., *In Search of Prosperity: Analytic Narratives on Economic Growth*. Princeton, N.J.: Princeton University Press.

Aghion, Philippe, and Peter Howitt. 1998. *Endogenous Growth Theory*. Cambridge, Mass.: MIT Press.

Approved Judgement of the Honourable Mr. Justice Cooke between Kensington International and the Republic of Congo in the High Court of Justice, Queens Bench Division, Commercial Court, Royal Court of Justice, Strand, London. November 28, 2005.

Bernard, Andrew B., J. Bradford Jensen, and Peter K. Schott. 2005. "Importers, Exporters and Multinationals: A Portrait of Firms in the U.S. that Trade Goods." Working Paper 11404. National Bureau of Economic Research, Cambridge, Mass.

Blomstrom, Magnus, Robert E. Lipsey, and K. Kulchyck. 1988. "US and Swedish Direct Investment and Exports." In Robert E. Baldwin, ed., *Trade Policy Issues and Empirical Analysis*, 259–97. Chicago, Ill.: University of Chicago Press.

CGD (Center for Global Development). 2007. "Commitment to Development Index." Washington, D.C.

Criscuolo, Alberto. 2007. "Driving Growth: How did Botswana, Mauritius, Cape Verde, and Taiwan overcome institutional capacity constraints?" Draft. Foreign Investment Advisory Service, Washington, D.C.

Desai, Mihir A., C. Fritz Foley, and James R. Hines, Jr. 2005. "Foreign Direct Investment and the Domestic Capital Stock." *American Economic Review* 95 (2): 33–38.

EIU (Economist Intelligence Unit). 2007a. *Country Report: Botswana*. London.

———. 2007b. *Country Report: Chile*. London.

Good, Kenneth. 1992. "Interpreting the Exceptionality of Botswana." *Journal of Modern African Studies* 30: 69–95.

Goodman, Peter S. 2007. "In N.C., A Second Industrial Revolution." *Washington Post*, September 3.

Grossman, Gene M., and Elhanan Helpman. 1991. *Innovation and Growth in the Global Economy*. Cambridge, Mass.: MIT Press.

Hanson, Gordon H. 2004. "What Has Happened to Wages in Mexico since NAFTA?" In Toni Estevadeordal, Dani Rodrick, Alan Taylor, and Andres Welasco, eds., *FTAA and Beyond: Prospects for Integration in the Americas*. Cambridge, Mass.: Harvard University Press.

ICMM (International Council on Mining & Metals). 2007. *The Challenge of Mineral Wealth: Using Resource Endowments to Foster Sustainable Development. Chile: Country Case Study*. London.

Kletzer, Lori G., James Levinsohn, and David Richardson. 2007. *Responses to Globalization: U.S. Textile and Apparel Workers*. Washington, D.C.: Peterson Institute for International Economics.

Lipsey, Robert E., and Herle Yahr Weiss. 1981. "Foreign Production and Exports in Manufacturing Industries." *Review of Economics and Statistics* 63 (4): 448–94.

Lipsey, Robert E., Eric D. Ramstetter, and Magnus Blomstrom. 2000. "Outward FDI and Parent Exports and Employment: Japan, the United States, and Sweden." Working Paper 7623. National Bureau of Economic Research, Cambridge, Mass.

Markusen, James R. 2005. "Modeling the Offshoring of White-Collar Services: From Comparative Advantage to the New Theories of Trade and FDI." Working Paper 11827. National Bureau of Economic Research, Cambridge, Mass.

Markusen, James R., and Keith E. Maskus. 2003. "General-Equilibrium Approaches to the Multinational Enterprise: A Review of Theory and Evidence." In E. Kwan Choi and James Harrigan, eds., *Handbook of International Trade*. London: Blackwell.

McKendrick, David G., Richard F. Donner, and Stephan Haggard. 2000. *From Silicon Valley to Singapore: Location and Competitive Advantage in the Hard Disk Drive Industry*. Stanford, Calif.: Stanford University Press.

Melitz, Marc J. 2005. "Comment." In Theodore H. Moran, Edward M. Graham, and Magnus Blomstrom, eds., *Does Foreign Direct Investment Promote Development?* Washington, D.C.: Center for Global Development.

Richardson, J. David. 2005. *Global Forces, American Faces: U.S. Economic Globalization at the Grass Roots*. Washington, D.C.: Institute for International Economics.

Romer, Paul. 1992. "Two Strategies for Economic Development: Using Ideas and Producing Ideas." In World Bank, *Proceedings of the World Bank Annual Conference on Development Economics*. Washington, D.C.

———. 1994. "New Goods, Old Theory, and the Welfare Costs of Trade Restrictions." *Journal of Development Economics* 43 (1): 5–38.

UNCTAD (United Nations Conference on Trade and Development). 2006. *World Investment Report 2006*. Annex tables A.1.2 and A.1.4. Geneva.

U.S. Senate. 2004. *Money Laundering and Foreign Corruption: Enforcement and Effectiveness of the Patriot Act: Case Study Involving Riggs Bank*. Report prepared by the Minority Staff of the Permanent Subcommittee on Investigations. Washington, D.C.

5 Getting the Focus Right: U.S. Leadership in the Fight against Global Corruption

Dennis de Tray and Theodore Moran

Corruption is bad for development, bad for poverty reduction, bad for business, and bad for the United States. Democrats and Republicans alike know this, and both sides of the aisle have taken up the cause. The United States was the first to pass a serious international anticorruption law, the 1976 Foreign Corrupt Practices Act (FCPA), while other countries were still letting their corporations deduct bribes as a business expense. The United States has been an active participant in the key conventions, symposiums, and international bodies on corruption, including the United Nations Convention against Corruption and the Financial Action Task Force. On aid delivery, good governance is a key criterion for access to grants from the Millennium Challenge Corporation (MCC), and the U.S. Senate Foreign Relations Committee, under Senator Richard Lugar's leadership, has pushed the multilateral development banks to reduce corruption and fraud in their operations.

These efforts notwithstanding, most observers agree that results have been less than hoped for. If the next administration is to strengthen U.S. leadership in the fight against global corruption and its drag on development, it must have a clear and unequivocal moral authority to lead this fight, have an evidence-based program that offers practical solutions rather than mere moral platitudes, and generate a

Dennis de Tray is the vice president for special initiatives and Theodore Moran is a nonresident fellow at the Center for Global Development.

dialogue that brings all the key players to the table through a multilateral process.

The starting point for any anticorruption strategy must be an understanding that those who engage in fighting corruption internationally live in glass houses. The United States can lead the fight against corruption only if the rest of the world sees us as holding our own firms, citizens, and politicians to high standards of conduct. Put simply, the rest of the world is unlikely to heed U.S, calls for good governance if it sees corruption in U.S. contract aid to countries such as Afghanistan, Iraq, and Pakistan, "legalized" corruption in the form of lobbying for bridges to nowhere and agricultural subsidies to a few rich farmers, or publicly funded contracts that never see the light of competition. In the fight against international corruption, the United States must lead by example.

Second, to offer practical, evidence-based solutions when dealing with corruption in developing countries, U.S. policy and approaches must rest on three lessons of history: good governance and the fight against corruption must be homegrown and cannot be forced by outsiders; the institutions needed to control corruption take considerable time to build; and development assistance is about improving lives, and corruption is but one of many constraints developing countries face. Clean governments, strong laws, good courts, and transparent processes are essential in the fight against corruption, but getting to these "best-practice" solutions must be seen as a long-term goal.

Finally, the United States, as powerful as it is, cannot go it alone if it is to be effective in the battle against international corruption. We must not only rebuild alliances with our traditional rich-country allies, but also bring to the table the rapidly growing developing countries that are transforming from being aid recipients to aid donors, and absorbers of foreign direct investment to providers of it. How one sees today's world depends on the lens through which one looks. China and India either rank 102nd and 146th respectively, in terms of per capita income, or are the world's second and third largest economies after the United States, in terms of purchasing power parity. The old order, based on the first way of ranking countries, no longer makes sense.

Assuming these prerequisites are in place, the next administration should focus on practical ways of reducing the impact of corruption in three areas of U.S. national interest:

1. Reducing corruption's drag on the capacity of international and national private sector development to create jobs, reduce poverty, and give all citizens a stake in their country's future.
2. Increasing the "value for money" from U.S. foreign assistance through a focus on transparency and outcomes.
3. Leading the effort to dampen the corrosive effects of global "bads" such as terrorism, illegal drugs, and global crime on developing countries.

In the following sections, we give our arguments for these priorities and for our specific recommendations. The discussion is summarized in the final section, which sets out a ten-step program to reestablish U.S. leadership in the fight against corruption.

Corruption and private sector development

Reducing poverty is the stated goal of most development assistance. Not long ago, this was taken to mean that growth in itself was somehow secondary, but there is now agreement in the development community that developing countries must grow or remain forever on the international welfare dole. The kind of growth needed to reduce poverty is growth that fosters private investment, allowing firms to flourish and expand, and workers to find productive jobs. In short, poverty-reducing growth requires a vibrant private sector.

The United States has been a consistent leader in putting the private sector firmly on the global development agenda. The next administration has the opportunity to strengthen U.S. effectiveness in promoting this priority. Finding effective ways to deal with the corruption that undermines and slows private sector development internationally and nationally is crucial to this effort. As we argue below, in some important areas, we know what needs to be done, but getting there will take the kind of strong global leadership only the United States can provide.

Although they overlap considerably, countries have not one but two private sectors: domestic and international. Much literature on private sector development has focused on the importance of foreign direct investment, especially in creating the exports that have led to middle-income status for some of the best known development success stories, such as China and much of East Asia. This focus on foreign direct investment is not misplaced for many developing countries (see chapter 4 by Moran). Foreign corporations bring capital and know-how that allow them to build plants and, often more important, to create chains of local firms as suppliers to those plants. Foreign and domestic companies both benefit. The next section considers ways of holding international corruption in check so that foreign direct investment can have the greatest development impact.

Getting the most out of global capital: closing loopholes in the Foreign Corrupt Practices Act

Corruption in international business transactions harms developing countries in many ways. By bypassing or undermining competitive bidding, it raises costs and lowers quality by awarding contracts to less efficient companies. Higher costs make already-struggling economies less competitive, and services to the poor more costly and less reliable. Corruption also enables firms to avoid the penalties that would otherwise be imposed if they abuse workers, damage the environment, or ignore regulatory requirements.

Corrupt payments have been so common in international business transactions that through 1995 many developed countries routinely allowed them to be deducted as a standard expense of doing business. In 1996, under pressure from the United States, and following U.S. leadership in the form of the 1976 FCPA, the Organisation for Economic Co-operation and Development (OECD) approved Tax Recommendations on the Non-Deductibility of Bribe Payments. This was followed in 1999 by the OECD-wide Anti-Bribery Convention, officially known as the Convention on Combating Bribery of Foreign Public Officials in International Business Transactions.

Are these efforts paying off? In the United States, the 2006 caseload of the head of the justice department's criminal division doubled in 2007. In some other countries—as illustrated by Germany's investigation of Siemens—concern about bribery by home-country firms is also on the increase. But recent research, some sponsored by the Center for Global Development, offers evidence from Africa, Asia, and Latin America showing that the OECD convention and the FCPA may be written too narrowly. The problem is that U.S., European, and Japanese multinationals have found a loophole, in both the OECD convention and the FCPA, that allows them to win contracts and obtain favorable treatment without fear of prosecution. Detailed investigation of international investment contracts shows U.S., European, and Japanese companies using sophisticated current-payoff-and-deferred-gift structures to relatives and friends of host-country officials that do not technically put them at risk of OECD-consistent home-country antibribery laws, or the FCPA.

The basic arrangement has been for the multinational to approach a prominent family member or close friend (a "connected party") of the host-country leadership about forming a partnership to develop the target investment project (or respond favorably when approached by a connected party about forming a partnership), loan that connected party the funds needed to take an equity stake in the project, and pay a dividend that is more than what was needed to service the original loan. This arrangement functions as a deferred gift—the loan to fund the equity stake of the connected party gets paid off via the dividend over time. The excess return above what is needed to service the loan is a current payoff.

Unlike a genuine equity investor, the connected party had no capital at risk, nor any responsibility to repay the loan. The equity stake came to this person for free; the only "service" that was required was to ensure that the foreign company was chosen to receive the infrastructure concession. In some cases, the connected party began to receive "dividends" as soon as the concession was awarded, before the project was even in operation. An added benefit to the international firm from these arrangements is that, because the return to cover the loan payments and the current payoff depend upon the project remaining profitable, the connected party has an ongoing interest in protecting the project from competition.

Particularly startling has been the discovery that some of these sophisticated payment mechanisms—as deployed by U.S. investors to obtain infrastructure concessions in the case of Indonesia—had been vetted by well-respected U.S. law and accounting firms as part of the investors' due diligence prior to committing funds, and reported to the U.S. Securities and Exchange Commission, without objection.

Ironically, the development impact of these arrangements is often more damaging than if the family members and associates had simply been given straight "commissions" upfront. Because their "take" depends on their returns as equity-holders, they will want projects in which they "invest" to generate the highest profits possible. These well-connected individuals will therefore work to ensure that their projects are protected against competition or regulation. This allows them to charge uncompetitively high prices over the often lengthy life of the concessions—high prices that end up being passed on to often poor households and businesses. Examples of projects that appear to have been handled in this manner include roads, ports, and power plants (box 5.1).

Why were these payoffs to family members, business associates, and cronies of developing-country ministers and presidents not illegal under home-country legislation consistent with the OECD convention or, in particular, with the FCPA?

The reason is that the scope of the OECD convention is extremely limited, requiring member states to pass domestic legislation that only criminalizes a straight payment to a public official by an international company to secure a contract. To contravene the convention, any pecuniary or other advantage must go to the foreign official; there is no mention of business associates, employees, business partners, or relatives. With regard to the FCPA, too, the Department of Justice is precise about the limited extent of the statute in its guide to the FCPA: "Recipient—The prohibition extends only to corrupt payments to a foreign official, a foreign political party or party official, or any candidate for foreign political office."[1] The word "only" seems to instruct parties that arrangements that do not involve direct payments to officials are not illegal.

What does the next president of the United States need to do? A 2007 Transparency International report notes that the United States leads the world

Box 5.1. Outbid by bribery, say firms

More than 40 percent of businesses in some of the world's leading economies believe they have lost a deal in the past five years because a competitor used bribery.

According to a recent survey commissioned by the U.K.-based political risk and security advisory firm Control Risks and international law firm Simmons and Simmons, businesses in these countries also see themselves as largely powerless to deal with bribery by their competitors. The most widely used means to hide bribes and circumvent the law was by using intermediaries, a number of those surveyed said. The survey also found that about a third of the executives surveyed believed that the use of bribery to obtain contracts was likely to rise over the next decade. The survey, "International Business Attitudes to Corruption," involved interviews with 350 firms based in Brazil, France, Germany, Hong Kong, the Netherlands, the United Kingdom, and the United States on the pervasiveness of corruption to obtain deals abroad.

Transparency International has conducted a survey of the propensity of companies in thirty leading exporting countries to bribe to obtain business abroad. Based on a survey of more than 11,000 business executives in 125 countries, it found that companies from China, India, Malaysia, Russia, South Africa, Taiwan, and Turkey were the most likely to bribe.

One of the most startling findings of the Control Risks/Simmons and Simmons report is that despite the governments of the OECD—often called "the rich-man's club"—having introduced antibribery legislation, many of those who were interviewed were unaware of the law.

The Control Risk/Simmons and Simmons survey finds that many businesses are wary of reporting bribery to governments in the countries where the governments are themselves corrupt.

Others say they would make informal queries to find out what happened and seek the help of their embassies. Most said they would avoid working again with the same customer if they heard a bribe had won business.

Source: Katzenellenbogen 2006.

in the number of investigations enforcing the OECD convention, with about 67 investigations out of a worldwide total of 128. The report also notes, "There have been some signs that the U.S. government has increased the number of staff assigned to this area. Nonetheless, the continued increase in cases and voluntary disclosures continues to strain Securities and Exchange Commission and Department of Justice resources."[2] There has been increased press coverage of U.S. enforcement of the FCPA, and the *Financial Times* has complained jokingly that "bribery is too much like hard work" these days.[3] The increased enforcement of the FCPA, although a good step, still does not protect against the type of arrangements we described above. The next U.S. president needs to make sure that, when the Securities and Exchange Commission and the Department of Justice enforce U.S. anticorruption legislation, they are enforcing something with teeth. We offer three steps that would strengthen U.S. efforts to reduce corrupt payments in international investment.

1. *Broaden the definition of corrupt payments.* The first step that the next president must take is to get the U.S. house in order, but in a way that does not put U.S. firms at a disadvantage relative to investors from less-scrupulous home countries. This means that the United States must not only enlarge the definition of "corrupt payments" in the FCPA to include family members, business partners, and cronies, but it must also push the OECD to broaden the Anti-Bribery Convention accordingly.

   A good starting point would be for both the FCPA and the OECD convention to adopt the language of the OECD Guidelines for Multinational Enterprises, which have already been accepted and approved by all OECD members. The guidelines state:

   > Enterprises should not, directly or indirectly, offer, promise, give, or demand a bribe or other undue advantage to obtain or retain business or other improper advantage. Nor should enterprises be solicited or expected to render a bribe of other undue advantage. In particular, enterprises should not offer, nor give in to demands to pay public officials or the employees of business partners any portion of a contract payment. They should not use subcontracts, purchase orders, or consulting agreements as a means of channeling payments to public officials, to employees of business partners, or their relatives or business associates.[4]

   The goal is to make it clear that payments to family members and personal associates will be treated—under certain conditions—as if they were payments to the official.

   What "certain conditions" would make such behavior impermissible? It is probably impossible—and inadvisable—to criminalize altogether any arrangement that involves a family member or personal associate. Family members and friends of leaders may have legitimate business or consulting roles to play in the economic life of the host country. Tests for impermissible behavior should therefore focus on whether there is a conflict of interest and whether a gift is being given. The tests might include, but would not necessarily depend upon, whether any favor or influence was sought or given in return. Investors would be required to disclose partnership and other ownership arrangements; the burden of proof would then fall on the investors to show value received, or promised, for any and all payments made.

The test for conflict of interest is whether there is the possibility of self-dealing, in which public and private interests or roles collide. The test of whether a gift is being bestowed could include the following: Is a genuine service rendered for any payment made, and is there a discernible proportionality (read "competitive price") between the value being given and the considerations being given in return? If the payment is made in the form of an equity partnership, does the recipient have to put any assets at risk?

Forbidden behavior would not have to be limited to whether there was a clear quid pro quo showing that the payment or the "gift" affected the awarding of the investment concession, or the structure of the terms. The creation of circumstances in which there was a conflict of interest, or gifts could be given to connected parties, could also be a standalone prohibition.

Tightening the wording of the FCPA and the OECD convention will help wring corruption out of transactions by firms that must abide by U.S. laws or OECD agreements, but what about the rest of the world? Until emerging market economies adopt similar laws, the United States needs to push efforts to reform international arbitration.

2. *Reform international arbitration procedures.* Broadening the definition of corruption in the FCPA and the OECD convention are the first necessary steps, but it is important not to leave U.S. and other OECD firms at a competitive disadvantage with respect to competitors from China, India, Russia, and elsewhere. Here, an evolution in investor-state arbitration procedures can constitute a powerful second tool for combating corrupt payments.

   Recent research has identified a trend in investor-state arbitrations in which investors find tribunals unwilling to enforce their contracts when those contracts have been achieved through corrupt means. Investor-state dispute settlement cases show a growing international acceptance of the principle—already widespread in domestic law—of rejecting the validity of any contract or permit obtained by corrupt means. While no U.S. president can dictate what independent arbitral tribunals do, the next administration should endorse the principle that where there is some reasonable basis for believing there could be corruption, whether raised directly by a party to the arbitration or by a third party (*amicus curiae*, for example), a tribunal should exercise its responsibility to investigate, and be prepared to deny the investor rights of contract enforcement if corruption is found.

There are limits to international arbitration. One major issue is that, in contrast to courts, arbitral decisions are not subject to *stare decisis*, the doctrine of following precedent and respecting past decisions. Although arbitrators do consider prior opinions—and there appears to be a growing acceptance, as noted above, that corrupt procurement of contracts is contrary to widely accepted norms of international public policy—there is no process for setting and following precedent because there is no appeals process to resolve conflicting decisions by tribunals. In addition, arbitral panels are not well equipped to pursue criminal investigations, which may make panels reluctant to take on issues of corruption.

Even with these problems, formal endorsement by the next administration of arbitrators' rights and responsibilities to deny investors recourse where corruption is evident could have a large impact in creating a level playing field among international investors from countries outside direct U.S. control and influence (China and Russia, two countries not known for tight enforcement of anticorruption regulations, come to mind). All investors, regardless of origin, will be forced to think twice about using bribes to obtain concessions if they understand that their rights will not subsequently be respected if, at any point in the long life of their projects, they find themselves engaged in investor-state arbitrations. In short, corruption at the beginning of operations could lead them to lose all the capital they invest over the life of their projects.

3. *Enhance transparency in payments made by international companies.* The third step in creating a genuinely effective international regime to combat corruption in international investment turns again to the weapon of transparency, but this time for relationships and payments associated with international investment concessions. The risk of exposure—with damage to reputation, loss of assets, and possible prosecution—can act as a great inhibitor on both sides of any corrupt relationship.

One of the most important contemporary efforts to promote the transparency of investor payments is the Extractive Industries Transparency Initiative (EITI), developed and promoted initially by the U.K. government. This initiative grew from the recognition that regular reporting by corporations of payments made to foreign governments—beginning with oil, gas, and mineral extraction—would aid efforts to end corruption, make producing countries and their energy or other resource supplies more stable, and enable citizens of these countries to hold their leaders to account for the misuse of their abundant natural resource wealth.

Five years after its launch, EITI has twenty-six out of fifty-three resource-rich countries as signatories, and it is supported by donor governments, including the United States, major extractive industry companies, civil society, and the international financial institutions. The challenge now is to make the EITI work. To do this is going to take a coordinated effort on the part of rich countries, poor countries, and the international community.

To this end, the next administration should work to expand the number of countries that endorse the EITI, and to ensure that developing countries that are currently endorsing the EITI establish concrete plans and specific timetables for implementation.

The EITI organization, at the same time, needs to put in place a system for validating the performance of participating countries against EITI criteria and their own agreed work plans (without this, the EITI currency is at risk of rapid depreciation). This requires as a start the establishment of criteria for credible independent auditors who can certify which countries qualify and to what degree.

The new president should enlist counterpart leaders from other developed countries in a campaign to give the major multilateral organizations, especially the World Bank, the wherewithal to support the EITI. For EITI to work, developing countries and civil society organizations will need technical and financial assistance to develop the necessary oversight and participation mechanisms. A part of this support needs to go to efforts to publicize and monitor payments not only at national levels, but also at subnational levels.

Unfortunately, the EITI does not currently apply to foreign direct investment outside of the extractive industries. As the EITI is strengthened, the United States should lead the charge in considering other areas in which an EITI-type process and arrangement might help shed the cleansing light of transparency on developing-country economic activities.

These three steps constitute the agenda for the next president to combat corruption in international investments. As he or she moves forward on implementing this agenda, there are some actions that can be taken immediately. The next president should begin by ordering the Overseas Private Investment Corporation and the Export-Import Bank of the United States to refuse to provide capital, guarantees, or political risk coverage to projects that do not pass the "smell test" of propriety, without waiting for changes in laws or final determination of whether crimes have been committed. The new administration should instruct the two organizations to be vigilant in prescreening projects to check for even the hint of corrupt relationships. Where problems of corruption exist, these agencies should be instructed to refuse to pay claims. (One of the Indonesian cases referred to above suggests that in the recent past, just the opposite was the case—support of a claim even in the face of strong evidence of wrongdoing.) The two organizations should as well use their access to investor records to forward indications of suspect behavior to the Department of Justice for investigation.

These are moves the United States can take unilaterally, but, as we say above, in today's world, unilateral action is unlikely to be enough. The next president will have to work closely with traditional rich-country partners of the United States to ensure that U.S.-based companies don't find themselves at a disadvantage in competing for business in developing and emerging economies. And, in today's world, this outreach has to extend to Brazil, China, India, and Russia—emerging market economies that are increasingly active in international business. These countries and others have to be a part of the conversation, not as second-class citizens but as full members of the international community. The next president should, early in his or her tenure, push for membership of these countries in two now-exclusive, rich-country clubs—the OECD and the Group of 7/8.

For some developing countries, especially for the poorer and smaller states (certainly Paul Collier's fifty-eight "bottom billion" countries), export-led growth driven by foreign direct investment is just not going to happen anytime soon, and domestic economic activities are likely to be about the only private sector game in town. Below, we turn to how the United States can help to cut the "corruption tax" for domestic small and medium-size firms, and for domestic investors in these countries.

Giving local business a chance: lowering the corruption tax

Just as U.S. leadership is essential in limiting the impact of corruption in foreign direct investment, it can also reduce corruption that hinders "domestic" private sector growth. Corruption slows such growth by taxing success. It is a common story in developing countries that successful micro and small firms soon become the targets of a host of government-backed gatekeepers whose main goal is often to extract what they can from businesses in return for allowing them to continue to function. Why "government-backed"? Because much of the corrupt activity affecting local private sectors—by tax authorities, customs officials, police, and health and safety inspectors—has as its foundation the gatekeeping roles and rights that government bestows on institutions and agencies.

The best known examples of publicly-backed gatekeepers are the ubiquitous traffic police to be found on roadways throughout developing countries. These are classic gatekeepers in that their efforts to enrich themselves result in no social good. Their presence actually worsens traffic flows as the vehicles they pull over to shake down block traffic. Equally omnipresent are the gatekeepers who control trade flows. Customs officials often neither raise revenues for the state, nor protect citizens from illegal imports. They're too busy making money. Moreover, the burden of gatekeeping corruption often falls most heavily on those countries that can least afford it. According to a recent World Bank analysis:

> More worrisome is that the incidence of bribes is higher precisely in the poorest countries, where development needs are most pressing. For example, whereas 9 percent of firms in Chile believe informal gifts are required to "get things done," 87 percent of firms in Burkina Faso are of that view. Similarly, two out of every three firms in Cameroon and the Democratic Republic of Congo state that they must pay bribes when meeting with tax officials. Finally, firms in Africa report having to pay higher bribes, as a percent of sales, than their counterparts in relatively-affluent Latin America, 2.7 vs. 1.4 percent, respectively.[5]

The bad news is that developing countries are replete with gates that breed corruption and slow private sector development. The good news is that we now know a great deal about these gates, not just where they are, but which ones matter to private sector participants and how much they cost businesses. We know this from two path-breaking surveys assessing business climates around the world.

The Doing Business surveys describe the rules businesses must deal with in 178 countries, including the cost of hiring and firing workers, the amount of time taken to register a business and the cost of this registration process, the licenses that businesses are required to obtain, the process of registering property, getting access to credit, and other key variables. These data allow us to measure the burden of regulation and its impact on competitiveness, and to compare the business environments in rich and poor countries.

A second data set—the Enterprise Surveys—consists of face-to-face interviews with managers and owners of businesses, and describes firms' actual experiences in fifty-five countries (more are on the way, according to the World Bank's Web site). Enterprise Survey data show that in many countries, businesses pay a significant portion of their sales revenues in bribes and have to spend valuable managerial resources lobbying the government in order to do business. The Enterprise Surveys confirm that regulations and other costs imposed by governments create serious roadblocks for the private sector.

The United States should not, indeed, cannot, dictate local regulations and policies in other countries, but it can lead an international effort to reduce corruption-inducing gatekeeping in developing countries. Efforts to reform the business climate for local firms dovetail with the U.S. agenda toward overall trade-and-investment liberalization emphasized in other chapters of this volume.

Lest we think that gates do not matter, or that removing them does not produce results, consider the experience of Vietnam, a Communist country built on control and not always known for its support of the private sector. Although the Vietnamese government may be slow to change, the country's people historically have rivaled their Chinese neighbors to the north for industriousness and ingenuity.

In 1999, the government came to the belated conclusion that it was losing its battle to control the private sector. With the stroke of a pen, the government changed Vietnam's costly and ineffective business licensing regime to a simple business registration requirement. A process that had taken months, considerable money, or both suddenly took a few days and no money. Business registrations went from under 6,000 in 1999 to nearly 15,000 in 2000. The moral: Businesses in developing countries want to be a part of the formal sector and want to be good citizens, but in many instances they can't because of heavy-handed and unhelpful government regulations. It is worth noting that the MCC (see box 5.2 in the next section) has used the "Business Start-up Sub-Indicator," which measures the time and regulatory cost to starting a business, as part of its eligibility criteria. Many countries have responded with regulatory reforms that have removed some gates.

U.S. leadership in pushing for the removal of gates in developing countries is essential, given its lead role in promoting private sector development, but again, the United States cannot go it alone. A lone U.S. voice on these matters may well be heard as political, imperialist, and bullying—and will not be effective. If the moral suasion needed to encourage developing-country governments to get rid of corruption-generating gates is to hit home, it must have a multilateral voice as well. U.S. support for the World Bank and other multilateral institutions as they work to improve local business environments is a critical part of this agenda and very much in the interests of the United States.

Corruption and effective development assistance

U.S. taxpayers have a long history of helping those around the globe who are less fortunate than themselves. Quite reasonably, they want assurances that the aid their taxes pay for is not being siphoned off through corruption. When governments and providers are corrupt, water taps run dry; power fails; schools go without repairs, and what classrooms there are don't have textbooks; health clinics crumble, and those that stand have no medicine or dispense counterfeit drugs that kill instead of cure. Poorly-educated, sick people struggling to survive cannot participate in their country's development.

With strong U.S. backing, multilateral development banks have strengthened the "fences" that ring their projects, putting more investigators in the field, increasing supervision dollars, and cutting projects off from government systems. These efforts have helped politicians to claim that they know where every dollar of our development assistance goes (even if that is seldom true), but they have done little to further the real fight against corruption or to encourage poor countries to develop the institutions needed to deliver results. Ring-fencing development projects is a bit like putting a burglar alarm in one among many houses. That house may be protected, but the bad guys will just go to the house next door. Dealing with corruption in developing countries requires patience, perseverance, and realism. This is a fight that does not lend itself to "blunt instrument" approaches.

As we say in the opening paragraphs of this chapter, the best and lasting way to reduce corruption in developing countries is to create strong institutions that promote transparency and accountability. Laudable as this goal is, it is very close to saying that in order to control corruption, developing countries need to develop. Institution-building solutions may be the right starting point for more advanced developing countries, such as the MCC crowd, but can poorer and weaker countries afford to wait for institutional solutions to their corruption problems?

A look at the countries that have shown and are showing success in creating professional civil services, honest court systems, and a free and open press suggests that the answer may well be that neither countries nor donors can afford to wait. Chile is often cited as an example of successful judicial reform, where some of the worst excesses of corruption—such as high court and trial judges selling sentences—have been reduced dramatically. An advanced middle-income developing country, Chile began its judicial reform in 1990, with the introduction of reforms that included the creation of the Judicial Academy to control the recruitment and career path of judges. It went on to reform other aspects of the judicial process and to eliminate functions that served as channels for corruption.

All this has made Chile one of the stars in Transparency International's Corruption Perceptions Index, ranking first in Latin America, on a par with the United States and right behind France and Belgium internationally. But even in the face of considerable progress, a 2006 report states there is still "much to be done"—and this after fifteen years of effort by a highly competent civil service, coupled with strong economic growth and rising national prosperity.

Hong Kong and Singapore also have strong records on government cleanup. Even in governance-challenged Africa, there are examples of success. Botswana has made significant strides in creating the institutional base for dealing with corruption, as have Rwanda and Uganda. But for many poor countries, especially those at the bottom of the development ladder, the institution-building road to reducing corruption will be a long, hard slog.

The message from Chile's experience is that even for top performers among developing countries, tackling corruption through institutional reform is a long-term project. Chile's story serves as an inspiration to donors and developing countries that institutional solutions to corruption can work, but it also underscores the need for patience, perseverance, and realistic expectations on the part of both parties.

Helping countries fight corruption by building effective institutions is the right strategy for countries with basic acceptable starting levels of governance. These are the middle-income, emerging market economies such as Chile and, more generally, countries that qualify for MCC grants. In fact, the United States has built its MCC program on an institutional platform, requiring countries seeking MCC funds to meet a number of institution-related eligibility criteria. One of these criteria focuses on corruption and governance. Although the jury is still out on whether the MCC's selection criteria are providing the hoped-for incentives (box 5.2), the prize of substantial additional development assistance for good institutional performers is an important addition to the U.S. development toolbox.

The problem, of course, is that by design, MCC criteria leave many of the toughest development challenges out of the running, often the poorest countries with the biggest governance and corruption challenges. If it took a country as advanced as Chile fifteen years to go partway in reforming its judiciary, what time frame should we have for the low-income countries of Africa or Central Asia or Indochina? Experience says decades, if not generations. In the meantime, what can be done to control corruption in the weak and fragile states that are the focus of so much international concern these days?

Two lessons from past development assistance efforts should guide the United States in its efforts to control corruption in such countries. The first is that building the institutional base to fight corruption is a long and complex process, one best approached with caution and humility. The second, and related, lesson is that better governance and lower corruption require country ownership and cannot be imposed from outside.

We have also learned that where systems—like the civil services, courts, regulatory agencies, and financial systems—are weak or dysfunctional, just making things better on paper doesn't work. The best written laws, the best

Box 5.2. The Millennium Challenge Corporation: a good start

Announced in 2002 and formally funded a year later, the Millennium Challenge Corporation (MCC) is, in the words of *Washington Post* commentator Michael Gerson (2007), "grown up foreign aid." The MCC approaches development by seeking out countries that meet certain criteria for need, capacity, and governance. A country's efforts to control corruption, as measured by the World Bank's "Control of Corruption" index, is one of the "hard hurdles" in assessing country eligibility, meaning, meet it or you don't get in. To be eligible for MCC financing, a country has to be above the median of its income group on this indicator.

Have the incentives created by the MCC borne fruit? The short answer is, "possibly." Ten out of the thirteen countries that have threshold programs targeting corruption improved their scores from 2005 to 2006. However, as a working paper by the Center for Global Development notes, "Many programs have not been underway long enough to show results, and even for those that have, it is extraordinarily hard to attribute an improvement in governance—particularly when defined as complexly as this indicator is—to any particular donor intervention" (Herrling and Rose 2007).

Although the jury may still be out on the overall effectiveness of MCC's incentives, there have been notable results in encouraging countries to get rid of gates. One of the MCC's subindicators is the number of days it takes to start a business. There is clear evidence that countries are responding to this cut-and-dried performance measure. The lesson seems to be that countries are eager to change policies in order to meet eligibility requirements, but that these policy changes work better when they are clearly articulated and simple to understand. Based on this experience, it is possible to imagine a reworked governance eligibility indicator that focuses on transparency issues. An indicator (or even supplemental evidence for eligibility) reporting the types of information a government makes public, such as national, regional, and local budgets, would be a good start.

Source: Gerson 2007.

regulations, the best designed anticorruption commissions, and the best trained auditors and judges will have no effect in weak states, except to give cover to donor agencies and government officials when asked what they are doing about corruption.

The United States must continue its efforts to improve developing country institutions—while continuing to encourage multilateral institutions such as the World Bank's International Development Association to do the same—but it needs to do so recognizing that even under the best of conditions, this is a challenge spanning decades. What can the next U.S. president do to hold corruption in check in the meantime?

1. *Ensure that developing-country citizens have the information they need to fight corruption.* Information is the starting point in the fight to give citizens a voice in the way their country's resources are used. Although not a guarantor of success, arming citizens with credible information gives them at least the wherewithal to take up the fight against waste and corruption. What information citizens receive and how they receive it will necessarily vary for countries at different levels of development. But in all cases, the international community, led by the United States, should insist that countries in which they do development business meet a minimum standard of transparency as the price of receiving assistance.

   There will be exceptions—mostly stemming from efforts to deal with humanitarian crises —where the international community must step in to save lives and avoid bloodshed, but for most other cases, a basis of transparency should be a *sine qua non* for international assistance. And, no, this is not robbing countries of sovereignty; in fact, just the opposite. It is the essential starting point for returning sovereignty to countries' citizens.

   Does information work in reducing the level and impact of corruption? Available evidence suggests it does, and in some pretty tough environments, too. In the Kyrgyz Republic, a country that ranks 150 out of 179 countries in Transparency International's Corruption Perceptions Index, local officials are not always known for good governance. In an effort to improve local services, the World Bank launched a village infrastructure program modeled after the successful Village Improvement and Kecamatan Development Program (KDP) in Indonesia (a country with a similarly challenging corruption ranking of 143 out of 179). The Kyrgyz project had a simple rule as its governance foundation. There had to be clear evidence that villagers were fully informed of the grant—its amount and how it was used. The results were quite remarkable. With minimal institutional changes, villagers started holding their leaders accountable. In one instance, a village head was actually forced to return funds to the public kitty by the local village council, a heretofore unprecedented event.

The Kecamatan Development Program is widely cited for its success in reducing corruption in public construction while also instilling a sense of ownership and power in citizens. As the anecdote in box 5.3 shows, the power of information does not stop at a project's boundaries.

2. *Insist on results even in weak and fragile states.* More transparency will help, but not unless there is increased accountability among developing-country leaders and officials. It is the combination of transparency and local accountability that makes the Indonesian, Kyrgyz, and similar projects work in reducing corruption and increasing impact. Unfortunately, as international aid agencies have dominated developing countries' policy agendas and fiscal space, donors have taken the mantle of accountability away from developing-country leadership and governments. This has led to a long tradition of aid recipients blaming the international community when things go wrong, when in many instances recipient governments and the people they serve should be looking at their own actions. Returning accountability to its rightful owners—the developing countries themselves—is essential if improved transparency is to lead to better governance and less corruption.

    Can this role reversal work? The argument most often given against making developing countries accountable is that their institutions are too weak to take on this role. The concern is valid if "take on this role" means doing it the way rich countries do, through well-functioning civil services, good investigative agencies, and strong, independent courts. But there are other ways in which developing countries can be held accountable. They can, for instance, be made accountable for results. An insistence that developing-country governments be accountable for delivering what they agree to deliver would complement efforts to improve transparency and also contribute to the longer term goal of building effective institutions.

    A good example of both the power of transparency and the value of this approach in building institutions can be found in a World Bank urban services project for the West Bank and Gaza. Under exceedingly difficult fiscal, political, and security circumstances, local authorities were able to find ways to keep critical urban services

Box 5.3. Spillovers from the Kecamatan Development Program in Indonesia—People learn

It was a brilliantly clear morning in Central Sulawesi when the villagers first spied the large pile of lumber. One of the delivery truck drivers stood lazily by the wood, smoking a cigarette that he blew over his steaming coffee. He'd come from Palu, the provincial capital. The golden lettering embroidered on his hat told the villagers that he and the silent man in the neatly pressed green safari suit, also sipping his coffee, worked for the Public Works Department there.

The villagers were curious. Just last year they had gotten funds from the Kecamatan Development Program (KDP) to build a stone road from their rice fields to the market route, and now here were the materials to repair a bridge. Had the government finally noticed their plight?

> "Friend, what is this wood for?"
> "It's to build a bridge."
> "How much wood is there? What did it cost?"
> "That's none of your business. Just be thankful that the government will be building you a bridge."
> "But we want to know. This is our new rule here. You have to come to the *balai desa* and tell us about the project. Then you have to post a signboard so that all of us know how much this bridge costs. If KDP does it, we want you to do it too."
> "You are mistaken. KDP is KDP and it has KDP rules. This is a government project and we follow our rules. Just be thankful that you are getting a bridge."

The villagers were troubled. That night the village elders met. Some people said they should just accept the wood because the village needed the bridge. But many more villagers were angry. This was now the era of *reformasi* and people had a right to know about projects.

Early the next morning, even before the first rays of sunlight pierced the dark clouds, the villagers had heaved the wood back onto a large truck owned by the son of the village council head. Two truckloads of villagers and scores of motorcycles joined the procession to the district parliament. When the first parliamentarians arrived for work that morning, they were met by a quiet delegation of villagers standing atop a large pile of wood wrapped in an enormous white cloth.

> "What is this?" they asked.
> "This is the cloth we use to wrap our dead," the village head replied. "And dead is what this project is. We would rather have no bridge and no wood than go back to the corrupt ways of the New Order. From now on, we only want projects that involve us in decisions. If KDP can do it, other projects can do it too."

And with those words, the villagers got back on their trucks and went home.

—Scott Guggenheim and Enurlaela Hasanah

from collapsing. The project used a local institution, the Municipal Development Fund (similar in concept to Paul Collier's Independent Service Authorities), and built in high levels of transparency. Municipal authorities were held responsible for delivery, by both the Municipal Development Fund and citizens. The result was a situation in which the water kept running (as did other services) in an extraordinarily politicized and uncertain environment. In a field fertile for corruption—with high unemployment and low wages—corruption was held in check just by keeping an eye on the right ball, focusing on outcomes and delivery. Of course, there was and is still considerable corruption in the West Bank and Gaza, but a combination of local involvement, transparency, and a focus on outcomes meant that critical development results were still achievable.

As with transparency, what countries agree to deliver and what donors expect them to deliver will vary with country circumstances, but even weak and fragile states can and should be held accountable for results. In fact, one of the added benefits of a focus on outcomes is that it introduces a much stronger element of practicality and realism into the discussion between donors and recipients. If donors control the money and the agenda, recipient countries have little incentive to decline a project, but if payment depends on performance, officials will not want to promise what they know they cannot deliver.

An example may help clarify how this approach would differ from what we've been doing. Let's say that a developing country government has a donor-funded program to build and repair local roads. The conventional approach, at least in projects financed through multilateral loans, is to provide heavy input in the design phase, and heavy oversight through large supervision budgets, much of this in the name of controlling corruption. Although this approach may or may not work for one-off, large-scale projects, it is inherently unworkable when a program has a national reach involving many players and many projects, typical of government programs and scaled-up donor-financed programs.

Instead, what if donors agreed with governments on what was to be produced? Community or district X wants to repair Y kilometers of local roads. Since basic wage and materials costs are known within reasonable bounds, it is not difficult to determine the grant needed to meet this end. As a number of projects have shown, some of them in very weak institutional environments, it is quite possible to require certain basic levels of transparency in the process of selecting roads to be repaired and in the use of funds. At the end of the first year of the project (the time period could vary), a physical and financial audit is performed (which would have to be simple) to determine whether what was agreed on was produced and at an acceptable standard. If yes, the community or district gets the next round of funding; if no, it does not. No use throwing good money after bad . . . and the recipient government could not argue otherwise.

Along similar lines, Center for Global Development President Nancy Birdsall and staff member Kate Vyborny are exploring the potential of a hands-off approach to aid delivery that would be sharply focused on results. Such progress-based aid would link aid flows to clear evidence of progress on the ground. For example, under progress-based aid for education, participating countries and donors would enter a contract in which donors would pay for educational attainments, say, $100 for each child who completes primary school and takes a standardized test. This approach would place full decisionmaking about the use of funds in the hands of developing-country governments, but they would be fully accountable for achieving the agreed-upon outcome. Under this arrangement, rather than donors trying to rein in governments on the corruption front, governments would be faced with a clear tradeoff: either curb corruption that undermines delivery of education, or don't get paid. U.S. and other taxpayers could be assured that they were receiving value for money.

This approach may not be appropriate in all cases—there may be some settings in which humanitarian needs dictate that donors step in and, as it were, do it themselves—but an insistence on results is appropriate in far more cases than the development community now recognizes. But how does this approach fight corruption? Won't the mayor's brother-in-law get the contract to fix the roads? Won't he skim off his "commission"? What we know from the Indonesian, Kyrgyz, West Bank, and other projects suggests that the answer is a qualified "no" if the following conditions hold: people in the community or district know the money was received; the community knows next year's allocation depends on using this year's well; and the outcome of the audits is made public.

Even with less micro-management of process, if outcomes are measurable in quantity and quality terms, if average unit costs are known, and if donors insist on the right to independent auditing and confirmation, the space available for corruption will be greatly reduced. To be sure, corruption will not be squeezed out of the system entirely. Indeed, the mayor's brother-in-law may still build the road.

> But the road will be built, and built to specs, or no money. Corruption that reduces critical development outcomes would have been held in check. That is the standard to which anticorruption efforts and programs should be held.
>
> How to ensure that audits are not corrupted? This is a real and serious challenge, one that some of the best minds in development are thinking about. Paul Collier, in his recent book, *The Bottom Billion: Why the Poorest Countries Are Failing and What Can Be Done About It,* argues for the creation in weak and fragile states of Independent Service Authorities (modeled after central banks, one of the few examples of a professionalized agency in most poor countries). These would be local institutions responsible for managing resource flows and the auditing process. The details are devilish and have to be worked out—but the concept is there and needs to be tried.

To ensure that U.S. taxpayers are getting value for their development dollars, the next president should embrace these two simple suggestions: insist on more transparency and concentrate on outcomes, not process, as the key elements of the formula to produce better public services and more government accountability.

If the United States is to succeed in moving these two suggestions from theory to practice, it must also recognize that getting developing countries to increase transparency and the rich countries to focus on results, not processes, needs a multilateral approach. Other providers of development assistance must also adopt the focus on outcomes rather than on processes. And the developing countries that must ultimately accept and implement these changes in development culture have to be at the table. That is what the multilateral system—the World Bank, the regional development banks, the United Nations Development Programme—does: It provides a forum for collective action where donors and recipients both have a voice.

"Global bads": part of the problem

> Poverty does not make poor people into terrorists and murderers. Yet poverty, weak institutions, and corruption can make weak states vulnerable to terrorist networks and drug cartels within their borders.[6]

As this quotation from the U.S. National Security Strategy shows, the United States has long known that global bads—like international crime, illegal drugs, terrorism, and smuggling—affect development and hence U.S. national interests. Global bads distort economies and markets, and erode the social networks that hold societies together; the fight against them diverts governments, both rich and poor, from basic service provision. Much of the money used to bribe officials and buy elections comes from them. They often pave the way for fragile states to become failed states (see chapter 12 by Patrick). If the United States wants progress on the international corruption front, it needs to find ways to reduce the impact of global bads.

The heroin trade from Afghanistan through Central Asia to Russia and Europe offers a telling example. It shows how the drug trade can undermine the economies of not only producing countries but of neighbors. As much as one-third of Afghanistan's gross domestic product comes from growing poppy and from illicit drugs such as opium, morphine, heroin, and hashish. Tajikistan, just to the north of Afghanistan, doesn't produce poppies, but by some estimates, one-third to a half of its economy depends in one way or another on the drug trade. Further north, in the Kyrgyz Republic, the last election was said to be bought by the drug barons who essentially "own" the country's south.

With the rest of the economy languishing, the drug trade is sometimes the only game in town. Once established, it is nearly impossible to eradicate, as Colombia has found. Development programs must create alternatives—even where surrounding conditions are not ideal in terms of governance, democracy, and human rights—or risk ceding more and more countries to the burgeoning illegal economy.

As Moises Naim shows in his insightful book, *Illicit: How Smugglers, Traffickers and Copycats Are Hijacking the Global Economy*, the illegal drug trade's global consequences extend well beyond developing-country borders. The revenue from the multibillion dollar industry is often the seed capital for a host of other activities that impose serious costs on the world. Drug money supports criminal networks; it creates narco-states where drug barons own the political process; it funds smuggling, human and otherwise; and it supports a vast industry of counterfeiting. The U.S. record in the fight against the illegal trade is not a happy one, but there are things we can do that will reduce the harm done.

1. *Launch a commission to review the U.S. approach to the war on drugs.* As a starting point, the next administration needs to reconsider the U.S. approach to fighting illegal drugs. The current U.S. strategy puts great store in supply interdiction and criminalizing drug use. As politically sensitive as any discussion of illegal drugs is, the next administration must step back and ask whether this strategy is paying off. The debate on how best to deal with the scourge of illegal drugs is

long and sensitive, highly emotionally charged, and well illustrated by a recent exchange between Willem Buiter and Joseph Califano.

Buiter, an economist at the London School of Economics, says there is little evidence that the criminalization of drugs has reduced the costs imposed on society, arguing that it has, in fact, increased these costs—through the crime generated and the financing created for other global bads, and also by making it more difficult for addicts to get treatment. Califano, the former U.S. secretary of health, takes the conventional line that drugs are bad and have to remain illegal, and that we need to redouble our interdiction and criminal prosecution efforts at every level.

The next administration needs to find a way to break this long-standing stalemate. An appeal to the facts of what we know about both sides of the argument would be a good place to start. A credible, nonpartisan, high-level commission would be the right next step, tasked with undertaking a thorough and objective review of U.S. and world antidrug efforts to study what is working and what is not, and to report back to the new president one year after his or her inauguration.

2. *Get serious about anti–money laundering.* As the new administration seeks new and better ways of fighting the war on illegal drugs, it can and should lead the charge to stem illicit financial flows by working to make dirty money useless money. Drug money and revenues from other illegal activities, including outright corruption, are next to worthless unless these funds can find their way into the legitimate financial system, that is, unless, the money is laundered. Reducing the possibilities for laundering money from illegal activities makes those activities less attractive. Equally important, effective anti–money laundering policies make it more difficult to use the dirty money to finance other global bads.

   The record on controlling money laundering is not good. In their aptly titled *Chasing Dirty Money: The Fight against Money Laundering*, Peter Reuter and Ted Truman conclude that, as of 2004, little was concretely known about either the extent of the problem or the effectiveness of efforts to stop it. But since the events of September 11, 2001, the United States has become much more concerned about international financial flows that come from illicit activities. The U.S. Treasury's 2005 Money Laundering Threat Assessment concludes that "the volume of dirty money circulating through the United States is undeniably vast," but that over the past decade "there has been considerable progress . . . most encouraging are interagency initiatives and task forces that, when properly coordinated, bring the talents, expertise, and resources of multiple agencies to bear on a problem with great effect."[7]

An effective campaign against money laundering has to be global, but it can start at home. Billions of dollars stolen from poor countries, earned through the sale of illegal drugs, are processed through rich-country banks. These banks "manage" the funds of some very shady characters, hiding behind proclamations of confidentiality concerns that let suspect clients get away with what almost amounts to indirect murder. It is difficult to know before the fact whether banks are still engaged in the types of activities that Riggs Bank and Citigroup performed for Augusto Pinochet, but the next U.S. president should not wait for a scandal before taking action. Rich-country banks are part of a system that helps translate ill-gotten gains into legitimate purchasing power. The 2004 bilateral agreement between Peru and the United States, which repatriated $20 million dollars forfeited from Vladimiro Montesinos and one of his associates, was a step in the right direction, but the process of asset repatriation is difficult and unwieldy, especially for under-resourced governments in developing countries.

The World Bank and the U.N. Office on Drugs and Crime have just launched a stolen-asset recovery initiative with the goal of encouraging governments to help repatriate some of the ill-gotten gains that kleptocrats hide in banks abroad. This excellent initiative will work only if the United States is truly behind it. So far, the United States has "signed up," as it were, but not taken a leadership role.

Chasing Dirty Money argues that the United States does have some effective laws in place to prevent this kind of money laundering. The United States requires that banks file suspicious activity reports when they suspect that their clients might be using accounts for money laundering. With a little analysis, the database created could produce a wealth of information concerning potential money laundering. More analysis of suspicious activity reports could produce new money-laundering investigations, and an analysis of which banks are not submitting an average number of reports might tip off investigators toward those banks which might, knowingly or unknowingly, be assisting criminals and kleptocrats. The Federal Bureau of Investigation is working to develop advanced technologies to exploit suspicious activity reports and other Bank Secrecy Act data by using computer software to identify financial patterns, link criminal activities, and display the activity in link analysis charts. The bureau is also implementing a next-generation electronic file management system that will help manage investigative, administrative, and intelligence needs while also improving ways to encourage information sharing with other agencies. This kind of program is an effective way of mobilizing already existing resources.

What needs to be done? We recommend that the next administration start by organizing an international review of bank secrecy laws around the world. This is a difficult area to legislate, but one that cannot be avoided if progress is to be made on slowing money laundering and pursuing stolen assets. Yes, legitimate parties have a right to confidentiality of assets, but that right must not provide sanctuary for those hiding dirty money. The right to individual privacy has to be balanced against the global public good of reducing the value of dirty money.

A look at the alleged amounts of assets stolen by corrupt officials in comparison with recovered assets makes the point. General Abacha of Nigeria is said to have stolen between \$3 billion and \$5 billion from the Nigerian people. So far, only a fraction of that money has been discovered and repatriated. Where is the rest? Some of it is surely in rich-country banks. Without a better balance between the right of individuals to confidentiality and the right of citizens to know, progress on stolen-asset recovery is likely to be limited.

Conclusion: ten steps for reducing the global consequences of corruption

Although everyone agrees that corruption is bad in its own right, ultimately, measures to reduce corruption should be evaluated in terms of how much they improve people's lives in developing countries. The United States should also remember that there are few quick wins in the fight against corruption; the next administration must be clear that it is in the fight for the long haul.

In this chapter we have set out an agenda for the next administration that attacks three aspects of international corruption that harm U.S. interests: corruption that slows private sector development; corruption that undermines development assistance; and global bads that fuel corruption and instability. Our recommendations involve changes in the way the United States approaches corruption and, importantly, the country's leadership role in getting the rest of the world to buy into these new approaches. We are specific where our knowledge base justifies specificity, and we call for quick action to settle old debates where that is the essential next step.

Our recommendations are the following:

To reduce corruption in international transactions

- Broaden the definition of corrupt payments. Close the loopholes in the FCPA and in the OECD Anti-Bribery Convention.
- Reform international arbitration procedures. Support an expanded scope for international arbitration to level the playing field in the application of anticorruption measures.
- Enhance transparency in payments made by international companies. Make the EITI work, and seek its expansion to other industries.
- Open up rich-country clubs to all the world's biggest economies. Start by opening up the OECD and the Group of 7/8 to the key large emerging economies.

To reduce corruption in domestic investment for poor countries

- Lead the fight to get developing countries to remove "gates." Get rid of bureaucratic restrictions and regulations that provide fertile ground for corruption and slow private sector development.
- Support the multilateral system, especially the World Bank, in its effort to improve local business environments. The U.S. voice on private sector corruption is important, but that voice will be more effective if it is heard as part of the multilateral system.

To make development assistance more effective

- Ensure that developing-country citizens have the information necessary to take up the fight against corruption. Develop and implement a minimum standard of transparency as the price of admission to the international aid table.
- Insist on results even in weak and fragile states. Move U.S. direct aid assistance to a platform on which countries resume responsibility for outcomes, and are held accountable for delivery.

To slow the spread of global bads

- Launch a commission to review the U.S. approach to the war on drugs. Look for an evidence-based replacement for the current approach, which is not working.
- Get serious about anti–money laundering. Too much dirty money passes through rich-country banks. Lead the charge to stop this, starting by organizing an international review of bank secrecy laws.

If implemented, these recommendations will reduce corruption's drag on development. If undertaken in partnership with other rich and poor countries through multilateral organizations such as OECD and the World Bank, they will, as well, restore the leadership position of the United States in shaping the world's development agenda.

Notes

1. USDOJ 2001.
2. Transparency International 2007.
3. Waldmier 2007.
4. OECD 2000, p. 24.
5. González, López-Córdova, and Valladares 2007.
6. White House 2002, introduction.
7. U.S. Treasury 2005, p. i.

References

Approved Judgement of the Honourable Mr. Justice Cooke between Kensington International and the Republic of Congo. 2005. High Court of Justice, Queens Bench Division, Commercial Court, Royal Court of Justice, Strand, London. November 28.

Buiter, Willem. 2007. "For the Sake of Liberty and Security: Legalise all Drugs." *Financial Times*. August 8, Opinion Section.

Califano, Joseph. 2007. "Drug Legalisation Is Playing Russian Roulette." *Financial Times*. August 16, Opinion Section.

Central Intelligence Agency. N.d. "The World Factbook: Afghanistan." Washington, D.C.

Collier, Paul. 2007. *The Bottom Billion: Why the Poorest Countries Are Failing and What Can Be Done About It*. New York: Oxford University Press.

Dinh Cung, Nguyen. "Vietnam's Licensing Reforms: A Work Still in Progress." World Bank Library. [http://info.worldbank.org/etools/docs/library/239807/Vietnam_s_licensing_ reforms.pdf].

Gerson, Michael. 2007. "One Tool America Needs." *Washington Post*. August 1.

González, Alvaro, J. Ernesto López-Córdova, and Elio E. Valladares. 2007. "The Incidence of Graft on Developing Country Firms." Policy Research Working Paper 4394. World Bank, Washington, D.C. [http://econ.worldbank.org/external/default/main?pagePK=64165259&theSitePK=469372&piPK=64165421&menuPK=64166093&entityID=000158349_20071112131416].

Guggenheim, Scott. "Crises and Contradictions: Understanding the Origins of a Community Development Project in Indonesia." World Bank Library. [http://siteresources.worldbank.org/INTINDONESIA/Resources/Social/KDP-Crises.pdf].

Herrling, Sheila, and Sarah Rose. 2007. "Control of Corruption and the MCA: A Preview to the FY2008 Country Selection." MCA Monitor Analysis. Center for Global Development, Washington, D.C.

Katzenellenbogen, Jonathan. 2006. "Outbid by Bribery, Say Firms." *Business Day Online*. October 9.

Moran, Theodore H. 2006. *Harnessing Foreign Direct Investment for Development: Policies for Developed and Developing Countries*. Washington, D.C.: Center for Global Development.

Naim, Moises. 2005. *Illicit: How Smugglers, Traffickers and Copycats Are Hijacking the Global Economy*. New York: Doubleday.

OECD (Organisation for Economic Co-operation and Development). 2000. *OECD Guidelines for Multinational Enterprises*. June. [www.oecd.org/dataoecd/56/36/1922428.pdf].

Reuter, Peter, and Ted Truman. 2004. *Chasing Dirty Money: The Fight against Money Laundering*. Washington, D.C.: Institute for International Economics.

Schwartz, Nelson D., and Lowell Bergman. 2007. "Payload: Taking Aim at Corporate Bribery." *New York Times*. November 25, Section C.

Transparency International. 2006. *Global Corruption Report*. Washington, D.C.

———. 2007. *Enforcement of the OECD Convention on Combating Bribery in Foreign Public Officials: Progress Report*. Washington, D.C.

USAID (U.S. Agency for International Development). 2005. *USAID Anticorruption Strategy*. Washington, D.C. [www.usaid.gov/our_work/democracy_and_governance/publications/pdfs/ac_strategy_final.pdf].

USDOJ (U.S. Department of Justice). 2001. *Lay-Person's Guide to the FCPA Statute*. Washington, D.C. [www.usdoj.gov/criminal/fraud/docs/dojdocb.html].

U.S. Senate. 2004. *Money Laundering and Foreign Corruption: Enforcement and Effectiveness of the Patriot Act: Case Study Involving Riggs Bank*. Report prepared by the Minority Staff of the Permanent Subcommittee on Investigations. July 15.

U.S. Treasury. 2005. *United States Money Laundering Threat Assessment*. Washington, D.C. [www.ustreas.gov/offices/enforcement/pdf/mlta.pdf].

Waldmier, Patti. 2007. "Bribery Is Too Much like Hard Work." *Financial Times*. October 17, page 12.

Wells, Louis T., and Rafiq Ahmed. 2007. *Making Foreign Investment Safe: Property Rights and National Sovereignty*. New York: Oxford University Press.

White House. 2002. *National Security Strategy of the United States*. Washington, D.C. [www.whitehouse.gov/nsc/nss.html].

World Bank. 2007. "Stolen Asset Recovery (StAR) Initiative: Challenges, Opportunities, and Action Plan." Washington, D.C.

6 Integration in the Americas: One Idea for Plan B

Nancy Lee

Once there was a shared strategy in the Americas to boost growth and spread its gains. April 2008 marked the tenth anniversary of the launch of negotiations in Santiago, at the second Summit of the Americas, for the Free Trade Area of the Americas, the plan to unite a market of 880 million people. Now support for the Free Trade Area of the Americas has effectively collapsed—a victim of the deadlocked Doha Round, globalization fears, ideological differences, regional leadership rivalries, the distractions of financial instability, and the lure of subregional approaches.

Should the United States care about the demise of a regionwide integration strategy? This chapter argues that it should, that the risks of failure to address extreme regional inequality (between and within countries) are increasingly evident. Warning lights are flashing in the hemisphere. Political polarization and the steep rise in crime and urban violence present real threats to stability in large and small countries. Market democracies in the region need an effective regional strategy to help them spread the benefits of growth to large excluded and disaffected populations. The lack of such a strategy helps create a vacuum that some seek to fill with undemocratic, statist models that risk a giant leap backward.

Nancy Lee is a visiting fellow at the Center for Global Development. For helpful comments and encouragement, she is grateful to Nancy Birdsall, Kim Elliott, Vijaya Ramchandran, and Dennis de Tray at the Center for Global Development; Peter Hakim at the Inter-American Dialogue; and Mark Medish at the Carnegie Endowment for International Peace. For excellent research assistance, she thanks Cindy Prieto and Selvin Akkus at the center and Julia Sekkel at the Inter-American Dialogue.

The experience of Europe and East Asia demonstrates that regional integration matters fundamentally for competitiveness, growth, and income convergence. In both those regions, the largest countries have led the pursuit of progressively deeper integration. The United States, with others, must lead the way in this hemisphere. The fifth Summit of the Americas in early 2009 looms as a challenge and opportunity in this regard.

Moreover, though further trade liberalization remains important, other economic policy challenges are emerging as binding constraints on growth and income convergence in the region. As free trade agreements confront growing resistance, the region needs to consider new integration models that help address these constraints in pragmatic, politically feasible ways. One possible model outlined here is a regional investment agreement designed to reduce microeconomic and other barriers confronting both domestic and foreign investors.

Why now?

Some may question the urgency of finding a viable path to regional integration after four years of growth averaging above 5 percent in Latin America, buoyed by good macroeconomic and exchange rate policies, more outward orientation, a strong global economy, high commodity prices, and rapid domestic credit growth.

It is true that incomes and consumption have risen in the recent boom, and formal job creation has picked up significantly. But there is a very long way to go. An estimated 49 percent of Latin American employment was still in the informal sector in 2005. And the surging exports that ignited recent growth are largely commodities. It is hard to sustain high, job-creating growth when so much economic activity is outside the legal system and when so much of the export boom consists of energy, minerals, and food. Crucially, Latin America differs from the most successful emerging market regions in a way that bodes ill for the future: Investment as a share of gross domestic product (GDP) remains discouragingly low (figure 6.1).

The progress made on some of the traditional barriers to investment and growth in the region[1]—weak macroeconomic policy, financial instability, and high formal trade barriers—has not for the most part been matched in the sphere of the microeconomic environment (figure 6.2).

Not only does the region (with some country exceptions) rank poorly in the World Bank's *Doing Business* indicators, it also has the lowest share of countries making reform progress of any region (figure 6.3). Do businesses worry about microeconomic barriers? Business surveys suggest they do: The top two obstacles cited to doing business in the region are mechanisms for coping with burdensome and nontransparent regulatory and tax

Figure 6.1. Gross capital formation, by region, 2000 and 2005

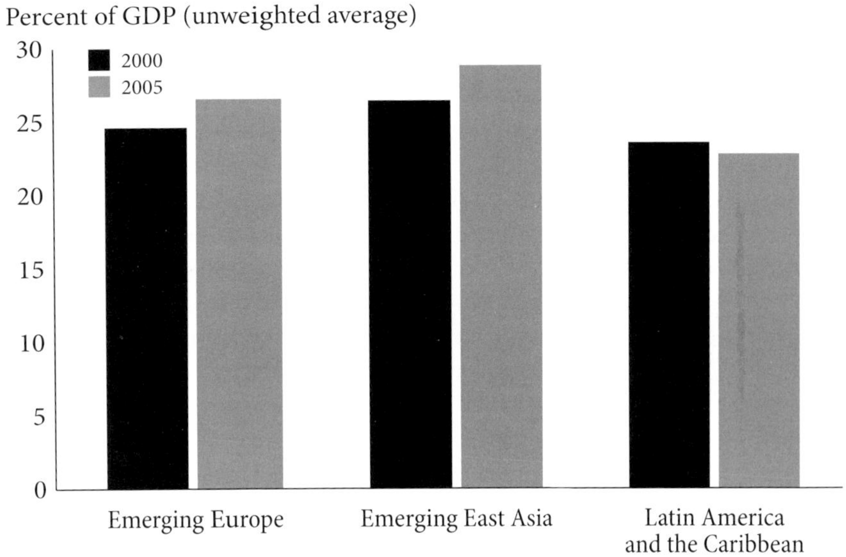

Note: Emerging Europe comprises Bulgaria, Czech Republic, Estonia, Hungary, Latvia, Lithuania, Poland, Romania, Slovak Republic, and Slovenia. Emerging East Asia comprises Cambodia, China, Indonesia, Republic of Korea, Lao People's Democratic Republic, Malaysia, Mongolia, Myanmar, Philippines, Thailand, Timor-Leste, and Vietnam. Latin America and the Caribbean comprises Argentina, Barbados, Belize, Bolivia, Brazil, Chile, Colombia, Costa Rica, Dominica, Dominican Republic, Ecuador, El Salvador, Grenada, Guatemala, Guyana, Haiti, Honduras, Jamaica, Mexico, Nicaragua, Panama, Paraguay, Peru, St. Kitts and Nevis, St. Lucia, St. Vincent and the Grenadines, Suriname, Trinidad and Tobago, Uruguay, and Venezuela.

Source: World Bank 2007a.

systems—choosing to remain in the informal sector and corruption (that is, bribing regulatory and tax officials). If all categories of obstacles associated with burdensome regulation and tax systems are combined, 53 percent of businesses cite these as the main obstacles to doing business (table 6.1).

Left in the dust

While regionwide integration progress in the hemisphere has ground to a halt, other parts of the world have forged ahead rapidly with their own strategies. More than ten countries in emerging Europe have joined the European Union in this decade and reaped striking growth and income benefits. Emerging East Asia is now knit together in cross-border production-sharing chains, shaped by foreign investment inflows, fed by parts and components trade, and facilitated by governments and regional organizations.

Figure 6.2. Business climate indicators for Latin America and the Caribbean countries, 2007

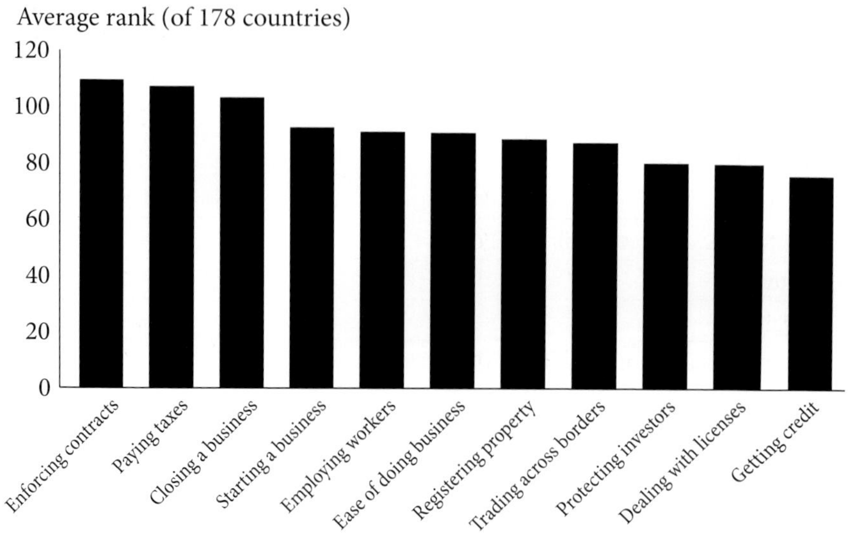

Source: World Bank 2007c.

Figure 6.3. Share of countries making at least one positive *Doing Business* reform in 2006/07

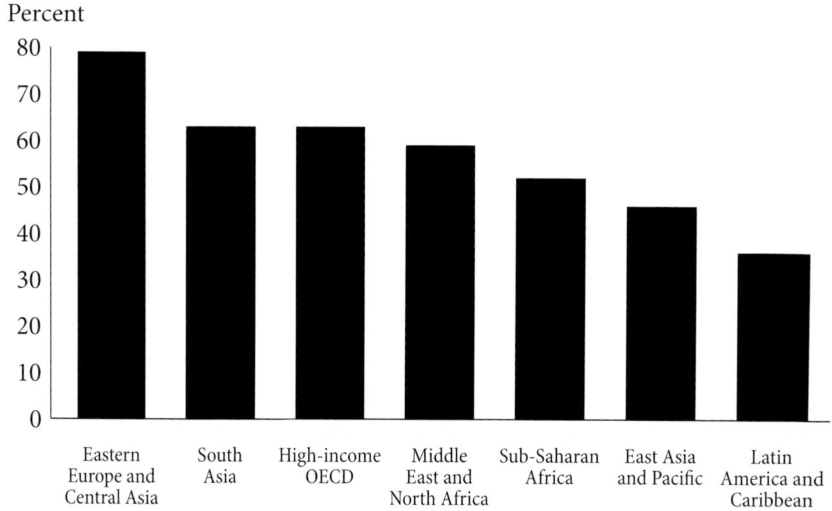

Source: World Bank 2007c.

Table 6.1. Main obstacles to doing business in Latin America and the Caribbean

	Firms citing problem as main obstacle (percent)
Informality[a]	18.1
Corruption[b]	11.4
Crime, theft, and disorder	10.9
Political instability	9.9
Access to financing (availability and cost)	9.7
Tax rates	9.1
Electricity	6.9
Skills and education of available workers	6.5
Tax administration	5.1
Labor regulations	4.0
Business licensing and operating permits	3.4
Customs and trade regulations	2.2
Transportation of goods, supplies, and inputs	1.1
Courts	0.9
Access to land	0.8

Note: Shaded categories collectively define obstacles associated with the quality of the regulatory regime and tax systems.
a. Covers the extent of informal and underreported operations (which compete with formal enterprises).
b. Covers informal payments associated with customs, taxes, licenses, regulations, and government contracts.
Source: World Bank 2006.

For these two regions, integration, especially its benefits for investment, has played a central role in turbo-charging growth and income convergence (figure 6.4).

Europe boosted investment climates through a top-down, formal enlargement process, with supranational institutions, economic systems reshaped in a common image, and massive aid. In East Asia, the role of governments and regional agreements has been to assist the regional investment strategies of private companies through trade facilitation, infrastructure development, and more recently "behind-the-border" reforms. Both approaches offer lessons for this hemisphere, though neither model is easily transferrable. The challenge is to find a third way—one that relies less on bureaucracies,

Figure 6.4. Income convergence

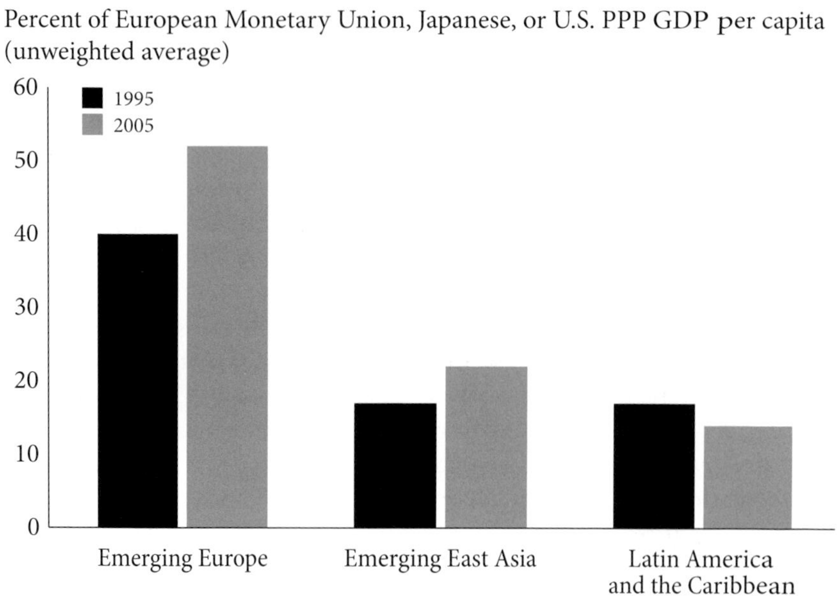

Note: PPP is purchasing power parity. Emerging Europe comprises Bulgaria, Czech Republic, Estonia, Hungary, Latvia, Lithuania, Poland, Romania, Slovak Republic, and Slovenia. Emerging East Asia comprises Cambodia, China, Indonesia, Republic of Korea, Lao People's Democratic Republic, Malaysia, Mongolia, Myanmar, Philippines, Thailand, Timor-Leste, and Vietnam. Latin America and the Caribbean comprises Argentina, Barbados, Belize, Bolivia, Brazil, Chile, Colombia, Costa Rica, Dominica, Dominican Republic, Ecuador, El Salvador, Grenada, Guatemala, Guyana, Haiti, Honduras, Jamaica, Mexico, Nicaragua, Panama, Paraguay, Peru, St. Kitts and Nevis, St. Lucia, St. Vincent and the Grenadines, Suriname, Trinidad and Tobago, Uruguay, and Venezuela.

Source: World Bank 2007a.

uniformity, and aid than the European Union but that takes a more systematic approach to reform than did East Asia.

A regional investment agreement

One possible approach that addresses the investment problem directly is a standards-based regional investment agreement or code. The idea is a collective effort to set standards for improving the quality of regulatory and tax systems affecting both domestic and foreign investors. As in the financial and trade worlds, a standards-based approach could spread good practice without requiring supranational governance (such as a common regulator). These standards could simplify and expedite systems for starting a business, paying taxes, obtaining licenses, registering property, dealing with border controls, and accessing credit and infrastructure services.

This approach is made possible by the enormous leap forward in the world's capacity to measure the microeconomic environment for investment using objective, verifiable indicators that are consistent across countries and regularly updated by third-party institutions such as the World Bank. Examples of such objective indicators range from the official costs of starting a business, to the number of procedures to obtain licenses, to the number of business tax payments required annually, to the time required for customs clearance, to the strength of creditor rights based on standardized criteria.

Countries could use a regional agreement to set common standards or benchmarks based on international norms for an agreed set of investment climate indicators. A notional source of such norms might be, for example, minimum or average practice in the member countries of the Organisation of Economic Co-operation and Development.

The aim would be to foster reforms consistent with a set of universally applicable principles such as:

- *Simplification.* Systems should be as simple as possible in terms of the numbers of steps, documents, and approvals needed.
- *Use of computerized systems.* Online applications and approvals standardize requirements, limit discretion and scope for corruption, and improve transparency and accountability.
- *Reduction of direct costs and fees.* Fees charged for procedures and approvals should be minimized and made transparent.
- *Time limits.* Reasonable limits should be set on the time needed for approvals and decisions.
- *Transparency.* Regulations, documents, and procedures should be standardized and published on websites, along with the authorities responsible for decisionmaking and enforcement.

The World Bank's annual *Doing Business* reports demonstrate that reforms consistent with these principles are well within the reach of low- and middle-income countries.

Beyond the microeconomic environment

Such an agreement could also serve as a flexible vehicle for addressing other major investment climate issues. It could, for example, include confidence-building standards to lock in macroeconomic policy improvements, such as limits on public debt and tax burdens. And it could be used to address the increasingly urgent challenge of strengthening standards for protecting the environment and labor (in ways perhaps more effective than are possible in trade agreements).

The region could consider something like the European Stability and Growth Pact standards limiting financial vulnerability. Members of the European Monetary Union must, for example, limit their ratios of public debt to GDP to 60 percent. While monetary union provided the direct policy impetus for debt limits in the European case, Latin America's history of debt problems offers a rationale for debt ceilings even without a common currency. The enforcement difficulties of the Stability and Growth Pact suggest the need to avoid overselling such limits, but most analysts agree that the pact has nevertheless had a significant restraining impact on fiscal and borrowing behavior.

Tax burdens remain a major issue in much of the region. Business taxes as a percentage of profits average 54.5 percent for Latin America and the Caribbean, compared with 38.8 percent for high-income countries.[2] And businesses in the region on average pay forty-nine different taxes, while businesses in high-income countries on average pay eighteen taxes.[3] The agreement proposed here could set a cap on the overall business tax burden from the combined effects of all taxes. It could function as a kind of alternative maximum tax (a mirror image of the U.S. alternative minimum tax). Businesses could calculate the combined tax burden across all taxes as a share of profits versus the share based on the alternative maximum tax rate and pay whichever is lower. In addition, the agreement could include commitments to consolidate the number of taxes paid by businesses to some threshold level.

With respect to the environment, common regional standards would help cross-border investors who produce for a variety of markets, and it would facilitate cross-border production-sharing. Companies may view the downside of mandatory standards in areas such as vehicle fuel mileage as offset at least partially by cross-country consistency and predictability.

Regarding labor protection, the International Labour Organization has already defined standards and conventions to which many countries in the region are signatories. The problem may not be a lack of standards but a lack of enforcement.[4] In this connection, the value added of a regional agreement may be its capacity to provide incentives and support for better performance. Here the idea is not to ease the burden on investors but to impose consistent obligations with respect to the treatment of labor so that countries with better regimes do not feel competitively disadvantaged.

Why multilateral?

Each country already has a clear incentive to undertake unilateral investment climate reform and race to the top. Although unilateral reforms make sense (as in the case of trade reforms), experience demonstrates that multilateral agreements can help drive reform and increase its benefits. They can lock in reform. They can help rationalize the reform approach to foster the critical mass of related reforms needed to achieve desired outcomes. They can spur countries to mobilize the machinery of government to identify specific steps needed for implementation. And they can better inform investors of policy progress, given the transparent process of negotiating multilateral agreements.

Why would one country in the region benefit from investment climate reforms in other countries? Fundamentally, for the same reason that Europe decided to move beyond reducing trade barriers to harmonizing systems. Better investment climates boost the supply response to reduced trade barriers. And faster investment-led growth in the neighborhood pulls others along. Growth is not a zero-sum game.

Moreover, there is a reciprocity argument that parallels the rationale for trade agreements. Competitiveness in a globalized economy requires investment strategies that do not stop at the home-country border. Companies pursuing efficient production sharing across borders, along with economies of scale, depend on supportive investment environments in neighboring countries. Each country therefore has an incentive to seek better treatment for its own companies in the region in exchange for offering better conditions at home for foreign (and domestic) investors.

Selective obligations and most-favored-nation treatment

The reforms contemplated here serve both domestic and foreign investors. For this reason, this approach could be pursued with more flexibility than has often been the case for multilateral agreements grounded solely in the logic of reciprocity. Countries could be given the freedom to sign on to one set of standards, say, the microeconomic standards, and not others, for example, the macroeconomic standards, without destroying the benefits of the agreement for other participating countries.

For reasons of economic efficiency and to maximize gains, it would make sense for the standards to be applied on a most-favored-nation basis. It would be distortive and burdensome to design one licensing system, for example, for domestic investors and foreign investors from participating countries, and another for investors from nonparticipating countries. To preserve the incentive to participate in the agreement, however, the mechanisms for promoting compliance, such as access to dispute settlement and capacity-building aid (which are discussed below), could be made available only to member countries.

Potential gains

The gains from such an agreement may be very large indeed. Cross-country studies suggest that major and comprehensive improvements in developing-country regulatory quality could boost per capita annual growth rates by around 2 percentage points.[5] As investment climate problems fall especially hard on micro, small, and medium-size firms,[6] attacking these obstacles could also advance equity in the region by helping newcomers to formal product and capital markets. And the evidence suggests that a better regulatory environment would likely substantially boost the growth response to lower trade barriers.[7] A regional investment agreement would therefore complement and expand the benefits of bilateral and subregional trade agreements.

Fostering compliance

Participating countries could consider a gamut of soft to hard options for promoting compliance with agreement commitments, ranging from transparency to peer review and dispute settlement options for investors and states. The simplest and least intrusive approach would be to construct a process for regular third-party reporting on country progress. Annual report cards could be published with the agreed standards and each country's actual performance. A notch up on the surveillance scale would be to institute a system of peer review. Countries could gather regularly to discuss each other's progress and perhaps issue assessments. The most ambitious approach would provide recourse to dispute settlement. An investor-to-state arbitration process could be made available to investors who allege failure by a state participating in the agreement to comply with agreed standards. This process could serve domestic as well as foreign investors if consistent with domestic law. In cases where states do not honor arbitration judgments, foreign investors could request their home countries to pursue state-to-state dispute settlement as a backup means of promoting agreement compliance.

Transition periods and capacity-building assistance

Generous transition periods and ample technical assistance could be offered to countries willing to make ambitious commitments and progress. It would be desirable to set relatively high performance standards but give countries that initially fall short the time they need to build the capacity to meet the standards. During the transition period, countries should have access to useful technical assistance to help them with the difficult task of strengthening their regulatory, policy, and legal institutions and systems. As this technical assistance would be directed at clearly defined goals (meeting specific agreement standards within a specified time frame), recipient countries are likely to ensure that it is productively used. The assistance could be provided by participating countries that already meet the standards, by the international financial institutions, or by both.

Launching discussions: initial steps and the U.S. role

To launch this effort, interested countries could begin by calling for exploratory discussions to define options for an agreement scope and structure that could generate broad support. Such a call might logically come from countries already focused on investment reforms but interested in expanding the benefits. Colombia, Guatemala, Mexico, and Peru, for example, have been named among the top ten global reformers by the World Bank in its *Doing Business* reports.

The United States would have much to gain from a successful agreement, which could significantly boost the region's contribution to U.S. growth and help level the regional playing field in such areas as environmental and labor standards. The United States could play a crucial role by responding positively and quickly to an initiative from interested emerging markets. There are three steps the United States could take to advance this effort:

- *Encourage the Inter-American Development Bank to take an active supporting role and engage the private sector.* As the largest shareholder of the Inter-American Development Bank, the United States could encourage the institution to convene discussions among interested countries. Such discussions should involve the private sector, both small and large firms, as a vital and logical partner in this effort. The Inter-American Development Bank could also provide essential technical input as it did in the early days of the discussions on the Free Trade Area of the Americas.
- *Mobilize aid for capacity-building technical assistance.* The United States could take the lead in mobilizing aid to help governments meet agreed regulatory, tax, and legal standards from its own institution-building aid budget and from the international financial institutions.
- *Work with others to use the Summit of the Americas process to advance discussions.* In 2009, the leaders of the region will gather in Trinidad and Tobago for the fifth Summit of the Americas. The summit provides an opportunity for leaders to give political impetus to discussions by supporting work on an agreement among interested countries. In the likely absence of agreement on resuming negotiations on the Free Trade Area of the Americas (just after the new U.S. administration takes office), pursuit of a regional investment agreement could supply one possible new way forward for progress toward integration in this hemisphere.

Notes

1. Zettelmeyer 2006.
2. World Bank 2007b.

3. World Bank 2007b.
4. Elliott 2007.
5. See, for example, Djankov, McLeish, and Ramalho 2006; Loayza, Oviedo, and Servén 2008.
6. Birdsall, De la Torre, and Menezes 2008, chapter 5.
7. See Bolaky and Freund 2004 and Haar and Price 2008, chapter 13.

References

Birdsall, Nancy, Augusto de la Torre, and Rachel Menezes. 2008. *Fair Growth: Economic Policies for Latin America's Poor and Middle-Income Majority.* Washington, D.C.: Center for Global Development and the Inter-American Dialogue.

Bolaky, Bineswaree, and Caroline L. Freund. 2004. *Trade, Regulations, and Growth.* Policy Research Working Paper 3255. Washington, D.C.: World Bank.

Desruelle, Dominique, and Alfred Schipke. 2007. *Economic Growth and Integration in Central America.* Washington, D.C.: International Monetary Fund.

Djankov, Simeon, Caralee McLeish, and Rita Ramalho. 2006. *Regulation and Growth.* Washington, D.C.: World Bank.

Elliott, Kimberly. 2007. "A Better Way Forward on Trade and Labor Standards." CGD Notes. Center for Global Development, Washington, D.C.

Gill, Indermit, and Homi Kharas. 2007. *An East Asian Renaissance: Ideas for Economic Growth.* Washington, D.C.: World Bank.

Haar, Jerry, and John Price, eds. 2008. *Can Latin America Compete? Confronting the Challenges of Globalization.* New York: Palgrave Macmillan.

ILO (International Labour Organization). 2006. *Panorama Laboral de América Latina y el Caribe 2006.* Lima: International Labour Organization, Regional Office for Latin America and the Caribbean.

IMF (International Monetary Fund). 2008. *World Economic Outlook, April 2008: Statistical Appendix.* Washington, D.C.: International Monetary Fund.

Loayza, Norman V., Ana María Oviedo, and Luis Servén. 2008. "Regulation and Macroeconomic Performance." In Norman V. Loayza and Luis Servén, eds., *Microeconomic Underpinnings of Growth.* Washington, D.C.: World Bank.

———. 2005. "The Impact of Regulation on Growth and Informality: Cross-Country Evidence." Policy Research Working Paper 3623. World Bank, Washington, D.C.

OECD (Organisation for Economic Co-operation and Development). 2007. *Latin American Economic Outlook 2008.* Paris.

Pastor, Robert A. 2001. *Toward a North American Community: Lessons from the Old World for the New.* Washington, D.C.: Institute for International Economics.

Studer, Isabel and Carol Wise, eds. 2007. *Requiem or Revival? The Promise of North American Integration.* Washington, D.C.: The Brookings Institution.

World Bank. 2006. Enterprise Surveys database. Washington, D.C.: World Bank.

———. 2007a. *World Development Indicators.* Washington, D.C.: World Bank.

———. 2007b. *Economic Performance in Latin America and the Caribbean: A Microeconomic Perspective.* Report 40717-LAC. Washington, D.C.: World Bank.

———. 2007c. *Doing Business 2008,* Washington, D.C.: World Bank.

Zettelmeyer, Jeromin. 2006. "Growth and Reforms in Latin America: A Survey of Facts and Arguments." Working Paper 06/210. International Monetary Fund, Washington, D.C.

7

U.S. Trade Policy and Global Development

Kimberly Ann Elliott

Cross-border commerce is critical to the economies of rich countries and can be an important tool for reducing poverty in developing countries. Rich-country barriers to exports from the poorest countries are ethically questionable, and they undermine U.S. interests by blocking opportunities for growth, thereby making these countries more vulnerable to epidemic diseases, terrorists, and transnational criminal organizations. Yet, despite the important links to development, U.S. trade policy is largely divorced from its foreign assistance and other development policies. Even though the Center for Global Development's 2007 Commitment to Development Index ranks the U.S. market as one of the most open in the world, the remaining U.S. barriers discriminate against developing countries. And U.S. trade preferences for developing countries, which are intended to spur trading opportunities and growth in those countries, are riddled with exceptions that undermine their development potential.

The proliferation in bilateral and regional trade agreements could also hurt poor countries if it undermines the nondiscrimination principle that has anchored the international trade system for six decades. These agreements, with differing rules and conditions, also increase transaction

---

Kimberly Elliott is a senior fellow jointly at the Center for Global Development and the Peterson Institute for International Economics. She thanks Selvin Akkus for research assistance and Nancy Birdsall, Dani Rodrik, Arvind Subramanian, Gary Hufbauer, Nancy Lee, Kate Vyborny, and other colleagues at the center for their comments and suggestions.

costs for business, offsetting some of the benefits of reduced import taxes, and divert trade away from smaller, poorer countries that are often excluded. And all too often, in asymmetric negotiations with much smaller developing countries, U.S. negotiators pursued the interests of U.S. exporters at the expense of development priorities, such as public health.

At the global level, the Doha Round of World Trade Organization (WTO) negotiations remained unresolved more than three years after the original completion date. Although most estimates suggest that the immediate economic gains would be modest, a successful Doha Round remains critical in order to maintain the WTO as a bulwark against discrimination and temptations to retreat from openness. This is especially important for the smallest and poorest countries, which benefit most from having an international trade system based on rules rather than on power. The United States also benefits from the WTO's nondiscrimination and dispute settlement process, but in providing support and leadership for the system, the United States also contributes to the provision of a global public good that benefits others at least as much.

To ensure that the international economic system remains open and that poorer countries have opportunities to engage, the next president's trade policy should:

- Treat market access for the poorest countries as development policy rather than trade policy and push Congress to fully open the U.S. market to exports from all least-developed countries and Sub-Saharan Africa.
- Rejuvenate the U.S. commitment to multilateralism and nondiscrimination and, as a first step, ensure that the Doha Round is completed and implemented expeditiously (Doha negotiations were still stalled as of this writing).[1]

As part of the latter initiative, the next president should seek a global moratorium on the negotiation of preferential trade agreements until members negotiate new rules to ensure that these agreements do not undermine the WTO. If this proves impossible and if U.S. policymakers resume negotiating such agreements, they should revise the content to ensure that they promote economic and social progress in developing countries, as well as the interests of U.S. exporters and investors. These are often, but not always, consistent.

Finally, U.S. anxieties about the effects of globalization are growing, and strong leadership will be crucial to maintain the openness of the U.S. economy and rebuild bipartisan support for a liberal trade policy. Thus, the next president must also strengthen social safety nets and address other critical gaps in domestic policy. This should include ensuring access to health care and pensions to reduce the costs of job loss, providing workers opportunities to acquire the skills they need to compete in a more fluid and demanding labor market, and repairing the holes in the safety net for those who lose jobs, for whatever reason.

This chapter begins by looking at U.S. trade policy toward poorer countries and how it could be more supportive of development. It then turns to the evolution of the multilateral system and why it is so important, especially for developing countries, and examines the development challenges posed by recent trends toward bilateral and regional trade agreements. Finally, it discusses the globalization-inspired anxieties that must be addressed to rebuild abroad support for open U.S. markets. It concludes with recommendations designed to ensure that trade policy serves the country's development agenda as well as its commercial interests.

U.S. trade policy and the poor: improving access to the U.S. market

Whatever happens in the Doha Round, it will not come close to eliminating the distortions in rich-country agricultural policies or the remaining barriers to labor-intensive manufactures. Moreover, while the average U.S. tariff is under 5 percent, the average for labor-intensive manufactures (textiles, apparel, footwear, and travel goods)—goods where developing countries have a natural advantage—is 13 percent (figure 7.1). And although the average tariff on raw materials and agricultural products is below 1 percent, this does not reflect the highly restrictive impact of the lingering quantitative restrictions on sugar, dairy products, tobacco, peanuts, and a few other agricultural products. Nor does it reflect the impact of U.S. subsidies on poor cotton farmers in West Africa. Yet these are sectors where many developing countries could export far more if allowed.

The United States has programs that provide preferential access for developing-country exports, but these only partially mitigate the regressive profile of U.S. trade policy. The main U.S. preference program, the Generalized System of Preferences, waives tariffs on many products for more than 140 eligible developing countries, but it excludes products designated as "sensitive," including most of the labor-intensive manufactures shown in figure 7.1, as well as key agricultural products. More generous preferences are granted to eligible least-developed countries, as designated by the United Nations, but important exclusions remain, especially on apparel and agriculture.[2]

The most generous preferences are provided under regional programs for Caribbean and Andean countries, and for Sub-Saharan Africa under the African Growth and Opportunity Act. These programs allow for the duty-free export of most sensitive products, including apparel, but only subject to

Figure 7.1. Average U.S. tariff, by category

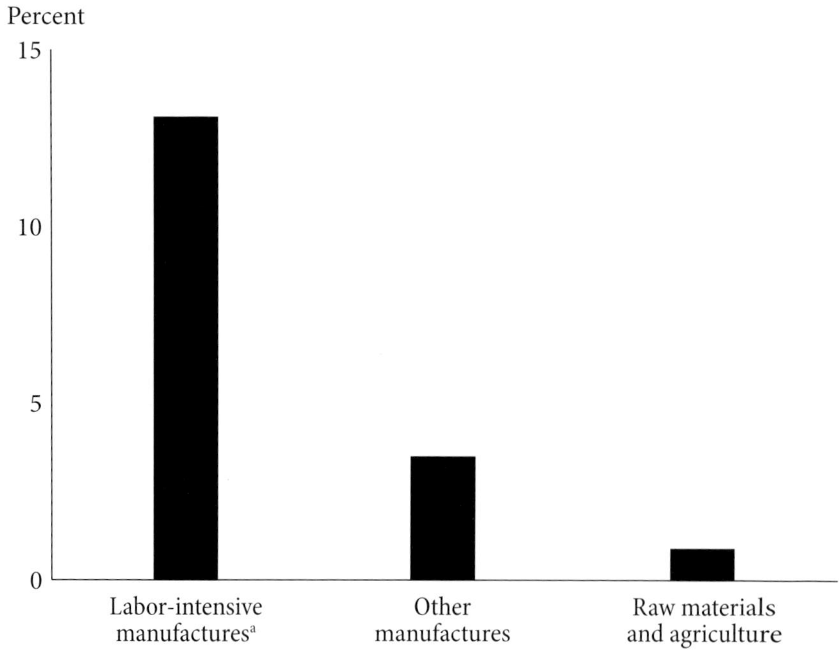

a. Includes textiles, apparel, footwear, and travel goods.
Source: Author's calculations based on data from the International Trade Commission's DataWeb (http://dataweb.usitc.gov).

strict conditions, and they also retain restrictions on agricultural products. Most notably, "rules of origin," nominally designed to ensure that products are not transshipped through preference-receiving countries merely to take advantage of duty-free treatment, are often manipulated to restrict access. The baseline rule of origin for apparel, for example, typically requires beneficiary countries to use U.S. fabric and other inputs if they want to export to the United States duty-free. Given high U.S. production costs and, in the case of Africa, high transportation costs, clothing exports would often not be feasible under this rule, and for that reason the regional programs allow for the use of non-U.S. components within limits (box 7.1).

The African Growth and Opportunity Act is the most flexible U.S. preference program; it allows countries with per capita incomes below $1,500 in 1998 (plus Botswana and Namibia) to use fabric from anywhere in the world in clothing exports, subject to a cap. Mauritius and South Africa, which are above the income threshold, can use local or regional fabric, again up to a cap. Thus far, five countries (Lesotho, Kenya, Madagascar, Mauritius, and Swaziland) account for 90 percent of apparel exports to the United States under the

Box 7.1. U.S. trade preference programs

All these programs have similar country-eligibility conditions, requiring that benefactors allow market access for U.S. exports, respect worker rights, and protect intellectual property, but specific product eligibility and related rules of origin differ.

Generalized System of Preferences

The U.S. Generalized System of Preferences program, like those of other developed countries, was created and implemented in the 1970s. Today, the program provides duty-free entry for some 3,400 products from 144 eligible beneficiary countries (defined by eight-digit tariff categories). An additional 1,400 tariff lines are duty-free for 43 least-developed beneficiary countries (as designated by the United Nations).

Exclusions: Key products are excluded by statute or because the president has identified them as "import-sensitive," including textiles and apparel; watches; footwear, handbags, luggage, and other leather goods; steel, glass, and ceramics; and electronics.

Rule of origin: 35 percent value-added; substantial transformation of imported inputs.

Expiration: The Generalized System of Preferences was renewed for two years as part of the omnibus tax and trade package passed by Congress at the end of 2006, meaning it will have to be renewed again in 2008.

African Growth and Opportunity Act

Originally passed in 2000, the African Growth and Opportunity Act has been expanded and revised three times, most recently at the end of 2006. The act provides enhanced access for thirty-nine of forty-eight eligible Sub-Saharan countries (others are excluded for political and human rights reasons).

Exclusions: Agricultural products subject to tariff-rate quotas (notably sugar, tobacco, and peanuts) and a few other import-sensitive products.

Rules of origin: Same as the Generalized System of Preferences for non–textile and apparel products. Only countries with an effective control system to prevent transshipment are eligible to export apparel. Textiles must be wholly formed in an eligible beneficiary country; in general, apparel must be assembled from U.S. textile inputs. Less-developed countries (per capita income less than $1,500) may use third-country fabric up to a cap of 3.5 percent of the total volume of U.S. apparel imports over the prior twelve months; others (Gabon, Mauritius, Seychelles, and South Africa) can use local or regional fabric within an overall cap of 6.44 percent of the volume of U.S. apparel imports. (Sub-Saharan African apparel exports in 2006 were 1.4 percent of U.S. apparel imports.)

Expiration: 2015 for the African Growth and Opportunity Act, 2012 for the third-country fabric rule.

(continued)

Box 7.1. U.S. trade preference programs (continued)

Andean Trade Preferences and Drug Eradication Act

The Andean Trade Preferences and Drug Eradication Act provides Generalized System of Preferences–plus benefits on 5,600 products for Bolivia, Colombia, Ecuador, and Peru, until free trade agreements are negotiated and implemented.

Exclusions: Agricultural products subject to tariff-rate quotas (notably sugar and canned tuna) and a few other import-sensitive products, including certain textiles, apparel, and footwear.

Rules of origin: Same as the Generalized System of Preferences for nonapparel products. Apparel using U.S. fabric and components is unlimited; apparel using regional fabric is limited to 5 percent of total U.S. imports. (Apparel exports in 2006 were 1 percent of U.S. apparel imports.)

Expiration: The act was extended at the end of 2006 for a few months pending completion and implementation of free trade agreements with some or all beneficiary countries; after much congressional debate the preferences were extended for all four Andean countries to February 2008 and then again to the end of 2008.

Caribbean Basin Initiative and Caribbean Basin Trade Partnership Act

The Caribbean Basin Initiative, which provides Generalized System of Preferences-plus benefits for eighteen Caribbean Basin countries, was expanded in 2000 to address trade diversion created by the North American Free Trade Agreement.

Exclusions: Agricultural products subject to tariff-rate quotas (notably sugar) and a few other import-sensitive products.

Rules of origin: Same as the Generalized System of Preferences for most non–apparel or textile products. Woven apparel must use U.S. fabric, and there are quantitative restrictions for knit apparel, including t-shirts, brassieres, and other apparel products. There are additional restrictions on various components, including thread and linings. The HOPE Act for Haiti, passed in 2006, allows the use of fabric and components from the United States, Haiti, or any free trade agreement partner or beneficiary of the Andean Trade Preferences and Drug Eradication Act or African Growth and Opportunity Act, up to a cap rising to 2 percent of total U.S. imports.

Expiration: The Caribbean Basin Initiative is permanent; the Caribbean Basin Trade Partnership expires September 30, 2008, and the HOPE Act in 2011.

Source: Office of the United States Trade Representative website (www.ustr.gov).

act, while total apparel exports are only 2.5 percent of the overall total (energy products are more than 90 percent). Several other countries, including Ethiopia, Malawi, Mozambique, and Zambia, export mainly farm products, and they have seen limited benefits from the act because of quantitative restrictions on sugar, tobacco, and peanut exports. The Western Hemisphere regional programs also include restrictive rules of origin on apparel and exclude important agricultural products. In short, even the most generous preferential access programs offered by the United States contain important restrictions that limit their development potential.[3]

Outside of Africa and the Western Hemisphere, there are fourteen least-developed countries that are not eligible for any of the regional preference programs, and four of them—Bangladesh, Cambodia, Lao PDR, and Nepal—pay average tariffs of over 15 percent because their exports are concentrated in apparel (figure 7.2). In dollar terms, Bangladesh and Cambodia pay as much in tariffs as do France and the United Kingdom on a fifteen-fold

Figure 7.2. Duties collected as a share of dutiable U.S. imports, by import source

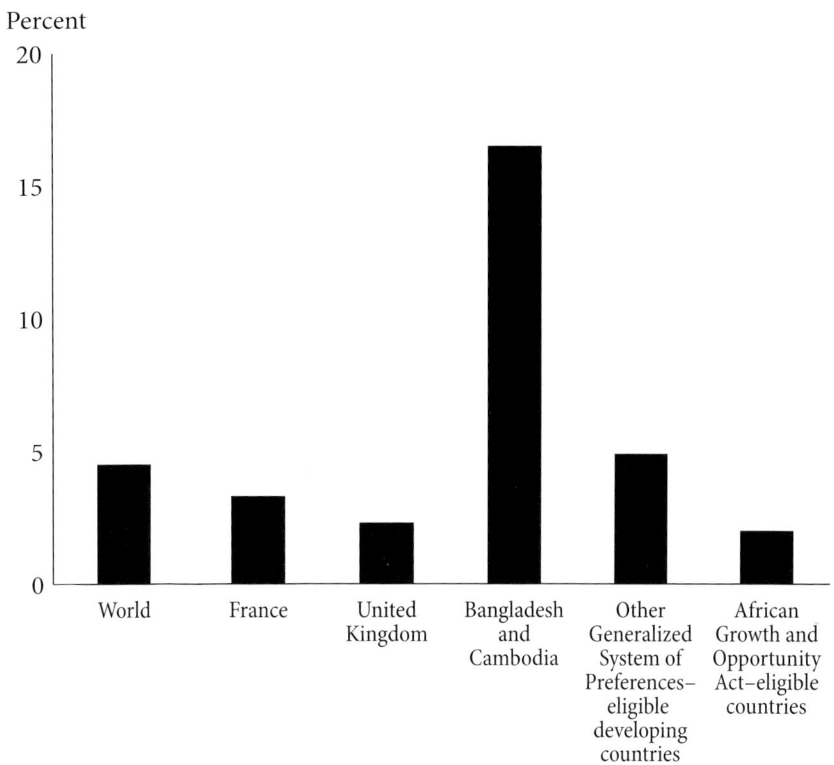

Source: Author's calculations based on data from the International Trade Commission's DataWeb (http://dataweb.usitc.gov).

larger value of imports. Indeed, the $850 million in import duties that these countries jointly paid to the United States in 2006 dwarfs the $120 million that they received in foreign aid.

As part of the Doha Round, in 2005, U.S. negotiators committed to provide "duty-free, quota-free" market access for the U.N.-designated least-developed countries, but only for 97 percent of products. That seemingly small exclusion would be enough, however, to essentially gut the offer, allowing continued restrictions on imports of sugar and other agricultural products from Africa, and the maintenance of tariff peaks on apparel imports from Bangladesh and Cambodia. This miserly approach undercuts U.S. leadership and is unnecessary because extending duty-free, quota-free treatment to the world's poorest countries would have little impact on U.S. producers. Dutiable imports from the least-developed countries that are eligible only for the Generalized System of Preferences (but not any of the regional programs) account for less than 1 percent of total U.S. imports and less than 7 percent of apparel imports.[4]

Support for the idea of granting duty-free, quota-free treatment to poor countries has been growing in recent months, though with differences over the countries that should be eligible. The Center for Global Development and several other nongovernmental groups filed a comment with the U.S. Trade Representative's Office recommending that the United States provide duty-free, quota-free treatment on 100 percent of tariff lines, rather than the 97 percent proposed by U.S. negotiators in 2005, to all least-developed countries, as well as certain other poor countries. The latter provision was intended to avoid removing benefits currently available to Sub-Saharan countries that are not among the least-developed countries under the African Growth and Opportunity Act as well as providing a mechanism to add benefits for countries just over the threshold, such as Sri Lanka, or fragile states, such as Pakistan. In November 2007 the HELP Commission, created by Congress to examine U.S. foreign assistance policies, offered an even broader proposal, recommending that duty-free, quota-free access be provided to those deemed eligible as either compact or threshold countries under the Millennium Challenge Account. The HELP Commission report also recommends that, "if possible," duty-free, quota-free access should be extended to "the poorest countries with a per capita gross domestic product . . . below $2,000." That would further expand the number of countries potentially eligible, including India but barely excluding China (based on 2006 World Bank data), and would be far more politically controversial than providing such access to least-developed countries and Sub-Saharan Africa. The Commission on Smart Power, created by the Center for Strategic and International Studies, simply recommended providing duty-free, quota-free access to all least-developed countries.[5]

Some are concerned that extending duty-free, quota-free access to all least-developed countries (and potentially a few other very poor countries, such as Sri Lanka, that are just above the threshold) would erode the advantage that apparel exporters eligible under the African Growth and Opportunity Act have relative to Bangladesh and Cambodia. Recognizing this concern, legislation proposed in the fall of 2007 by Democratic Congressman Jim McDermott (Washington) and a bipartisan group of House colleagues caps duty-free apparel access for those countries at 2007 levels. Passage of legislation along these lines would be an important step forward, but these countries are also extremely poor, and, like Africa and many other developing countries, they are threatened by competition from China when U.S. and European Union safeguards on China's textile exports are lifted this year. A better approach than continuing to discriminate against a small number of least-developed countries would be to provide increased financial assistance to help Africa address the serious supply-side constraints that limit its competitiveness in international markets.[6] Such "aid for trade," along with duty-free, quota-free access for their agricultural exports, would do more to help Africa maintain apparel exports, and also promote export diversification.

To fully realize the development potential of U.S. preferential access programs, Congress should also make them permanent and reform the rules of origin to make them simpler and less restrictive. Embracing 100 percent duty-free, quota-free access for the poorest countries would also put pressure on Japan to open its market for rice and other agricultural products, as well as help to ensure that the European Union does not renege on its pledge to provide access to its market for "everything but arms" exports from least-developed countries.

Multilateralism and the WTO: challenges for the system

Improved access for the products of the poorest and most vulnerable countries will do even more to promote development if it is embedded in a strong, well-functioning, rules-based multilateral system. The WTO is the best protection that small developing countries have from protectionist backsliding or bullying by more powerful trading partners. Moreover, because the system is founded on the principle of nondiscrimination, even the poorest countries, without resources to fully participate themselves, can benefit from the efforts of others. For example, West African cotton exporters will benefit from any reduction in U.S. cotton subsidies that results from Brazil's successful legal challenge at the WTO.

Until the 1970s, the "Quad"—Canada, the European Community, Japan, and the United States—were the key players in the General Agreement on Tariffs Trade (GATT), which developed core rules for international trade. Developing-country members generally accepted the system because they were asked to do little in terms of opening their own markets, yet they could reap the benefits of cuts by the rich countries under the most-favored-nation principle, which requires that any tariff cut granted to one GATT member be extended to all others.[7] But that lack of participation also meant that sectors of interest to developing countries—agriculture, clothing, and other low-wage manufactures—were mostly left off the liberalization agenda. At the same time, some developing countries were growing rapidly and becoming more attractive markets for rich-country exporters and investors, and the nature of those exports was also changing, with more emphasis on services and products based on intellectual property.

The culmination of these trends was the Uruguay Round of GATT negotiations, launched in 1986, in Punta del Este, Uruguay, and completed at the end of 1993, three years after the original deadline. This round was the first in which developing countries were fully engaged in the negotiations and expected to eventually accept all of the new rules under what was termed a "single undertaking." Developing countries still received "special and differential" treatment, in that they cut their tariffs less and over a longer period of time. They also were given longer phase-in periods to implement new rules. Moreover, countries had to accept the full agreement in order to join the newly created WTO.

But in the words of Canadian trade negotiator Sylvia Ostry, the Uruguay Round's "Grand Bargain turned out to be a Bum Deal for developing countries."[8] In exchange for agreeing to include services, accept new rules to protect intellectual property, and remove impediments to foreign investors, developing countries were supposed to receive increased market access for agricultural products, textiles, and clothing. But the expected benefits from the agricultural agreement proved to be illusory because the new rules were too loosely defined and countries were able to evade reform. And when China joined the WTO in 2001, the elimination of bilateral quotas on textiles and apparel turned out to be more a problem than a boon for many smaller developing countries that had problems competing in a more open market. At the same time, implementation of new rules on reforming customs procedures turned out to be more costly than anticipated, and controversy grew steadily over the Agreement on Trade-Related Aspects of Intellectual Property Rights (TRIPS) because of the potential impact on access to affordable drugs in developing countries that had not previously recognized patents on pharmaceutical products.[9]

Developing-country perceptions about the results from the Uruguay Round led to what Michael Finger calls the "imbalance overhang," which has turned into a major obstacle in the new round of negotiations launched in Doha, Qatar, in November 2001.[10] Achieving a balanced outcome in this round is made even more difficult by the fact that the rich countries have relatively little left to offer in a reciprocal bargain. Average tariff rates in the Quad countries have fallen to around 5.5 percent in Canada, the European Union, and Japan, and around 4 percent in the United States. But agricultural tariffs are much higher on average in the Quad countries, and quantitative restrictions and export subsidies, which are prohibited in all other sectors, will again pose obstacles for developing-country exporters if the current spike in agricultural prices proves as short-lived as in past cycles (box 7.2). And, though the quotas have been eliminated, tariffs on textiles and clothing also remain well above the average for other imports.

In essence, while overall trade policies in the United States and other rich countries are relatively open, they discriminate against precisely the sectors where many developing countries have a comparative advantage. Preferential access programs mitigate this regressivity to some degree but not entirely, and certain issues can only be addressed globally. For example, the farm bill that was passed by Congress in May 2008 mostly retained or even raised trade-distorting subsidies, despite record high commodity prices, and ignored WTO rulings and demands from trading partners for reform. Although it will not be easy, it appears that only a multilateral bargain can convince Congress to reduce those subsidies. At the same time, even though agriculture accounts for a small share of global trade, addressing the remaining barriers is necessary if not sufficient for inking a deal in the Doha Round. Box 7.2 discusses priorities for rich-country reform in the midst of the food crisis that suddenly flared in early 2008.

As of the spring of 2008, fragile hopes for completing the negotiations revived, but the prospects for agreement remained uncertain. Nevertheless, completing the Doha Round remains important to ensure that the international trade system remains one that is based on rules rather than on power, including protection under the dispute settlement system and to ensure that nondiscrimination remains the core principle for relations among most countries.

More strains on the system: bilateral and regional trade agreements

Prior to the 1984 free trade agreement with Israel, the United States had been an unwavering supporter of the multilateral system. It generally supported European efforts to deepen and expand the scope of its regional customs union for political and foreign policy reasons, but avoided bilateral or regional negotiations itself. But beginning in the 1980s, in part because of frustration

Box 7.2. The Doha negotiations, the food crisis, and U.S. policy

With commodity prices skyrocketing and food riots breaking out in several countries in spring 2008, some observers questioned whether an agreement to reduce rich-country farm subsidies and trade barriers still made sense. Reasons that the Doha negotiations on agricultural liberalization should forge ahead include:

- Other economic and systemic benefits of the Doha Round would be lost without an agreement on agriculture.
- Estimates of the price effects of a feasible Doha agreement are in the low single digits, a trivial amount when compared with recent price increases.
- Rich-country subsidies are countercyclical, meaning they provide little or no relief in times of high prices while dampening the incentives for producers in developing countries to increase production when prices are low.
- Providing tens of billions of U.S. taxpayer dollars to large farmers with above-average incomes is an incredibly inefficient mechanism for transferring a small amount to consumers in developing countries.
- High commodity prices provide a window of opportunity to reform U.S. (and European) farm policies, by removing production-distorting subsidies and freeing up money for research and development to boost productivity and create new varieties, which might also benefit developing country producers, and to improve rural infrastructure.
- Subsidies for nonfood commodities, such as cotton, or for tropical commodities, such as sugar, are unlikely to be reduced outside a broad reform that addresses the other commodities as well.

The farm bill that was being debated in Congress in early 2008 seemed determined to miss the opportunity, retaining and even increasing traditional commodity subsidies.

Effectively responding to the food crisis also requires action in a number of other areas:

- Sharp increases in emergency food aid to address immediate problems of hunger and malnutrition.
- Reforms in U.S. food aid to remove the requirement that it be "in-kind" and to allow cash to be used to purchase and deliver food from wherever it is most efficient to do so.
- Restraint by countries in restricting food exports to dampen domestic inflation because it worsens the problem for importing countries and dampens incentives for farmers at home to increase future production.
- Creation of safety nets in developing countries to provide food-for-work, cash, or other targeted assistance to those in need.
- Removal of U.S. and European subsidies and mandates for the current generation of biofuels and more money for research into development of the next generation.
- Increased investments in agriculture and rural development in developing countries.

Finally, even if the framework for an agreement for the Doha Round is reached this year, final adoption and implementation would not occur until 2010 at the earliest and would be phased in over several years, mitigating any upward pressure on food prices.

with the GATT/WTO system, U.S. policymakers began to respond more positively when allies and trading partners sought bilateral trade agreements to ensure their access to the U.S. market and to cement their foreign relations with the United States (table 7.1).

These bilateral agreements raise a number of troubling issues from a development perspective. Some countries will inevitably be excluded and those smaller, poorer countries that make less attractive partners can expect to suffer some degree of trade diversion. A continued proliferation of these agreements, not just by the United States but around the world, could also detract attention from and undermine support for the multilateral system.

The developing countries that negotiate preferential agreements also pay a price. And the smaller, poorer, or more dependent on the U.S. market a partner is, the more likely it is that the bargaining process will be tilted in favor of the United States. So why are developing countries keen to secure free trade agreements with the United States? Traditional trade theory says that the smaller partner will reap the largest share of the gains from such agreements because the efficiency and welfare-enhancing restructuring triggered by trade liberalization will have a relatively larger effect in the smaller economy. The smaller partner may also be able to reap economies of scale by gaining additional access in the larger country's market. Many developing economies also hope to use free trade agreements to lock in domestic economic reforms and thereby send a positive signal to potential foreign

Table 7.1. Status of U.S. bilateral free trade agreements, mid-2008

Agreements signed and approved by Congress	Agreements signed but not yet approved by Congress	Negotiations launched but no agreement concluded
Israel (1984)	Colombia	Free Trade Agreement of the Americas
Canada (1988)	Republic of Korea	Malaysia
North America (1993)	Panama	Southern African Customs Union (SACU)
Jordan (2001)		Thailand
Singapore (2003)		United Arab Emirates
Chile (2003)		
Morocco (2004)		
Australia (2004)		
DR-CAFTA (Dominican Republic, Costa Rica, El Salvador, Guatemala, Honduras, Nicaragua; 2005)		
Bahrain (2006)		
Oman (2006)		
Peru (2007)		

Source: Office of the United States Trade Representative website (www.ustr.gov).

investors. Finally, many are eager to cement their access to the U.S. market or to offset the trade-diverting effects when neighbors negotiate free trade agreements (an important dynamic in the Western Hemisphere).

For smaller countries, however, the asymmetry in potential benefits brings with it an asymmetry in bargaining power over specific elements of the agreement. And, to date, U.S. negotiators have taken a traditional mercantilist stance, demanding far-reaching concessions in agricultural, high tech, and services sectors where the United States is competitive, and resisting concessions in its own sensitive import-competing sectors. Countries with significant access through regional preference programs, such as the Dominican Republic, and the Andean and Central American countries, have negotiated free trade agreements essentially to ensure continued access to the U.S. market and have gained little additional access in sensitive agricultural sectors, such as sugar, or textiles and apparel. The costs of this market access "insurance" can be high—developing countries often must agree to special mechanisms to protect foreign investors, to accept rules to protect intellectual property that are stricter than those in the WTO, and to forgo the use of capital controls.

Despite the variety of questionable provisions in these bilateral trade agreements from the perspective of developing countries, the weight of the debate in the United States has been on the provisions on worker rights and environmental protections (box 7.3). Although trade-related labor and environmental standards are important politically in the United States and are useful in ensuring that trade is sustainable and that its benefits are broadly shared, the impact of enforcing these provisions through U.S. trade agreements is likely less than either the proponents or critics believe. Improved implementation of fundamental worker rights in developing countries party to trade agreements is unlikely to have large effects on labor costs and, therefore, would have little effect on trade flows or jobs and wages in the United States. At the same time, there is substantial evidence suggesting that using trade sanctions to enforce core labor standards in other countries is not effective. Although sanctions are appropriate for egregious violations of fundamental worker rights that are related to trade, technical and financial assistance to governments that have the will, but lack the capacity, to effectively enforce labor standards is more likely to promote sustainable improvements.[11]

On May 10, 2007, Democratic and Republican congressional leaders and representatives of the Bush administration, led by U.S. Trade Representative Susan Schwab and Treasury Secretary Henry Paulson, reached an agreement that addresses some of the weaknesses in U.S. bilateral trade agreements. The agreement retains the sanctions-focused approach to enforcing international labor standards in free trade agreements but makes these provisions

Box 7.3. The politics of U.S. free trade agreements

After two relatively uncontroversial free trade agreements, with Canada and Israel in the 1980s, President George H. W. Bush negotiated the North American Free Trade Agreement (NAFTA) involving Mexico. It was the first time the United States had negotiated with a country that had much lower wages and weak labor and environmental standards. Completed at the end of the first President Bush's term, newly elected Democratic President William Clinton had to submit NAFTA to Congress for ratification. Under intense pressure from key constituencies to renegotiate or reject the deal, Clinton opted for supplemental "side agreements" to protect worker rights and the environment. A large majority of Republicans ultimately voted in favor while a majority of Democrats voted against, and the agreement passed by roughly 30 votes. Just weeks after seeing NAFTA ratified, the multilateral Uruguay Round was completed and Congress approved the agreement a year later by a 142-vote margin, with majorities of both parties voting in favor.

The NAFTA compromise on labor and the environment satisfied no one, however. Proponents of standards wanted them to be stronger than what was agreed with Mexico and to be in the core of the agreement, rather than in side agreements. The business community and most Republicans opposed linking trade to social issues, arguing that increased trade contributes to growth, which in turn leads to improved labor and environmental conditions. After the Republicans captured the Congress in the 1994, these partisan disagreements blocked renewal of "fast-track" trade authority, which commits the Congress to vote on trade agreements expeditiously and without amendment. Without the fast track, trade partners are usually reluctant to negotiate for fear that Congress will make changes that unravel carefully negotiated bargains. Trade policy was largely stymied for the rest of Clinton's term.

The debate over whether and how to include labor (and environmental) standards in trade agreements was managed but not resolved when Congress finally approved fast-track legislation (now called trade promotion authority) for the new Republican president, George W. Bush, in 2002. But the bill passed by just three votes and with only twenty-five Democrats voting in favor. Subsequent votes on free trade agreements varied widely, depending largely on the status of worker rights in the trading partner country. Agreements with high-wage partners Australia and Singapore, and with Chile, Morocco, and Bahrain, which had passed significant labor law reforms before or during free trade agreement negotiations, were passed by an average margin of 178 votes with 100 Democrats voting in favor (on average). The agreement with Central America and the Dominican Republic was the most controversial and passed by only two votes in the House with just fifteen Democrats voting in favor.

When the Democrats won control of Congress in the 2006 midterm elections, the political dynamic changed sharply. The Bush administration had completed free trade agreement negotiations with Colombia and Peru and was in the midst of negotiations

(continued)

Box 7.3. The politics of U.S. free trade agreements (continued)

with Panama and the Republic of Korea. The new Democratic leadership made it clear that changes would have to be made in several areas, including labor and the environment, before the agreements could be brought up for a vote. The agreement reached on May 10, 2007, between the Bush administration and congressional leaders strengthened the provisions on labor and environmental standards and made other changes sufficient to contribute to approval of the free trade agreement with Peru at the end of 2007. As of early 2008, a nontrade controversy over a political leader in Panama was holding up that agreement; the free trade agreement with Colombia was in limbo because of concerns about murders of union leaders; and the free trade agreement with the Republic of Korea seemed furthest from passage because of old-fashioned concerns over U.S. access to the auto and beef markets.

Source: Hufbauer and Schott 2005; Elliott 2000; Destler and Balint 1999; Destler 2005, 2007; Elliott and Freeman 2003.

more consistent with international norms and revises some poorly crafted language that might have encouraged signatories to lower their labor (or environmental) standards to ensure compliance with the trade agreement. Importantly, the agreement also loosens the provisions that previously required even low-income countries to adopt laws protecting intellectual property, including patents on drugs, that were stronger than what had been agreed in the WTO.[12] But the May 10, 2007, agreement does not address the prohibition on capital controls, nor does it loosen the restrictions on clothing and agriculture.

Although a renewed emphasis on multilateral agreements would be desirable, it is unlikely that the bilateral and regional trade genie can be put back in the bottle and the May 10, 2007, agreement does not go far enough in fixing the problems with U.S. free trade agreements. The problem of exclusion and the potential for trade diversion are inherent in preferential trade agreements, but they can be mitigated through the agenda, described above, of expanding preferences for poorer countries and ensuring that the multilateral system remains strong and effective. The new president should also amend existing agreements to ensure they conform to the May 10, 2007, template, especially for intellectual property, and also address other provisions that could undermine development in poorer partner countries.

Domestic challenges to an open U.S. trade policy

Opening the U.S. market to the poorest countries should be politically feasible because they are too small in trade terms to be threatening and their development too important to U.S. interests to ignore. Allowing poor countries a fair shot at exporting their goods is also the right thing to do. Unfortunately, U.S. leadership in maintaining an open, rules-based trading system is being increasingly challenged at home. The U.S. economy is far more exposed to global economic forces than earlier in the post–World War II period, and an increasing share of its trade is with low-wage countries. Although the exact causes are hotly debated, these trends are correlated with increasing income inequality and growing anxiety about average Americans' living standards, and globalization is an easy scapegoat.

Over the post-war period, the effective tax on imports dropped sharply, as duties collected fell from nearly 60 percent of dutiable imports in 1932 (20 percent of all imports) to just 4.6 percent in 2005 (1.4 percent of total imports). Two-thirds of that drop came as a result of Secretary of State Cordell Hull's efforts to unwind the 1930 Smoot-Hawley tariffs through negotiated reductions under the Reciprocal Trade Agreements Act of 1934. The GATT cut remaining tariffs by another 75 percent after it was created in 1948 (figure 7.3) and by 2005 70 percent of U.S. imports paid no duty at all.[13] At the same time, the international exposure of the U.S. economy nearly tripled, with total trade in goods and services rising from under 10 percent of gross national product in 1960 to nearly 30 percent in 2005 (figure 7.4).

By one estimate, increased integration in the global economy (which is the result of both technological and policy changes) has raised U.S. incomes by 10 percent, roughly $1 trillion in today's economy.[14] This gain is derived both from lower prices on a variety of products (from clothing to computers and other electronics) and from the pressure on firms to improve productivity, which contributed to above-average growth with low inflation in the 1990s.

In recent decades, however, this policy-induced opening has also been associated in the public mind with other economic trends that have created anxiety. Though the causal relationships are more complex than is generally assumed, the U.S. trade balance turned sharply negative in the 1980s and, after a brief recovery in the latter part of that decade, plunged again in the late 1990s (figure 7.5). Over roughly the same period, the share of U.S. imports (excluding those from major oil exporters) that originated in other rich countries dropped from 60–70 percent in the mid-1980s to under 50 percent in 2006. China's import share in the U.S. market quadrupled over that same period, while Mexico's doubled (figure 7.6).

Coincident with these trends, manufacturing employment fell from a 1979 peak of 19 million workers—26 percent of nonagricultural private sector employment—to 14 million workers and 13 percent of private employment. But manufacturing value added increased more than four-fold over the same period, underscoring the contribution of productivity growth to these trends.

Figure 7.3. Duties collected as a share of dutiable imports and total imports

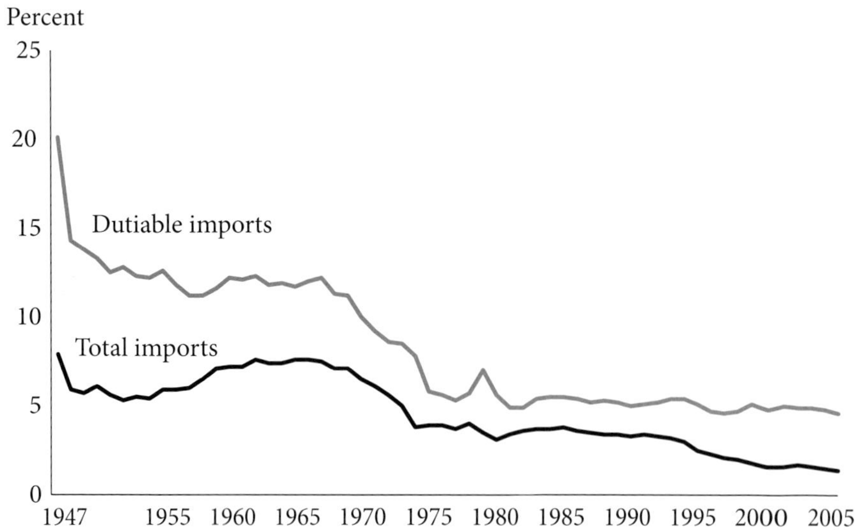

Source: U.S. International Trade Commission 2006.

Figure 7.4. U.S. trade in goods and services as a share of GDP

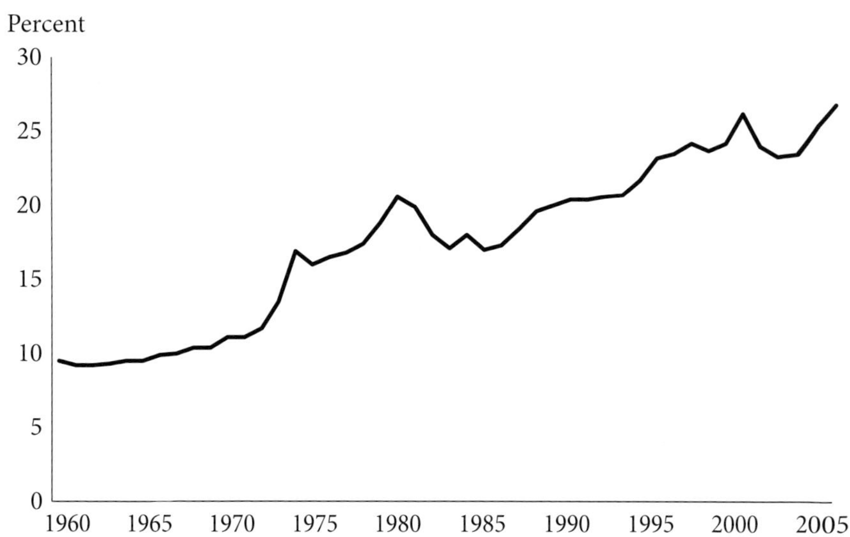

Source: White House 2008.

Figure 7.5. U.S. trade balance as a share of GDP

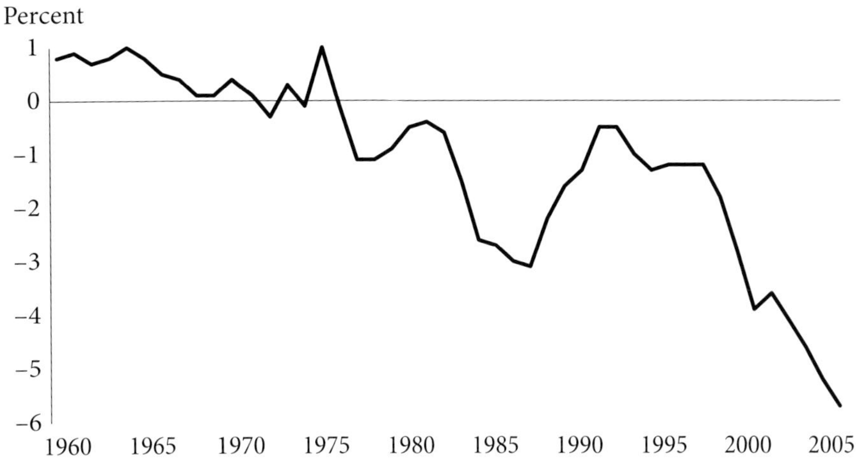

Source: IMF 2007.

Figure 7.6. U.S. imports, by source

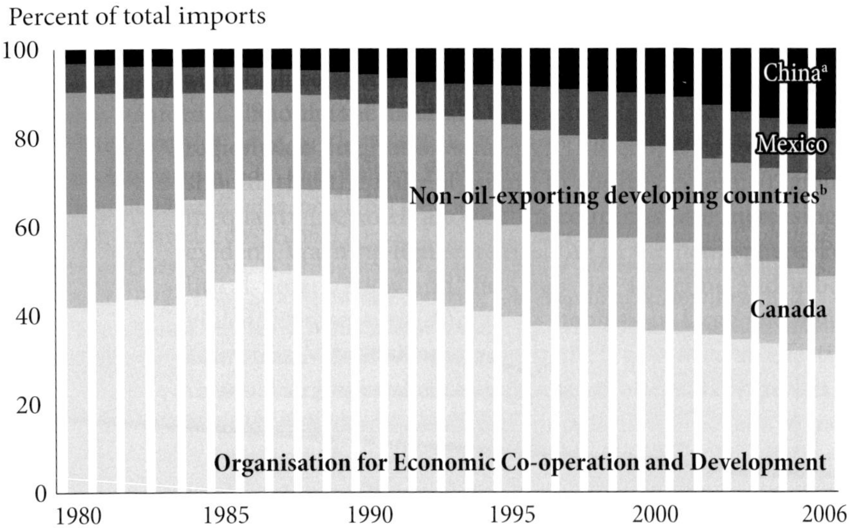

Note: Excludes imports from Organization of the Petroleum Exporting Countries, except Indonesia, which is included in non-oil-exporting countries.

a. Includes Hong Kong and Macao.

b. Includes all developing countries except China, Czech Republic, Hungary, Republic of Korea, and Mexico.

Source: IMF 2007.

Even with improved productivity, however, average weekly earnings in the private sector, in 1982 dollars, fell from $332 in 1973 to $276 in 2005.[15] The top 20 percent of households did well over this period, and the top 5 percent extremely well, but the bottom 20 percent of households fared less well (figure 7.7).

Robert Lawrence finds that little of the increase in inequality can be attributed to trade.[16] Nevertheless, these trends have contributed to increasing anxiety on the part of many Americans and their congressional representatives about the effects of increasing trade, and globalization more broadly, on jobs, wages, and increasing inequality in the United States. While an overvalued dollar, relatively stronger U.S. growth, and, recently, oil prices have been principal factors explaining the rapid growth in imports and the trade deficits in both the 1980s and the early 2000s, trade policy has been a more tangible and easier target for the concerns.

Figure 7.7. U.S. inequality

Ratio of income received by the richest 20 percent of households to income received by the poorest 20 percent

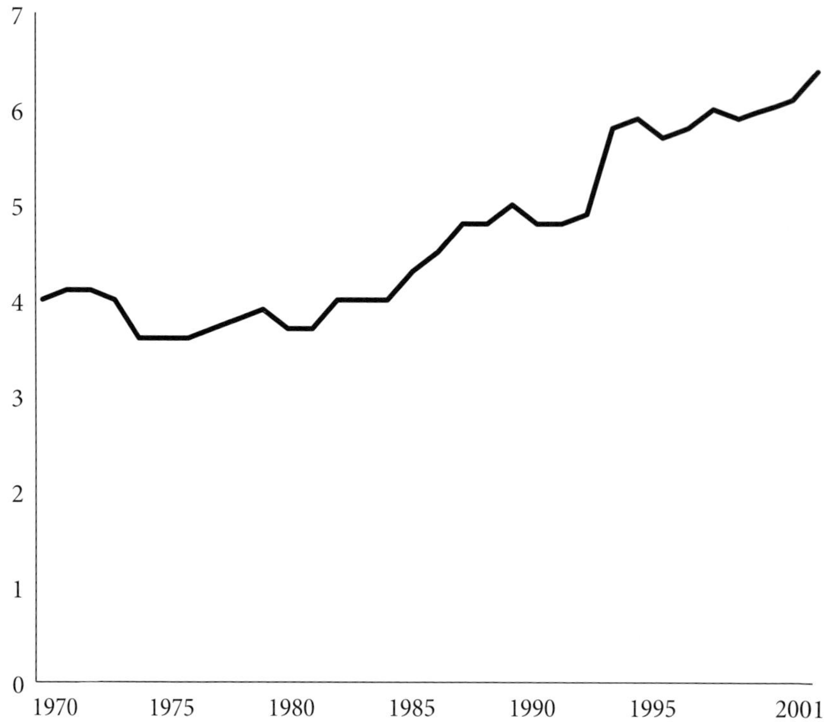

Source: U.S. Department of Commerce 2002.

Interestingly, the even sharper plunge in the trade balance since 1999 (see figure 7.5) has thus far attracted a less severe and more diffuse response, including increased unwillingness to move forward on trade, but little of the traditional protectionist backlash that was seen in the 1980s. A partial explanation for the difference is that trade, foreign investment, and other capital flows are now such an important part of the U.S. economy that most recognize that it would simply be too costly to engage in old-fashioned protectionism. Indeed, careful analysis of public opinion polls over a number of years generally shows that Americans understand the benefits of trade, in terms of lower prices and greater variety, but that they weigh the costs more heavily.[17] Until those costs are addressed seriously, views on trade will remain ambivalent at best.

A trade policy for U.S. and global prosperity

The United States cannot lead the world toward greater peace and prosperity if it turns its back on globalization. A renewed commitment to multilateralism, along with improved preferential access for the poorest, will help to make U.S. trade and development policy consistent and coherent. The benefits for the poorer developing countries from a successful conclusion to the Doha Round are not so much the direct economic effects as the longer-run political and systemic effects.[18] Multilateral trade negotiations are also less controversial politically than deeper and more extensive bilateral agreements with low-wage partners. But a liberal trade policy cannot regain momentum if policymakers do not address the concerns that a rapidly changing economy, stimulated by globalization, generates in so many citizens.

The next president can put the United States on the right path with a package that includes the following:

- Preferential market access for the poorest that is treated as development policy rather than trade policy.
- A renewed commitment to the WTO and multilateralism.
- Domestic policies that equip workers to take advantage of globalization's opportunities, as well as a stronger safety net to cushion the pain of dislocation.

Some have suggested there is a conflict between the first two parts of the package. U.S. negotiators and exporters are frustrated that some developing countries, including the least-developed countries that are not being asked to undertake any liberalization commitments, are blocking progress in the Doha Round because multilateral tariff liberalization would erode the advantage that they get from preferential access. These developing countries are correct that preference erosion would be one effect of a successful round, but analysis shows that it would affect a relatively small number of countries and products and that the export revenue losses could be compensated for by donors at relatively low cost. These countries may be slowing the negotiations down, but they are ultimately unlikely to block an agreement. The real problem is getting the big players—Brazil, China, and India—to contribute more to the negotiations.

Moreover, developing countries that expect to gain little from the round in the short run, and who fear preference erosion, also have reasons to contribute to a successful conclusion. First, a multilateral agreement is the only way that agricultural export subsidies and domestic support will come under the discipline of international rules, which remains important to provide incentives for increased production in developing countries. Second, a multilateral round is the most effective way to address barriers among developing countries, which is increasingly important as trade between developing countries grows. Finally, the smallest and poorest countries gain the most from having a trade system based on rules rather than size and power.

The details of each part of the package depend on what happens between the time this is written and when the new president is inaugurated. The key elements are described here.

Preferential market access for the poorest as development, not trade, policy

The U.S. Generalized System of Preferences, which is available for most developing countries (including Brazil and India, but excluding China) is likely to remain riddled with exceptions because of opposition to lower tariffs from domestic import-competing sectors; that is, it will continue to be shaped primarily from a trade policy perspective. But the least-developed countries are in desperate need of opportunities and assistance to help them grow and reduce poverty. Moreover, they account for only 1 percent of total U.S. imports and less than 10 percent of clothing imports and pose little threat to U.S. business. It is in the self-interest of the United States to help these countries, including by providing the broadest possible market access and treating preferences as development, rather than trade, policy.

While thirty-four of the U.N.-designated least-developed countries are in Sub-Saharan Africa and receive nearly complete access under the African Growth and Opportunity Act (as does Haiti under the HOPE Act), there are fourteen least-developed countries that receive only Generalized System of Preferences benefits, and even the African Growth and Opportunity Act imposes tight restrictions on sugar, dairy, tobacco, and peanuts.[19] The development potential of U.S. trade preferences is also undermined because they have to be renewed every few years, which creates uncertainty, increases risk, and discourages investment. Preference programs also have restrictive rules of origin and are complicated and difficult to use.

Reform of these programs to maximize their development potential should include three key elements:

- Simplifying the various programs by bringing the Generalized System of Preferences and the regional programs together under a single umbrella with common eligibility conditions and less restrictive rules of origin.
- Making the consolidated program permanent (though individual countries would continue to graduate from the program as they develop).
- Providing full duty-free, quota-free market access for all least-developed and Sub-Saharan African countries (except those excluded for foreign policy or other reasons, such as Burma).

In addition, to address concerns that the current benefits received by countries eligible for preferential access under the African Growth and Opportunity Act would be eroded by extending duty-free, quota-free treatment to other least-developed countries, especially Bangladesh and Cambodia, African low-income countries should be eligible for less restrictive rules of origin and should receive targeted aid to address supply-side challenges that undermine export competitiveness.

Reviving the WTO

If the Doha Round goes back into hibernation later this year (as many expect), the new president should act quickly to get things moving again. The goal should be to conclude the round by early 2010, with implementation starting in 2011. A return to a traditional negotiating agenda, based on the papers put forward by the chairs of the Agricultural and Non-agricultural Market Access negotiating committees, Crawford Falconer and Don Stephenson, respectively, provides a reasonable basis for an agreement with the following benefits:

- Elimination of the European Union's agricultural export subsidies; lower levels of the most trade-distorting subsidies that the U.S. government can provide to farmers when prices drop.
- A cut in agricultural tariffs in rich countries of roughly 50 percent, albeit with higher levels remaining on sensitive products.
- A cap on rich-country tariff peaks on manufactured products, including on labor-intensive goods, below 10 percent.
- Reduced uncertainty for exporters through caps on most developing country tariffs at around 20 percent; modest cuts in actual applied tariffs in many cases.

Among other benefits, a successful negotiation could also constrain the fishing subsidies that are contributing to crashing stocks around the world, contribute to climate change and pollution abatement through a sectoral agreement to eliminate barriers to imports of environmental technologies, and encourage developing countries to take steps to facilitate trade through improved customs procedures and reduced documentation requirements.

Developing countries would also benefit from, and should have an interest in, opening their markets to top-quality financial, communications, and transportation services, because they are essential to development of a modern economy. But services have not been a good fit for the traditional reciprocal bargaining structure of the WTO, and relatively little is expected from the Doha Round in this area. Bernard Hoekman and colleagues identify the following obstacles to progress[20]:

- The data on barriers to trade in services are sparse, and for that reason the potential costs and benefits of liberalization are uncertain and difficult to measure.
- Trade in services is more complex than trade in goods, often involving foreign investment and movement of people, and services are more heavily regulated in most countries than goods.
- Many developing countries either have few services exports or the ones they have (for example, tourism or call centers) face few barriers.

Hoekman and other experts have therefore concluded that the best that is likely to be feasible in the WTO context is to lock in current levels of openness. A parallel track should then be created to provide technical and financial assistance to help developing countries with regulatory and other reforms that would make them more comfortable in opening up to foreign service providers in the future, perhaps unilaterally.

Currently, the political will does not appear to exist in any of the major countries—developed or developing—to conclude a more ambitious Doha Round, and almost all of the statistical models suggest that the immediate economic benefits from a feasible bargain will be relatively small, especially if little is done on services. Expeditious conclusion of the round is nevertheless worthwhile and important, especially for smaller, poorer countries. In addition to the modest but real gains outlined above, conclusion of the round would help maintain the credibility of the rules-based system by signaling that major players remain committed to it. Therefore, it would be better for least-developed countries to pressure their more advanced developing-country "allies" to make concessions that would allow the round to come to a successful conclusion than to join them in blocking the round because they are concerned about relatively small and short-term losses due to preference erosion.

Bolstering support for trade through domestic reform

If a foundation is to be laid for a more ambitious WTO round in the future, the political environment in the United States and other key countries will have to change. Although there is much discussion these days about the need for "aid for trade" to help developing countries with infrastructure, customs reform, and other capacity-building needs, the United States also needs to devote significant resources to rebuild the social infrastructure necessary to support open trade here at home. The details must be left to others more knowledgeable about these issues, but the broad outlines of the package are well known.

The safety net for dislocated workers in the United States is small relative to other countries, and the size of the holes in it are growing. Total funding for trade adjustment assistance programs is only around $1 billion a year, and it goes to only around 150,000 people a year, while an even smaller number of workers benefit from recent innovations in the program, notably the tax credit to maintain health insurance and wage insurance to partially offset lower wages in a new job.[21] These figures are in striking contrast to the more than $10 billion a year, on average, that the U.S. Department of Agriculture paid out in farm subsidies in 2003–05, most going to large operations with household incomes above the national average.[22] Over time, trade adjustment assistance programs that work well should be extended to workers dislocated for any reason, not just trade. The primary objection is cost, but careful estimates show that it would not be that high, especially relative to the estimated gains from globalization. Coverage of the unemployment insurance system has also dropped sharply, as has the support that it provides, and it is past time to modernize the system to reflect today's economy.[23]

It will take longer to develop and implement the broader domestic policy improvements that are needed, but the work should begin in the first year of the new president's term. Globalization and rapid technological change demand greater flexibility on the part of firms and workers, which makes the current reliance on employer-based health insurance and pensions increasingly obsolete. Employers are already cutting back on these benefits, and fear of losing insurance and pensions, as well as income, are major sources of anxiety related to job loss. Health care is also a major issue in the campaign, and addressing that problem is a logical place to begin. Another result of the combination of globalization and technological change is that it puts a premium on skills, meaning that better preparation and training of workers, from K–12, through college and beyond, is essential.[24]

Tax policy can also play an important role in addressing inequality. Ed Gresser reminds us that President Woodrow Wilson wanted to move away from trade taxes and toward income and estate taxes, in part, to create a more progressive system for funding the federal government. Tariffs in Wilson's day contributed about half of government revenue, whereas they are trivial today. But then as now, import duties tended to weigh more heavily on basic items consumed disproportionately by the poor. Gresser quotes Benton McMillin, ambassador to Peru and a former representative from Tennessee, as noting, "Heretofore we have taxed want instead of wealth."[25]

Conclusion

Until Americans feel that they have the tools to cope with globalization, trade policy will remain on shaky ground. The domestic agenda will likely take several years to accomplish, and although the work should begin immediately in the next president's first term, other steps should also be taken to get trade policy moving in the right direction. The Generalized System of Preferences and preferences for the Caribbean and Andean regions expire this year and are typically extended for a few years at a time. If that happens again this year, the new president should propose an overhaul of all U.S. preference programs that would make them permanent, simplify the rules of origin, and expand product coverage, including by providing full duty-free, quota-free access for exports from the least-developed countries and Sub-Saharan Africa. This should be accompanied by broadly defined aid for trade, including for infrastructure, to ensure that poor countries are able to take advantage of market access opportunities. The Doha Round, if not already done, should also be concluded as quickly as possible. Together, these policies would help to sustain U.S. prosperity and to spread it more widely in the poorest parts of the world.

Notes

1. Approval of any agreement would require new "trade promotion authority" legislation, which allows the president to negotiate trade agreements that the Congress commits to vote on expeditiously and without amendment. Because specific scenarios for how that might be achieved depend on political alignments coming out of the election, it is not addressed here.
2. There are fifty UN-designated least-developed countries with per capita incomes below $750 and with other features of vulnerability, such as small size or volatile exports (www.un.org/special-rep/ohrlls/ldc/ldc%20criteria.htm). Not all are currently eligible for U.S. preferences because of their failure to meet other eligibility criteria, for example human rights and democracy conditions in Burma.
3. An early assessment of the African Growth and Opportunity Act and recommendations for how to strengthen its development potential may be found in Cline 2003; see also Elliott 2007c.

4. The U.S. Trade Representative asked the U.S. International Trade Commission to investigate the potential effects of granting duty-free, quota-free access to least-developed countries, but the report has not been published for "national security" reasons; Bouët, Mevel, and Orden (2007) estimate that, in the context of a realistic Doha agreement, granting duty-free, quota-free access on 100 percent of products would reduce U.S. production of either textiles or apparel by less than 1 percent, relative to the scenario where 3 percent are excluded.
5. The public comment filed in March 2007 by the Center for Global Development and several other nongovernmental organizations is available on the center's Web site (www.cgdev.org/doc/commentary/Market_Access.pdf). See also HELP Commission 2007 and Armitage and Nye 2007.
6. On the need for assistance to confront supply-side constraints to trade in Africa, including energy, roads, and other infrastructure, see chapter 3 by Ramachandran; Buys, Deichmann, and Wheeler 2006; and the address by Tanzanian President Jakaya Mrisho Kikwete at the Center for Global Development in December 2007 (www.cgdev.org/doc/events/12.14.07/President_Kikwete_Transcript_12.14.07.pdf).
7. There are two exceptions to this rule. Article XXIV of the original GATT allows countries to preferentially cut tariffs for partners in a customs union or a trade agreement that covers "substantially all trade." In the 1970s, GATT members also agreed that richer countries could provide better than most-favored-nation access for developing countries under the Generalized System of Preferences.
8. Ostry 2005, p. 3.
9. On agriculture, see Elliott 2006 and 2007a; on the elimination of the Multi-Fiber Arrangement managing textile and apparel trade, see Bhattacharya and Elliott 2005; and on intellectual property, see chapter 8 by Fink and Elliott.
10. Finger 2007.
11. Elliott and Freeman (2003) analyze these issues in detail; see also Elliott 2007b.
12. See Destler 2007 on the May 10 agreement and chapter 8 by Fink and Elliott on the TRIPS-plus provisions in free trade agreements.
13. The tariff data are from the U.S. International Trade Commission, Statistical Services Division, Office of Investigations, March 2006 (www.usitc.gov). See also Destler 2005. This figure differs slightly from the figure cited above because it is from a different source.
14. Bradford, Grieco, and Hufbauer 2005.
15. White House 2007.
16. Lawrence 2008.
17. Scheve and Slaughter 2001.
18. On the debate over the size and distribution of the potential benefits from trade liberalization, see Bouët 2006 for a detailed analysis of the various models and estimates, and Elliott 2005 for a brief summary of the key issues.

19. This proposal would not apply to countries, such as Burma, that are subject to sanctions for foreign policy reasons.
20. See Hoekman and Mattoo 2007; Hoekman, Mattoo, and Sapir 2007.
21. The trade adjustment assistance figures are from the U.S. Department of Labor, Employment and Training Administration Web site (www.doleta.gov/); see also Rosen 2006.
22. See the farm subsidies database compiled by the Environmental Working Group (www.ewg.org/featured/8). Steven Pearlstein captured the disparity well in commenting on the explanation of a Republican member of the House Agriculture Committee who voted for a farm bill that would further increase subsidies while voting against an expansion of the Trade Adjustment Assistance program: "Let me get this straight: A $20 billion-a-year farm bill that provides income guarantees of as much as $1 million a year every year to 3 million farmers is an affordable and efficient use of taxpayer money, while it is 'runaway spending' if the government spends $1.6 billion a year to provide as much as $26,000 in income support to any of 40 million workers who might lose their jobs because of trade and outsourcing" (Pearlstein 2007).
23. Kletzer and Rosen 2005 and 2006.
24. Mann 2006.
25. Gresser 2007, p. 66.

References

Armitage, Richard L., and Joseph S. Nye, Jr. 2007. *A Smarter, More Secure America: Report of the CSIS Commission on Smart Power*. November. Washington, D.C.: Center for Strategic and International Studies.

Bhattacharya, Debapriya, and Kimberly Elliott. 2005. "Adjusting to the MFA Phase-out: Policy Priorities." CGD Brief. Center for Global Development, Washington, D.C.

Bouët, Antoine. 2006. "What Can the Poor Expect from Trade Liberalization? Opening the 'Black Box' of Trade Modeling." MITD Discussion Paper 93. Markets, Trade, and Institutions Division, International Food Policy Research Institute, Washington, D.C.

Bouët, Antoine, Simon Mevel, and David Orden. 2007. "Missed Opportunities? Understanding the Effective and Potential Consequences of a Doha Agreement on Developing Countries." Unpublished.

Bradford, Scott, Paul L. E. Grieco, and Gary Clyde Hufbauer. 2005. "The Payoff to America from Global Integration." In C. Fred Bergsten, ed., *The United States and the World Economy: Foreign Economic Policy for the Next Decade*. Washington, D.C.: Peterson Institute for International Economics.

Buys, Piet, Uwe Deichmann, and David Wheeler. 2006. "Road Network Upgrading and Overland Trade Expansion in Sub-Saharan Africa." Policy Research Working Paper 4097. World Bank, Washington, D.C.

CGD (Center for Global Development). 2007. Commitment to Development Index. [www.cgdev.org/section/initiatives/_active/cdi/].

Cline, William R. 2003. "Trading Up: Strengthening AGOA's Development Potential." CGD Brief 2 (3) (June). Center for Global Development, Washington, D.C.

Destler, I. M. 2005. *American Trade Politics*. Washington, D.C.: Peterson Institute for International Economics.

———. 2007. "American Trade Politics in 2007: Building Bipartisan Compromise." IIE Policy Brief. Peterson Institute for International Economics, Washington, D.C.

Destler, I. M., and Peter J. Balint. 1999. *The New Politics of American Trade: Trade, Labor, and the Environment*. Washington, D. C.: Peterson Institute for International Economics.

Elliott, Kimberly Ann. 2000. "(Mis)Managing Diversity: Worker Rights and US Trade Policy" *International Negotiation* 5:97–127.

———. 2005. "Looking for the Devil in the Doha Agricultural Negotiations." CGD Brief. Center for Global Development, Washington, D.C.

———. 2006. *Delivering on Doha: Farm Trade and the Poor*. Washington, D.C.: Center for Global Development and Peterson Institute for International Economics.

———. 2007a. "Agriculture and the Doha Round." CGD/IIE Brief. Center for Global Development, Washington, D.C.

———. 2007b. "A Better Way Forward on Trade and Labor Standards." CGD Notes. March. Center for Global Development, Washington, D.C.

———. 2007c. "Trade Policy for Development: Reforming U.S. Trade Preferences." CGD Brief. Center for Global Development, Washington, D.C.

Elliott, Kimberly Ann, and Richard B. Freeman. 2003. *Can Labor Standards Improve under Globalization?* Washington, D.C.: Peterson Institute for International Economics.

Finger, Michael J. 2007. "Developing Countries in the WTO System." Paper prepared for Cordell Hull Institute, Roundtable on Doha Round Hiatus and Lessons for Developing Countries. October 1.Washington, D.C.

Gresser, Edward. 2007. *Freedom from Want: American Liberalism and the Global Economy*. Brooklyn, N.Y.: Soft Skull Press.

HELP Commission. 2007. *Beyond Assistance: The HELP Commission Report on Foreign Assistance Reform*. December. Washington, D.C.: U.S. Commission on Helping to Enhance the Livelihood of People around the Globe.

Hoekman, Bernard, and Aaditya Mattoo. 2007. "Regulatory Cooperation, Aid for Trade and the GATS." *Pacific Economic Review* 12(4): 399–418.

Hoekman, Bernard, Aaditya Mattoo, and Andre Sapir. 2007. "The Political Economy of Services Trade Liberalization: A Case for International Regulatory Cooperation?" *Oxford Review of Economic Policy* 23(3): 367–91.

Hufbauer, Gary Clyde, and Jeffrey J. Schott. 2005. *NAFTA Revisited: Achievements and Challenges*. Washington, D.C.: Peterson Institute for International Economics.

IMF (International Monetary Fund). 2007. *Direction of Trade Statistics*. Washington, D.C.

Kletzer, Lori G., and Howard Rosen. 2005. "Easing the Adjustment Burden on US Workers." In C. Fred Bergsten, ed., *The United States and the World Economy: Foreign Economic Policy for the Next Decade*. Washington, D.C.: Peterson Institute for International Economics.

———. 2006. "Reforming Unemployment Insurance for a Twenty-First Century Workforce." Hamilton Project Discussion Paper. September. Brookings Institution, Washington, D.C.

Lawrence, Robert Z. 2008. *Blue Collar Blues: Is Trade to Blame for Rising US Income Inequality?* Policy Analyses in International Economics 85. January. Washington, D.C.: Peterson Institute for International Economics.

Mann, Catherine L. 2005. "Offshore Outsourcing and the Globalization of US Services: Why Now, How Important, and What Policy Implications." In C. Fred Bergsten, ed., *The United States and the World Economy: Foreign Economic Policy for the Next Decade*. Washington, D.C.: Peterson Institute for International Economics.

Ostry, Sylvia. 2005. "The Multilateral Agenda: Moving Trade Negotiations Forward." MCIS Briefings. November. Munk Centre for International Studies at Trinity College, University of Toronto.

Pearlstein, Steven. 2007. "Here Passing the Plate, There Passing the Buck." November 21, p. D1. *Washington Post*.

Rosen, Howard. 2006. "Trade Adjustment Assistance: The More We Change the More It Stays the Same." In Michael Mussa, ed., *C. Fred Bergsten and the World Economy*. Washington, D.C.: Peterson Institute for International Economics.

Scheve, Kenneth, and Matthew Slaughter. 2001. *Globalization and the Perceptions of American Workers*. Washington, D.C.: Peterson Institute for International Economics.

U.S. Department of Commerce. 2002. "Historical Income Tables: Income Inequality." From the current Population Survey, Annual Demographic Supplement. Bureau of the Census, Washington, D.C.

U.S. International Trade Commission. 2006. "Value of U.S. Imports for consumption, Duties Collected, and Ratio of Duties to Values, 1891–2005." Statistical Services Division, Office of Investigations, Washington, D.C.

White House. 2007. *Economic Report of the President: 2007 Report Spreadsheet Tables*. Tables B-12, B-46, and B-47. [www.gpoaccess.gov/eop/download.html].

———. 2008. *Economic Report of the President: 2008 Report Spreadsheet Tables*. Tables B-1 and B-24. [www.gpoaccess.gov/eop/tables08.html].

8 Tripping over Health: U.S. Policy on Patents and Drug Access in Developing Countries

Carsten Fink and Kimberly Ann Elliott

U.S. technological prowess can play an important role in promoting global development, while advancing U.S. interests and prosperity. Although achieving these goals depends on continued strong public support for innovation, including protection for intellectual property (IP), it also requires that the fruits of innovation be broadly shared. But often there is a tension between protecting IP and diffusion, and nowhere is this more evident than in pharmaceutical products. Patent protection provides a period of market exclusivity that permits firms to raise pharmaceutical prices above competitive levels and thus recoup their research costs, creating incentives for them to innovate. At the same time, high prices reduce access by putting products beyond the means of many customers, and the small size of markets in poor countries means that patents alone are not sufficient to spark innovation for diseases, such as malaria, that affect only these countries.

Without creative public policy, it is clear that markets alone will not suffice to achieve broad diffusion. But U.S. policies in this area have been neither consistent nor coherent. For over two decades, they have tilted heavily in the direction of narrow commercial interests at the expense

---

Carsten Fink is a visiting senior fellow at the Groupe d'Économie Mondiale at Sciences Po, and Kim Elliott is a senior fellow, jointly, at the Center for Global Development (CGD) and the Peterson Institute for International Economics. This chapter draws heavily on Fink (2008). The authors thank Nancy Birdsall, Christoph Spennemann, Jayashree Watal, Keith Maskus, and participants in a CGD staff lunch for useful comments.

of the social interest in broad diffusion.[1] Although strong IP protection has played an important role in supporting the technological innovations central to American prosperity, IP protection can also be too strong, stifling innovation and impeding socially desirable levels of access.[2]

Beginning in the 1980s, U.S. negotiators demanded that trade agreements include universal rules for IP protection. The most significant result was the Agreement on Trade-Related Intellectual Property Rights (TRIPS) at the World Trade Organization (WTO), which requires members, regardless of their level of development, to adopt and enforce laws providing minimum levels of protection to all forms of intellectual property. TRIPS attracted particular opprobrium over its provisions requiring developing countries to adopt patent protection for pharmaceutical products, reducing competition from generics and thereby raising drug costs. Although TRIPS includes provisions designed to mitigate potential threats to public health, questions remain about their efficacy. Bilateral agreements, negotiated with even greater U.S. leverage, have required, until recently, that even low-income trading partners adopt IP protections comparable to those in the United States and with few of the flexibilities in TRIPS.

U.S. policy is increasingly facing pressure to change from a variety of key players: Microsoft, Apple, and other high-tech companies are lobbying for changes in U.S. patent laws; American producers of generic pharmaceuticals want to expand their market share at home and abroad; and nongovernmental organizations are concerned about health problems in developing countries and want greater access to life-saving medicines for the poor. This pressure appears to be having an effect: on May 10, 2007, the Democratic leadership in the House of Representatives and the Bush administration signed an agreement that eased some of the "TRIPS-plus" provisions in pending and future bilateral trade agreements that make it difficult for developing countries to override pharmaceutical patents in the interest of public health.

The next U.S. president can do much more. He or she should come down clearly in favor of a new policy that better balances public health needs in developing countries and private incentives for innovation. U.S. ingenuity should be used to create, expand, and strengthen mechanisms that spur as well as disseminate innovations to address public health problems in developing countries. Specifically, the next president should

- Make clear through words and deeds that the United States supports the right of developing countries to use the flexibility provided in TRIPS to protect public health.
- Provide technical, logistical, and financial assistance to ensure that low-income countries can effectively use the flexibility provided by TRIPS, including through legal reforms, demand pooling, and bulk purchasing.

- Respect the right of middle-income countries to use compulsory licensing, and launch an international dialogue on burden sharing in the financing of pharmaceutical research and development.

Evolving rules: a short history of TRIPS and U.S. free trade agreements

Rules governing IP rights for pharmaceutical products are now embedded in the WTO's TRIPS Agreement and in numerous bilateral trade agreements. At their core, these rules determine whether drugs are supplied under temporary monopoly or in a competitive market that includes generic producers. This section summarizes evolving global IP regimes for pharmaceutical products, focusing on their effect on developing countries. There are three main points:

- Although TRIPS has limited the supply of certain pharmaceutical products in developing countries, developing-country governments have considerable legal flexibility to implement rules that can help to mitigate this negative impact.
- Because TRIPS rules on pharmaceutical patents were not fully phased in for developing countries, other than the least-developed, until 2005, the full impact of the new rules will materialize only over the next decade.
- IP provisions in U.S. bilateral free trade agreements have contained little flexibility and, if enforced, could have severe consequences in poor countries. Some of the worst provisions were rolled back in May 2007, but the previous rules could still be harmful to countries, such as Honduras and Nicaragua, that signed agreements before the changes were made.

The TRIPS Agreement

An agreement setting universal standards for the protection of IP (along with new rules on services trade and a narrow agreement on trade-related investment measures) was the price that U.S. and other rich-country negotiators demanded of developing countries for agreeing to eliminate global textile and apparel quotas and reduce barriers to agricultural trade in the Uruguay Round of trade negotiations.[3] The resulting TRIPS Agreement covers copyright and trademarks, but the most controversial provision is the obligation requiring all WTO members to eventually provide twenty years of patent protection for inventions in all fields. In other words, countries could no longer exclude pharmaceutical products from eligibility for patent protection—as had been the practice in a number of large developing countries such as Argentina, Brazil, and India.

Although all WTO members have to accept the same minimum standards, TRIPS provides substantial flexibility to countries in implementing them. For example, countries that did not provide for patents on drugs as of January 1, 1995, when TRIPS became effective, did not have to extend protection to pharmaceuticals patented elsewhere prior to that date. And TRIPS provisions entered into force on a staggered schedule: Developed countries were expected to be in compliance as of January 1, 1996, while developing countries and countries in transition (under certain conditions) had until 2000. Least-developed countries do not have to implement the TRIPS rules on pharmaceutical patents until 2016, with the possibility of a further extension.

In addition, developing countries, other than least-developed countries, that did not recognize pharmaceutical product patents prior to TRIPS could choose to delay implementation until January 1, 2005. From the beginning of the transition period in 1995, however, they had to create a "mailbox" to accept applications for drug patents from pharmaceutical companies, and as of 2000, they were to grant exclusive marketing rights on those products if so requested. In practice, many developing countries, including some of the least developed, had patent protection in place prior to TRIPS (as a result of colonial legacies or external pressure), and only thirteen countries notified the WTO that they were creating mailboxes, including Brazil and India.[4]

The use of these flexibilities by India, one of the world's leading producers of generic medicines, allowed it to continue exporting many products that would otherwise have come under market exclusivity. However, the share of medicines supplied under exclusive rights is beginning to rise, including in countries that were previously able to import generics from India and other suppliers, and the full impact of the TRIPS-induced legal changes will be seen over the next decade.

Finally, even after full implementation of TRIPS, countries retain important flexibilities that could help them mitigate potential negative effects, if they have the technical and legal capacity to use the flexibilities effectively. At the most basic level, governments have substantial latitude in deciding what is patentable, subject to "the normal tests of novelty, inventiveness and industrial applicability."[5] WTO members also retain the right to issue compulsory licenses—government authorizations to use patented subject matter without the consent of the patent holder under certain conditions. Such licenses are considered on their individual merit and are generally permitted

> . . . only if an unsuccessful attempt has been made to acquire a voluntary license on reasonable terms and conditions within a reasonable period of time; the requirement to pay adequate remuneration in the circumstances of each case, taking into

> account the economic value of the license; and a requirement that decisions be subject to judicial or other independent review by a distinct higher authority.[6]

The provision requiring efforts to first negotiate a voluntary license can be waived in the case of national emergency or in cases of public noncommercial use—for example, providing medicines on a nonprofit basis through public health clinics. The provision requiring remuneration based on the economic value of the license can be waived if it is part of a judicial or administrative remedy for anticompetitive practices.

It is important to emphasize that TRIPS does not restrict compulsory licenses to emergency situations, as is often wrongly asserted in press reports on global IP rules. Emergency or public use situations merely trigger the additional flexibility of not having to first negotiate with the patent holder to obtain a voluntary license.

But concern that these flexibilities are insufficient has grown, especially in the face of increasing demand for expensive, patented antiretroviral drugs to treat HIV/AIDS in Africa. One particular concern has been the requirement in TRIPS Article 31 that production under compulsory licenses be predominantly for domestic use. This has meant that many poor countries without local production capacity cannot easily obtain antiretrovirals because countries with generic production capacity are constrained in exporting them.

WTO members first addressed concerns regarding IP protection at the ministerial meeting in November 2001 that launched the current Doha Round of trade negotiations. In addition to the ministerial communiqué, which emphasized that the new round should pay particular attention to the needs of developing countries, attendees issued a separate declaration affirming that "the TRIPS Agreement does not and should not prevent members from taking measures to protect public health," including through the use of compulsory licenses.[7] The declaration also committed WTO members to negotiate a solution to the problem of how countries without production capacity could effectively exercise the compulsory license option.

The acrimony over the implementation of TRIPS quickly resumed, however, as U.S. negotiators blocked agreement on revisions to the compulsory licensing rules for many months, insisting that any change should apply only to a narrowly restricted list of diseases. Finally, in an effort to avoid stalemate at the ministerial meeting in Cancun in September 2003, the United States dropped its demand for limiting the diseases to which the revision could be applied and agreed to a waiver of TRIPS obligations so that WTO members without manufacturing capacity could import generic drugs—what is known as the August 2003 Decision.[8] The procedures for implementing the decision are summarized in box 8.1.

Box 8.1. Implementing the August 2003 Decision

In Cancun in 2003, the United States agreed to a waiver of TRIPS obligations to allow WTO members that lack manufacturing capacity to import generic drugs. The procedures for invoking this waiver involve a number of steps, but they should not pose a substantial problem for any but the weakest or most corrupt governments. Provisions designed to prevent diversion of medicines produced under the waiver could raise costs and be more burdensome, but the decision recognizes that possibility and provides flexibility in implementing them. The procedures are summarized below, first for importing countries and then for exporting countries.

An *eligible importing member* is one that has notified the TRIPS Council of its intent to use the system.

- To invoke the waiver, the importing country must submit a notification that
    - Specifies the name and expected quantities of the product needed.
    - Affirms that it has established that it has no capacity, or insufficient capacity, to meet its needs.
    - Confirms that it has or will grant a compulsory license if the product is patented in that country.
- To prevent diversion, the importer "shall take reasonable measures within their means, proportionate to their administrative capacities . . . to prevent re-exportation."

On the last point, the decision provides that developed-country members "shall" provide technical and financial cooperation to help developing and least-developed members implement this provision.

Most *industrialized countries* and some upper-middle-income countries have stated that they will not use the system as an importer, while others (mainly Eastern European economies in transition) have stated that they would do so only in cases of national emergency or extreme urgency. *Least-developed countries* are automatically regarded as eligible importers that lack sufficient production capacity, without submitting any notification. They do, however, have to meet the other conditions.

An *eligible exporting member* must issue a compulsory license to produce drugs for export to eligible importing members. Exporting members typically have to amend their laws to do so. Among countries with generic capacity, Canada and India have notified the WTO that they have made the necessary changes to their laws. Other conditions include the following:

- Distinguishing the product as subject to the waiver through special packaging or color or shape of the product, "provided that such distinction is feasible and does not have a significant impact on price."
- Prior to shipment, posting on a Web site the quantities being supplied and to whom, and any distinguishing characteristics.

- Notifying the TRIPS Council that a license has been granted under the waiver and providing information similar to that provided on the Web site.
- Paying adequate remuneration to the patent holder (importing countries do not have to pay additional remuneration when they must also issue a compulsory license).

Source: Adapted from the August 30, 2003, decision of the World Trade Organization General Council (www.wto.org/english/tratop_e/trips_e/implem_para6_e.htm).

In sum, TRIPS—the result of multilateral trade negotiations that ended more than ten years ago—has now been phased in for all but the poorest countries, and its effects on the supply of patented pharmaceutical products are growing. TRIPS flexibilities currently available to developing countries include the following:

- Patents granted anywhere in the world prior to 1995 do not have to be recognized in countries recognizing patents after that date.
- Countries not granting product patents for pharmaceuticals before TRIPS went into effect could delay implementation until 2005.
- Least-developed countries do not have to implement TRIPS rules on drug patents until 2016.
- After implementation of TRIPS, countries can issue compulsory licenses.
- Countries without domestic production can get a waiver to import drugs under a compulsory license issued by the exporting country under the August 2003 Decision.

Even though developing countries have the legal option to resort to compulsory licensing to have drugs produced competitively, it remains uncertain how effectively they can make use of this option, especially if commercial and other obstacles continue to block exports of generic medicines from China, India, and other exporters, as discussed below.

U.S. free trade agreements

As a global leader in technology, the United States has a comparative advantage in IP-based industries, such as software, entertainment, and pharmaceuticals. Thus, it is no surprise that strong protection against pirates and copycats has been a priority of U.S. policymakers from both parties for more than two decades. A Democratic Party majority passed an omnibus trade act in 1988 that created the "Special 301" process for monitoring trading partners' levels of IP protection and using threats of trade sanctions to pressure them to provide greater protection. Democratic and Republican presidents alike have vigorously adhered to that process. And the Reagan, Bush I, and Clinton administrations enthusiastically pursued the Uruguay Round negotiations on TRIPS.

While collective opposition from many developing countries forced compromises on IP issues in the WTO, resulting in the flexibilities described above, U.S. negotiators have been more successful in pushing stronger IP provisions in bilateral negotiations of free trade agreements. Since the end of the Uruguay Round, the United States has negotiated free trade agreements with seventeen trading partners, including three agreements awaiting congressional approval as of mid-2008 (see chapter 7 by Elliott). The IP provisions were among the most contentious issues in many of these negotiations and in negotiations that have not been concluded with several other countries, such as Brazil (in the context of the Free Trade Area of the Americas), the countries of the Southern African Customs Union, and Thailand.[9]

Although there is some variation, these stronger IP provisions (known as "TRIPS-plus" provisions) share key elements. Most notably, U.S. negotiators generally seek to extend the length of the patent term to compensate for delays in regulatory approvals; to allow for patents for new uses of existing compounds; to limit the grounds for issuing compulsory licenses; to force drug regulatory agencies to play a role in enforcing patent rights, even though they typically have no expertise in that area; and to create another layer of market exclusivity through rules for the protection of pharmaceutical test data, further complicating the use of compulsory licensing.[10]

The adoption of TRIPS-plus standards in U.S. free trade agreements received much criticism internationally and among nongovernmental organizations for contradicting the spirit of the 2001 Doha Declaration on the TRIPS Agreement and Public Health and for undermining the flexibility for developing countries in addressing public health needs.[11] After the Democrats won control of both houses of Congress in the November 2006 elections, the House leadership launched negotiations with the Bush administration to change the free-trade-agreement framework to reflect Democratic concerns, mainly on labor and environmental protections but also on IP. The resulting May 10, 2007, bipartisan agreement rolls back the most damaging TRIPS-plus provisions.[12] Among other things, the agreement gives governments discretion in deciding whether to extend a patent's term to compensate for delays in obtaining approval to market a new product, rather than making it mandatory. Similarly, drug regulators would not be required to deny marketing approval based on a drug's patent status, provided that there are other means for patent holders to assert their rights. Crucially, the agreement removes provisions that could have blocked the ability of countries to make effective use of compulsory licensing.[13] In addition to responding to criticisms from development advocacy organizations, such as Oxfam, the changes on IP were reportedly influenced by the U.S. generic pharmaceuticals industry, which wants to expand its export markets.[14]

The immediate impact of the bipartisan trade deal is limited because it applies only to the free trade agreement negotiated with Peru and those with Colombia and Panama, if approved by Congress. However, the deal marks an important political shift in U.S. trade policy toward greater sensitivity to public health concerns in global IP rules and may herald additional policy changes in the future.

Innovation, access, and developing-country concerns

Patents are important to the pharmaceutical industry because it must invest large amounts of money into research and development of new drugs with no guarantee that a particular product will pass regulatory muster for safety and quality, or be a success in the marketplace. Moreover, the marginal costs of producing a new drug, once it has been developed, are relatively small, and competitors can reverse-engineer and produce many drugs at much lower cost than the innovators faced in creating them. Patents address this problem by providing a period of market exclusivity during which firms can charge a higher price than in a fully competitive market and thereby recoup costs, thus giving companies an incentive to innovate.

An alternative approach would be to have the public sector pay for the research and development using tax revenues and then disseminate resulting discoveries widely for commercialization by any company. Governments have generally opted in favor of the patent system because, with patents, decisions on investments are guided by information produced by markets about what consumers want and are willing to pay for. Reliance on market mechanisms also opens the potential rewards of innovation to all and avoids the danger that incentives will be limited to those individuals, institutions, or ideas that may be in political favor at a given time.

Patents are thus a powerful tool for spurring innovation, but problems can arise when patent protection is too strong. Moreover, patents offer little incentive to invest in research and development for drugs for which there is only a small commercial market—either because the diseases treated by these drugs are rare or the potential patients are poor. And patents can raise the price of drugs in developing countries, thus reducing access.

Patents and incentives for innovation in small, poor markets

By one estimate, only about $6 billion of the $100 billion spent annually on pharmaceutical research and development are aimed at the concerns of developing countries.[15] This is not surprising given the fact that high-income countries account for the vast majority of pharmaceutical sales (table 8.1).

Table 8.1. Global sales of prescription medicines (retail and hospitals)

	2001		2006	
Income group	Value ($ billions)	Percent of total	Value ($ billions)	Percent of total
Low-income (4 countries)	5.9	1.3	9.1	1.4
Middle-income (23 countries)	43.6	9.9	88.6	13.3
High-income (25 countries)	391.6	88.8	569.3	85.4
Total	441.0	100.0	667.0	100.0

Note: Values may not sum to totals because of rounding.

Source: IMS Health.

Low-income countries, including most countries in Africa and South Asia, account for just over 1 percent of worldwide sales.[16]

In principle, the skewed distribution of pharmaceutical purchasing power would not pose a problem in the allocation of research-and-development funding if rich and poor countries faced similar health burdens. Indeed, there are a number of diseases to which large populations in both rich and poor countries are vulnerable—called "type 1" diseases by the World Health Organization. Examples of such diseases are measles, hepatitis B, diabetes, cardiovascular disease, and tobacco-related illnesses. But while deaths from communicable diseases have been substantially reduced in rich countries, they still account for a large share of the disease burden in poor countries (table 8.2). "Type 2" diseases are those, such as HIV/AIDS and tuberculosis, that occur in rich and poor countries but are far more present in poor countries.[17] Diseases classified by World Health Organization as "type 3" occur overwhelmingly or exclusively in poor countries, such as African sleeping sickness and river blindness. Patents alone clearly do not offer adequate incentives for investing in research and development to address type 3 diseases, and may not in the case of some type 2 diseases either, with AIDS being a striking exception.

Moreover, the development of drugs will be without concern for whether delivery systems are well designed for effective use in poorer countries (for example, whether they need refrigeration). Commercial incentives are such that pharmaceutical companies are more likely to direct investment toward treatments for erectile dysfunction than toward treatments for malaria. Reflecting these incentives, patenting related to tropical diseases, for example,

Table 8.2. Leading causes of death by income group, 2005 (percent of total)

Type of disease	High-income countries	Middle-income countries	Low-income countries
Communicable diseases	7	14	48
HIV/AIDS, malaria, and tuberculosis	0.4	5	14
Respiratory infections	4	3	10
Noncommunicable diseases	88	75	43
Cardiovascular diseases	38	37	23
Cancer	26	16	7

Source: WHO 2006a.

has never exceeded more than about 0.5 percent of overall pharmaceutical patenting.[18]

Thus, a role for the public sector in drug development to address neglected diseases in developing countries is both necessary and desirable. A number of foundations and official donors have entered into collaborative agreements with private pharmaceutical companies to develop treatments for specific diseases. These public-private partnerships can involve the patenting of research outputs, while upfront contractual arrangements ensure the distribution of medicines at preferential or cost-based prices to low-income countries. An example is the Global Alliance for Tuberculosis Drug Development, funded by the Bill & Melinda Gates Foundation, the Rockefeller Foundation, and a number of bilateral government donors. Three drugs are undergoing clinical trials under this initiative, with Bayer, Novartis, and Chiron (a biotechnology company) as private partners.[19]

"Pull" mechanisms, such as innovation prizes, can complement this "push" approach to innovation. A Center for Global Development working group, created to study the problem of inadequate vaccine development, wrote a detailed proposal aimed at creating a market for vaccines through advance purchase commitments.[20] Under the proposal, governments or philanthropic organizations commit upfront to buying a set amount of a product at a set price if it is successfully developed, thus reducing uncertainty about future demand and lowering the risk of the investment in research and development.[21] A pilot project on an advance market commitment to develop a vaccine for pneumococcal disease is being tested by the GAVI Alliance and the World Bank, with $1.5 billion in funding from

Canada, Italy, Norway, Russia, the United Kingdom, and the Bill & Melinda Gates Foundation.[22]

Prices and access in developing countries

High prices reduce access to medicines in poor countries because health insurance coverage is limited and patients often pay for drugs out-of-pocket. Prior to TRIPS, a few developing countries, most notably India, had developed strong generic drug industries by limiting patent protections (see box 2), making medicines more affordable. Strengthening patent protection eliminates such competition, leading to higher prices in most cases. For example, data from Médecins Sans Frontières (2007) shows that the annual price of a triple-combination antiretroviral dropped from more than $10,000 per patient in mid-2000 to $99 in 2007, after several generic companies began selling it. Although many of these countries have public health programs for HIV/AIDS, tuberculosis, and malaria, the reach of these programs is not universal and, with limited resources, depends in part on the price governments pay for needed medicines.

Higher prices for patented drugs can also sometimes be mitigated through government policies that encourage the use of off-patent therapeutic substitutes when available, for such ailments as cardiovascular problems or pain. But for other diseases—particularly those confronting drug resistance, such as HIV/AIDS, tuberculosis, and malaria, and those for which pharmaceutical treatments are relatively new, such as cancer and diabetes—off-patent substitutes are less likely to exist and the price effects will be greater. Overall, the World Health Organization's Essential Medicines List includes only fourteen patented drugs, eleven of which are antiretrovirals. However, it is possible that the list underplays the access problems posed by patents because affordability is one of the key issues considered in compiling the list.[23]

In theory, drug patents need not pose a major obstacle to drug access in developing countries—if drug companies are willing to charge different prices in different markets, taking into account a country's per capita income.[24] A profit-maximizing firm fares better—and more people have affordable access to drugs—if it charges lower prices in markets where patients are more price-sensitive, which is more likely to be the case in poorer countries. But this strategy requires that markets be "segmented" to prevent re-export of the low-price product back to the high-price market.

In the real world, countries have simultaneously adopted policies that undermine strict market segmentation, while trying to maintain it with respect to relations between developed and developing countries. The European Union, for example, allows "parallel trading" whereby a patented drug sold at a lower price in any member country can be exported and resold in any other member country. But parallel imports from outside the European Union are not allowed, and additional steps have been taken to guard against parallel imports of reduced-price drugs from poor countries.[25] The European Union and some other governments also use external "reference pricing," examining prices in other markets when setting the prices that public health systems pay for drugs. Although both types of policies are generally restricted to imports from, or reference to prices in, countries at a similar level of income, publicly known international price differentials may create political pressures on drug companies to lower prices in countries where prices are high, such as the United States.[26]

Some pharmaceutical firms offer discounts on some drugs for developing-country use, particularly for treating HIV/AIDS. For example, the pharmaceutical company Abbott offers a key antiretroviral to low-income and lower-middle-income countries for $1,000 per patient per year, and for $500 to least-developed countries and Africa.[27] But differential pricing is still not systematically used.

Moreover, market-based differential pricing is likely to remain ad hoc and imperfect because of a lack of information about market demand, potentially high fixed costs in obtaining regulatory approval in some smaller markets, and differences in negotiating skills and leverage. Given weaknesses in insurance markets, it is also possible that pharmaceutical firms choose to price products in developing countries at levels that higher-income elites can afford, rather than at levels based on average incomes. For some people, countries, and diseases, drugs will be unaffordable even at prices that cover only marginal costs, meaning subsidies will be needed to ensure access.

Finally, pharmaceutical policy itself can play an important role in promoting rational and cost-efficient drug use. As noted above, many therapies have off-patent substitutes, and governments can encourage the use of generics through public clinics and reimbursement programs. Direct price controls, if used carefully, can also be an effective tool to reduce prices for patented medicines from the free-market levels. Indeed, the majority of countries—both developed and developing—regulate pharmaceutical prices in some way. But, as with compulsory licensing, a collective action problem arises if widespread and uncoordinated price controls cause firm profits to fall below the level needed to cover research-and-development costs, thereby leading to a reduction in investment. Going forward, the next president should initiate a dialogue involving all parties on mechanisms that can help to equitably spread the burden of research-and-development costs.[28]

It is true that access to medicines depends on a number of other factors besides patents and prices—notably, the efficiency of drug distribution systems and the availability of complementary health services. Moreover, drug access has to be considered in the context of overall health policy. In particular, governments and donors need to carefully consider how to allocate scarce resources between treatment and prevention policies. For example, some economists are concerned that the costs of treating HIV/AIDS, even at the lowest drug prices, could leave inadequate resources for prevention and for other health concerns.[29] In addition, other communicable and noncommunicable diseases such as heart diseases and diabetes account for a significant and growing share of the health burden in most developing countries. Governments need to carefully analyze the effect of drug prices on access and health outcomes in both private and public markets, and act accordingly.

Exploiting the flexibilities under TRIPS

Developing countries' experiences with TRIPS

Developing countries have been using the flexibilities of TRIPS to cushion its negative effects on access. India delayed pharmaceutical patent protection, and its companies continued to export a variety of generic drugs before the amended patent legislation was approved in March 2005 (box 8.2). On July 19, 2007, Rwanda became the first country to notify the WTO of its intention to use the August 2003 Decision to import an antiretroviral drug. Canada approved a compulsory license shortly thereafter for the generic manufacturer Apotex to supply it.[30]

In addition, several developing countries have granted compulsory licenses for antiretrovirals, many of them with very little press attention; among them are Zimbabwe (2002); Malaysia (2003); Indonesia, Mozambique, and Zambia (2004); and Eritrea and Ghana (2005). In most cases, the licenses were for government use in public treatment programs and allowed for the purchase of generic medicines—often from India, which did not begin recognizing patents until mid-2005. Patent-holding companies therefore continued to enjoy market exclusivity in private markets (where such private markets existed).

The recent compulsory licensing cases of Brazil and Thailand generated substantially more media interest and strong reactions from pharmaceutical patent holders, on the one side, and health activists, on the other. Brazil had previously used the threat of compulsory licensing in its price negotiations with pharmaceutical companies prompting Roche, for example, to offer a 40 percent price reduction on its AIDS drug nelfinavir in 2001. In 2007, however, the Brazilian government could not reach agreement with Merck on a price discount for efavirenz, a more recently patented, second-line AIDS drug, and it issued a compulsory license. Going further, Thailand issued three government-use licenses within a two-month period. As an important precedent, one of those licenses pertained to a non-AIDS drug, clopidogrel, produced by

Box 8.2. Intellectual property developments in India

India hosts one of the world's most dynamic pharmaceutical industries (Fink 2001). Having experienced rapid growth at more than 15 percent a year in the 1990s, the industry's overall production value in 2003 stood at $7 billion. The sector is made up of more than 20,000 companies, though the bulk of production is accounted for by 250 to 300 large companies. Exports have grown rapidly and pharmaceuticals now represent India's second largest export industry. Companies such as Cipla, Dr. Reddy's Laboratories, and Ranbaxy have become household corporate names in international pharmaceutical markets. The U.S. Food and Drug Administration has approved more than 100 Indian drug manufacturing facilities—the largest number outside the United States.

Much of the success of the Indian industry can be traced to the Indian Patent Act of 1970, which abolished patent protection for pharmaceutical products. Indian companies excelled at quickly reverse-engineering new pharmaceutical compounds patented abroad and producing quality products at competitive prices, including active pharmaceutical ingredients. It is thus not surprising that the implementation of the TRIPS pharmaceutical obligations proved controversial in India—involving several rounds of legislative reforms, acrimonious debate, and even one WTO dispute.

India initially opted for the "mailbox" transition mechanism, allowing pharmaceutical companies to file patent applications for examination after India extended full pharmaceutical product patent protection as required by TRIPS in 2005. The March 2005 amendments to India's Patent Act implemented many of the flexibilities contained in TRIPS and, significantly, contained a provision permitting Indian manufacturers to continue generic production of those drugs for which mailbox patents are granted—as long as the Indian producer had made significant investments in production prior to 2005 and paid the patent holder a "reasonable" royalty. The WTO compatibility of this provision is murky, but no country has challenged it after two years. It is also unclear how many pharmaceutical compounds were affected by this provision, but it may serve to reduce the number of medicines subject to market exclusivity in the short term.

Another form of flexibility in TRIPS allows countries fairly broad latitude in determining what is eligible for a patent. India's new patent law came to a critical test in 2006, when the multinational company Novartis sued the government, alleging that India's standard of patentability, requiring a high degree of novelty, was unconstitutional and not in compliance with TRIPS. Previously, the Indian Patent Office in Chennai had rejected Novartis's patent application for the leukemia drug Gleevec/Glivec on the grounds that the claimed molecule was only a new form of a known substance that did not show any enhanced efficacy. Novartis's court challenge quickly stirred heavy protest from health activists and politicians all around the world. Among others, the European Parliament and several U.S. Congressmen called on the company to drop the case. In 2007, the Chennai High Court dismissed Novartis's challenge, saying that the law's standard of patentability is constitutional and that the court had no jurisdiction on whether Indian patent laws complied with TRIPS rules.

Sources: Amin 2007, IMS Health 2006, and Sampath 2006.

Sanofi-Aventis to fight heart disease.[31] Abbott, the patent holder for one of the AIDS drugs, raised the stakes for countries seeking compulsory licenses by announcing that it would not launch new drugs in Thailand.

Still, many developing countries have not (or not yet) incorporated available flexibilities under TRIPS into their national laws, and critics argue that the flexibilities meant to cushion the negative effects of TRIPS are too difficult for many countries to use effectively.[32] Indeed, it is surprising that, as of the end of September 2007, only eleven countries had ratified the 2005 amendment of the TRIPS Agreement that codifies the August 2003 waiver allowing countries without production capacity to import drugs under compulsory license (seven of the eleven countries are high-income countries).[33] And many least-developed countries that have patent laws that predate—and are as strong or stronger than—the TRIPS rules have not modified their laws to take advantage of the extension of the deadline to 2016 for them to implement TRIPS.

It is not clear whether this is because of administrative difficulties or other costs, including pressure from the United States and other rich-country governments, or because it is not a priority for these governments. One possibility is that drug companies, in addition to Abbott, never bothered to file patents in many of the least-developed countries. In other cases, some poor countries are receiving heavily discounted supplies or donations of patented drugs. And as noted, the impact of TRIPS-induced patent reforms is just starting to be felt in many countries because the phased implementation was completed for all but the least-developed countries only in 2005.

As new medicines addressing health concerns of developing countries come onto the market, controversies over drug prices are bound to intensify and more countries may resort to compulsory licenses. Also, chronic diseases already surpass infectious diseases as causes of death and ill-health in middle-income countries and are growing rapidly in low-income countries. As the markets in these countries grow with rising incomes, the debate over the fair share of research-and-development costs that these countries should pay will also intensify.

At the same time, broader geographic patent coverage of new drugs will render the use of compulsory licenses more difficult. In the most recent cases, including Brazil and Thailand, governments relied at least temporarily on importation of licensed generic medicines from India, where they were still available. As more drugs come under patent protection in developing countries, including China and India, it will become harder for governments to use compulsory licensing to draw on existing generic supplies.

How difficult will it be for a government to use compulsory licenses in the absence of existing generic supplies? Depending on the pharmaceutical compound in question, it may take a year or more for a generic manufacturer to reverse-engineer and deliver a quality product. Finding generic companies willing to take on the business risk involved may not be easy. Use of the August 2003 Decision entails additional procedural requirements and the cooperation of governments, but these hurdles seem manageable in relation to the commercial constraints involved. We address both in what follows.

How the United States can help developing countries make use of TRIPS flexibilities

Although it is not always clear why many developing countries have not yet taken steps to incorporate the flexibilities available under TRIPS into their national laws and regulations, there are steps that the United States could take to ensure that legal and administrative obstacles are not to blame. For example, a patent registry—an online database showing which drugs have been patented and where—would be useful for determining the scope of the problem and identifying countries where legislative reforms may be needed. Given the need for coordination across ministries, and in some cases across countries, a registry would also be helpful to governments seeking to issue a compulsory license.

For countries that need to make legislative changes, a report prepared for the U.K. Department for International Development recommended that the World Health Organization or the World Intellectual Property Organization develop a model law for incorporating TRIPS flexibilities that countries could adapt as needed.[34] In addition, the Doha Declaration on TRIPS and public health states that least-developed countries need not enforce patent rights prior to 2016, even if filed under patent laws adopted before the Uruguay Round agreement (WTO 2001). Depending on the legal system, some countries may be able to take advantage of this flexibility by executive order, but others may need to amend local laws to do so.

Perhaps more important than legal obstacles are the potential commercial obstacles to compulsory licensing. Countries that have no domestic production capacity may have problems taking advantage of the August 2003 Decision if the volume of drugs needed is too small to entice generic producers in the exporting country to go to the trouble of obtaining a compulsory license. Small batches would also tend to drive up production costs. Demand pooling and bulk purchasing are among the options for overcoming these constraints. For example, the Clinton Foundation, with $100 million in funding from UNITAID (the international drug purchase facility created by Brazil, Chile, France, Norway, and the United Kingdom), was able to negotiate substantial discounts on antiretrovirals in part by promising to purchase large volumes of the drugs to be provided to twenty-seven countries. Roughly another forty countries that are members of the Clinton Foundation's

Procurement Consortium, including some at middle-income levels, will also be able to buy drugs at the discounted prices.[35]

Somewhat ironically, the least-developed countries could also emerge as a new source of generic medicines, given that TRIPS does not yet require them to protect or enforce pharmaceutical patents. In some of the least-developed countries, some pharmaceutical production capacity is already available, though it typically does not extend to the technologically more complex production of active pharmaceutical ingredients, and companies often do not meet standards of quality and compliance with good manufacturing practices. At the same time, the market opportunity created by the special status of the least-developed countries under TRIPS may well lead technologically more advanced generic producers to invest in the least-developed countries, helping to alleviate these constraints.

In the long run, free use of compulsory licenses raises a collective action problem. Even though most developing countries are individually too small to materially affect the bottom line of research-based pharmaceutical companies, as a group they can. Indeed, developing countries benefit from new treatments against diseases that hit rich as well as poor countries. It seems only fair—and economically desirable—for at least the middle-income countries to share the burden of research-and-development costs. In an ideal world, such burden sharing would be achieved through differential pricing, whereby prices depend on a country's level of income. But the obstacles to economically optimal pricing are substantial, and evidence to date suggests that this approach can only go so far. Under current circumstances, and given the limited impact of developing-country markets on incentives to invest in research and development, it seems hard to deny individual countries the right to determine for themselves whether free-market prices imply the right level of burden sharing. They clearly have the right to do so under TRIPS. That said, it would be desirable in the long term to develop an international framework that could lead to more objective criteria for differential pricing or for triggering the use of compulsory licenses.

Recommendations for the next president

Until quite recently, U.S. policy on trade-related IP focused narrowly on promoting commercial interests, with little regard for potential public health or other effects on developing countries. The next president should proclaim a new approach that brings public and private interests into better balance. The new policy should be founded on two key conclusions from the analysis of IP protection noted briefly here and discussed elsewhere in more detail (see note 2 for sources):

- *The strongest possible patent rights are not optimal for society as a whole,* and at some level, IP protection can stifle rather than stimulate innovation.
- *Patents provide little incentive to innovate if the potential market is too small or too poor,* so poor countries have little to gain and stand to lose from stronger IP rules.

As a first step toward restoring balance to U.S. health and trade policies, the next president should, within the first 100 days of taking office, announce a clear policy that recognizes the rights of developing countries to implement TRIPS in a way that is consistent with public health priorities and the flexibilities that are included in the WTO agreement to that end.

U.S. negotiators reluctantly agreed to the 2001 Doha Declaration affirming the need for a balance between IP and public health, and then undermined that commitment through TRIPS-plus provisions in free trade agreements. In addition, U.S. officials have put political pressure on countries to discourage the use of compulsory licenses. For example, even though the U.S. Trade Representative acknowledged that Thailand's compulsory licenses complied with WTO rules, the U.S. Trade Representative's Special 301 Report later elevated Thailand to the Priority Watch List, alleging "lack of transparency and due process" in the issuance of the licenses.[36] The Thai government had, however, engaged in extensive discussions with the patent holders on pricing before issuing the compulsory licenses, even though it was not required to do so under TRIPS rules.[37] Nonetheless, in a meeting with the Thai health minister, U.S. Commerce Secretary Carlos Gutierrez expressly demanded that Thailand abandon the issuance of the compulsory licenses.[38]

Second, building on the May 2007 bipartisan agreement between the administration and the congressional leadership, the new president should issue, as soon as possible after taking office, a "Domestic Doha Declaration" that includes the following elements:

- Clarification that the United States respects the rights of countries under the TRIPS Agreement and will not interfere with WTO-consistent compulsory licensing policies[39]
- A commitment to abide by the more accommodating IP provisions negotiated by the Bush administration and congressional leadership in future free trade agreements, as well as directing the United States Trade Representative to amend existing free trade agreements to incorporate these provisions.

Over the medium run, the new president should also take the following steps:

- Submit legislation to Congress to implement the August 2003 Decision to allow U.S. generic companies to export to countries with insufficient manufacturing capability if these countries wish to make use of compulsory licenses

- Provide technical, logistical, and financial assistance to ensure that low-income countries can effectively use the flexibilities provided by TRIPS, including through legal reforms, demand pooling, and bulk purchasing
- Respect the right of middle-income countries to use compulsory licensing, and launch an international dialogue on burden sharing in the financing of pharmaceutical research and development.

More broadly, "fixing" U.S. policy on TRIPS and other trade-related IP issues goes only part of the way toward ensuring that U.S. policy is supportive of better health outcomes in developing countries. The new president should also increase support for initiatives seeking to promote research and development into diseases that primarily affect developing countries—and to ensuring that any innovations in this area are made available as quickly as possible (see chapter 1 by Levine). The United States should not do this unilaterally; it should cooperate with the World Health Organization in finding new models for innovation into developing-country diseases—including public-private partnerships and innovation prizes, as well as advance market commitments.[40] Also, the next president should pay careful attention to the global effects of any reforms in domestic health care policy (see chapter 1 by Levine).

Conclusion

In sum, if the president taking office in January 2009 wants to rebuild the reputation of the United States as a benign rather than malign hegemon, he or she will need to take action on two fronts related to access to essential medicines in developing countries. First, the president will need to reverse the policy of pushing for stronger IP protection in developing countries; respect their right to use the flexibilities provided under TRIPS for promoting public health, including the use of compulsory licenses; and take other steps to facilitate access to affordable drugs. Second, and equally important, the president will need to ensure that the U.S. government supports schemes to spur innovation in treatments for diseases that mainly affect developing countries.

Notes

1. Maskus 2006.
2. For a review of economic research on the nexus between IP protection and economic development, see Maskus 2000, and Fink and Maskus 2004.

3. In chapter 7, Elliott describes how this grand bargain turned into a bum deal from the perspective of developing countries.
4. Other countries that created mailboxes were Argentina, Cuba, Egypt, Kuwait, Morocco, Pakistan, Paraguay, Tunisia, Turkey, United Arab Emirates, and Uruguay. See WTO 2006.
5. See WTO n.d.
6. WTO n.d.
7. See WTO 2001.
8. In 2005, WTO members agreed to amend the TRIPS Agreement in light of the August 2003 Decision. The amendment will take effect, and will replace the waiver for those accepting it, when it has been ratified by two-thirds of members. In the meantime, for those not accepting the formal amendment, the August 2003 waiver continues to apply (WTO 2008). See Abbott 2005 and Fink 2005b for a more detailed treatment of the decision.
9. For examples of the press coverage on this issue, see Agence France-Presse, July 24, 2007, and Bangkok Post, April 17, 2006, on Thailand; Canadian Press, April 21, 2005, on Brazil and the Free Trade Area of the Americas; and Reuters, April 17, 2006, on southern Africa.
10. Abbott (2004) and Fink and Reichenmiller (2005) offer a more detailed overview of the different TRIPS-plus provisions found in U.S. free trade agreements, while Maskus (2006) focuses on the IP chapter in the pending agreement with Colombia. In addition to IP obligations, the Australia-U.S. and the Korea-U.S. free trade agreements establish separate, mainly procedural, rules for pharmaceutical reimbursement decisions under government-operated health care programs. For instance, governments must permit pharmaceutical manufactures to apply for an increased reimbursement amount, based on the submission of evidence on a product's safety and efficacy. On balance, these rules may strengthen the bargaining position of research-based pharmaceutical companies in reimbursement decisions, though their precise relevance is not yet clear.
11. See, for example, the press release of Médecins Sans Frontières on U.S.-Thai free trade agreement negotiations, May 21, 2004 (www.accessmed-msf.org/resources/press-clips/press-clip-detail/article/ips-thailand-us-freer-trade-weakens-access-to-hivaids-drugs/); and Oxfam International 2007. The WHO also approved a resolution at its assembly meeting in May 2006, urging member states "to encourage trade agreements to take into account the flexibilities contained in the Agreement on Trade-Related Aspects of Intellectual Property Rights and recognized by the Doha Ministerial Declaration on the TRIPS Agreement and Public Health" (www.who.int/gb/ebwha/pdf_files/WHA59/A59_R24-en.pdf). Accessed October 18, 2007.
12. The Consumer Project on Technology provides a copy of the agreement, as well as reactions and analysis of these issues (www.cptech.org/ip/health/trade/).

13. See CPATH 2007.
14. See Intellectual Property Watch 2007a and Generic Pharmaceutical Association 2007.
15. Levine, Kremer, and Albright 2005, p. 18.
16. It is true that the shares shown in table 8.1 reflect a bias in the availability of sales data: the low-income group includes only four countries and the middle-income group just thirty-six countries. The size of this bias is likely to be small, however. Using the IMS Health data and population figures from the World Bank, we calculated per capita sales for the different income groups and then applied the resulting figures to the total population in those groups (including the countries for which no sales data are available). The share of high-income countries decreases by no more than 1.3 percentage points. A second bias may stem from the fact that price discounts extended by pharmaceutical companies are not always captured by IMS audits, inflating sales figures in some countries. Educated guesses suggest that this type of sales inflation may be more pronounced in developed countries, though its precise empirical significance is not clear. Finally, sales data from IMS are incomplete, because hospital sales are not recorded in some countries and sales to the public sector are generally excluded. However, it is not clear whether these omissions would necessarily have led to an upward bias in the global market share of high-income countries.
17. See WHO 2006b. At the 2006 World Health Assembly, WHO members requested the establishment of an Intergovernmental Working Group on Public Health, Innovation, and Intellectual Property with a mandate "to prepare a global strategy and plan of action on essential health research to address conditions affecting developing countries disproportionately." The working group is to present its plan to the Assembly gathering in mid-2008.
18. See Lanjouw and Cockburn 2000, and De Francisco and Matlin 2006.
19. See the information made available by the TB Alliance on its Web site (www.tballiance.org/home/home.php). Other public-private partnerships include the International AIDS Vaccine Initiative, the International Partnership for Microbicides, the South African AIDS Vaccine Initiative, the European Malaria Vaccine Initiative, the Malaria Vaccine Initiative, the Medicines for Malaria Venture, the Areas Global Tuberculosis Vaccine Foundation, the Foundation for Innovative New Diagnostics, and the Drugs for Neglected Diseases Initiative (WHO 2006b).
20. Table 2.1 of the report of this working group surveys twelve different approaches that might be used to encourage commercial investment in the development of drugs for developing country markets. See Levine, Kremer, and Albright 2005.
21. See Kremer 2002 and Levine, Kremer, and Albright 2005 for more detailed discussion of this mechanism.
22. See AMC 2007 for information on the initiative and see chapter 1 by Levine for a specific proposal in this area.

23. The WHO's list is available at www.who.int/medicines/publications/essential-medicines/en/index.html. For a critique of the methodology used in compiling the list, see the December 1, 2006, letter from James Love, director of the Consumer Project on Technology, to WHO Director-General Margaret Chan (www.cptech.org/blogs/ipdisputesinmedicine/2006_12_01_archive.html).
24. See Ridley 2005, Danzon 2007, and Danzon and Towse 2003.
25. Council Regulation (EC) 953/2003 of May 26, 2003 (http://eur-lex.europa.eu/LexUriServ/site/en/oj/2003/l_135/l_13520030603en00050011.pdf).
26. Danzon and Towse (2003) argue for confidential rebates to encourage companies to use differential pricing, but they also note that restrictions on parallel imports and external reference pricing would accomplish the same result.
27. See information available on the company's Web site: "Access and Affordability to Abbott's HIV Medicines," updated April 10, 2007 (www.abbott.com/static/content/document/aids_care.pdf) and "The Abbott Commitment Philosophy" (www.abbott.com/global/url/content/en_US/40.5.10:10/general_content/General_Content_00327.htm).
28. Grace (2003) surveys an even broader array of potential policies aimed at ensuring affordable access for essential medicines.
29. These issues are addressed in more detail in chapter 1 by Levine.
30. See the WTO Document IP/N/9/RWA /and ICTSD 2007.
31. See Fink 2005a, Oh 2006, Reichman and Hasenzahl 2002, and "Health Care and Intellectual Property: Compulsory Licensing" (www.cptech.org/ip/health/cl/). In late 2007, Thailand announced that it was considering issuing compulsory licenses for another twenty drugs for the treatment of chronic diseases, such as hypertension and diabetes (Intellectual Property Watch 2007b).
32. See Musungu and Oh 2005.
33. See WTO 2008. The amendment will not come into force until it has been ratified by two-thirds of WTO members.
34. Notably, the World Bank has published a guide and model documents for implementation of the August 2003 Decision. See Abbott and Van Puymbroeck 2005.
35. See www.clintonfoundation.org/050807-nr-cf-hs-ai-pr-clinton-foundation-and-unitaid-announce-price-reductions-on-16-aids-medicines-for-66-developing-countries.htm
36. See USTR 2007a and 2007b.
37. See Government of Thailand 2007.
38. Bangkok Post 2007.
39. In 2000, President Clinton issued an executive order effectively prohibiting the U.S. government from seeking TRIPS-plus standards in Sub-Saharan African countries that could interfere with access to treatments for HIV/AIDS.
40. Such models are being discussed in a WHO Intergovernmental Working Group on Public Health, Innovation, and Intellectual Property. The

recommendations of this group may generate momentum toward new initiatives and policy reforms at the international level.

References

Abbott, Frederick M. 2004. "The Doha Declaration on the TRIPS Agreement and Public Health and the Contradictory Trend in Bilateral and Regional Free Trade Agreements." Occasional Paper 14. Quaker United Nations Office, Geneva.

———. 2005. "The WTO Medicines Decision: World Pharmaceutical Trade and the Protection of Public Health." *The American Journal of International Law* 99: 317–58.

Abbott, Frederick M., and Rudolf Van Puymbroeck. 2005. "Compulsory Licensing for Public Health: A Guide and Model Documents for Implementation of the Doha Declaration Paragraph 6 Decision." Working Paper 61. World Bank, Washington, D.C.

AMC (Advance Market Commitments for Vaccines). 2007. "Five Nations and the Bill & Melinda Gates Foundation Launch Advance Market Commitment for Vaccines to Combat Deadly Disease in Poor Nations." Press Release. February 9. Washington, D.C. [www.vaccineamc.org/media/launch_event_01.html].

Amin, Tahir. 2007. "India's Patent Act on Trial." *BRIDGES* 11 (1): 15. [www.ictsd.org/monthly/bridges/BRIDGES11-1.pdf].

Bangkok Post. 2007. "Drop Drug Policy, U.S. Tells Thais." May 23.

CPATH (Center for Policy Analysis on Trade and Health). 2007. "Peru & Panama FTA Changes." San Francisco, Calif. [www.cpath.org/sitebuildercontent/sitebuilderfiles/2007_new_trade_policy_details5-10-07.pdf].

Danzon, Patricia. 2007. "At What Price?" *Nature* 449: 176–79.

Danzon, Patricia, and Adrian Towse. 2003. "Differential Pricing for Pharmaceuticals: Reconciling Access, R&D and Patents." *International Journal of Health Care Finance and Economics* 3: 183–205.

De Francisco, Andrés, and Stephen Matlin, eds. 2006. "Monitoring Financial Flows for Health Research 2006: The Changing Landscape of Health Research for Development." Global Forum for Health Research, Geneva.

Fink, Carsten. 2001. "Patent Protection, Transnational Corporations, and Market Structure: A Simulation Study of the Indian Pharmaceutical Industry." *Journal of Industry, Competition and Trade* 1 (1): 101–21.

———. 2005a. "Entering the Jungle of Intellectual Property Rights Exhaustion and Parallel Importation." In Carsten Fink and Keith E. Maskus, eds., *Intellectual Property and Development: Lessons from Recent Economic Research*. Oxford, U.K.: Oxford University Press / Washington, D.C.: World Bank.

———. 2005b. "Intellectual Property and Public Health: The WTO's August 2003 Decision in Perspective." In Richard Newfarmer, ed., *Trade, Doha, and Development: Window into the Issues*. Washington, D.C.: World Bank.

———. 2008. "Intellectual Property and Public Health: An Overview of the Debate with a US Perspective." Working Paper. Washington, D.C.: Center for Global Development.

Fink, Carsten, and Keith Maskus. 2004. *Intellectual Property and Development: Lessons from Recent Economic Research*. Oxford, U.K.: Oxford University Press / Washington, D.C.: World Bank.

Fink, C., and P. Reichenmiller. 2005. "Tightening TRIPS: The Intellectual Property Provisions of Recent U.S. Free Trade Agreements." Trade Note 20. World Bank, Washington, D.C.

Generic Pharmaceutical Association. 2007. "New Trade Policy for America." Press Release. May 31. [www.gphaonline.org/]. Arlington, Va.

Government of Thailand. 2007. "Facts and Evidences on the 10 Burning Issues Related to the Government Use of Patents on Three Patented Essential Drugs in Thailand." White Paper. Ministry of Public Health and the National Health Security Office of the Government of Thailand, Bangkok. [www.moph.go.th/hot/White%20Paper%20CL-EN.pdf].

Grace, Cheri. 2005. "A Briefing Paper for DFID: Update on China and India and Access to Medicines." DFID Health Resource Centre, Department for International Development, London.

ICTSD (International Centre for Trade and Sustainable Development). 2007. "Canada Issues Compulsory License for HIV/AIDS Drug Export to Rwanda, in First Test of WTO Procedure," *BRIDGES Weekly Trade News Digest* 11 (32). September 26. [www.ictsd.org/weekly/07-09-26/story2.htm].

IMS Health. 2006. "Intelligence 360: Global Pharmaceutical Perspectives 2006." Norwalk, Conn.

Intellectual Property Watch. 2007a. "Observers Watchful of U.S. Trade Impact on Medicines Access." July 24.

———. 2007b. "Thailand: 20 More Drugs in Pipeline for Possible Compulsory Licenses." November 2. [www.ip-watch.org].

Kremer, Michael. 2002. "Pharmaceuticals and the Developing World." *Journal of Economic Perspectives* 16 (4): 67–90.

Lanjouw, Jean O., and I. Cockburn. 2000. "Do Patents Matter?: Empirical Evidence after GATT." Working Paper 7495. National Bureau of Economic Research, Cambridge, Mass.

Levine, Ruth, Michael Kremer, and Alice Albright. 2005. *Making Markets for Vaccines: Ideas to Action*. Report of the Advance Market Commitment Working Group. Center for Global Development, Washington, D.C.

Maskus, Keith. 2000. *Intellectual Property Rights in the Global Economy*. Washington, D.C.: Institute for International Economics.

———. 2006. *Reforming U.S. Patent Policy: Getting the Incentives Right*. Council Special Report No. 19. New York: Council on Foreign Relations Press, November.

Médecins Sans Frontières. 2007. *Untangling the Web of Price Reductions: A Pricing Guide for the Purchase of ARVs for Developing Countries*. 10th edition. Geneva.

Musungu, Sisule, and Cecilia Oh. 2005. "The Use of Flexibilities in TRIPS by Developing Countries: Can They Promote Access to Medicines?" Study 4C. Commission on Intellectual Property Rights, Innovation and Public Health. World Health Organization, Geneva.

Oh, Cecilia. 2006. "Compulsory Licenses: Recent Experiences in Developing Countries." *International Journal of Intellectual Property Management* 1 (1/2): 22–36.

Oxfam International. 2007. "All Costs, No Benefits: How TRIPS-Plus Intellectual Property Rules in the US-Jordan FTA Affect Access to Medicines." Briefing Paper 102. Oxford, U.K.

Reichman, Jerome, and Catherine Hasenzahl. 2002. "Non-Voluntary Licensing of Patented Inventions: History, TRIPS, and Canadian and United States Practice." *BRIDGES* 6 (7): 3. October. [www.ictsd.org/monthly/bridges/BRIDGES6-7.pdf].

Ridley, David B.. 2005. "Differential Pricing of Pharmaceuticals and the Role of International Organizations." *Pharmacoeconomics* 23(7): 651–58.

Sampath, Padmashree Gehl. 2006. "Indian Pharma within Global Reach?" Working Paper 2006-031. United Nations University, Maastricht Economic and Social Research and Training Centre on Innovation ad Technology, Maastricht, The Netherlands.

USTR (U.S. Trade Representative). 2007a. Letter by USTR Susan Schwab to Congressman Thomas Allen, January 17. Washington, D.C. [www.cptech.org/ip/health/c/thailand/letter.pdf].

———. 2007b. "2007 Special 301 Report." [www.ustr.gov/Document_Library/Reports_Publications/2007/2007_Special_301_Review/Section_Index.html.

WHO (World Health Organization). 2004. "The World Medicines Situation." Geneva.

———. 2006a. "Projections of Mortality and Burden Of Disease 2006."

———. 2006b. "Public Health, Innovation and Intellectual Property Rights." Report of the Commission on Intellectual Property Rights, Innovation, and Public Health. Geneva.

WTO (World Trade Organization). 2001. "Declaration on the TRIPS Agreement and Public Health." [www.wto.org/English/thewto_e/minist_e/min01_e/mindecl_TRIPS_e.htm].

———. 2006. "Pharmaceutical Patents and the TRIPS Agreement." [www.wto.org/english/tratop_e/trips_e/pharma_ato186_e.htm].

———. 2008. "Members Accepting Amendment of the TRIPS Agreement." [www.wto.org/english/tratop_e/trips_e/amendment_e.htm].

———. n.d. "Overview: The TRIPS Agreement." Patents. [www.wto.org/english/tratop_e/trips_e/intel2_e.htm#patents].

9 Don't Close the Golden Door: Making Immigration Policy Work for Development

Michael Clemens and Sami Bazzi

International movements of people can spark and sustain the development process in poor countries, helping people climb out of poverty. Creating opportunities for poor people to improve their lives is in our interest. Doing so promotes our values, enhances our security, and restores an image of the United States that is faltering abroad. The United States has a long and incomparable history of welcoming people in search of advancement, since long before Emma Lazarus's poem celebrating the "golden door" was affixed to the base of the Statue of Liberty in 1903.

Some view the phenomenon of migration as a sign of failed development, which causes people to leave their home countries because of a lack of opportunity and, in the process, harm the places they leave by taking their skills and labor with them. But there is an entirely different way to see the international movement of people. It is a view in which the movement of people between the United States and the rest of the world is so much at the heart of the global development process that, rather than being a sign of failed development, it is actually a form of development. A careful look at how the United States itself developed and has interacted with the poorest places in the world reveals that from the beginning of our history—and now more than ever—the movement of people is at the heart of complex development processes all around the world.

Michael Clemens is a research fellow and Sami Bazzi is a research assistant at the Center for Global Development. They would like to thank Lauren Weeth for helpful discussions about U.S. immigration policy.

The next president of the United States has an opportunity to advance a migration agenda that is one of several pillars of our leadership position on global development. Our economy's spectacular growth over the last century has given us a far greater ability to offer opportunities to low-income workers than we did when we first became the land of opportunity. Although many Americans have legitimate concerns about the effects of immigration on our economy and society, a careful look at the evidence suggests that we can give enormously more opportunity to many more low-income people. Doing this makes us stronger, not weaker.

It is easy to see how high-skilled immigrants create jobs and prosperity in this country. Immigrants play a key role on Wall Street and in Silicon Valley, and their skills and drive help keep the United States in a leadership position in many global industries. What is somewhat harder to see, but no less real, is that lesser-skilled immigrants create jobs and prosperity too. About sixty million people have come to this country to stay since 1900, and our unemployment rate today is almost exactly equal to what it was then. The unequivocal lesson of history is that there is no tradeoff whatsoever between enormous, largely low-skilled immigration and jobs for people already here. We are also far more materially prosperous than we were in 1900. The only way this is possible is if all those new arrivals have been part of our strength. They frequently perform jobs that complement those done by people who arrived before them; they typically work very hard, and they make a large range of goods and services cheaper and better for others here, greatly contributing to the prosperity of our families and businesses. Being open to them is the development strategy that has built the United States into the richest country the world has ever known, and we need to maintain that proven strategy.

Maintaining that strategy will take strong, wise leadership on this divisive issue—and leadership on migration is not political suicide. The idea that Americans are more resistant than ever before to migration is quite wrong. The Gallup organization has asked Americans the same question every year since 1965, when the foreign-born share of the population was far lower than it is today: "Should immigration be kept at its present level, increased, or decreased?" The fraction of people saying "increased" is more than twice as high today as it was in 1965. And whereas 65 percent said "decreased" in 1993, that fell to just 39 percent by 2006—during a period when immigration soared.

Today the United States regulates the movement of workers from poor countries by two broad standards: one for high-skilled workers and another for the low-skilled. Entry for well-educated workers is easier than for those with only a basic education, but skilled-worker visas are capped at one-third the level of just seven years ago. Employers' requests exhausted all the skilled-worker visas for fiscal year 2008 in a single day in early 2007, leaving perhaps hundreds of thousands of educated and potentially very productive workers to remain at home with far lower productivity or to go to other, more welcoming rich nations. This is bad for the U.S. economy, to be sure. But it also reduces the opportunities available to people from poor countries struggling to build a professional career and, contrary to conventional wisdom, may even do harm to prospects for those who would not have moved.

Low-skilled workers from poor countries are even more severely restricted. Around half of the low-skilled workers who enter the United States to stay enter as unauthorized migrants—about half a million every year—despite risks to personal safety, high costs, and the insecurity of an undocumented life.[1] The vast majority of the rest are given residence for the goal of family reunification, not for the goal of promoting U.S. economic growth or of allowing low-skilled workers from poor countries greater opportunity. The current policy of the United States, in broad strokes, is to run a large program staffing its farms, construction sites, janitorial positions, domestic assistant positions, and factory floors with many millions of workers obliged to live in the shadows, partially outside the social and fiscal institutions that weave the American social contract.

Vast numbers of people who would jump at the chance to come to the United States cannot, and we are more closed to low-skilled migrants than we have been in the past: in 1910, 15 percent of Americans were foreign-born. Today it is only 12 percent, despite the fact that we can offer much more opportunity to low-skilled workers than ever before: those who came a century ago typically doubled or tripled their real incomes; today low-skilled workers can achieve salaries in the United States between five and twenty times their best option at home.

Crucially, the world is much different and people are far more mobile than they were in the nineteenth century. Back then, movement often meant permanent settlement. In recent decades, temporary movements of workers shape many labor markets. The United States is far out of step with this enormous global trend; we ourselves, and developing countries as a whole, are the losers. The most glaring example is the Immigration Reform and Control Act of 1986. This law, rather than create legal pathways for established patterns of temporary and circular movement of workers at the border, opted instead to illegalize them—causing millions of Mexicans and others to stay here permanently and illegally rather than temporarily.[2] We missed an enormous opportunity to bring workers out of the shadows, help our economy remain strong, and foster development-friendly links with poor communities south of the border. We must do better, and we can. This chapter gives many specific steps the next president can take to get us on the right path.

Why migration is a development issue

The movement of people across borders shapes the entire world's development process in ways that can be difficult to see at first. Five of these are the changed decisions by those who might have moved but did not, interactions between those who moved and those who did not, return migration, effects of the pure absence of those who moved, and enormous opportunities for the migrants themselves.

1. Broadened horizons for those who stay behind

The prospect of migration changes the decisions of people who do not migrate. Anyone who grew up in rural America understands that the existence of faraway urban centers, and the fact that some people from rural areas leave to work in those centers, shapes rural communities. For example, one of the reasons rural Americans insist on quality schools for their children is so that some of those children can have opportunities in colleges and jobs far away. Those good schools end up helping even the kids who do not leave.

Similar things happen in developing countries. The Philippines, for example, is a very poor country that sends more nurses to work in rich countries than any other country in the world. Most foreign-born nurses in the United States are from the Philippines, as are the majority of all nurses in oil-rich Saudi Arabia. One result of this outward migration is that an enormous system of high-quality nursing education has arisen in the Philippines to prepare (mostly) low-income women to take advantage of these opportunities.

But does this outward migration of nurses mean that the Philippines lacks nurses? No. There are about six times as many nurses per capita in the Philippines than there are in countries at a similar level of income, more even than in the United Kingdom or Austria—two of the richest countries in the world.[3] What makes this seeming paradox possible is that large numbers of people whose education decisions were shaped by the migration opportunity did not leave the Philippines. This is hard to see because it is not easy to know why people make the choices they do. But it is happening on an enormous scale all over the world.

The prospect of migration can change people's decisions in other ways that are difficult to quantify but no less real. For example, why are Latin American athletes and musicians in the United States revered by so many children in their countries of origin, just as athletes and musicians of humble origin are revered by many children in inner-city U.S. neighborhoods? Perhaps it is because seeing people like themselves achieve spectacular material success inspires them to think of themselves as potentially successful, and it reminds them that poverty need not be their fate. Shifts in self-esteem can spread even to the poorest corners of developing countries.

2. Interaction between workers abroad and the poor countries they come from

People working abroad interact extensively with their countries of origin. They send enormous amounts of money home; they help build trade and investment ties between the United States and the rest of the world; they serve as conduits for spreading U.S. technology and ideas to the world; and they make it easier for other people from their countries to find work here.

People working in the United States sent $45 billion in unrequited transfers to Latin America in 2006.[4] This vastly exceeds all U.S. development assistance in the same year, not just to Latin America but to the whole world ($23 billion).[5] Remittances are roughly one-fifth of gross domestic product in Albania, El Salvador, and Haiti. Sums this massive have a large positive effect on welfare in the countries of origin.

But cash gifts are just the beginning of the story. Other, perhaps far more important, interactions occur between diasporas and home countries. Indian and Taiwanese immigrants to the United States, for example, have been crucial to the formation of manufacturing and information technology hubs in those countries, by serving as intermediaries, commercial ambassadors, investors, and conduits for technology transfer. Chinese entrepreneurs in California were the first to commission the manufacture of IBM-compatible computers from Taiwanese firms such as Acer, Compeq, and Mitac in the 1980s. This blossoming of high-tech industry helped induce tens of thousands of Taiwanese engineers to return to Taiwan from the United States in the 1990s. In other words, earlier migration was part of the process of developing home industries and retaining skilled workers. Migration did not affect Taiwan's development; it has been part of Taiwan's development. Likewise, Indian engineers working at U.S. firms were the first to outsource software services to their home country, which encouraged others to do the same and sparked rapid economic growth in Bengaluru, Hyderabad, Mumbai and elsewhere.[6] Investment capital also flows through migrant networks: Small firms in Mexico that are attached to migrant networks face a lower cost of capital, and thus reap greater profits, than those that are not.[7] One of Africa's most important cellular telephone networks was built and financed by Mohamed Ibrahim, a naturalized U.K. citizen who left his native Sudan at age 26.

There is a common theme here. We know from our own history that analogous patterns have been part and parcel of our own process of slowly developing into a very rich country over centuries. The development of the whole country, not just its urban areas, has been driven by people born in rural areas who moved to urban areas to make their mark and never went back: John D. Rockefeller, Abraham Lincoln, Thomas Edison, and countless others. These people built networks of trade and investment, shaped ideas, and brought new technologies to every corner of the country—and the whole nation benefited, not just the cities they spent their careers in. Such linkages did not "affect" our development process; they have been an intrinsic part of it. We should expect nothing fundamentally different at the global level, where the United States is a hub for world commerce, ideas, and capital, just as New York City has been a hub for commerce, ideas, and capital to all fifty states.

3. Knowledge, skills, and savings brought home from abroad

Many immigrants from poor countries return home bringing with them savings, skills, raised expectations, and familiarity with U.S. institutions. In the 2005/06 academic year, over half a million foreign students were enrolled in U.S. institutions of higher education, including 77,000 from India and 6,200 from Nigeria.[8] A large fraction of those trained in the United States do not remain here: of the foreign students that received a U.S. doctorate in 1991, 42 percent had left the country by 2001.[9] Although this departure rate was only 14 percent for Indian students, it was 50 percent for Turks, 53 percent for Africans (outside South Africa), and 59 percent for Peruvians. The large majority of these departures represent returns to the country of origin.[10]

These movements have significant positive effects on development. People who receive an advanced degree here and go home carry with them not only skills acquired in the world's top system of tertiary education but also firsthand experience of U.S. institutions and raised expectations for their colleagues and institutions at home. Although the effects of this are inherently difficult to measure, one recent study finds that democratic reform has progressed substantially more in developing countries that have sent more students to universities in democratic countries such as the United States.[11]

Behind many of the best-known examples of positive change in developing countries stand international migrants. Return migrants from the United States in key leadership positions of the Indonesian government—Widjojo Nitisastro, Ali Wardhana, and others popularly known as the "Berkeley Mafia"—are widely credited with helping to sustain Indonesia's three decades of growth and poverty reduction beginning in the 1960s.[12] Most economists agree that economic reforms championed by a group of Chilean return migrants from the United States in the 1970s—Sergio de Castro, Pablo Baraona, and several other colleagues known collectively as the "Chicago Boys"—contributed to Chile's being the fastest-growing major Latin American economy for the last thirty years.[13] Lee Kwan-Yew, who guided Singapore's transformation into an emerging economy of global importance, is a return migrant from the United Kingdom. Chung-Mou "Morris" Chang founded the world's largest silicon foundry in Taiwan after a twenty-five-year U.S. career at Texas

Instruments. Deng Xiaoping, the Chinese leader from 1978 to the early 1990s, whose economic reforms led to the largest and fastest reduction of poverty in history, was a return migrant from France. Mohandas K. Gandhi studied and worked for twenty-seven years in South Africa and the United Kingdom before returning to shape his homeland. Recently important and admired developing-country leaders who lived and studied abroad for long periods before leading their governments include Nobel laureate José Ramos Horta of East Timor, Ellen Johnson-Sirleaf of Liberia, and Joaquim Chissano, the former Mozambican president who in 2007 won the Mo Ibrahim Foundation's Prize for Achievement in African Leadership.

Of course there is nothing magical or automatically "good" about return migrants; Khalid Sheikh Mohammed, who orchestrated several major terrorist attacks including the destruction of the World Trade Center from bases in South Asia, lived and studied in North Carolina. Nevertheless, a close look at nearly all developing countries where sustained economic growth has occurred since World War II reveals important movements of people in key public and private sector positions to and from rich countries.

4. The pure effect of migrants' absence

It is often assumed that migrants, especially the high-skilled, harm rather than help the places they leave. But there is evidence that, on the contrary, migration can have some positive effects on the people who stay behind. For example, very large movements of labor out of particular countries, especially specific sectors in those countries, can raise wages there; when labor is scarce, its price rises. This has been documented in very large emigrations, such as the nineteenth-century exodus from Ireland,[14] and late twentieth-century emigration from Mexico[15] and Puerto Rico.[16] Movements on such a large scale are unlikely, of course, in most of today's poor countries, though emigration rates in parts Morocco, the Philippines, and Vietnam are of the same order of magnitude. Nevertheless, surges of emigration from certain sectors can raise wages within that sector even if most of the country stays put. There is suggestive but incomplete evidence that sector-specific wages among Pakistani skilled construction workers and Filipino manufacturing workers have increased due to large increases in out-migration.[17]

Again, this is not just an international phenomenon; hundreds of economically depressed counties in the United States, in the Deep South, Heartland, Rust Belt, and Great Plains, have lost about a third of their collective population since the 1930s. Precisely this freedom of movement meant that per capita income in those places did not decline significantly with respect to the national average.[18] In contrast, tsarist Russia severely restricted the internal movement of its poorest farmers from the sixteenth to the eighteenth centuries, and it has been argued that this is one of the chief reasons for its impoverishment relative to Western Europe and the United States by 1900.[19]

New evidence also suggests that emigration of skilled workers in particular does not necessarily make poor countries worse off. It is certainly true that the absence of skilled émigrés who provided key services to society prior to departure—risk-taking entrepreneurs, scientists, honest politicians, health care professionals, and so on—can tend to make access to those services more difficult for people remaining in the countries of origin, to some degree. For such reasons the British government has banned recruitment of doctors and nurses from most developing countries, including all of Africa, and developing countries such as South Africa have enacted punitive measures against émigré health professionals.

But does forcibly restricting movement result in better delivery of important services in developing countries? First, it is important to remember that entrepreneurs, scientists, and doctors from poor countries are indeed people, with aspirations and rights of their own. Policy measures to prevent "human resources" from being "drained," "poached," or "exported" reduce them from human beings to mere commodities. Second, the full consequences of restricting movement must be carefully considered. Some of India's most important high-technology entrepreneurs have worked abroad for extended periods. Would the industry that is one of India's most dynamic engines of growth be where it is today if those people had been blocked at the airport from leaving India in the first place?

Once again, we have an intuitive sense of these complexities from our national experience. Would West Virginia have done well for itself by forcing Harvard professor Henry Louis Gates Jr. to remain in the small mill town where he was born? To what extent would the economic development of U.S. inner cities be advanced by forcing their most skilled and talented young people to reside there, even if in some cases it was against their wishes?

Using the blunt tool of migration restrictions on skilled workers in order to promote development in faraway, complex places is extraordinarily difficult and likely to produce unintended consequences. All forms of coercion carry the same risks, even when they sound less coercive than actually restricting the movement of skilled professionals. These include the frequently advocated policies of bans on recruitment (that is, forcing U.S. employers not to provide information about U.S. jobs to people in foreign countries) and "self-sufficiency" in high-skill sectors (that is, eliminating U.S. jobs available to the foreign-born by ensuring that they are exclusively filled with U.S.-born workers).

Box 9.1. African health professionals

One of the most frequently cited arguments for limiting the ability of developing-country professionals to emigrate is the case of emigration of African doctors and nurses. Health professionals are scarce in Africa, and their services are certainly needed. But it is not clear that forcibly restricting their movement will result in better health for Africans. The question we should ask is: What set of policies will help Africans live longer, healthier lives?

Consider two alternative policies open to an African country interested in better health outcomes for its citizens:

Policy package A: "Train and trap"

1. Heavy subsidies for training of physicians and registered nurses.
2. Abysmal subsidies to post-training compensation of caregivers (terrible working conditions, no performance incentives, miniscule rural service incentives, few advancement opportunities, extreme overregulation, widespread corruption).
3. Comparatively inadequate subsidies beyond high-level caregivers for crucial areas like public health, sanitation, disease prevention, and community-level health workers.
4. Blunt, mostly ineffective coercion to force highly trained health professionals to remain within the borders of the country they happened to be born in, reserving lucrative professional jobs abroad for people who happened to be born in those countries.

Policy package B: "Reward desired behaviors"

1. A broad shift from subsidizing training to subsidizing practice and performance (lift bans on private training, encourage rural service and physical presence in public clinics with meaningful incentive schemes, target performance subsidies for highly trained professionals at centers of excellence, greatly shift subsidies toward paying for mid-level community care plus public health prevention efforts and sanitation).
2. Elimination of counterproductive overregulation in the health sector (bans and limits on private training, restrictions on independent practice by mid-level professionals, and so on).
3. Decoupling of the health profession from the civil service (some health ministries cannot hire because of onerous obligations to civil servants).
4. Building of bridges with international companies and organizations to facilitate the movement of health professionals as an enormous, unprecedented opportunity for Africans' professional development.

The Philippines has embraced key elements of Policy B, sending far more nurses per capita abroad than any African country—and yet it still has far better indicators of basic public health outcomes, and far more nurses per capita, than Africa collectively. And for the most part the Philippines does not lose massive public training investments from

(continued)

Box 9.1. African health professionals (continued)

that movement, because it has encouraged a system of training that permits many nurses to pay for their own educations. In the process, it has created otherwise unthinkable professional opportunities for hundreds of thousands of (mostly) low-income women. There is no reason why Africa cannot follow this example, led by countries with the institutional capacity to implement such schemes—like Botswana, Morocco, and South Africa, which are today among the countries most concerned about health worker emigration.

The main policy concern should lie with creating easy and effective mechanisms for the beneficiaries of training to cover a greater share of the cost of training. In some countries this may mean new credit instruments; in others, a limited period of required post-graduate service; and in others still, a bilateral agreement for transfer of tax revenue from destination country to sending country. What all such measures have in common is that they seek to expand, not reduce, the range of choices available to professionals in poor countries.

Source: Clemens 2007.

5. Immediately improved living standards for those who find work abroad

Obtaining a job in a rich country makes a certain number of poor people much better off—immediately, massively, and almost certainly. If economic development is the construction of systems of exchange that make people progressively better off, then jobs in rich countries are not an alternative to development—they are a form of economic development for some people from poor countries. What is largely invisible to the rest of us is the fact that, even when working conditions for immigrants in the United States are hard, for the vast majority of immigrants conditions are better here than where they came from.

To claim that substantial numbers of immigrants "get it wrong" and come here by the millions to make themselves worse off is to believe that immigrants are quite stupid. One hears claims of this sort frequently: a recent National Public Radio story claimed that "most" Filipino laborers in the United States "would rather be somewhere else,"[20] while an editorial in *The New Republic* compared today's Mexican agricultural laborers to nineteenth-century African-American slaves.[21] This is simply false. Nearly all of today's immigrants freely choose to come here, having judged where they would rather be, much better than anyone else could judge for them. And the typical Mexican laborer in the United States makes roughly five times what he or she could make at home.[22] Of all the Mexican-born people in the world who earn more than the paltry sum of $10 per day, 43 percent live in the United States.[23] By this reasonable standard of poverty, departure to the United States has been not just one route out of poverty for lucky individual

Mexicans. It has been one of the principal routes out of poverty available to any Mexican.

The United States obviously cannot employ the whole world. But our extraordinarily strong economy—the richest in the world, and in all of human history—can employ many people from many countries. And better jobs for the poorest people on earth are economic development.

Migration as a route out of poverty is very familiar from our national story. Best known is the frontier homesteading of the nineteenth century. Less known, but at least as important, is the epochal movement of about one million African-Americans born in the South to cities of the North and West, beginning in the 1920s and 1930s—known as the "Great Migration." At the heart of the economic development process for many African-Americans born in western Mississippi was departure for distant centers of economic activity in prosperous cities. Generating those opportunities through movement did not affect the process of development for those Mississippians; it was development for them.

A snapshot of current migration policy debates

In late June 2007, after several months of intense formal deliberation and nearly 800 pages of documentation, the U.S. Senate effectively tabled the Comprehensive Immigration Reform Act of 2007,[24] which had emerged as a compromise on three previous bills: the Secure America & Orderly Immigration Act (the McCain-Kennedy Bill), the Comprehensive Enforcement & Immigration Reform Act of 2005 (the Cornyn-Kyl Bill), and the earlier Comprehensive Immigration and Reform Act of 2006. The Comprehensive Immigration Reform Act was the most concerted attempt at wholesale immigration reform in over a decade, but it never reached a final vote. As of January 2006, an estimated 11.6 million unauthorized immigrants were residing in the United States,[25] and pressure for congressional action on immigration policy had been mounting for several years.

Z-visas and point systems

Largely credited to twelve senators,[26] the Comprehensive Immigration Reform Act focused on many provisions, including border enforcement, employee hiring practices, temporary worker programs, family reunification, visa and green card opportunities for undocumented immigrants, and educational opportunities for children of those immigrants. While bipartisan proponents portrayed the bill as a victory for all stakeholders including the migrants, conservative interest groups attacked several of the bill's key components, notably the "Z-visa" provision.

At the core of the bill, the proposed Z-visa would have provided a means for over 10 million unauthorized immigrants to obtain a path to legal citizenship.[27] For hard-line opponents, the Z-visa amounted to simple amnesty for lawbreakers. Others questioned whether millions of unauthorized immigrants would comply with the required provisions. Polling conducted by the New Media Foundation around the time of the debate over the bill in June 2007 found that, in fact, a majority (83 percent) of the unauthorized Latino immigrant population in the United States would be willing to comply with the chief provisions of the Z-visa.[28] Surveyed individuals, however, frequently expressed serious reservations about the bill's requirement that they return to their home countries in order to complete their application for permanent residency. Under the proposed bill, only the spouses and children of immigrants residing in the United States would be eligible for family visas. These stipulations, proponents argued, would arrest the "chain immigration" phenomenon whereby distant relatives outside the nuclear family attain visas on grounds of family reunification.

The chief architects of the Comprehensive Immigration Reform Act also introduced a novel point system that would determine employment visa acquisition. Currently, work visas for skilled laborers are sponsored directly by employers, and the details of each contract are negotiated privately and bilaterally before the employer applies to the federal government on behalf of the applicant. The proposed point system would be similar in spirit to that employed in other OECD countries.[29] But according to a study by the National Foundation for American Policy, basic flaws in the proposed system would have made entry difficult for broad classes of professionals, including "nurses, . . . renowned actors, athletes, physicians in rural areas, factory managers, certain executives and possibly even Nobel Prize winners."[30]

Temporary workers

The initial stages of the Comprehensive Immigration Reform Act included proposals for a new Y-visa that would have enabled 400,000 temporary laborers to enter the United States annually for a period of two years, after which time they would have been required to return to their home countries for one year before reapplying for the visa. By the end of the debate in late June, however, the number of potential Y-visas had been reduced to 200,000 and the program had been set to expire just five years after getting under way. Opposition centered on the lack of adequate immigration enforcement mechanisms to address visa overstays, and the impact of additional immigration allowances on wages and employment of low-skill native workers.

Two aspects of the major temporary worker proposals directly addressed these concerns. First, the temporary laborers would have likely engaged in some degree of self-enforcement so long as they had reasonable assurance of subsequent opportunities to return to the United States after the required return to their home countries. Second, the proposed program would give strong incentives for immigrants' home-country governments to engage more actively in managing the flow of emigrants to the United States. Particular provisions stipulated that home-country governments would have risked future reductions in the visa quotas allocated to their countries if current migrants were found to have overstayed.[31]

"In-sourcing" brains (and jobs)

Despite the breadth of issues covered by the Comprehensive Immigration Reform Act, substantive consideration of immigration policy toward highly skilled foreign workers had largely been neglected. The behemoths of the high-tech industry, with Bill Gates leading the charge, have lobbied consistently over the past several years for streamlined green card procedures and an elimination of the cap on H1-B visas for highly skilled professionals. The H1-B system, they claim, is broken. Most tellingly, since 1994, nearly 100,000 green cards reserved for H1-B visa holders have gone unused, a state of affairs frequently attributed to funding limitations at U.S. Citizenship and Immigration Services. By September 2007, the agency came under fire for its perceived unwillingness to streamline the visa backlog, given that associated fees provide nearly 20 percent of the agency's annual budget.[32] At the time of this writing, annual H1-B visas were limited to 65,000 (with an additional 20,000 reserved for those with graduate degrees from the United States),[33] down greatly from the cap of 195,000 in the year 2000. Over 120,000 applications were submitted on a single day in April 2007, instantly exhausting all 65,000 visas for fiscal year 2008. The 2007 Comprehensive Immigration Reform Act proposed a return to the 2000 level of 195,000 per year.

The consequences of this low cap on H1-B visas are only beginning to emerge. Excessive red tape and an increasingly low ceiling on the number of annual H1-B visas granted has driven high-skilled workers from the Indian subcontinent and East Asia to Canada and Australia in recent years. This raises the possibility that U.S. immigration policy could strengthen our competitors; Microsoft's recent decision to expand operations in British Columbia has been linked directly to the collapse of immigration reform in the United States.[34] Bill Gates and others have argued that the solution to the shortage of skilled professionals lies not in any proposed point system but rather in a substantial increase (or even an "infinite" increase, to quote Gates's testimony before Congress in March 2007[35]) in the cap on H1-B visas in the near term.

Refugees

In accordance with the Immigration and Nationality Act of 1965, each year the president submits a proposal to Congress for the maximum number of refugees to be admitted in the forthcoming fiscal year.[36] Refugee admissions were at their highest in the first few years after the Refugee Act of 1980 and the collapse of the Soviet Union. Between 1990 and 2000, nearly 95,000 refugees were admitted to the United States annually.[37] Since September 11, 2001, however, the United States has significantly curtailed its annual admission of refugees and asylum seekers. Admissions have only slowly recovered in recent years with nearly 41,000 refugees admitted in 2006.

At the same time, it has become much easier for previously admitted refugees and asylum seekers to obtain permanent residence. The REAL ID Act of 2005 indefinitely removed the annual cap of 10,000 green cards available to this special class of immigrants, and in 2005 and 2006 alone, nearly 140,000 such immigrants already residing in the United States won permanent residence. Today, a refugee who has resided continuously in the United States for at least one year has immediate access to a visa number.

Despite these new favorable policies toward existing refugees, the United States still lags behind other industrialized countries' humanitarian immigration programs. According to the Commitment to Development Index rankings for 2007, the United States actually ranks near the bottom (seventeenth) of the twenty-one major donor countries in terms of what the United Nations High Commission for Refugees identifies as "refugee burden sharing."[38] Although the United States hosts a large stock of refugees, smaller industrialized countries such as Sweden and Switzerland generally bear a far greater share of the global refugee burden relative to the size of their populations.

This huge disparity has been most glaring in recent years as a single town in Sweden received twice as many Iraqi refugees as the United States allowed into the entire country in 2006.[39] In the four years after the far less disastrous 1991 Gulf War, the United States had accepted nearly 4,000 Iraqi refugees annually, but since 2003, no more than 300 refugees have been allowed from Iraq in any given year. To be sure, U.S. refugee policy is doing a great deal to help people from the poorest countries; the share of African nationals in U.S. refugee admissions has risen from an annual average of 11 percent in the late 1990s to almost 50 percent today, for example.[40] But the United States can, and should, do more.

Enforcement and splintered local efforts

Perhaps the most uncontroversial piece of the Comprehensive Immigration Reform Act package, border enforcement was the first issue to meet legislative enactment in the wake of the late June no-vote. In late July 2007, under the sponsorship of Arizona Senator John Kyl (one of the early proponents of the act), the Senate ratified a $3 billion increase in the federal budget for border enforcement. This increase in specific border security enforcement could generate the renewed confidence in federal immigration policymakers needed to move forward on other components of immigration reform.

The collapse of the Comprehensive Immigration Reform Act has brought the deficiencies of federal immigration policy to the fore. In the vacuum left by consistent federal inaction on immigration policy, state legislatures across the country have begun taking immigration policy into their own hands. In the first seven months of 2007, fifty state legislatures considered 1,404 bills related to immigration policies, resulting in 170 enacted into law, up dramatically from the total enacted in 2006.[41] These bills have mostly been aimed at curbing immigrant access to jobs and public services. Although state-specific immigration legislation is not inherently problematic, some of the most crucial policy reforms regarding visa legislation simply cannot take place without federal leadership and oversight.

An agenda for the next U.S. president

A president who treats migration policy as part of his or her development policy must be a leader. It is not enough simply to "enforce our laws." Our laws do not always serve us well, or serve the cause of justice. President James Buchanan had a responsibility to lead, not just to enforce laws allowing African-Americans to be owned by other Americans. President Calvin Coolidge had a responsibility to lead, not just to enforce laws that placed anyone sipping a beer in violation of the U.S. Constitution. Laws that impose questionable ethics on unstoppable historic forces need to be shaped in a way that makes the world a more just place. The buck stops with the chief executive.

One fundamental principle of action should be that movement and linkages between the poorest countries and the United States are at the heart of the global development process. The United States can and should maintain its centuries-long role as an engine of economic progress for the world, and this can and should be done in a way that those lucky enough to have been born here find acceptable. We cannot "save" the world, but we can do much more for many more. Today's immigrants are not poorer in absolute terms than many of the nineteenth-century immigrants who are ancestors of so many of us: The real wages of construction workers in India across the twentieth century are similar to those in poor parts of Europe in the early- to mid-nineteenth century. If today's immigrants are poorer relative to those already here than earlier immigrants were, it is because we have become enormously wealthier and stronger than we were back then. This gives us greater ability, and responsibility, to continue our traditions than ever before.

A second principle of action is that the United States cannot choose to have no links with developing countries. The disparities in our world have become so large that no attempt to keep "them" out has any hope of working, as the South African architects of apartheid discovered. Our laws and policies must reflect the real world, and it falls to the president to help Americans understand this.

Indeed, the disparities between the world's poorest and the opportunities we offer—enormously larger than they were when we first became the land of opportunity—mean that we can offer more opportunity now than at any time in our history. This new ability to help, however, comes at a time of new reluctance to help. Low-skilled workers' real wages in the United States, while roughly ten times the world average, have recently been stagnant, and overseas wars have contributed to a feeling of pessimism about the poorer parts of the world. Leadership can move the United States and the world a few steps closer to a win-win scenario on migration. There are five key steps.

1. Forge a broad understanding of our tradition of opportunity

The evidence is clear: Migration is one of the most important sources of poverty reduction for a large number of developing countries. A president who wishes to build an immigration policy that continues our precious tradition of offering opportunity to poor, hard-working people needs to talk clearly and authoritatively with Congress and with the American people. Overall, our economy is doubtlessly strengthened by the labor that today's immigrants provide, in the same way and for the same reasons that the poor and hard-working immigrants who flooded in at the end of the nineteenth century helped us become the world's industrial superpower in the twentieth century. Abundant, emotionally charged anecdotes of workers being displaced by immigrants are as numerous today as they were in the newspapers of 1900, but the leader of this country cannot let anecdotes cloud the big picture. Now, as back then, immigrants frequently choose different jobs than people whose families have been here longer—they complement the work we do, rather than take work away from us.

This is why the latest economic research[42] finds that the surge in immigration from 1990 to 2004 had a small, positive effect on the overall wages of all native-born U.S. workers of 1–2 percent, and a small negative effect on the least-educated native-born, high school dropouts, of –1.1 percent. Competing with this strand of research is another, older strand[43] finding that a generation of enormous immigration from 1980 to 2000 decreased the overall wages of all native-born workers by just 3 percent compared with what they would have been otherwise, with a change of –8.9 percent for high school dropouts, and that all immigration between 1990 and 2004 had a cumulative effect of zero percent on the average worker and –4.2 percent on wages of native-born high school dropouts.[44] This latter, more negative finding depends crucially on the assumption that immigrants are perfect substitutes for native-born workers of the same education level.

In other words, the broad finding of the best economics literature is that massive immigration of all types over many decades has not lowered the wages of the average American worker at all. It also finds that this large inflow may cumulatively have lowered wages for native-born high school dropouts by a few percentage points, although even this small effect is slightly exaggerated because it does not account for the fact that immigration probably contributed to lower prices (especially for foodstuffs) and that lower wages for high school dropouts may have caused fewer people to become high school dropouts. Meanwhile, during the period 1990–2004, the United States admitted 13.4 million permanent immigrants[45] and 161 million temporary nonimmigrants[46] from developing countries, thereby raising their wages by 200 percent, 400 percent, or even 1,000 percent in some cases. This inflow also generated a cumulative total remittance outflow of at least $600 billion,[47] dwarfing our charitable efforts at foreign aid. This vast contribution to global development has not come at a substantial cost to our overall domestic prosperity, by any reasonable standard. It falls to the president to help Americans understand this.

Similarly, the president must be clear with the public that the consensus of careful research finds no meaningful burden of immigrants on public finances. Anecdotes about crowded Arizona emergency rooms aside, the overall effect of immigrants on this strong, prosperous nation's social services and state coffers is small. Unauthorized Mexican immigrants, for example, use health services in California at much lower rates than U.S.-born Latinos.[48] The Congressional Budget Office determined that the cumulative impact of all recent unauthorized immigration on state and local budgets is "modest," increasing expenditures in the vast majority of districts by less than 5 percent. Even that small increase is mostly offset by corresponding increases in local revenue.[49] The most serious research available finds that the fiscal impact of immigrants themselves is roughly zero over their lifetimes—they contribute to the system roughly what they take out—and that their children are large net contributors to the system.[50] Incarceration rates are much lower among immigrants than among otherwise comparable U.S. citizens[51]—which was not the case, by the way, in the age of mass European immigration to this country.[52] Immigrants even have higher credit scores than otherwise comparable U.S. citizens.[53] Temporary guest workers, moreover, have the clear potential to contribute more to the system than they take out, thus becoming part of a complex and long-term solution to the crises faced by Social Security and Medicare as our population continues to age.

Finally, and importantly, the president must make it clear that national security does not require halting immigration (even if that were feasible); instead, it requires knowing who is coming and going. Our current policy of dramatically restricting the number of low-income people who can come here to work simply drives migration underground. Every year roughly half a million people come here illegally to stay, and even more arrive illegally but do not stay.[54] The government has no idea who those people are. Keeping those movements in the shadows clearly and directly lowers our security. Increasing legal channels for movement is compatible with higher security, and it might be a necessary part of higher security.

2. Craft an economically sound policy toward guest workers

There are currently just 150,000 legal slots for authorized temporary low-skilled workers to enter the country each year (H-2 visas). Meanwhile, roughly three times that many workers enter the country each year without any authorization. Enforcement is not the answer to this situation: between 1986 and 2002 the budget dedicated to patrolling the Mexican border increased about 1,000 percent and the number of border patrol officers tripled—but unauthorized entries are at an all-time high.[55] Our strong economy unquestionably demands those workers, and they are willing to work. The solution is to create a legal pathway for those people to give us their labor. It makes economic sense, to be sure. But it is also more humane and safer—for the workers, about 400 of whom died trying to cross the border secretly in 2007,[56] and for the United States: Our current policy of forcing massive movements underground ensures that we have no idea who is entering our country. Creating legal channels for movement vastly increases our ability to monitor entries and know who is here. Simple enforcement of current, wildly unrealistic regulations also works against our foreign policy: According to Peter Hakim of the Inter-American Dialogue, "Regardless of its intent, the erection of [a] barrier—which is often compared to the Berlin Wall—would make it plain to most Latin Americans that Washington no longer views the region as a serious partner or collaborator, but mainly as a source of unwanted problems."[57]

The president should push hard for the establishment of a temporary guest-worker program to create a legal pathway for temporary migrants to work in the United States. This would allow hundreds of thousands more people access to opportunities here—helping them, their families, and the places they come from. It would do little to rile opponents of "amnesty" because it would not address the status of those who have broken laws in the past, but rather would create a legal path to limited but substantial opportunity for new migrants. It would placate those concerned about consumption of unpaid public services because it would confer strictly limited rights to public services, and those that were provided could be paid for by employers (health care, yes; Social Security, no).[58] And it would partially placate those concerned about displacement of U.S. workers because the number of workers and industries in which they were authorized to work could be flexible over time. Crucially, the program would have to be complemented by better enforcement of individual identification, such as upgrading systems to detect false Social Security numbers. The president should place this at the heart of the reform.

The first thing that the president must explain to America is that the alternative to such a plan is not "no movement." The alternative to an expanded legal pathway for labor movement is continuation of the hundreds of thousands of annual clandestine, dangerous unauthorized border crossings every year. Creating this number of visas would not be opening the door any further, but simply watching a door that is already open and can never be completely closed, so that we impose less suffering on others and so that we know who is here and what they have and have not paid for.

The second thing that the president must explain to the American people is that we live in a much more mobile world than ever before. Many Mexican migrants would prefer not to stay constantly or permanently in the United States, but they remain here precisely because there is no legal channel for them to ever return if they depart even briefly. Prior to the 1986 Immigration Reform and Control Act, the goal of most Mexican migrants was to work abroad seasonally and temporarily. But increased border enforcement under the act caused more than two million of these workers to remain permanently in the United States under the act's amnesty provision.[59] That is, the massive illegalization of seasonal, temporary movements has contributed enormously to the population of lasting, permanent unauthorized residents. The president must explain to Congress and voters that the formula of interdiction-plus-amnesty has been tried and has failed. It is time for a bold new formula, the creation of a legal channel for the temporary movements that most migrants desire. Legalizing large numbers of temporary movements is quite separate from amnesty, but the two issues are related in that guest-worker visas will reduce the need for future amnesties.

The United Kingdom has recently discovered, with a bold experiment of its own, that labor movement from even very poor parts of Eastern Europe can be truly circular when it occurs legally. As of May 2004 anyone from the ten new European Union countries[60] could come to work in the United Kingdom, though eight of those countries (the "A8") are subject to special registration and other limitations. From May 2004 to March 2006, about 400,000 citizens of A8 countries came to work legally in the United Kingdom, most of them from Poland. The majority of those arrivals had already returned home by early 2007, even though their visas have no duration limit. Those who remain have had no discernible impact on U.K. wages or unemployment rates[61] and may have actually lowered the natural rate of unemployment.[62] Fewer than 1 percent of these applied for public benefits such as jobseeker's allowance, income support, and state pension credit, and all but a tenth of those applications were immediately thrown out.[63] The success of the U.K. experiment has led other European Union states that opposed free movement from the A8 countries to subsequently drop their barriers, including Finland, Italy, and Spain.[64]

With all of these factors in mind, the United States should create a guest-worker scheme on the scale of between 300,000 and 500,000 nonimmigrant temporary admissions per year; 300,000 is the number proposed by Princeton University's Douglas Massey,[65] and 500,000 is the number of current annual unauthorized arrivals.

3. Greatly raise or eliminate caps on high-skilled worker visas

The president should explain to Congress why limits to skilled-worker visas are bad for the United States, bad for migrants, and bad for the countries migrants come from. Shutting the door to skilled workers, aside from eliminating hundreds of thousands of professional opportunities for educated and highly productive people from developing countries who wish to work in the United States, also lowers our productivity and threatens our ability to remain a center of innovation and job creation. Skilled workers have become ever scarcer as we have entered the information age—so scarce that it has become a major contributor to our recent sharp rise in income inequality.[66] In other words, in the twenty-first century, our ill-considered attempts to cut ourselves off from the world actually divide us from one another.

In 2007 the United States issued just 65,000 H-1 visas for temporary skilled workers with private sector jobs.[67] This ludicrously low number—down two-thirds from the level of just five years ago—was so highly oversubscribed that the entire one-year allotment ran out in a matter of hours. At the time of this writing, proposals are floating around Congress to raise this cap to 115,000, or at most 180,000. But even these higher ceilings are scandalously low. Relative to their sizes, other industrialized countries are issuing dramatically more skilled-worker visas. If Australia, Canada, and New Zealand issued the same number of skilled-worker visas in proportion to their populations as they do now, but were the same size as the United States, Canada would offer about half a million per year, Australia would give over one million, and New Zealand would give over two million.[68] The European Union is getting into this game now as well, establishing the new "Blue Card" explicitly to compete with the United States for high-skilled workers from around the world.

These numbers tell us three things: First, much larger inflows of skilled workers will not harm us, as they have not harmed our friends. Second, other countries are stepping in to take advantage of this costless, invaluable resource because we are not. Third, the United States economy has the strength to offer professional job opportunities to hundreds of thousands and perhaps millions of skilled, educated people from developing countries every year at no cost.

The most recent proposals for legislative reform called for the creation of a point system reminiscent of Canada's. Employers were unenthusiastic, as the change would mean that control of which skilled workers are admitted would be largely transferred from employers to government bureaucrats. The numbers of skilled workers who would be let in under the proposed U.S. point system is so difficult to ascertain that even a careful, detailed study could not predict the number.[69] But exactly how the system is changed to let in more skilled workers is less important than that it be thus changed. The president must lead on this issue; forcibly keeping out the world's brightest and most productive workers is a national embarrassment, as well as being a development obstacle.

The United States should raise the number of visas it grants to high-skilled workers to levels comparable to those of our international competitors, which is to say between half a million and one million per year—or higher.

The next president should also order the Department of Education, Department of Labor, Social Security Administration, and Internal Revenue Service to explore the possibility of bilateral treaties with major sending countries for skilled migrants, providing for portable retirement benefits for return migrants in order to remove obstacles to going home when they choose to. Such agreements should also explore innovative and context-specific ways for emigrants to pay for the education they receive, especially including U.S. government and U.S. employer support for private tertiary training facilities in key sending countries.

4. Do our fair share for refugees

The United States hosts more refugees and asylum-seekers from developing countries than any other country in the world, which by itself is something to be proud of. But we are also much larger and economically stronger than any other developed country. And relative to the smaller sizes of their populations and economies, all but a handful of the other developed countries host many more refugees than we do. They do this while maintaining their national prosperity and cohesion, revealing that we could lend much more of our strength to those who need it most. Today, refugees comprise about 0.2 percent of the U.S. population, while Sweden manages to host five times that many as a share of its population—while maintaining a secure, equitable, and wealthy society. Countries like Canada and the United Kingdom host a number of refugees comprising about 0.5 percent of their populations; we can, and should, do at least that.

The number of refugees the United States may admit each year is set directly by the president.[70] This is one area where the next president can quickly and easily change the lives of some of the neediest people on earth with the stroke of a pen and without consulting anyone else. It can be done at negligible cost to our national strength; indeed, U.S. influence in global affairs would be strengthened by such an unequivocally humanitarian act, based on our world-renowned tradition of welcoming the tired and poor.

The next president should order the State Department's Bureau of Population, Refugees, and Migration to increase annual admissions of refugees and asylum-seekers from the current average of around 50,000 to between 100,000 and 150,000. This would bring our country into line with international standards and with our own historical precedent. Even after this large increase, there would be only somewhat more than roughly 100,000 annual refugee admissions that the Reagan, Bush, and Clinton administrations averaged throughout the 1980s and 1990s.[71] That number is in line with the recommendations of leading national and international refugee advocates.[72]

5. Know who is moving in and who is moving out

The United States collects reliable data on arrivals of persons because this is what most voters are concerned about. But we collect very poor data on departures, the circular movements of temporary workers, and financial flows from migrants to the rest of the world because voters are not as interested in these movements and flows. But some of the most important U.S. contributions to global development have been to give temporary and permanent work opportunities to tens of millions of people born in poor countries, to thereby generate about one-quarter of official global remittance flows, and to provide higher education to public and private sector leaders in developing countries all over the globe. Understanding the full impacts of labor mobility is impossible without knowing who is coming in as well as who is moving out.

For decades, anyone wanting to measure flows of trade or investment between countries has had ready access to minutely detailed statistics in large international databases. There is no such tool for migration researchers. How many high-skilled foreign-born professionals residing in the United States left for other countries last year? No one knows. Even the countries with the largest migrant populations and the best statistics—France, the United Kingdom, and the United States—do not carefully track departures. This is a little like collecting statistics on imports but not on exports, though more bizarre because people are so much more important than commodities. How many temporary workers moved back and forth between rich and poor countries in 2003? No one can tell you, because there is no standard international definition of what constitutes "temporary" migration. This is tantamount to every country in the world using irreconcilable definitions of "goods" and "services" in their trade statistics. It is a scandal.

It is possible to do better. Years of effort in the middle of the twentieth century gave us superb statistics on trade and investment, and it is easy to measure the American contribution to global development through these channels. We have successfully worked with other countries to accurately track both inflows and outflows of capital, and to create standardized definitions of goods, services, and financial flows. We can do the same for movements of people. This too requires leadership. The president should direct the Bureau of the Census, the State Department, and Citizenship and Immigration Services to work together to lead international efforts at collecting and compiling migration statistics that are as good as our trade statistics.

Conclusion

Keep the big picture in sight. International movement can bring much more opportunity to others without substantial harm to anyone. The population of the United States in 1900 was around seventy-five million. That was a time of intense concern about immigration: A *New York Times* headline on April 15 of that year warned of an unprecedented "army" of poor, uneducated immigrants at our doorstep. Then, the fraction of our population that was foreign-born was much higher than today. After 1890 the Bureau of the Census had officially declared that the frontier no longer existed, and many felt that the country was simply full.

Imagine going back in time and telling the American public that, over the course of the twentieth century, roughly sixty million more people were going to come and stay[73]—that is, 80 percent of the population at the time, in new immigrants—plus tens of millions more who came for a while and did not stay. People would have been terrified of what that would mean to the privileged position they enjoyed in the world. Yet that is precisely what happened, and here we are today: the richest nation the world has ever seen. Back then, who could have foreseen the emergence of Silicon Valley and its contribution to global development through circular migration and diaspora-linked flows of information and commerce? Who could have predicted that by 2007, foreign workers in the United States would be sending home almost $50 billion a year—which, converted to the dollars of 1900, was about one-sixth the size of the entire U.S. economy? Or that by 2007 around a fifth of each graduating class of Harvard University would be foreign nationals[74] and that over one million foreigners would come to study in the United States each year?[75] All of these things happened. Though they might once have been seen as threats to our strength, they are today part of our strength.

In short, few envisioned the degree to which we have grown economically strong while retaining and enhancing our ability to provide opportunities to low-income people from all over the world. We have proven our ability to do so. It is something liberals can embrace because it effectively and enormously reduces poverty, and it is something conservatives can embrace because it is one of our longest and grandest traditions. The next president of the United States has a historic opportunity to turn today's shameful disarray into tomorrow's win-win breakthrough.

Notes

1. MPI 2007.
2. Durand, Massey, and Parrado 1999.
3. WHO 2005, pp. 50–52.
4. IADB 2007.
5. OECD 2006a. Workers' remittances, to be sure, are not a form of "development assistance"—they are transfers of earned money primarily to family members, not altruistic charity any more than a holiday gift to one's mother is "charity." But they are without doubt a very major source of development finance for the migrants' countries of origin. Much ink has been spilled over whether remittances substantially affect countries' exchange rates or whether remittances are spent on schooling or televisions, but these are second-order questions.
6. Saxenian 2002; Pandey and others 2006.
7. Woodruff and Zenteno 2007.
8. IIE 2006.
9. Finn 2003.
10. NSB 2003 (table 2-12, pages 2–36) shows that 41 percent of Turkish science and engineering doctoral recipients return home (thus about four-fifths of the 50 percent who depart for any other country), and 10 percent of Indian recipients (thus over two-thirds of the 14 percent who depart).
11. Spilimbergo 2007.
12. Their stories are documented in Thee Kian Wie 2003, among others.
13. Their experience is documented in Valdés 1995, among others.

14. O'Rourke 1994.
15. Mishra 2007.
16. Borjas 2008.
17. Lucas 2005, pp. 99–100.
18. Pritchett 2006, p. 49.
19. Landes 1999, pp. 240–42.
20. Sullivan 2007.
21. *New Republic* 2007.
22. The well-respected Mexican Migration Project has established this with detailed surveys of migrants since 1982, as have several other sources.
23. Clemens and Pritchett 2008.
24. The bill was introduced into the 110th Congress, 1st Session of the Senate by Majority Leader Harry Reid (D-NV) on May 9, 2007. To much less public fanfare, the House of Representatives was also debating immigration reform in its Security Through Regularized Immigration and Vibrant Economy (STRIVE 2007) Act, introduced on April 3, 2007.
25. Hoefer, Rytina, and Campbell 2007.
26. Prominent in the group are Mel Martinez (R-FL), Jon Kyl (R-AZ), Edward Kennedy (D-MA), Dianne Feinstein (D-CA), Lindsey Graham (R-SC), Arlen Specter (R-PA), John McCain (R-AZ), and Ken Salazar (D-CO).
27. The bill stipulated that, in order to obtain legal status, unauthorized aliens must first pay a fine of $2,000 and back taxes on previous earnings. Applicants would also have been required to undergo a background check and have no criminal record. They would have been provided with the Z-visa for eight years, after which time they would be required to return to their home countries to obtain a green card.
28. See NAM 2007, for full details of the study, including methodology and executive summaries. Because Latino immigrants make up the grand majority of the undocumented population (see Hanson 2006) and under the given time constraints, the authors did not ensure that other unauthorized immigrant populations were captured in the sampling frame.
29. For example, New Zealand has had a points-based system since 1991, Canada since 1967, Australia since 1984, and Switzerland since 1996. The United Kingdom plans to launch its program in 2008.
30. Anderson 2007.
31. In addition to the temporary workers program, the Development, Relief, and Education for Alien Minors Act (the DREAM Act) has emerged as a feasible and less controversial policy reform. The proposed action would have provided a pathway to legal status for undocumented immigrant students who (a) came to the United States before the age of 16, (b) have resided in the United States continuously for at least five years, and (c) have a GED or high school diploma.

Each year, nearly 65,000 undocumented immigrants graduate from high school and have little prospect of attending state universities because of stipulations in the Illegal Immigration Reform and Immigrant Responsibility Act of 1996, which make it difficult for universities to provide in-state tuition fees for undocumented aliens. The DREAM Act would reverse these provisions and also guarantee legal status to families of immigrant members of the military. The latter provision has garnered strong support for the DREAM Act from officials in the Department of Defense. In the wake of the demise of the Comprehensive Immigration Reform Act, Democratic senators, led by Richard Durbin (D-IL), capitalized on Defense Department interest by offering the DREAM Act as an amendment to the defense appropriations bill for 2008. The bill, Senate Amendment 2237, proposed by Durbin, remains in its Senate draft version at the time of writing and has not yet passed.

32. *Washington Post* 2007, p. A1. The article states that in June of 2006, "U.S. immigration officials were presented a plan that supporters said could help slash waiting times for green cards from nearly three years to three months and save 1 million applicants more than a third of the 45 hours they could expect to spend in government lines. It would also save about $350 million. The response? No thanks. Leaders of U.S. Citizenship and Immigration Services rejected key changes because ending huge immigration backlogs nationwide would rob the agency of application and renewal fees that cover 20 percent of its $1.8 billion budget, according to the plan's author, agency ombudsman Prakash Khatri."
33. Note that there is no limit on H1-Bs for nonprofits, government research laboratories, or universities.
34. McDougall 2007.
35. Gates 2007.
36. See, for example, U.S. State Department 2007. Refugees are generally admitted to the United States under one of three priorities, the precise categories of which change annually. Priority one concerns general refugee and asylum seekers as stipulated by the United Nations High Commission for Refugees; priority two comprises groups identified by the U.S. government as being of special concern (such as religiously persecuted groups in former Soviet states and Russia); priority three comprises reunification of refugees living in the United States and their families abroad.
37. Calculated from table 13 in DHS 2007.
38. Determined by the number of refugees and asylum seekers and weighted by the size of the host countries' economies, the "refugee burden sharing" index ranks the United States much lower than most of the European countries. See the Commitment to Development Index Web site (www.cgdev.org/section/initiatives/_active/cdi).

39. Ekman 2007.
40. Calculated from table 14 in DHS 2007.
41. NCSL 2007.
42. Ottaviano and Peri 2007. Note also the evidence that immigrants compete for jobs primarily with other immigrants rather than incumbent residents, reported in Bohn 2007 (chapter 3).
43. See, for example, Borjas 2003.
44. Borjas, Grogger, and Hanson 2008.
45. OIS 2004, table 3.
46. OIS, multiple years.
47. The World Bank (2007) estimates that cumulative total remittance outflow from the United States to all other countries during 1990–2004 (inclusive) was $387 billion. These figures on officially recorded remittances omit a large fraction of true total outflows, much of which do not pass through official channels, according to Ratha and Shaw (2006). Ratha and Shaw estimate that remittance outflows from the United States to developing countries alone were roughly twice the level of the total recorded official outflows to all countries; $600 billion is thus a conservative estimate of cumulative total remittance flows from the United States to developing countries alone during 1990–2004.
48. Ortega and others 2007.
49. CBO 2007.
50. See, for example, Lee and Miller 2000; and Auerbach and Oreopoulos 1999.
51. Butcher and Morrison Piehl 2007.
52. Moehling and Morrison Piehl 2008.
53. U.S. Federal Reserve 2007.
54. MPI 2007.
55. Massey 2005.
56. *New York Times* 2007. See also CBP 2006.
57. Hakim 2007.
58. Polls show that support for immigration restrictions is much higher among higher wage earners in states where public programs are more accessible to immigrants (such as California) than in states where they are less accessible (such as Texas). See Hanson 2005.
59. Durand, Massey, and Parrado 1999.
60. Cyprus, Czech Republic, Estonia, Hungary, Latvia, Lithuania, Malta, Poland, Slovakia, and Slovenia.
61. Blanchflower, Saleheen, and Shadforth 2007.
62. Blanchflower and Shadforth 2007.
63. U.K. Home Office 2006.
64. BBC 2007.
65. Massey 2005.

66. Goldin and Katz 1999.
67. Educational institutions and nonprofits are exempted from this cap.
68. Canada issues 40,000–50,000 skilled-worker visas per year (CIC 2007, p. 76), Australia about 70,000 and New Zealand about 30,000 (OECD 2006b, pp. 133–37).
69. Anderson 2007.
70. Martin 2005.
71. DHS 2007, table 13.
72. See, for example, Refugees International 2008.
73. U.S. Bureau of the Census 2007.
74. Balakrishna 2007.
75. Batalova 2006.

References

Anderson, Stuart. 2007. "The Point System's Impact on Foreign Nurses and Other Potential Immigrants." National Foundation for American Policy, Arlington, Va. [www.nfap.com/pdf/0706pointsystem.pdf]. Accessed September2007.

Auerbach, Alan J., and Philip Oreopoulos. 1999. "Analyzing the Fiscal Impact of US Immigration." *American Economic Review* 89 (2): 176–80.

Balakrishna, Aditi. 2007. "2,058 Accepted into Class of 2011." *Harvard Crimson*. March 29. [www.thecrimson.com/article.aspx?ref=517933]. Accessed February 2008.

Batalova, Jeanne. 2006. "Spotlight on Foreign Students and Exchange Visitors." Migration Policy Institute, Washington, D.C. [www.migrationinformation.org/USfocus/display.cfm?ID=489#5].

BBC (British Broadcasting Corporation). 2007. "EU Free Movement of Labour Map." January 4. [http://news.bbc.co.uk/1/hi/world/europe/3513889.stm]. Accessed November 2007.

Blanchflower, David G., and Chris Shadforth. 2007. "Fear, Unemployment, and Migration." Working Paper 13506. National Bureau of Economic Research, Cambridge, Mass.

Blanchflower, David G., Jumana Saleheen, and Chris Shadforth. 2007. "The Impact of the Recent Migration from Eastern Europe on the UK Economy." Discussion Paper 2615. Institute for the Study of Labor, Bonn. [http://ftp.iza.org/dp2615.pdf].

Board of Governors of the U.S. Federal Reserve System. 2007. "Report to the Congress on Credit Scoring and its Effects on the Availability and Affordability of Credit." Washington, D.C.

Bohn, Sarah. 2007. *Immigration and Wages in the U.S. Labor Market*. Doctoral Dissertation. Department of Economics, University of Maryland, College Park, Md.

Borjas, George J. 2003. "The Labor Demand Curve Is Downward Sloping: Reexamining the Impact of Immigration on the Labor Market." *Quarterly Journal of Economics* 118(4): 1335–74.

———. 2008. "Labor Outflows and Labor Inflows in Puerto Rico." Forthcoming. *Journal of Human Capital*.

Borjas, George J., Jeffrey Grogger, and Gordon H. Hanson. 2008. "Imperfect Substitution between Immigrants and Natives: A Reappraisal." Working Paper 13887. National Bureau of Economic Research, Harvard University, Cambridge, Mass.

Butcher, Kristin, and Anne Morrison Piehl. 2007. "Why Are Immigrants' Incarceration Rates So Low? Evidence on Selective Immigration, Deterrence, and Deportation." Working Paper 13229. National Bureau of Economic Research, Cambridge, Mass.

CBO (U.S. Congressional Budget Office). 2007. *The Impact of Unauthorized Immigrants on State and Local Budgets.* Washington, D.C.

CBP (U.S. Customs and Border Patrol). 2006. "CBP Border Patrol Seize over 1.1 Million Pounds of Narcotics through the Third Quarter of Fiscal Year." Press Release. June 30. [www.cbp.gov/xp/cgov/newsroom/news_releases/archives/2006_news_releases/062006/06302006.xml]. Accessed February 2008.

CGD (Center for Global Development). 2007. "Commitment to Development Index." [www.cgdev.org/section/initiatives/_active/cdi].

CIC (Citizenship and Immigration Canada). 2007. *Facts and Figures 2006.* Ottawa.

Clemens, Michael. 2007. "Do Visas Kill? Health Effects of African Health Professional Emigration." Working Paper 114. Center for Global Development, Washington, D.C.

Clemens, Michael A., and Lant Pritchett. 2008. "Income per Natural: Measuring Development as if People Mattered More Than Places." Working Paper 142. Center for Global Development, Washington, D.C.

DHS (U.S. Department of Homeland Security). 2007. "Refugees and Asylees." *Yearbook of Immigration Statistics 2006.* Washington, D.C.: U.S. Department of Homeland Security. [www.dhs.gov/ximgtn/statistics/publications/YrBk06RA.shtm]. Accessed February 2008.

Durand, Jorge, Douglas S. Massey, and Emilio A. Parrado. 1999. "The New Era of Mexican Migration to the United States." *The Journal of American History* 86 (2): 518–36.

Ekman, Ivar. 2007. "Cold Comfort in Sweden for Iraqi Refugees." *International Herald Tribune.* June 13.

Finn, Michael G. 2003. "Stay Rates of Foreign Doctorate Recipients from U.S. Universities, 2001." Oak Ridge Institute for Science and Education, Oak Ridge, Tenn. [http://orise.orau.gov/sep/files/stayrate03.pdf]. Accessed February 2008.

Gates, William. 2007. Written Testimony of William H. Gates, Chairman, Microsoft Corporation, before the Senate Committee on Health, Education, Labor, and Pensions. March 7, 2007. [http://help.senate.gov/Hearings/2007_03_07/Gates.pdf]. Accessed February 2008.

Goldin, Claudia, and Lawrence F. Katz. 1999. "The Returns to Skill in the United States across the Twentieth Century." Working Paper 7126. National Bureau of Economic Research, Cambridge, Mass.

Hakim, Peter. 2007. "U.S. Policy towards Latin America." Statement of Peter Hakim, President of the Inter-American Dialogue, before the Subcommittee on the Western Hemisphere of the House Committee on Foreign Affairs. March 1. [www.internationalrelations.house.gov/110/hak030107.htm]. Accessed February 2008.

Hanson, Gordon H. 2005. *Why Does Immigration Divide America?* Washington, D.C.: Institute for International Economics.

———. 2006. "Illegal Migration from Mexico to the United States." *Journal of Economic Literature* 44 (4): 869–924.

Hoefer, Michael, Nancy Rytina, and Christopher Campbell. 2007. "Estimates of the Unauthorized Immigrant Population Residing in the United States: January 2006." August. Office of Immigration Statistics, U.S. Department of Homeland Security, Washington, D.C.

IADB (Inter-American Development Bank). 2007. *Sending Money Home: Leveraging the Development Impact of Remittances*. Washington, D.C.

IIE (Institute of International Education). 2006. *Open Doors 2006. Report on International Educational Exchange. Leading 20 Places of Origin, 2004/05 & 2005/06*. Washington, D.C.

Landes, David S. 1999. *The Wealth and Poverty of Nations*. New York: W.W. Norton & Co.

Lee, Ronald, and Timothy Miller. 2000. "Immigration, Social Security, and Broader Fiscal Impacts." *American Economic Review* 90 (2): 350–54.

Lucas, Robert E. B. 2005. *International Migration and Economic Development* Northampton, Mass.: Edward Elgar.

Martin, David A. 2005. *The United States Refugee Admissions Program*. Washington, D.C.: U.S. Department of State. [www.state.gov/documents/organization/36495.pdf]. Accessed February 2008.

Massey, Douglas S. 2005. "Beyond the Border Buildup: Towards a New Approach to Mexico-U.S. Migration." *Immigration Policy in Focus* 4 (7). September. Washington, D.C.: American Immigration Law Foundation.

McDougall, Paul. 2007. "Microsoft's Canada Plan Highlights Need for Immigration Reform." *Information Week*'s Outsourcing Weblog. July 9. [www.informationweek.com/blog/main/archives/2007/07/microsofts_cana.html]. Accessed February 2008.

Mishra, Prachi. 2007. "Emigration and Wages in Source Countries: Evidence from Mexico." *Journal of Development Economics* 82 (1): 180–99.

Moehling, Carolyn, and Anne Morrison Piehl. 2008. "Immigration and Crime in Early 20th Century America." Working Paper 13576. National Bureau of Economic Research, Cambridge, Mass.

MPI (Migration Policy Institute). 2007. "Annual Immigration to the United States: The Real Numbers." *Immigration Facts* 16 (May 2007). [www.migrationpolicy.org/pubs/FS16_USImmigration_051807.pdf]. Accessed February 2008.

NAM (New America Media). 2007. "Historic Poll of Undocumented Immigrants from Latin America." [http://news.newamericamedia.org/news/view_article.html?article_id=5f47289d59c786e1f07c3eb69707b8a4]. Accessed September 2007.

NCSL (National Conference on State Legislatures). 2007. "States Pick up Congress' Slack on Immigration." Press Release. August 6. [www.ncsl.org/programs/press/2007/pr070806immigration.htm]. Accessed September 2007.

New Republic. 2007. "Nuevos Braceros." June 18.

New York Times. 2007. "Immigrant Deaths Near Border Fall." November 8.

NSB (National Science Board). 2003. *Science and Engineering Indicators 2002*. Vol. 1. Arlington, Va.: National Science Foundation.

O'Rourke, Kevin. 1994. "The Economic Impact of the Famine in the Short and Long Run." *American Economic Review* 84(2): 309–13.

OECD (Organisation for Economic Co-operation and Development). 2006a. *Development Co-operation Report*. Supplement to the Statistical Annex.

———. 2006b. "Managing Migration—Are Quotas and Numerical Limits the Solution?" In *International Migration Outlook 2006*. Paris.

OIS (Office of Immigration Statistics). 2004. *Yearbook of Immigration Statistics 2004*. Table 3: Immigrants Admitted by Region and Country of Birth: Fiscal Years 1989–2004. Washington, D.C.: U.S. Department of Homeland Security.

———. Various years. *Yearbook of Immigration Statistics*. Table 22: Nonimmigrants Admitted by Selected Class of Admission and Region and Selected Country of Last Residence. Washington, D.C.: U.S. Department of Homeland Security.

Ortega, Alexander N., Hai Fang, Victor H. Perez, John A. Rizzo, Olivia Carter-Pokras, Steven P. Wallace, and Lillian Gelberg. 2007. "Health Care Access, Use of Services, and Experiences among Undocumented Mexicans and Other Latinos." *Archives of Internal Medicine* 167 (21): 2354–60.

Ottaviano, Gianmarco, and Giovanni Peri. 2007. "Rethinking the Effects of Immigration on Wages." Working Paper 12497. National Bureau of Economic Research, Cambridge, Mass.

Pandey, Abhishek, Alok Aggarwal, Richard Devane, and Yevgeny Kuznetzov. 2006. "The Indian Diaspora: A Unique Case?" In Yevgeny Kuznetzov, ed., *Diaspora Networks and the International Migration of Skills: How Countries Can Draw on Their Talents Abroad*. Washington, D.C.: World Bank.

Pritchett, Lant. 2006. *Let Their People Come: Breaking the Gridlock on Global Labor Mobility*. Washington, D.C.: Center for Global Development.

Ratha, Dilip, and William Shaw. 2006. "South-South Migration and Remittances." Working Paper 102. World Bank, Washington, D.C. [http://go.worldbank.org/QOWEWD6TA0].

Refugee Council USA. 2008. "Advocacy Spotlight." [www.rcusa.org/index.php?page=advocacy-spotlight]. Accessed February 2008.

Refugees International. 2008. "Resettlement." [www.refintl.org/content/issue/detail/6703]. Accessed February 2008.

Saxenian, AnnaLee. 2002. "Transnational Communities and the Evolution of Global Production Networks: The Cases of Taiwan, China and India." *Industry and Innovation* 9 (3): 183–202.

Spilimbergo, Antonio. 2007. "Democracy and Foreign Education." Working Paper 07/51. International Monetary Fund, Washington, D.C.

Sullivan, Michael. 2007. "Leaving the Philippines in Search of Jobs." Weekend Edition Saturday, National Public Radio. August 18.

Thee Kian Wie, ed. 2003. *The Indonesian Economy, 1950s–1990s*. Canberra: Australian National University / Singapore: Institute of Southeast Asian Studies.

U.K. Home Office. 2006. *Accession Monitoring Report: May 2004–March 2006*. [www.ind.homeoffice.gov.uk/6353/aboutus/accessionmoniotoringreport7.pdf]. Accessed February 2008.

U.S. Bureau of the Census. 2007. *The 2007 Statistical Abstract: Historical Statistics*.

U.S. Federal Reserve (Board of Governors of the Federal Reserve System). 2007. *Report to the Congress on Credit Scoring and Its Effects on the Availability and Affordability of Credit*. Washington, D.C.: U.S. Federal Reserve.

U.S. State Department. 2007. *Proposed Refugee Admissions for Fiscal Year 2006. Report to Congress*. Washington, D.C.: U.S. Department of State. [www.state.gov/g/prm/refadm/rls/rpts/52366.htm]. Accessed October 2007.

Valdés, Juan Gabriel. 1995. *Pinochet's Economists: The Chicago School of Economics in Chile*. New York: Cambridge University Press.

Washington Post. 2007. "Immigration Agency Mired in Inefficiency." May 28. [www.washingtonpost.com/wp-dyn/content/article/2007/05/27/AR2007052701118.html]. Accessed September 2007.

WHO (World Health Organization). 2005. *Health Systems Statistics 2005*. [www.who.int/healthinfo/statistics/whostat2005_healthsystems_en.pdf]. Accessed September 2007.

Woodruff, Christopher, and Rene Zenteno. 2007. "Migration Networks and Microenterprises in Mexico." *Journal of Development Economics* 82 (2): 509–28.

World Bank. 2007. "Remittances Data." [http://go.worldbank.org/QOWEWD6TA0]. Accessed February 2008.

10

Modernizing U.S. Foreign Assistance for the Twenty-first Century

Sheila Herrling and Steve Radelet

The world has changed dramatically since the end of the Cold War and the dissolution of the Soviet Union. Global economic inequality has risen, exacerbating destabilizing tensions and creating resentment among those left behind. Diseases such as HIV/AIDS and malaria claim millions of lives each year, weaken fragile economies, and threaten our interests and those of our friends and allies. September 11th made clear the significant security threats from weak and failing states. The war in Iraq has substantially damaged the image of the United States abroad, undermined our ability to lead the world on critical issues, and created significant tensions with many of our friends and partners. Although the process of globalization and the spread of new technologies have created tremendous opportunities, they have also created significant challenges, particularly for those who start from a position of disadvantage and who believe—rightly or wrongly—that the rich have rigged the rules to favor themselves at the expense of the poor. Democracy is taking root in low-income countries in Africa, Asia, and Latin America, but its hold is tenuous and its future in doubt in some cases.

Meeting these challenges requires a new vision of U.S. global leadership based on the strength of our core values, ideas, and ingenuity. It calls for an integrated foreign policy

---

Sheila Herrling is a senior policy analyst and Steve Radelet is a senior fellow at the Center for Global Development. Thanks to Sami Bazzi and Rebecca Schutte for their help in preparing this chapter and to Nancy Birdsall and Dennis de Tray for comments on earlier drafts.

that promotes our values, enhances our security, helps create economic and political opportunities for people around the world, and restores the United States' faltering image abroad. We cannot rely exclusively or even primarily on defense and security to meet these goals. Instead, we must make greater use of all the tools of statecraft through "smart power," including diplomacy, defense, trade, investment, intelligence, and a strong and effective foreign assistance strategy.[1]

In today's world, foreign assistance is a vital tool for strengthening U.S. foreign policy and restoring U.S. global leadership. Foreign policy experts on both sides of the political aisle now recognize the importance of strong foreign assistance programs. But they also recognize that our foreign assistance programs are out of date and badly in need of modernization to meet the challenges of the twenty-first century.

The Bush administration deserves credit for taking several steps to increase the amounts of foreign assistance and begin to change how it is managed. It sharply increased total U.S. aid from $12.6 billion in 2001 to $23 billion in 2006 (measured in constant 2005 dollars), although the vast majority of the increase went to Afghanistan, Iraq, and other allies in the war on terror.[2] It introduced several new programs, most prominently the President's Emergency Plan for AIDS Relief and the Millennium Challenge Account. And during its second term, it introduced several organizational changes through the so-called F process, including naming a new director of foreign assistance and bringing the U.S. Agency for International Development (USAID) more closely under the direction of the State Department.

But these changes fall far short of what is needed to modernize U.S. foreign assistance programs and make them more effective in achieving today's U.S. foreign policy goals—and may be moving in the wrong direction in several key areas.[3] Today's challenges require a fundamental rethinking of the purposes, scope, and organization of our foreign assistance programs, and the legislation underlying them. The next U.S. president should follow five steps.

1. Develop a National Foreign Assistance Strategy that elevates global development as critical to our national interest and lays out the principal missions and mandates for foreign assistance.
2. Reform the organizational structure by merging most foreign assistance programs and related development policy instruments into a new cabinet-level department, and strengthening the organization by expanding and deepening the professional staff, revamping delivery mechanisms, and building a serious monitoring and evaluation system.
3. Rewrite the outdated and unwieldy 1961 Foreign Assistance Act in order to streamline procurement rules, earmarks, and restrictions,

and to reestablish a strong partnership between the executive branch and Congress that allows greater flexibility to the former provided there is greater accountability and responsiveness to the latter.

4. Place a higher priority on multilateral channels of assistance.
5. Increase the quantity and improve the allocation of assistance because, even with recent increases, U.S. foreign assistance is not large enough or unencumbered enough to meet our major foreign policy goals.

Aid is no panacea. Stronger and larger foreign assistance programs alone will not be enough to achieve U.S. foreign policy goals. As discussed in other chapters in this book, policies affecting trade, migration, capital flows, governance, and climate change, among others, all influence our relationship with low-income countries, and the most important factors in the development process are the policies of developing countries themselves. This chapter focuses on foreign assistance not because it is the key to development, but because stronger, more effective aid programs alongside other policy tools can help the United States further its own interests and help low-income countries at the same time.

Aid before September 11th

Foreign aid first emerged as an important foreign policy tool during the Truman administration and has since been used to address a wide range of national security and development objectives. The first great U.S. foreign assistance program, the Marshall Plan, was aimed at rebuilding Western Europe after World War II, in part as a bulwark against Soviet expansion. President John F. Kennedy vastly expanded U.S. foreign assistance by establishing the Peace Corps, USAID, and the Alliance for Progress. All three programs were part of the Cold War arsenal aimed both at stemming the spread of communism and at encouraging development in some of the world's poorest countries. In the late 1960s, Vietnam was the largest recipient of U.S. foreign aid. By the early 1980s, the Reagan administration was financing El Salvador, Guatemala, Honduras, the Philippines, and Zaire—none paragons of democracy, but all fighting various communist threats. In the late 1970s, aid emerged as a major tool for supporting a second important foreign policy goal: Middle East peace. As part of the Camp David accords, the United States significantly increased aid to Egypt and Israel; these two countries were the largest recipients of U.S. foreign assistance for two decades.

Alongside these security interests, U.S. foreign assistance made important contributions to development. U.S. support played an important role in the Green Revolution, which provided the foundation for Asia's economic miracle, as well as in the rapid expansion of childhood immunization programs and the efforts to fight smallpox, river blindness, polio, and diarrheal diseases. The United States provided significant support to rapidly growing countries such as Botswana, Indonesia, the Republic of Korea, and Taiwan (and more recently Ghana, Mozambique, Tanzania, and several other countries). But alongside the successes were failures in which vast amounts of aid were spent with little achievement.

There are inherent tensions between the many disparate goals of foreign aid, especially between supporting short-term political and security needs and encouraging longer-term development. It is hardly surprising that aid did not always spur development, because that often was not its principal aim. In many countries that the United States supported during the Cold War, neither the United States nor the recipient government cared much about development. These tensions are a prime reason for the perceived ineffectiveness of aid over the years and are at the heart of the difficulties in strengthening our assistance programs.

After the Cold War, foreign aid lost much of its *raison d'être,* and the political support it had—always thin, even during the Cold War—waned sharply. Critics, led by Senator Jesse Helms, charged that foreign aid had little impact on economic development and was only "lining the pockets of corrupt dictators, while funding the salaries of a growing, bloated bureaucracy."[4] No one articulated a compelling vision of the purposes of foreign assistance, how it related to broader U.S. foreign policy and national security interests, and how aid policies should be executed. In the early and mid-1990s, Senator Helms and others called for the elimination of USAID or its merger into the State Department.

Under attack from Congress, net U.S. foreign assistance (or "official development assistance," as it is called in international circles) fell from $14.3 billion in 1990–94 to $9.5 billion in 1995–97 (in constant 2005 dollars; see figure 10.1).

For several years, the United States fell behind Japan as the largest provider of foreign assistance. Aid fell from 0.9 percent to 0.5 percent of the federal budget, and from 0.2 percent to 0.1 percent of U.S. national income, putting the United States at the bottom of the donor list by this measure (figure 10.2). USAID's staffing shrunk, and the organization changed from having a strong voice in development policy with broad expertise to becoming essentially a contracting agency that outsources assistance programs to private contractors.

Due in part to strong support and advocacy by civil society and other groups, the United States increased funding for debt relief, child health, and other development programs during the Clinton administration's second term. Between 1997 and 2001, foreign assistance increased 55 percent (in real terms), and assistance to Sub-Saharan Africa increased 62 percent. But there was no overriding strategy or clear set of objectives to guide the design and delivery of foreign assistance programs.

Figure 10.1. U.S. net official development assistance, 1980–2006

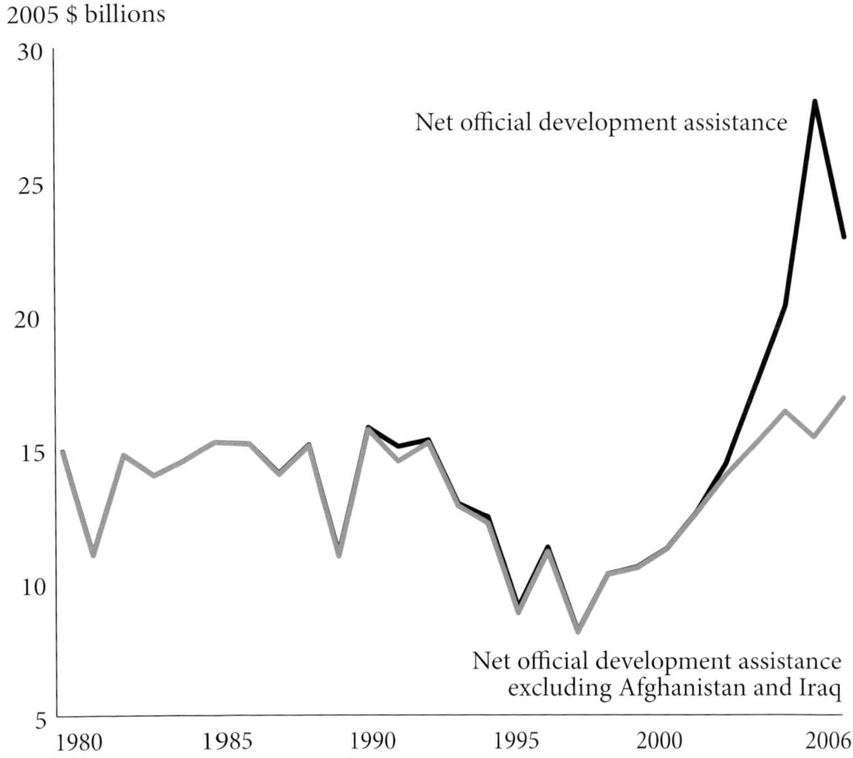

Source: Organisation for Economic Co-operation and Development–Development Assistance Committee database on annual aggregates.

Foreign assistance since 2001

Since September 11th, foreign assistance has reemerged as an important strategic tool of U.S. foreign policy. The Bush administration rapidly expanded assistance from $11.2 billion in 2000 to $22.9 billion in 2006 (the 2005 figure was even higher due to a one-time large debt relief deal for Iraq). There were four major prongs to the expansion.

Afghanistan, Iraq, and the growing role of the Department of Defense

First, the United States dramatically increased aid to Afghanistan, Iraq, and other "frontline" states such as Jordan and Pakistan. The largest increases by far have been for Iraq, which received $11.2 billion in 2005 and $4.7 billion in 2006 (including about $4 billion in debt relief). Aid to Iraq accounted for nearly one-third of all U.S. foreign assistance during those two years. Funding

Figure 10.2. U.S. net official development assistance, 1970–2006

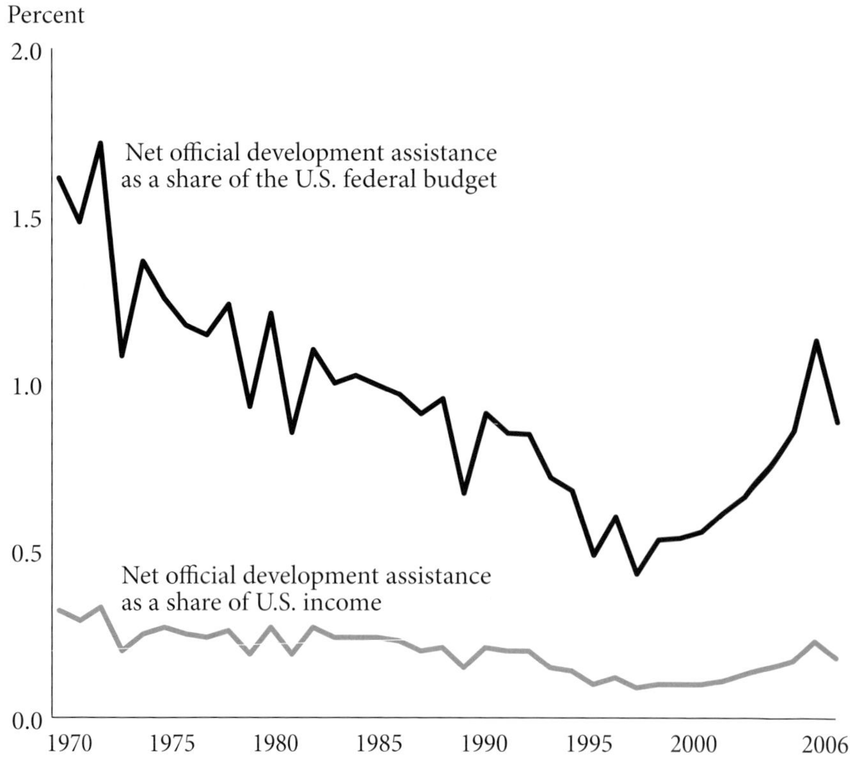

Source: International Monetary Fund World Economic Outlook database, Executive Office of the President of the United States, and Organisation for Economic Co-operation and Development–Development Assistance Committee's database on annual aggregates.

for Afghanistan reached $1.3 billion in 2005 and $1.4 billion in 2006, making it the second largest recipient of U.S. assistance (table 10.1). Excluding assistance to Afghanistan and Iraq, the increase in foreign assistance between 2000 and 2005 was much smaller, growing from $11.2 billion to $16.8 billion in real terms.

The increase in aid to Afghanistan and Iraq has been accompanied by a shift in the responsibilities for oversight of these assistance programs to the Department of Defense, which is now is responsible for 22 percent of U.S. foreign assistance (up from less than 6 percent in 2002), making it one of the largest foreign assistance agencies within the U.S. government.[5] This shift has raised significant concerns both about further fragmentation of programs across the U.S. government and about the lack of experience in the Department of Defense to implement development programs.

Table 10.1. Top 10 recipients of bilateral U.S. net official development assistance, 2005 and 2006 (2005 $ millions)

Recipient	2005	2006	Average
Iraq	11,228	4,646	7,937
Afghanistan	1,318	1,364	1,341
Sudan	759	718	738
Colombia	449	699	574
Congo, Dem. Rep.	144	815	479
Ethiopia	609	307	458
Nigeria	99	765	432
Pakistan	323	464	394
Jordan	353	320	337
Egypt	402	190	296

Source: Organisation for Economic Co-operation and Development–Development Assistance Committee database on annual aggregates.

Millennium Challenge Account

The second component of the Bush administration's expansion of foreign aid was the introduction of the Millennium Challenge Account in 2002, an innovative program that represents a sharp break in the way the United States provides aid. The Millennium Challenge Account selects a relatively small number of recipient countries based on independent policy indicators focusing on governance, education and health, and economic policies; and provides them with much larger sums of money than other programs do. The administration established a new organization, the Millennium Challenge Corporation, to run the program. Once countries qualify, the recipient countries set priorities, design the programs to be funded, and implement them. This approach places much more responsibility for development programs with the recipient country. In return for this flexibility, the Millennium Challenge Corporation—in theory—demands greater accountability for achieving results, including being willing to cut off funding when programs fail. This has yet to be tested.

The Bush administration had the opportunity, in conjunction with establishing the Millennium Challenge Account, to try to strengthen and modernize USAID (and U.S. foreign assistance programs more broadly). Its decision to establish a new organization, rather than have USAID administer the program, was widely interpreted as a vote of no confidence in USAID. There was a clear advantage in establishing a new entity: It was authorized under new legislation and, therefore, escaped many of the onerous burdens (such as tied aid, sectoral earmarks, and heavy reporting requirements) of the Foreign Assistance Act. But the move added to the fragmentation of foreign assistance programs across the executive branch and weakened the authority of USAID.

The Millennium Challenge Account has shown, and continues to show, great promise but also growing pains. By the end of 2007, fifteen countries had signed compact proposals totaling $4.8 billion, and another 18 countries had signed threshold agreements totaling nearly $400 million. There are many signs of "the Millennium Challenge Corporation effect" in which potential recipients work hard to improve their scores on the indicators in order to be selected for the program. However, the appropriated funding of about $1.7 billion a year has been far below the administration's initial promise of $5 billion a year.[6] Perhaps most importantly, actual implementation of programs has been slow—by the end of 2007 the administration had disbursed just $150 million.

President's Emergency Plan for AIDS Relief

The third major prong was the establishment of the President's Emergency Plan for AIDS Relief, announced by the president in the 2003 State of the Union Address and enacted into law in May of that year (see chapter 11 by Over). The initiative called for an increase in U.S. funding for international HIV/AIDS of $10 billion over five years, from $5 billion to $15 billion, of which $1 billion would go to the Global Fund to Fight AIDS, Tuberculosis, and Malaria. It named fifteen countries with high HIV/AIDS prevalence rates as the focus of the program. The President's Emergency Plan for AIDS Relief was a huge step forward for an administration that had voiced skepticism in its early days about the potential for effective programs in Africa, and reflected a broad shift in the foreign policy community that the HIV/AIDS pandemic constituted a moral crisis and a significant threat to U.S. foreign policy interests.

The President's Emergency Plan for AIDS Relief has enjoyed strong bipartisan support and is generally seen as being successful so far. The program has contributed (alongside other donors' programs) to putting over one million people on antiretroviral therapy, helped provide care for over two million orphans and vulnerable children, and (although they don't like to publicize it) has become one of the largest distributors of condoms in the world. But the program is awkwardly run. Because it funds a diverse set of programs across many executive branch agencies, the administration created an Office of the Global AIDS Coordinator in the State Department to oversee and coordinate programs run out of the State Department, USAID, and the Department of

Health and Human Services, including both the Centers for Disease Control and Prevention and the National Institutes of Health. The program has also been criticized for overemphasizing abstinence-only initiatives, relying too heavily on treatment programs and too little on prevention, and sending too small a share of its funding to the Global Fund. And there are concerns about the growing imbalance between the amount of funding for HIV/AIDS programs relative to funding for other health programs and systems or support for broader economic development programs; and about the long-term implications of life-long antiretroviral support. Nevertheless, the program's initial success ensures that it will receive strong support and probably increased funding in any new administration.

Debt relief

The fourth main component of the increase was debt relief, building on the debt relief programs started during the Clinton administration. Debt relief is accounted for differently from other components of official development assistance. The value of debt relief is the charge to the creditor country's budget for writing off the debt in the year of the debt relief, and it does not represent new funding to the recipient. Of course debt relief is beneficial to the debtor because it represents a future cash flow savings (in the form of debt service that has been forgiven). But the official development assistance accounting for debt relief can be misleading because it shows a large amount of assistance in the year of the write-off, even though it is not an immediate cash inflow to the debtor. Moreover, because it is a one-time deal, it is typically followed by a sharp decline in measured official development assistance in the following year.

Debt relief affects official development assistance figures every year, but three sizeable debt deals had an unusually large effect on recent numbers. Debt relief to Nigeria added $597 million to U.S. official development assistance in 2006; Iraq added an enormous $3.9 billion in 2005; and the Democratic Republic of the Congo added $1.4 billion in 2003 and an additional $689 million in 2006 (all in constant 2005 U.S. dollars). Debt relief added $4.4 billion to U.S. official development assistance in 2005 and an additional $2 billion in 2006, accounting for more than 12 percent of U.S. official development assistance over the two years.

Excluding assistance for Afghanistan and Iraq and debt relief, global U.S. official development assistance increased from $10.6 billion in 2000 to $14.8 billion in 2006, an increase of about 40 percent. By comparison, in the previous three years it increased 44 percent from $7.3 billion in 1997 to $10.6 billion in 2000.

One striking feature of all of the expansion in foreign assistance has been the emphasis on bilateral rather than multilateral programs. The administration has made some efforts at the World Bank and the African Development Bank, notably the push for more grant financing (first proposed by the Clinton administration[7]), further debt relief, and performance benchmarks for the institutions. And the United States was a key player in the establishment of the Global Fund, providing about 30 percent of its funding and playing a major role in its policy direction. Nevertheless, the Bush administration's primary focus has been on bilateral rather than multilateral foreign assistance initiatives. The share of bilateral programs in total foreign assistance for the United States—already high at 76 percent in 2000—increased sharply to 90 percent in 2006. U.S. funding for multilateral aid agencies actually fell by 7 percent in nominal terms during the Bush administration, from an average of $2.7 billion in 1998–2001 to $2.5 billion in 2002–06, despite the increases in overall U.S. foreign assistance. In real terms, U.S. multilateral contributions fell 16 percent. The United States has moved from being the largest funder of the World Bank to its second largest behind the United Kingdom. Within other donor countries and the multilateral agencies, there was a widespread perception (whether accurate is almost beside the point) that the United States was intentionally trying to weaken multilateral agencies in favor of its own bilateral programs.

The lack of attention and funding for multilateral programs represents a major missed opportunity for the United States to better leverage its aid dollars, because larger U.S. contributions to the multilaterals typically are followed by increased contributions by other members. It also weakens the ability for the United States to provide positive leadership in strengthening and shaping these agencies. The United States is undoubtedly still the strongest single voice within these agencies, but it often appears to lead by brute force (or not lead at all) rather than by building consensus. A strong multilateral approach would also reduce the burden on recipient countries because they would have to work with fewer donor agencies. In many countries, the most effective way for the United States to support development programs should be through existing multilateral channels rather than through bilateral programs, but doing so will require a change in strategic approach.

The need for deeper reform

The Millennium Challenge Account, the President's Emergency Plan for AIDS Relief, and the increases in funding were significant accomplishments, but they did not add up to an overall strategy for or fundamental restructuring of U.S. foreign assistance. By the middle of the Bush administration's second term, there was widespread recognition both inside and outside the administration that partial changes were not enough, and that deeper changes were necessary to strengthen and modernize U.S. foreign assistance programs to better meet today's foreign policy challenges.[8] This was recognized not just within Washington's Beltway—polls show a clear shift among Americans to much more favorable views about the role of foreign assistance in achieving important foreign policy goals (box 10.1).

At the core of the challenge is the fact that today's foreign assistance programs are hopelessly outdated. They date back to the Kennedy administration and were designed for a different time and different purposes. Over the years, various programs have been added in different agencies, with the result that our foreign assistance programs are highly fragmented with little coordination across the twenty or so executive branch agencies that administer them. Sometimes these agencies work at cross-purposes, with different objectives and techniques. At other times they aim to achieve the same goals but duplicate each others' efforts without realizing it. Each agency has its own processes, rules, and procedures, which creates confusion and puts significant strain on recipient countries. Many programs are subject to heavy bureaucracy that ensures that a large proportion of aid money never gets close to its intended recipients. Aid flows are also heavily earmarked by Congress and subject to myriad executive branch directives, procedural rules, and

Box 10.1. Americans support foreign assistance

Key polls show that regardless of political affiliation, gender, or race, a majority of Americans support foreign assistance and see it as a way to help restore U.S. credibility and make the world a safer place.

- **83%** of respondents agree that effective foreign assistance can be successful in improving U.S. image abroad and making the country safer (ASP 2007).
- **52%** of Republicans and **77%** of Democrats want the Bush administration to put more emphasis on diplomatic and economic methods, rather than military might, to combat terrorism (ASP 2007).
- **68%** of respondents are dissatisfied with the position of the United States in the world today—up from **51%** in 2005 (PIPA/Knowledge Networks 2006).
- **68%** of respondents want their elected representatives to increase the priority of fighting HIV/AIDS; **57%** want to increase the priority of building goodwill to the United States by giving food and medical assistance. (PIPA/Knowledge Networks 2006).

On average, respondents supported increasing the budget for helping poor countries develop their economies from $7.3 billion to $24.8 billion and increasing funding for humanitarian and disaster assistance from $1.4 billion to $26.8 billion (PIPA/Knowledge Networks 2006).

restrictions that add significantly to administrative costs, slow the delivery process, and weaken effectiveness.

Moreover, there is little accountability for achieving results. Much of our foreign assistance is spent on countries with governments that are not serious about development or in pursuit of objectives that have little to do with development. Monitoring and evaluation systems are weak and tend to focus on whether funds are spent, rather than whether programs achieved important strategic or development objectives.

To some extent these problems can be traced to the structures and procedures of USAID and other agencies that administer our assistance. But much of the problem lies with the diffusion of programs across agencies and with the elaborate web of legislation and directives from Congress and the White House under which USAID labors. The Foreign Assistance Act of 1961, amended many times, specifies several dozen different goals, priority areas, and directives. These multiple goals are more than just an administrative burden: they make it difficult for USAID to implement effective programs and achieve clear results. Problems with the legislation and multiple executive branch directives are at the heart of many of the concerns about U.S. foreign assistance, including heavy bureaucratic requirements, slow disbursements, and a large portion of aid dollars directed at Washington's priorities rather than the greatest needs of recipient countries.

These problems have led to a significant weakening of USAID, which once was considered one of the premier foreign assistance agencies in the world. Its staff is less than half the size of what it was fifteen years ago, and it has lost many skilled staff with significant development expertise and experience. It operates today much more as a contracting agency than as an organization that can provide strong input to U.S. policies and programs in developing countries around the world to face the challenges of the twenty-first century. Despite these problems, USAID has managed to support many successful programs over the years, but the agency is a shadow of its former self and its programs are less effective than they could be.

The "F process"

The Bush administration papered over some of these problems in its first term, and chose to introduce new programs with new structures rather than tackle the deeper issues. But in its second term it began to recognize that more fundamental changes were needed. In January 2006 Secretary of State Condoleezza Rice initiated a set of reforms, dubbed the "F process," that established a new position, director of foreign assistance, with the rank of deputy secretary of state; partially integrated assistance programs managed by the State Department and USAID; and led to the introduction of a new

"Foreign Assistance Strategic Framework" announced in May 2006. The State Department and USAID began to implement many of these changes in the context of the president's fiscal year 2008 budget process.

The F process has several positive elements. First, the naming of a director of foreign assistance was aimed at bringing greater coherence across significant parts of U.S. assistance programs, and is designed to enhance communication and coordination across State and USAID programs. Second, the Strategic Framework is a solid initial step toward articulating and achieving five clear and distinct goals for foreign assistance programs. It assigns all recipient countries into one of five categories (Rebuilding, Developing, Transforming, Sustaining Partnerships, or Restrictive), reflecting current assessments of those countries' circumstances. Third, the F process attempts to reorient the budget so that it is more in line with the five goals and with country needs.

Although the reform process has several positive elements, it does not add up to a coherent and comprehensive strategy. There are several major concerns. First, the substance of the reforms was at best incomplete because a large number of programs were omitted. The F process covers only programs controlled by State and USAID, only indirectly includes the Millennium Challenge Corporation and the President's Emergency Plan for AIDS Relief, and excludes programs run by more than a dozen other executive branch agencies involved in foreign assistance. It is silent on how the United States can better leverage its foreign assistance dollars through multilateral agencies. The Congressional Research Service estimates (based on the fiscal year 2005 budget) that the director of foreign assistance will manage just 55 percent of the foreign assistance budget, with the Department of Defense controlling 19 percent and other agencies managing 26 percent.[9] In short, the scope of the reforms has been limited to what the State Department can carry on its own without coordinating with other executive branch agencies or Congress. As a result, the best it can achieve is incomplete and partial reforms.

Second, the process of reform was far from ideal. By not including Congress in the deliberations, the administration missed the opportunity to build greater consensus on the path forward and to redress some of the weaknesses in the Foreign Assistance Act. In the absence of agreement with Congress on objectives, earmarks, procurement, personnel rules, and key strategies, the reforms fall far short of what is needed. Predictably, the reforms came up squarely against existing legislation during the budget process: the reforms envisage a country-based budgeting process, while existing authorities provide for sector-based allocations. By not involving Congress, the administration significantly undermined its own reform process.

Third, the administration restricted much of the discussion during the first year of planning to a small number of people, leading to substantial confusion and misunderstanding. Although communication has improved since then, many key people felt marginalized from and uninformed about the process, which created resentment and further undermined support.

Fourth, although appointing a director of foreign assistance to coordinate across programs is welcome, putting that person under the direct control of the secretary of state raises significant concerns. The State Department has expertise in diplomacy and foreign policy but not in economic development or poverty reduction. Moreover, while there are units and personnel within State that focus on long-term objectives, the department is driven primarily by a focus on short-term objectives and immediate needs. As a result, there is a danger that foreign assistance spending will shift towards addressing short-range and rapidly changing diplomatic and political concerns and away from achieving long-term development and institutional changes in recipient countries. Despite the fact that the new strategic framework calls for funding for democracies and countries with strong governance, a large share of current funds go to political partners with weak governance. The history of U.S. assistance to such countries—Haiti under the Duvaliers, the Philippines under Marcos, and Zaire under Mobutu—suggests that achieving development results or strengthening governance systems usually takes a back seat to short-term political expediency. Giving much greater control over these programs to the State Department is likely to exacerbate that problem.

Modernizing and strengthening U.S. foreign assistance

Partial reforms are not the solution. Making U.S. aid programs more effective requires a bold, ambitious vision for updating these programs for the twenty-first century and strengthening America's role in the world. There are five key steps that should be taken.

1. Develop a national foreign assistance strategy

The first step is to develop a comprehensive strategy that lays out the principal objectives and basic framework for foreign assistance as part of our broader policies for engaging with the world. The 2006 F process Strategic Framework went part of the way toward achieving this goal, but because it did not include all agencies and did not fully incorporate the views of Congress and others, it was incomplete.

A broader framework should be developed that lays out key objectives and priorities, describes the major programs that will be used to meet these objectives, and details strategies for coordinating and communicating across agencies. It should lay out broad guidelines for assistance programs in different kinds of recipient countries, including well-governed countries; failed, failing, and fragile states; and middle-income countries with much less need for development assistance. It should describe how foreign assistance programs will be coordinated and integrated with other policy tools for working with low-income countries (those in trade, migration, and investment), and should summarize the budgetary requirements necessary to achieve those goals. It should lay out how our bilateral assistance programs can work with important multilateral initiatives at the World Bank, African Development Bank, Global Fund, and other key multilateral organizations. Developing this strategy should not be a one-time process: Each administration should be expected to renew and revise the strategy as a Quadrennial Global Development Review, much like the Quadrennial Defense Review Report of the Department of Defense.[10]

2. Reform the organizational structure

U.S. foreign assistance cannot be fully effective when programs are spread among nearly twenty agencies with different objectives and implementing procedures, and when its key agency (USAID) has been severely weakened over time. There is broad agreement that rectifying the fragmentation and institutional weaknesses are at the heart of modernizing and strengthening foreign assistance to meet today's challenges. There are four broad alternatives:

- Create a new cabinet-level Department for Global Development.
- Fundamentally rebuild and reinvigorate USAID, or create a new subcabinet or independent agency for foreign assistance programs.
- Merge all foreign assistance programs into the State Department.
- Name a cabinet-level coordinator for all foreign assistance programs.

The best option for strengthening foreign assistance as a vital foreign policy tool would be to create a new cabinet-level Department for Global Development. We discuss the strengths and weaknesses of each option in turn.

Creating a new cabinet-level Department for International Development. This option would streamline the bureaucracy, reduce duplication, and strengthen our ability to align major programs with our key objectives. It would establish development as the primary mission of U.S. foreign assistance, elevating development to a more equal standing with diplomacy and defense as the three key pillars of U.S. foreign policy. It would bring nearly all aid programs under one roof, with the exception of debt relief (which would remain at the Treasury Department) and aid aimed primarily at supporting political allies (such as the current "Economic Support Fund" and military training programs), which would remain under the authority of the State Department. In so doing, it would allow for the independence necessary to focus on long-term development and guard against pressures to achieve short-term political goals. The new department would have a mandate for policy coherence on the full range of U.S. policies—trade, climate change, migration, debt—affecting low-income countries. It would facilitate the professionalization of a core of development expertise within the U.S. government on issues of public health, climate change, agriculture, institutional development, education, infrastructure, clean water, and other development issues. A new independent department—coupled with new legislation that would change management authorities and strengthen monitoring and evaluation efforts, as discussed below—would facilitate changing the incentives within development programs so that professionals can focus on achieving results in ways that the other options would not allow (especially merging all programs into the State Department, which would muddle rather than clarify incentives). The United Kingdom took this step several years ago, and its foreign assistance programs are now considered among the best of the bilateral donors.

Opponents of this option argue that a new department would create too much independence from and competition with the State Department, that the secretary of state should have full control over nondefense foreign policy issues, and that a development department would always be weak compared with State. Others debate this conclusion, and believe that strong coordination at the cabinet level can ensure consistency in foreign policy without usurping the role of the secretary of state, as with other departments involved in foreign policy.

The United States rarely creates new cabinet agencies, and the most recent experience—the creation of the Department of Homeland Security—did not go smoothly. But its creation was aimed at bringing together a wide range of disparate agencies with different purposes and objectives, while forming a department for development is aimed at bringing together programs that are much more similar. Perhaps a more instructive comparison is the separation of the former Department of Health, Education, and Welfare into the Department of Education and the Department of Health and Human Services. Most observers view the separation as a key step toward elevating the importance and strengthening the effectiveness of both agencies, based on the recognition that they were aimed at achieving different underlying objectives.

Ultimately this option is the ideal way to strengthen and modernize foreign assistance programs and elevate the importance of investing in development as part of a stronger and smarter foreign policy. It will be a heavy lift, politically, to achieve, and it will take significant efforts on the part of both the new administration and Congress. But it would create a powerful new instrument for U.S. global leadership in making a stronger and safer world. The change in attitudes and newly placed importance on foreign assistance programs in recent years on Capitol Hill, within the executive branch, and among Americans more broadly make this the best opportunity in decades to take the fundamental steps necessary to modernize and rebuild our foreign assistance programs.

Fundamentally rebuilding and reinvigorating USAID (or a strong successor agency). Under this option, the United States would build a strong subcabinet agency with responsibility for most aid programs, new underlying legislation, a direct relationship with the Office of Management and Budget on budget issues, and the ability to rebuild a strong staff with broad development expertise. Many of the programs administered by other executive branch agencies would be folded into this agency. This could be done either through a deep restructuring and rebuilding of USAID or by creating a strong successor agency. The head of the agency would also hold the title of director of foreign assistance (as under the F process reforms). A board of directors, chaired by the secretary of state, would oversee operations (much like the board of the Millennium Challenge Corporation) and ensure compatibility with broad foreign policy goals. The agency would significantly increase its size (while the staff size for other agencies currently administering programs would shrink) and aim to attract a strong cadre of development professionals to work not just on managing contracts but on analyzing and developing U.S. policies for engagement in low-income countries around the world.

If done right, this option would bring many, but not all, of the benefits of a fully separate cabinet-level department. It would be easier politically (although it would not be easy by any means), and it would ease the concerns of some about maintaining the primacy of the secretary of state. It would create a strong voice within the U.S. government on issues related to development and poverty reduction, and enable the United States to regain a leadership role on these issues internationally. It would lead to much more effective programs than the current structure, or than under a merger with the State Department. For these reasons, it may be an acceptable second choice if a new cabinet agency is not possible

But it is not as strong an option as a new agency. It would not have the same authority or independence, would not be able to attract the same caliber of professional staff, and would not be able to speak with the same stature as a cabinet agency, either in Washington or around the world.

Merging all programs into the State Department. This option has support among some foreign policy experts. Several European governments organize their aid programs in this way, and the F process was based on this idea. Advocates see foreign assistance as a foreign policy instrument that should be fully under the control of the secretary of state, and argue that merging all programs into State would streamline bureaucracy and allow for better coordination across programs.

However, merging foreign assistance programs into the State Department (or merging both into a new department) will likely weaken rather than strengthen aid programs. There are fundamental differences in the objectives, required expertise, and time frames that are relevant for most of the work of the State Department compared with implementing foreign assistance and development programs. The State Department at its core is oriented toward achieving immediate political and diplomatic objectives. The goals of development are quite different, requiring a much longer time horizon and focusing on supporting low-income country efforts to build institutions, train a professional workforce, deliver health and education services, and implement appropriate economic policies. Although the State Department thinks long-term and has many strong strategic planners, the department is fundamentally driven by crisis management and by a focus on meeting the immediate needs of the day, not by the long-term engagement in institution building needed for development.

Giving the State Department greater control over foreign assistance is likely to lead to an even greater share of funding going toward political and strategic allies as a *quid pro quo* for other actions where cooperation is needed immediately, rather than focused on long-term development. The United States has a long history of providing large amounts of foreign assistance to allies to meet short-term political objectives where little was achieved in terms of development. Although some funding for these purposes is important for other foreign policy goals, moving all foreign assistance programs under the direction of the State Department would threaten to push the balance even further in that direction and undermine the achievement of development goals. Of course, the United States should provide assistance to its political allies when circumstances merit it, but this funding should come out of different accounts controlled by the State Department with a clear mission of political support and should not be confused with development assistance.

Moreover, while the State Department has many skilled professionals with strong diplomatic skills, it does not have the expertise necessary to design and implement effective economic development programs and analyze the full set of options for U.S. engagement in low-income countries. It might be possible to build this expertise, but within the department, the development experts would likely always be seen as second-tier to more traditional foreign policy experts and diplomats. The historical record is not supportive: The State Department has been gradually assuming more responsibility for assistance programs for fifteen years but has not built much expertise nor put development experts on a par with traditional diplomats. The experience of the U.S. Information Agency is also instructive. The agency was folded into the State Department in 1999, and there is widespread agreement that the effectiveness of our information programs suffered as a result.

The majority report of the HELP Commission (2007) concluded that these problems could be overcome through a hybrid of this option that would entail merging all of the functions of the State Department and USAID into a new cabinet department called the International Affairs Department. This would reorganize the entire set of international affairs operations, not just foreign assistance, and would be designed to give more prominence and stature to development programs. Although there is appeal to the idea that more than foreign assistance programs need modernization to meet today's foreign policy challenges, ultimately the proposal does not overcome the problems and concerns listed above, and would be unlikely to strengthen foreign assistance programs in the long run.

It clearly is important to properly align foreign assistance programs with broader U.S. foreign policy goals. But this does not require that foreign assistance come under the direct authority of the State Department. U.S. policies in defense, international finance, trade, and intelligence are all important foreign policy tools, but it is for a purpose that they are established independently from the State Department (as was the U.S. Information Agency until 1999). Achieving long-term success in supporting development and good governance systems in recipient countries demands programs that are coordinated across agencies and consistent with our foreign policy goals, and yet independent of direct control by the State Department to ensure the effectiveness of these programs.

Naming a cabinet-level coordinator. The president could designate one person to be responsible for coordinating across the executive branch all aid programs and other policies affecting developing countries. This option would build on the Bush administration's initial step of naming a director of foreign assistance, but would expand it to include all agencies with foreign assistance programs, and would elevate it by giving it a more senior rank. This alternative would be the easiest to implement, but it is highly unlikely to make any significant difference over the long run. Without deeper changes, the coordinator would not have authority over the budgets and personnel in the many agencies that provide assistance. As with other "czar" positions, the coordinator's effectiveness would depend heavily on individual personalities and relationships with the president. It is likely that a coordinator at the National Security Council will be necessary to synchronize assistance programs—wherever they end up—with other policies that affect low-income countries.

But on its own, a cabinet-level position of coordinator is not a long-term solution to modernize U.S. foreign assistance programs.

Steps needed regardless of the organizational structure. Several supporting steps will be necessary to strengthen assistance programs regardless of the organizational structure that is ultimately decided.

- First, the new administration and Congress must rewrite the Foreign Assistance Act, as discussed below. Rewriting the legislation is not an alternative to reform; it is at the core of it. Another round of reforms or reorganization at USAID that does not address the underlying problems in the legislation will not get the job done.
- Second, the United States must beef up its development expertise both in number and with specialists in specific areas in order to improve the analysis of U.S. policies affecting low-income countries. The weakening of USAID has led to a significant reduction in development expertise within the U.S. government as a whole, and that weakness must be addressed in any reform effort.
- Third, any new organization must have a direct relationship with the Office of Management and Budget on budget issues, rather than having its budget go through the State Department.
- Fourth, the U.S. must develop a much wider range of programmatic approaches across the wide spectrum of countries: failed and failing states, post-conflict countries on the rebound, fragile states that are showing some promise, and "Millennium Challenge Corporation–type" countries with stronger governance. Aid programs should differ in the scope of activities, the length of commitment, the involvement of the recipient government in design and implementation, and involvement of nongovernmental agencies. The right approaches in democratic Ghana, post-conflict Liberia, and fragile Sudan clearly must differ. The Millennium Challenge Corporation began this differentiation, and the F process attempted to move it further, but there is much more to be done.
- Fifth, the U.S. must establish stronger monitoring and evaluation systems for its foreign assistance programs. With only a few exceptions, monitoring and evaluation systems are weak and provide little feedback into ongoing or new programs. The United States needs strong monitoring and evaluation processes aimed at keeping programs on track, guiding the allocation of resources toward successful activities and away from failures, and ensuring that the lessons learned—from both successes and failures—inform the design of new programs. This will require much stronger internal

mechanisms. In addition, it is crucial that measures of ultimate impact be conducted independently of the designers and implementers of the programs. For that reason, regardless of institutional design, the United States should support and ultimately join the International Initiative for Impact Evaluation, which would join together foreign assistance providers from around the world to provide professional, independent evaluations of the impact of development initiatives.[11]

3. Rewrite the Foreign Assistance Act

The amended Foreign Assistance Act of 1961 is more than 500 pages long and includes a complex web of rules, regulations, and multiple objectives and directives. Writing a new Foreign Assistance Act is central to clarifying the main mission, mandate, and organizational structure for U.S. foreign assistance. It would provide the opportunity to throw out the morass of personnel, procurement, and contracting regulations and other rules that undermine the effectiveness of USAID and other agencies, and to reduce the extensive amount of earmarking and "tied aid"—much of it well-intentioned—that severely cripples the ability of agencies to effectively allocate funds to the highest priority areas.

Rewriting the act would also provide the opportunity to strengthen and clarify the budget process. The budget should be at the center of designing clear priorities and tradeoffs for allocating foreign assistance funds. However, because foreign assistance activities are scattered throughout several accounts with different authorizations, it is difficult to determine where and how we spend our assistance dollars.

Writing a new Foreign Assistance Act undoubtedly will be a difficult, time-consuming, and risky process, as there are many groups that will fight to protect their interests and there is a danger in opening a Pandora's box. But there is little chance of modernizing the U.S. foreign assistance program and making it an effective tool for today's challenges in the absence of new legislation.

4. Place a higher priority on multilateral channels of assistance

The United States provides a very small share of its foreign assistance—just 10 percent in 2006—through multilateral channels; other major donors average 33 percent. This imbalance is a missed opportunity for the United States to leverage its funding and to exert greater influence over the programs and priorities of the major multilateral agencies. The United States provides 15–20 percent of the funding for the major multilaterals, and other shareholders look to the United States to take the lead in determining their own funding levels. Many shareholders feel that the United States has abandoned the multilaterals. There is no question that the performance of the major multilateral agencies can be strengthened. But the United States can only play a diminished role in the debates and efforts to reform these organizations when it provides such a small share of funding to the multilateral agencies.

The next administration should work more closely with and strengthen multilateral channels of foreign assistance, and allocate a greater share of funding for these organizations. Responsibility for the multilateral development banks currently rests with Treasury, and could shift over to a new cabinet department (or strong subcabinet agency). There are pros and cons to such a shift. Moving this responsibility would allow for stronger coordination between our bilateral and multilateral approaches and would place authority for multilateral development bank policy in the context of the full range of development policies affecting low-income countries, but it would separate it from International Monetary Fund and debt relief policies, which would remain at Treasury. The Treasury Department does not have strong expertise in development, but neither does USAID currently have strong expertise in economic growth and the U.S. role in multilateral development agencies. Placement of this responsibility could work either way, but it will require beefing up the expertise in either Treasury or USAID, and will require strengthening channels of communication and joint decisionmaking between the two agencies.

5. Increase the amount and improve the allocation of funding

More money by itself will not help the United States to better achieve its foreign policy goals in developing countries. But more money, better spent, is an important part of the answer. The steps outlined above, coupled with improved allocation of funding across countries and programs, are central to spending U.S. funds more effectively, but additional funding also will be necessary. Although the increases in funding in recent years are welcome, they were on top of a very low base, and are inadequate for the United States to fight poverty, state failure, and instability in low-income countries around the world.[12]

Conclusion

The Bush administration made much of elevating development to one of three prongs of its foreign policy alongside defense and diplomacy. However, a huge imbalance remains: The defense budget accounted for 21.5 percent of the administration's fiscal year 2008 budget request, while funding for development-related assistance was just 0.4 percent.[13] Although there is no question that the defense budget should be larger than development funding, a ratio of 50:1 is clearly out of balance at a time when stronger and more diversified foreign policy tools are required to achieve today's objectives. Not only are the relative amounts out of balance, the level of spending to achieve development objectives is still too low. As one example, net official development assistance from the United States to Sub-Saharan Africa in 2006 amounted to about $6.6 billion, equivalent to about $9 per African, hardly enough for the United States to play a lead role in helping countries battle poverty.

This view is now widely shared by foreign policy experts, including those outside the traditional development community. Secretary of Defense Robert Gates forcefully made the case for more funding for operations outside his department:

> Funding for non-military foreign-affairs programs has increased since 2001, but it remains disproportionately small relative to what we spend on the military and to the importance of such capabilities . . . The total foreign affairs budget request for the State Department is $36 billion—less than what the Pentagon spends on health care alone . . . What is clear to me is that there is a need for a dramatic increase in spending on the civilian instruments of national security—diplomacy, strategic communications, foreign assistance, civic action, and economic reconstruction and development.[14]

U.S. foreign assistance also can be strengthened by improving the allocation of funding. Forty-four percent of U.S. foreign assistance spending goes to just six countries—all allies in the war on terror or the war on drugs. The other 56 percent is spread among nearly 100 other countries. One of the most striking patterns is that the United States provides 40 percent of its assistance to middle-income countries, and just 34 percent to low-income countries (table 10.2). On average, other donors do the reverse: they provide 25 percent to middle-income countries and 51 percent to low-income countries. The United States provided middle-income Macedonia with an average of $28 per person per year between 2002 and 2004, while much poorer Nicaragua received just $12. Cyprus received $14 per person, while Bangladesh received just $0.46 per person. Between 2002 and 2004, for the eighty-one countries classified by the World Bank as low income (with per capita incomes below about $1,500), the median amount of assistance provided by the United States was about $3.50 per person per year in the recipient country. For thirty lower-middle-income countries (with per capita incomes between approximately $1,500 and $3,000), the median received was $5.43 per person. For countries with

Table 10.2. Share of U.S. bilateral foreign assistance, 2006

Recipients	Share of bilateral foreign assistance funding (percent): From the United States	Average from other Development Assistance Committee donors
Largest six recipients	44	41
Low-income countries	35	51
Middle-income countries	41	25
Sub-Saharan Africa	26	42
Multilateral[a]	10	33

a. The figures for multilateral assistance are shares of total U.S. net official development assistance flows.

Source: Organisation for Economic Co-operation and Development–Development Assistance Committee database on annual aggregates.

incomes greater than $3,000, the median was $10.56 per capita—more than three times larger than for low-income countries. The United States provided Jordan with assistance amounting to $100 per capita between 2002 and 2004, and Israel received $90 per capita. No single low-income country other than Afghanistan or Iraq received as much as $30 per person, and only a handful received more than $15 per person.

In addition, U.S. assistance goes to poorly governed countries with weak policies almost as much as it does to countries with stronger governance, better policies, and a demonstrated commitment to development. Relatively well-governed Tanzania received just $2 in aid per person from the United States, on average, between 2002 and 2004, while poorly governed Angola received more than four times as much at $9 per person. Ghana, another relatively well-governed country, received only about $4 per person, while Eritrea received $17 per person. Although U.S. government rhetoric strongly supports democracies, it spends a relatively small share of our foreign assistance supporting them. It also spends a relatively small share of its funding in Sub-Saharan Africa, the world's poorest continent. The United States can and should do a much better job of getting the right kind of assistance in the right amounts to the right countries to fight poverty, address some of the root causes of state failure, and support democracies around the world.[15]

Taking on these challenges will not be easy. Modernizing development assistance into an effective instrument for smart and strong U.S. global leadership will require major organizational and legislative changes and changing bureaucratic mindsets. Several attempts at modest reorganization or rewriting the Foreign Assistance Act have been made in the last two decades; all fell short because of lack of support in either the administration or on Capitol Hill. But today there is strong backing on both sides of the aisle for elevating the importance of development, with growing consensus around missions, mandates, and strategies. There is a certain Nixon-goes-to-China flavor in the Bush administration's embrace of development programs that has opened the door for a true bipartisan effort. It is time to take advantage of this rare opportunity to modernize and strengthen U.S. development assistance to more effectively combat poverty, widen the circle of development and prosperity, fight terrorism, and further other U.S. strategic interests abroad.

Notes

1. The term "smart power" was originally coined by Nossel 2004. See also Center for U.S. Global Engagement 2007 and Armitage and Nye 2007.
2. All references to amounts of foreign assistance in this chapter are based on data for "official development assistance" as reported by the United States and other countries to the Organisation for Economic Co-operation and Development. This is the standard international source for information on foreign assistance. These figures capture amounts of aid actually disbursed (as opposed to committed) and include assistance for humanitarian and development assistance but not military assistance. These figures differ from numbers drawn from the U.S. budget, which typically include amounts appropriated or authorized rather than amounts disbursed.
3. For earlier discussions, see Radelet 2003; Patrick 2006; Brainard 2006; HELP Commission 2007; and Lancaster 2008.
4. Helms 2001.
5. OECD–DAC 2006. See also Patrick 2006.
6. The fiscal year 2008 appropriation was $1.5 billion, down from $1.7 billion the previous two years. For ongoing analyses of key issues involving the Millennium Challenge Corporation, see the Center for Global Development's "MCA Monitor" Web site (www.cgdev.org/section/initiatives/_active/mcamonitor).
7. See Summers 2000.
8. For other discussions on the need for deeper reform, see Radelet 2003 and 2004; Brainard 2006; Patrick 2006; HELP Commission 2007; and Lancaster 2008.
9. Nowels and Veillette 2006.
10. Radelet (2004) and Patrick (2006), among others, earlier have called for developing a strategy along these lines.
11. For more on this proposal, see CGD 2006.
12. For more analysis on these points, see Bazzi, Herrling, and Patrick 2007.
13. Bazzi, Herrling, and Patrick 2007.

14. Gates 2007.
15. Gates 2007.

References

Armitage, Richard L., and Joseph S. Nye, Jr. 2007. *A Smarter, More Secure America*. Report of the CSIS Commission on Smart Power. November. Washington, D.C.: Center for Strategic and International Studies.

ASP (The American Security Project). 2007. "*America and the World: Evolving Attitudes on National Security and Foreign Policy*." Poll conducted April 30–May 8. [www.americansecurityproject.org/issues/reports/america_and_the_world_evolving_attitudes_on_national_security_and_foreign_policy_data].

Bazzi, Samuel, Sheila Herrling, and Stewart Patrick. 2007. "Billions for War, Pennies for the Poor: Moving the President's FY 2008 Budget from Hard Power to Smart Power." Center for Global Development, Washington, D.C.

Brainard, Lael, ed. 2006. *Security by Other Means: Foreign Assistance, Global Poverty, and American Leadership*. Washington, D.C.: Brookings Institution Press.

Center for U.S. Global Engagement. 2007. "Smart Power: Building a Better, Safer World." Washington, D.C.

CGD (Center for Global Development). 2006. "When Will We Ever Learn? Closing the Evaluation Gap." [http://www.cgdev.org/section/initiatives/_active/evalgap].

Gates, Robert. 2007. Landon Lecture. November 26. Kansas State University, Manhattan, Kansas. [www.defenselink.mil/speeches/speech.aspx?speechid=1199].

Helms, Jesse. 2001. "Towards a Compassionate Conservative Foreign Policy." Speech at the American Enterprise Institute, January 11, Washington, D.C. [www.aei.org/publications/pubID.17927,filter.all/pub_detail.asp].

HELP Commission (U.S. Commission on Helping to Enhance the Livelihood of People). 2007. *Beyond Assistance*. Washington, D.C.

Lancaster, Carol. 2008. *George Bush's Foreign Aid: Transformation or Chaos?* Washington, D.C.: Center for Global Development.

Nossel, Suzanne. 2004. "Smart Power." *Foreign Affairs* 83 (2): 131–42.

Nowels, Larry, and Connie Veillette. 2006. "Restructuring US Foreign Aid: The Role of the Director of Foreign Assistance." Congressional Research Service, Washington, D.C.

OECD-DAC (Organisation for Economic Co-operation and Development–Development Assistance Committee). 2006. *Peer Review of the United States*. Paris.

Patrick, Stewart. 2006. "U.S. Foreign Aid Reform: Will it Fix what is Broken?" Center for Global Development, Washington, D.C.

PIPA (Program on International Policy Attitudes)/Knowledge Networks. 2006. *What Kind of Foreign Policy Does the American Public Want?* Poll conducted October 6–15. [www.worldpublicopinion.org/pipa/pdf/oct06/SecurityFP_Oct06_quaire.pdf].

Radelet, Steve. 2003. "Bush and Foreign Aid." *Foreign Affairs* 82 (5): 104–17.

———. 2004. "U.S. Foreign Assistance after September 11th." Testimony before the House International Relations Committee. February. Washington, D.C.

Summers, Lawrence. 2000. "Statement to the Development Committee at of the World Bank and the International Monetary Fund." September 25. Prague.

11 Opportunities for Presidential Leadership on AIDS: From an "Emergency Plan" to a Sustainable Policy

Mead Over

The acquired immune deficiency syndrome, or AIDS, was unknown as recently as the 1980s. Now this "syndrome" is known to be caused by the human immunodeficiency virus, or HIV, and is the most notorious disease in the world. In the United States, children study the HIV/AIDS epidemic in primary school and learn HIV-prevention methods in high school.[1] Among some poor, illiterate populations in the severely affected countries of Africa, more people correctly identify sex as a means of HIV transmission than know that mosquitoes transmit the ancient scourge of malaria, which kills almost as many Africans.

The notoriety of the AIDS epidemic can be attributed to many factors. The fact that it first came to attention as a disease that primarily affected gay men in the United States and other rich countries is certainly one important reason; gay men proved to be extraordinarily articulate in publicizing the ravages of the disease and in lobbying for public resources to study and treat it. The long incubation period of the virus allowed persons living with AIDS to speak and write about their suffering

---

Mead Over is a senior fellow at the Center for Global Development. He is grateful for comments by Martha Ainsworth, Michael Bernstein, Nancy Birdsall, Jimmy Kolker, Ruth Levine, Michael Merson, Phil Musgrove, Nandini Oomman, John Stover, Steve Radelet, and Steve Rosenzweig; for the editorial suggestions of Lawrence MacDonald and Parul Subramanian; and for the expert research assistance of Martina Tonizzo. The views expressed in this chapter—and any remaining errors—are those of the author.

for years—possibilities that were less available to people suffering from more quickly fatal illnesses.

The appearance in these personal narratives of both sex and death contributed to their fascination. HIV-infected blood supplies spread the disease to many transfusion recipients in rich countries and led to scandals and more publicity. The creation of a specialized international agency—called first the Special Programme on AIDS, then the Global Programme on AIDS, and currently the Joint United Nations Programme on HIV/AIDS (UNAIDS)—provided salaried positions for people whose job it was to publicize this sole disease. The novel challenges of research on what causes the disease, one of a class of little understood pathogens called "retroviruses," engendered enthusiasm in the medical and biological research communities. Based on this rapidly evolving research, multinational pharmaceutical firms discovered new drugs to combat the disease and profited from selling the drugs in rich countries and sometimes in poor countries. And last, but not least, was the fact that the virus and its consequences seemed to spread in many parts of the world despite what seemed like the best efforts to control it.

Although the AIDS epidemic is no longer a growing public health problem in the United States or other rich countries, UNAIDS estimates that, worldwide, the virus infects more than 33 million people and causes more than 2 million deaths each year.[2] While the robust economic growth of heavily affected countries such as Botswana and South Africa suggests that AIDS does not have immediately catastrophic impacts on economic growth,[3] the fact that it can reduce life expectancy by decades is itself a catastrophic impact on economic well-being and development. AIDS is decimating the professional classes of the worst-affected countries.[4] Furthermore, the long-term impact of lower life expectancy and high rates of orphanhood are still unknown. One study has suggested that by the year 2080, orphanhood in South Africa might reduce its income per capita to less than half its current level.[5] Growing awareness of these impacts of AIDS may have contributed to President Bush's decision to propose an initiative to combat AIDS in poor countries in the same 2003 State of the Union address in which he announced his intention to invade Iraq.[6]

Origins of the President's Emergency Plan for AIDS Relief

In response to President Bush's proposal, the U.S. Congress launched the Global AIDS Initiative by passing the U.S. Leadership Against HIV/AIDS, Tuberculosis, and Malaria Act on May 27, 2003.[7] The act required the president to establish the Office of Global AIDS Coordinator within the Department of State, rather than the U.S. Agency for International Development, which had managed previous U.S.-funded AIDS assistance. The coordinator,

Ambassador Randall Tobias, fulfilled his mandate to present to Congress the Five-Year Global AIDS Strategy on February 23, 2004, titled "The President's Emergency Plan for AIDS Relief" (PEPFAR). This strategy establishes three objectives: to encourage bold leadership at every level to fight HIV/AIDS; to apply best practices within U.S. bilateral HIV/AIDS prevention, treatment, and care programs; and to encourage partners to coordinate efforts to ensure the most effective and efficient use of resources. The strategy proposed fifteen "focus" countries for HIV/AIDS assistance (table 11.1).

As a result of PEPFAR, the United States became the largest single contributor in the struggle to control the international AIDS epidemic in 2006 and 2007.[8] In 2006, the United States committed $2.6 billion for AIDS, which was 47 percent of the $5.6 billion total from all donors, with the Netherlands the second largest donor at 17 percent. The United States accounted for 41 percent of the $3.9 billion that was actually disbursed, with the United Kingdom the second largest donor at 20 percent (figure 11.1). Most of this money was channeled through PEPFAR, which can properly be described as the "largest global health initiative directed at a single disease that any nation has ever undertaken."[9] For comparison, in inflation-adjusted dollars, the United States is spending more than 100 times as much per year now on AIDS in poor countries as it spent between 1967 and 1979 on the eradication of smallpox.[10]

The most remarkable achievement of the PEPFAR program has been its contribution to the provision of AIDS treatment to more than 1.3 million patients in its fifteen focus countries by September 2007.[11] Furthermore, PEPFAR was able to accelerate constantly until March 2007, adding more patients in each six-month period than it had in the previous six months (figure 11.2). However, it is sobering to note that the number of new infections in this period in the focus countries averaged about 1.4 million each year—about three times the number of people who started therapy in the last year to which the data extend.

The U.S. Foreign Assistance Program, which funds PEPFAR, is also the biggest single funder of the Global Fund to Fight AIDS, Tuberculosis, and Malaria, and the second biggest funder (after the United Kingdom) of the World Bank, two important multilateral sources of AIDS financing. In addition, U.S. tax laws favoring the creation and operation of philanthropic foundations have enabled U.S. foundations to dominate the world of foundation giving to fight AIDS.

Build on the President's Emergency Plan for AIDS Relief

President Bush's AIDS policy established a record of success on AIDS treatment with which the actions of the next president will inevitably be compared. Presidential candidates choose to ignore AIDS policy at their peril.

Table 11.1. Selected economic and health indicators of the President's Emergency Plan for AIDS Relief focus countries

Country	Population	Income status	GDP per capita ($)	Life expectancy (years)	Adult HIV/AIDS prevalence (% of ages 15–49)		Number of physicians in 2003/04
					Point estimate	Range	
Botswana	1,765,000	Upper-middle	8,920	35	24.1	[23.0–32.0]	715
Côte d'Ivoire	18,154,000	Low	1,390	47	7.1	[4.3–9.7]	2,081
Ethiopia	77,431,000	Low	810	48		[0.9–3.5]	1,936
Guyana	751,000	Lower-middle	4,110	63	2.4	[1.0–4.9]	366
Haiti	8,528,000	Low	1,680	52	3.8	[2.2–5.4]	1,949
Kenya	34,256,000	Low	1,050	47	6.1	[5.2–7.0]	4,506
Mozambique	19,792,000	Low	1,160	42	16.1	[12.5–20.0]	514
Namibia	2,031,000	Lower-middle	6,960	46	19.6	[8.6–31.7]	598
Nigeria	131,530,000	Low	930	44	3.9	[2.3–5.6]	34,923
Rwanda	9,038,000	Low	1,300	44	3.1	[2.9–3.2]	401
South Africa	47,432,000	Upper-middle	10,960	52	18.8	[16.8–20.7]	34,829
Tanzania	38,329,000	Low	660	44	6.5	[5.8–7.2]	822
Uganda	28,816,000	Low	1,520	48	6.7	[5.7–7.6]	2,209
Vietnam	84,238,000	Low	2,700	72	0.5	[0.3–0.9]	42,327
Zambia	11,668,000	Low	890	37	17	[15.9–18.1]	1,264

Note: GDP is gross domestic product.

Source: Institute of Medicine 2007, (tables 2-3 and 2-4, pp. 59–61).

Figure 11.1. Donor-country disbursements for combating AIDS, 2006

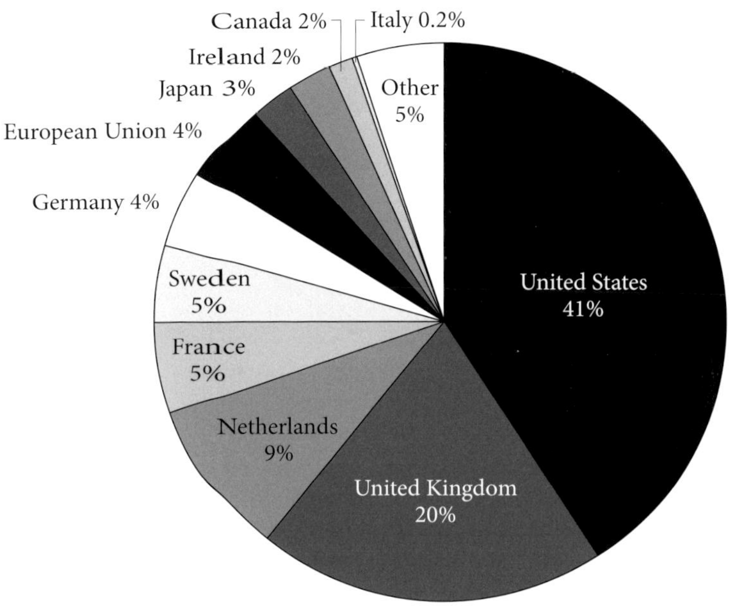

Source: Kates, Izazola, and Lief 2007.

They can quietly continue the country on its present course. They can withdraw support from AIDS patients, risking a backlash of cynicism about the country's will to respect its commitments. Or, as outlined below, they can address the weaknesses of existing U.S. AIDS policy and, in so doing, strengthen the U.S. reputation for contributing to the solution of global problems.

The attempts to expand U.S. support for AIDS treatment during the Clinton administration were justified on national security grounds. An innovation of the Bush presidency was to largely eschew national security as a justification for PEPFAR; President Bush chose instead to use the program as the prime international exhibit for his presidency's vaunted philosophy of "compassionate conservatism." As its name signifies, PEPFAR was originally justified primarily as an emergency plan. However, PEPFAR is creating entitlements that cannot be assumed by most of the recipient countries and are hard to justify on investment grounds.[12] These features of PEPFAR suggest that it is really an international transfer program, comparable perhaps to U.S. food assistance.[13] Programs to redistribute resources from rich-country taxpayers to the poor in developing countries constitute state-supported international welfare programs.

Figure 11.2. Number of people receiving U.S.-supported AIDS treatment in the focus countries

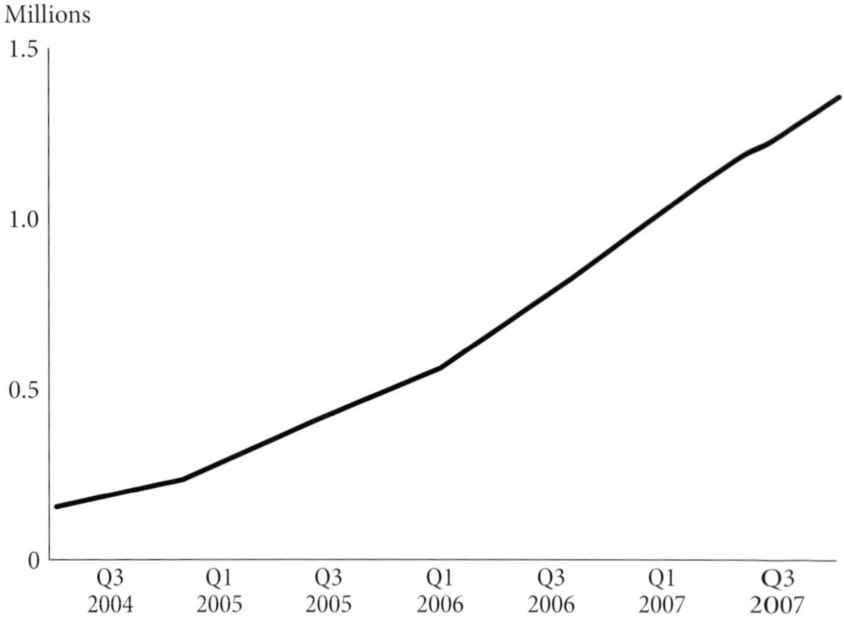

Source: OGAC 2007.

Recommendations to the next president are grouped under three headings:

- Managing the AIDS treatment entitlement.
- Preventing the future need for treatment.
- Ensuring the "AIDS transition."

1. Managing the AIDS treatment entitlement

The term "entitlement" applies to a government expenditure program that engenders the expectation that current beneficiaries will continue to receive funding in future years. The expectation is created partly by the language of the authorizing legislation, which typically endows beneficiaries with the "right" to a continued flow of payments, and partly by the perception that the beneficiaries are vitally dependent on continuation of the funding. The domestic U.S. program that is most commonly described as an "entitlement" program is Social Security, any reduction of which entails a grave reputational and political risk for the politicians who propose it. Because the beneficiaries of PEPFAR's treatment component are foreign nationals, they are endowed legally with neither the right to continued funding nor the right to vote against U.S. politicians who would reduce their benefits. Nevertheless, because these beneficiaries are vitally dependent on continued AIDS treatment and linked to an international network of articulate AIDS treatment advocates, any withdrawal of treatment funding that threatens their lives will expose the U.S. government to reputational risk at home and abroad and may threaten U.S. politicians at the ballot box.

To avoid the reputational risk of failing to support AIDS treatment, the next president must wisely manage the treatment entitlements inherited from the current administration. This chapter recommends four ways to do so:

- Maximize the success of ongoing treatment.
- Reduce the cost of treatment.
- Limit the expansion of AIDS treatment entitlements.
- Support the creation of a Global Health Corps.

Maximize the success of ongoing treatment. As an assistance program expands and matures, it can become encumbered by leaks and inefficiencies. In the case of AIDS treatment, these problems can mean loss of patient life, increased resort to second-line therapies, and increased transmission of drug-resistant strains of HIV. To prevent U.S.-funded AIDS treatment from suffering this fate, the United States must ensure the effective supervision of AIDS treatment personnel and supplies in the focus countries. Furthermore, the United States should provide small startup funds for the formation of patient-managed adherence support organizations.[14] Such groups could help slow the development of drug resistance not only for antiretroviral medications but also for medications against malaria and tuberculosis, and even for antibiotics. Such demand-side mechanisms can help ensure quality treatment in the private sector, where command and control supervision does not reach.

Reduce the unit costs of treatment. Although the continuing drive to extend treatment to almost all who need it will drive up unit costs, U.S. support for AIDS interventions should work to bring these costs down in other ways. The new president should collaborate with the program of the World Health Organization to certify generic versions of antiretrovirals for use in PEPFAR countries, and also cooperate with the Clinton Foundation's efforts to lower drug prices through long-term contracts for large quantities. (See box 11.1 for a suggested pilot initiative to administer cheap palliative drugs in poor countries.) As a last resort, when patent holders fail to sufficiently reduce their prices for poor countries, the United States should support compulsory licensing of AIDS drugs by poor countries and by third-party countries, such as Canada, which can then export them to poor countries. The United States

Box 11.1. A promising technical option for fulfilling the President's Emergency Plan for AIDS Relief's original goal to provide palliative care

Those who have experienced the extreme pain of cancer or the terror associated with severe lung congestion, either personally or vicariously through the illness of a patient or loved one, well understand the benefits of palliation. Pain relief benefits not only the patient but also the patient's family. It diminishes the stigma with which sick people might otherwise be regarded and frees both the patient and the patient's supporters to focus on their overarching challenges, such as maximizing the effectiveness of treatment, maintaining the functions of the household, or, in cases where treatment has failed, coming to terms peacefully with end-of-life issues such as leave-taking and inheritance.

In recognition of the importance of pain relief, the original President's Emergency Plan for AIDS Relief (PEPFAR) legislation mandated that a portion of each country's allocation be spent on palliative care. But in attempting to fulfill this mandate, PEPFAR has been handicapped by precautionary rules established in poor countries to prevent the diversion of medicinal opiates and analgesics toward the illegal drug trade (Koshy and others 1998; Rhodes and Grossman 1997).

A technical innovation that is close to approval offers the hope of dramatically improving pain relief for cancer and AIDS patients in poor countries without running the risks of diversion that are inescapable with liquid morphine and other potent opiates.

The breakthrough comes in the form of a small ceramic tablet (the size of a shirt button), impregnated with hydromorphone (a potent morphine derivative), that can be implanted beneath the skin of a patient (Lesser and others 1996). By properly matching the geometric construction of the tablet to the pain relief requirements of the patient, it is possible to alleviate most pain for thirty days, when a new tablet can be implanted. The technology of constructing the tablets and impregnating them with hydromorphone is so simple and fast that pain relief can be provided as cheaply by this method as it could by morphine injections. The cost is expected to be only a few dollars for a thirty-day tablet.

We recommend that renewal of U.S. support to AIDS treatment and care include explicit provisions for piloting the distribution of pain management medication, including these hydromorphone impregnated tablets, which can be prescribed and administered in a controlled setting in each of the fifteen focus countries. Based on the results of these pilot programs, each country could then propose a plan for scaling up the distribution of analgesics, so that no one suffering from extreme pain is deprived of relief.

—Mead Over, Center for Global Development; Stuart Grossman, The Sidney Kimmel Comprehensive Cancer Center at Johns Hopkins University; and Julette-Marie F. Batara, Philippines Institute of Neurosciences

should cease using bilateral trade agreements to constrain the use of compulsory licenses for treating diseases that are specific to poor countries (see chapter 8 by Fink and Elliott).

Limit the expansion of AIDS treatment entitlements. In view of the reputational risk to the United States associated with AIDS treatment entitlements, the new president should moderate the expansion of entitlements to new beneficiaries, while upholding and strengthening existing ones. Several strategies for limiting the imprudent expansion of entitlements are available. First, the president should resist any pressure to expand the number of focus countries targeted by PEPFAR. This group of countries already accounts for almost half of existing AIDS cases and more than half of new cases worldwide. The United States should concentrate on doing a good job in these countries at least through the next two presidential terms, leaving the remaining countries to be dealt with by other donor countries, the Global Fund, and other mechanisms.[15] If the United States and its partners succeed in reducing the impact of AIDS in the fifteen focus countries, spillovers to other countries would benefit the rest of the world, whereas poor performance in these countries would cast a shadow on AIDS control efforts everywhere. Examples of benefits that would spill over from focus countries to their neighbors include low generic drug prices, lessons about what works in treatment and prevention, reduced stigma for AIDS patients, and safer norms of sexual behavor.

Limiting the expansion of AIDS treatment in the fifteen focus countries to the rate of increase that PEPFAR has achieved up to now would require the AIDS treatment budget to grow to about $5 billion a year in 2016 and $7 billion a year in 2020 (figure 11.3a). This rate of expansion saves from $7 billion a year in 2016 to $10 billion per year in 2020, compared with the aggressive uptake scenario (figure 11.3b)—money that can be spent on urgently needed HIV prevention and on strengthening the health care systems of the recipient countries.[16]

The two right panels of table 11.2 present the numerical projections under historical and rapid uptake, assuming incidence declines at 5 percent a year. Over the five-year period of the proposed PEPFAR reauthorization (2009–13), AIDS treatment expenditures are predicted to total $25.8 billion. Congress has recently authorized that 80 percent of $50 billion, or $40 billion, be spent on AIDS, of which more than 20 percent ($8 billion) should be spent on HIV prevention and another substantial portion on care and support for patients and their orphaned children (box 11.2). Furthermore a large, but unknown, proportion of the $40 billion would flow to the Global Fund for AIDS, Tuberculosis, and Malaria. Thus $25.8 billion represents up to 25 percent more AIDS treatment expenditure than has yet been authorized. These

Figure 11.3. Projected cost of AIDS treatment and funding gap, 2006–2020

3a. Historical uptake at 18 percent of unmet need each year

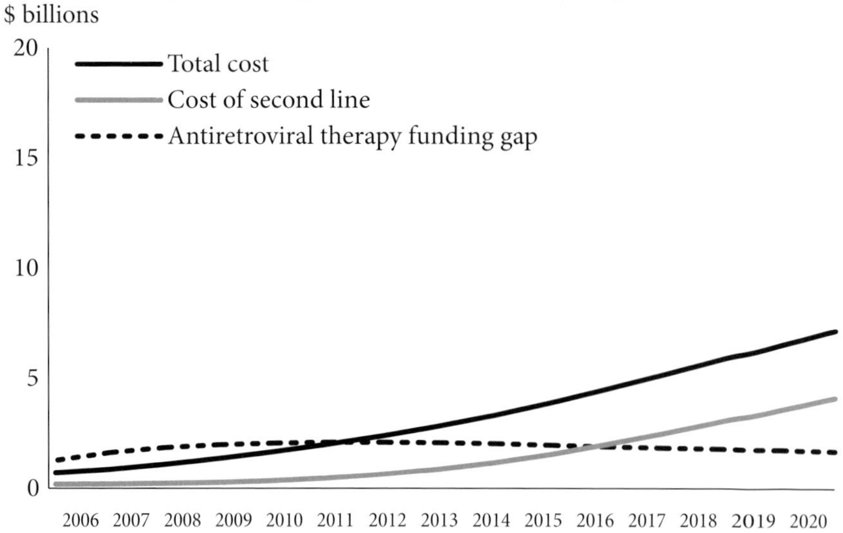

3b. Aggressive uptake at 95 percent of unmet need each year

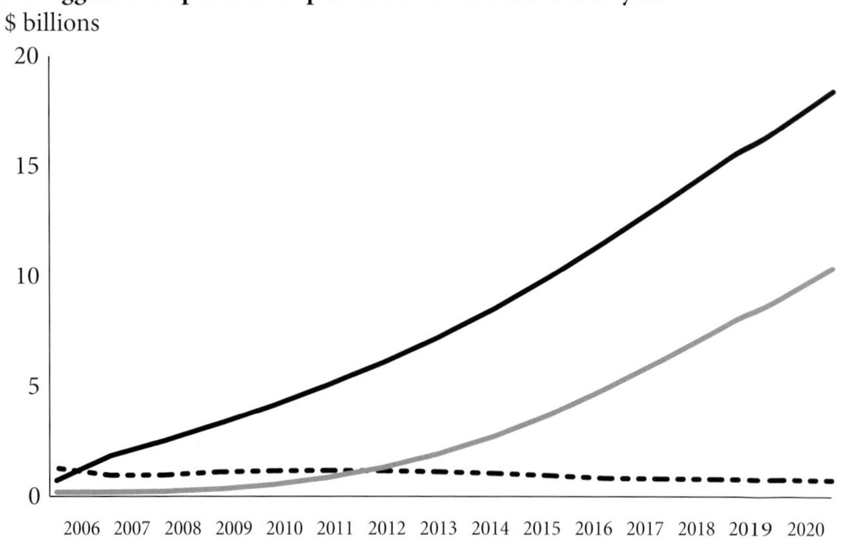

Source: Over 2008.

Table 11.2. Projected annual costs of AIDS treatment in the focus countries by uptake and prevention scenarios (in 2006 $ thousands)

	Cost at historical uptake and 90 percent reduction in incidence each year				Cost at historical uptake and 5 percent reduction in incidence each year		
	1st line	2nd line	Total cost		1st line	2nd line	Total cost
2006	529,785	191,727	721,512	2006	529,785	191,727	721,512
2007	673,329	201,623	874,952	2007	673,329	201,623	874,952
2008	874,949	227,439	1,102,388	2008	874,949	227,439	1,102,388
2009	1,093,394	274,306	1,367,700	2009	1,093,394	274,306	1,367,700
2010	1,303,451	353,146	1,656,597	2010	1,316,705	353,146	1,669,851
2011	1,493,607	474,165	1,967,772	2011	1,537,707	474,165	2,011,872
2012	1,659,169	645,144	2,304,313	2012	1,752,010	646,776	2,398,786
2013	1,799,050	871,376	2,670,426	2013	1,956,904	879,399	2,836,303
2014	1,914,054	1,155,985	3,070,039	2014	2,150,721	1,179,388	3,330,109
2015	2,005,932	1,500,249	3,506,181	2015	2,332,462	1,553,030	3,885,492
2016	2,076,820	1,903,999	3,980,819	2016	2,501,578	2,005,589	4,507,167
2017	2,128,992	2,324,288	4,453,280	2017	2,657,823	2,493,208	5,151,031
2018	2,164,638	2,756,281	4,920,919	2018	2,801,161	3,012,715	5,813,876
2019	2,185,840	3,195,719	5,381,559	2019	2,931,717	3,560,905	6,492,622
2020	2,194,497	3,638,869	5,833,366	2020	3,049,732	4,134,636	7,184,368
Total	24,097,507	19,714,316	*Least costly* 43,811,823	Total	28,159,977	21,188,052	49,348,029
By presidential term							
2009–2012	5,549,621	1,746,761	7,296,382	2009–2012	5,699,816	1,748,393	7,448,209
2013–2016	7,795,856	5,431,609	13,227,465	2013–2016	8,941,665	5,617,406	14,559,071

	Cost at rapid uptake and 90 percent reduction in incidence each year				Cost at rapid uptake and 5 percent reduction in incidence each year		
	1st line	2nd line	Total cost		1st line	2nd line	Total cost
2006	529,785	191,727	721,512	2006	529,785	191,727	721,512
2007	1,635,364	201,623	1,836,987	2007	1,635,364	201,623	1,836,987
2008	2,307,005	227,439	2,534,444	2008	2,307,005	227,439	2,534,444
2009	2,970,273	335,242	3,305,515	2009	2,970,273	335,242	3,305,515
2010	3,528,288	537,685	4,065,973	2010	3,604,610	537,685	4,142,295
2011	3,989,774	857,925	4,847,699	2011	4,206,920	857,925	5,064,845
2012	4,366,528	1,308,550	5,675,078	2012	4,775,381	1,317,404	6,092,785

(continued)

Table 11.2. Projected annual costs of AIDS treatment in the focus countries by uptake and prevention scenarios (continued)

	Cost at rapid uptake & 90% reduction in incidence each year				Cost at rapid uptake & 5% reduction in incidence each year		
	1st line	2nd line	Total cost		1st line	2nd line	Total cost
2013	4,669,214	1,896,367	6,565,581	2013	5,308,801	1,935,101	7,243,902
2014	4,907,290	2,624,207	7,531,497	2014	5,806,506	2,727,520	8,534,026
2015	5,089,106	3,491,710	8,580,816	2015	6,268,233	3,708,719	9,976,952
2016	5,222,058	4,496,040	9,718,098	2016	6,694,088	4,890,296	11,584,384
2017	5,312,678	5,530,143	10,842,821	2017	7,084,481	6,156,945	13,241,426
2018	5,366,727	6,583,190	11,949,917	2018	7,440,050	7,500,065	14,940,115
2019	5,389,291	7,645,843	13,035,134	2019	7,761,645	8,911,297	16,672,942
2020	5,384,857	8,710,115	14,094,972	2020	8,050,268	10,382,518	18,432,786
Total	60,668,238	44,637,806	105,306,044	Total	74,443,410	49,881,506	*Most costly* 124,324,916
			By presidential term				
2009–2012	14,854,863	3,039,402	17,894,265	2009–2012	15,557,184	3,048,256	18,605,440
2013–2016	19,887,668	12,508,324	32,395,992	2013–2016	24,077,628	13,261,636	37,339,264

Source: Author's calculations based on assumptions in Over (2008).

projections include estimates of the variable cost per patient in each country, but do not include any fixed cost per country or per treatment site. See Over (2008) for more details on the projections.

A second strategy open to the president for limiting the growth of U.S. entitlements is to increase the proportion of U.S.-financed AIDS funding that passes through multilateral institutions, including the Global Fund and the World Bank. Not only does this strategy shift the entitlement from the U.S. government to the multilateral institution, it can also benefit the recipient nations and patients by stimulating competition on the ground among institutions providing AIDS treatment and prevention. The ongoing HIV/AIDS Monitor project of the Center for Global Development, which compares the performance of the three largest AIDS funders in three countries, already shows how recipient countries benefit when evaluators can compare the funders to one another.[17]

Figure 11.4 shows the percentage of AIDS financing that passes through the Global Fund for each of the donor members of the Organisation for Economic Co-operation and Development. The United States is ranked sixth in the group, passing only about 17 percent of its resources through the Global Fund. There is room for substantial expansion here.

Box 11.2. How do the president and Congress think the President's Emergency Plan for AIDS Relief should be restructured?

The law creating the President's Emergency Plan for AIDS Relief (PEPFAR) gave it legal authority for a five-year period that expires at the end of 2008. With that date quickly approaching, Congress is expected to reauthorize the AIDS initiative for another five years. A variety of stakeholders have offered recommendations on how PEPFAR should be reformed. The views of two particularly important and influential actors—President Bush and the U.S. Congress—are summarized below.

President Bush

In May 2007, President Bush announced his support for $30 billion in funding for the next phase of PEPFAR. He also proposed a set of goals for "PEPFAR II" that would place greater emphasis on prevention than PEPFAR I did, and would slow the rate at which PEPFAR was enrolling new patients for treatment. Specifically, he has called for PEPFAR II to support treatment for 0.5 million additional people, prevention of 5 million new infections, and care for 2 million people. The relative weighting of these goals is consistent with the recommendations in this chapter, although the prevention target is less ambitious than the proposal here.

President Bush has also called for the U.S. government to sign agreements called "partnership compacts" with countries receiving PEPFAR funds in order to ensure that governments are investing their own resources in AIDS programs; formalize the relationships between PEPFAR and other stakeholders such as the government, other donors, civil society, and the private sector; and implement AIDS programs in a way that supports broader development objectives, including gender equality and economic growth. The executive branch has not yet offered more details about how these partnership compacts will be implemented or which countries will be asked to sign them.

U.S. Congress

The House and Senate have both drafted bills that call for $50 billion in funding for AIDS, tuberculosis, and malaria over the next five fiscal years. Most of that money—roughly 80 percent—would go for AIDS programs. The Global Fund would receive up to one-fifth of the total, $10 million over five years. The remaining bilateral AIDS funding would largely be free of the type of funding directives ("earmarks") that were mandated in the first five years of PEPFAR.

Congress has accepted President Bush's proposed targets for prevention and care, but they have changed the treatment target to 1 million and have added a new target—train 140,000 health workers. The Senate bill also includes targets on preventing mother to child transmission and pediatric AIDS treatment.

The bills to reauthorize PEPFAR emphasize the importance of prevention more than the original bill did. The original bill called for PEPFAR to spend 20 percent of its funding on prevention; the new PEPFAR bills stipulate that 20 percent should be the minimum

(continued)

Box 11.2. How do the president and Congress think the President's Emergency Plan for AIDS Relief should be restructured? (continued)

spent on prevention. Both bills have also increased the prevention target—which has gone from preventing 7 million infections to preventing 12 million infections—more significantly than the treatment target, which has changed from treating 2 million people to 3 million people. Whereas the first phase of PEPFAR included a provision stating that two-thirds of sexual prevention funding had to be used for abstinence and be faithful activities, the current bills have no such provision, but they do call for half of sexual prevention funding to be used for "behavior change" programs—a term that has not yet been clearly defined but clearly includes abstinence and be faithful activities.

As recommended in this chapter, the two bill calls for more funding for operations research and an increased emphasis on strengthening health systems. The Senate bill also mandates that PEPFAR conduct an impact evaluation to examine the effect of PEPFAR programs on indicators like incidence, prevalence, and mortality. Other key features of the two bills include a clear recognition that PEPFAR must address the special vulnerabilities of women and girls, and better integration of nutrition and HIV programs.

—*Michael Bernstein, HIV/AIDS Monitor team, Center for Global Development*

Support the creation of a Global Health Corps. As the United States continues to extend AIDS care in the PEPFAR countries, the burden on the existing health care systems will grow increasingly onerous. From the current levels of more than $10,000 per physician, expansion will soon require expenditures of up to $100,000 per physician each year. This additional burden, on top of existing health care needs, threatens to divert resources away from patients suffering from other health problems.[18]

One obvious answer to this problem is for the United States to support general health system strengthening such as that documented in Rwanda by a presentation at the Institute of Medicine, but more is needed.[19] The president should support the creation and deployment of a Global Health Corps such as that proposed in box 1.3 of chapter 1 by Levine. A key feature of this corps would be to go beyond providing AIDS treatment and offer to address the most serious gaps in the health care needs of the host country. By responding to requests to send U.S. health care personnel to PEPFAR countries, the president would demonstrate the willingness of the United States to engage its most valuable resource—its own people—in the struggle against the health problems of the PEPFAR countries.

2. Preventing the future need for treatment

The old proverb that an ounce of prevention is worth a pound of cure has never been more true than it is now with the AIDS epidemic.[20] The president

Figure 11.4. Bilateral and Global Fund resources for AIDS

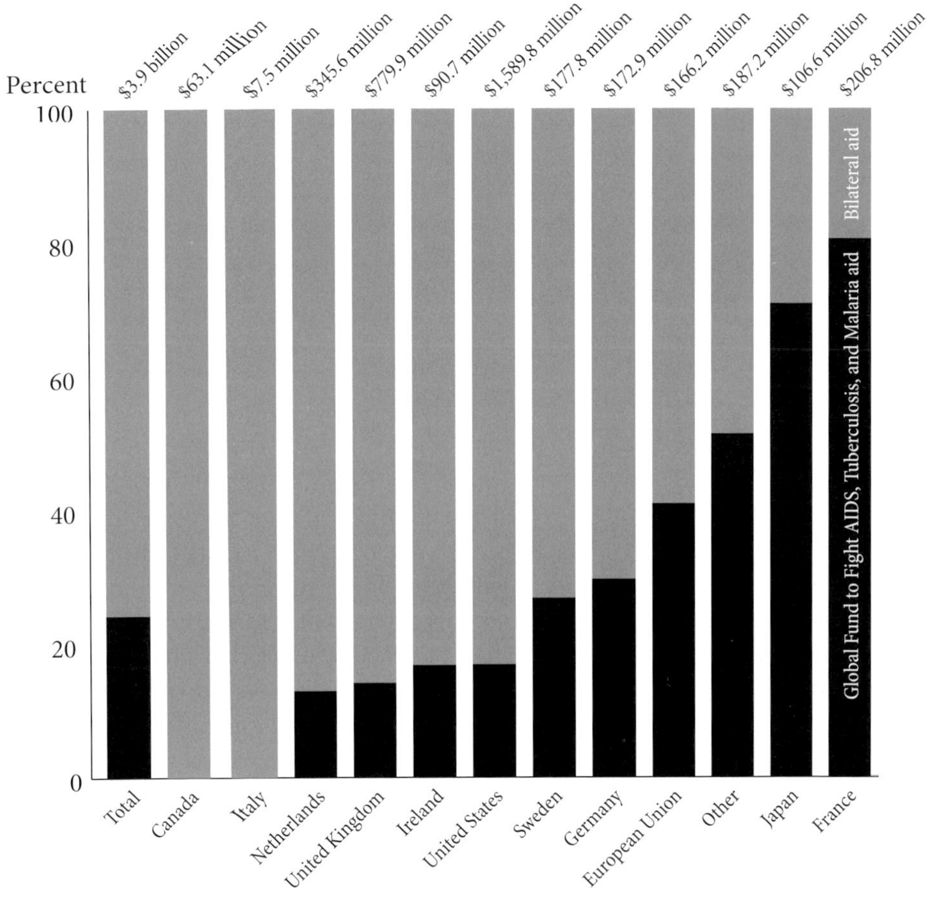

Source: Kates, Izazola, and Lief 2007.

should propose a dramatic new objective: prevention of 90 percent of annual infections in the focus countries by the year 2012. Given the current number of new infections each year in the PEPFAR countries at about 1.4 million, this goal would commit the United States to reducing this number to about 140,000 by the year 2016. Establishment of such a goal recognizes the superior cost-effectiveness of prevention in the long run and commits the United States to developing and applying interventions and measurement tools that would advance the prevention agenda and measure its progress.[21]

Because every new HIV infection adds to the AIDS treatment burden within five to ten years, it is becoming a fiscal imperative to slow the progress of HIV infection. Figure 11.3 above showed how the treatment burden would grow under two different uptake scenarios if HIV infection rates fell by only 5 percent each successive year. Figure 11.5 shows the effects of a more dramatic decline of 90 percent each year. If the United States is able to help the focus countries to slow the growth of HIV by this much starting in 2008, and the rate of treatment uptake is maintained at 18 percent of unmet need each year, by 2020 the cost of treatment will be smaller by about $1.4 billion a year—releasing resources for discretionary foreign assistance objectives.[22]

The imperative to strengthen HIV-prevention programs is reinforced not only by the cost of treatment but also by the possibility that access to treatment may, in itself, speed infection. Free access to widely available and demonstrably effective treatment can engender complacency leading to the disinhibition of risk behavior among those who are not yet in treatment or even HIV-infected. Following the Hippocratic injunction to "first, do no harm," the United States must strengthen HIV prevention programs at least in the focus countries.

A possible unintended consequence of the rapid and effective rollout of antiretrovirals in PEPFAR countries may be to attract immigration from neighboring countries where AIDS treatment is less accessible. PEPFAR should, therefore, contribute to prevention programs in these neighboring countries to eventually slow any influx into PEPFAR countries.

Much has been written about prevention strategies and this is not the place to review all the options. It is depressing and even scandalous that after more than twenty years of donor-funded prevention efforts, so few prevention interventions have been rigorously evaluated.[23] Five neglected prevention strategies that seem both technically and politically feasible, based on current knowledge, deserve particular attention in PEPFAR countries:

- Improved targeting of prevention efforts in places frequented by those at most risk of contracting and transmitting the infection.
- Mobilization, for HIV prevention, of the people who receive U.S.-funded AIDS treatment.
- Expansion of access to male circumcision.
- Integration of family planning services with HIV testing and AIDS treatment.
- Reorientation of HIV testing toward in-home services for couples, rather than facility-based testing of individuals.

Target HIV-prevention efforts to hot spots. The first step in a successful prevention campaign is to gather the epidemiological data to determine where and among whom HIV infections are spreading most rapidly. As the Institute of Medicine points out in its assessment of PEPFAR's implementation, PEPFAR has never done the basic survey work that would be required to monitor its own progress on prevention:

Figure 11.5. Projected cost of AIDS treatment and funding gap with a 90 percent reduction in new infections, 2006–2020

5a. Historical uptake at 18 percent of unmet need each year

$ billions

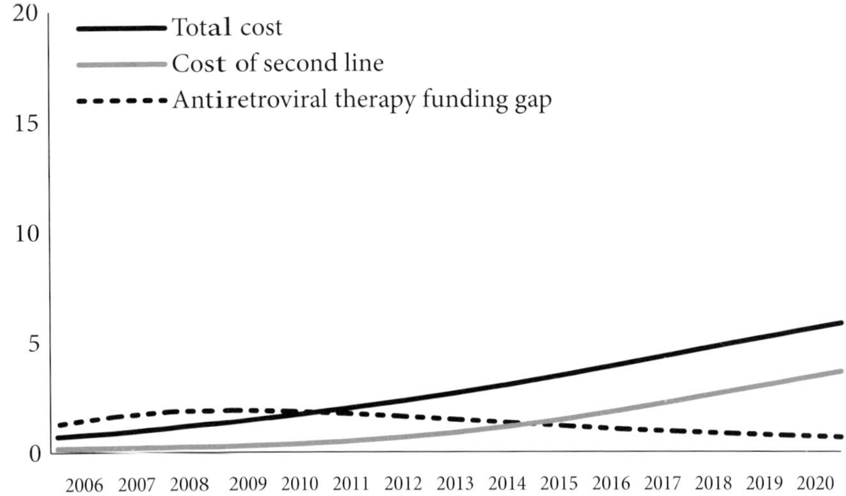

5b. Aggressive uptake at 95 percent of unmet need each year

$ billions

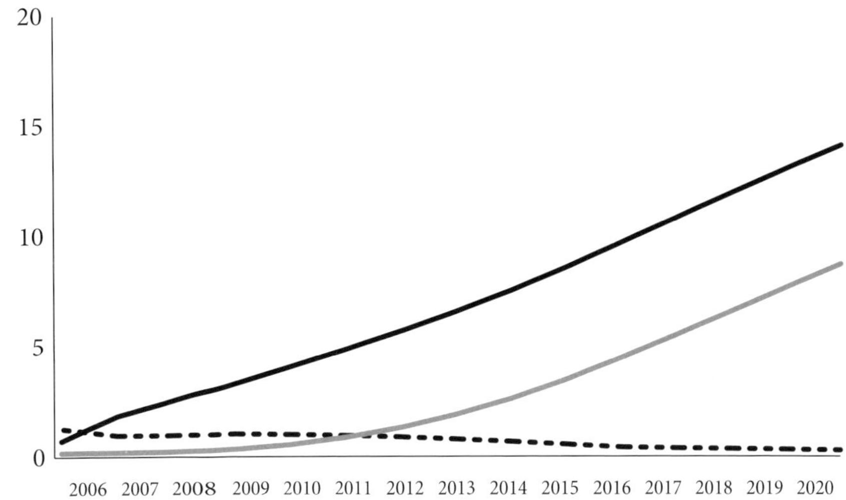

Source: Over 2008.

> PEPFAR and other U.S. government-funded programs before it have supported the collection, analysis and appropriate application of both sentinel and behavioral surveillance data in many of the focus countries . . . However, only a few of the countries have conducted behavioral surveys focused specifically on high-risk populations. Without behavioral data on these populations, it is difficult for countries and donors to know what specific factors are driving each epidemic and what particular interventions would be the most successful for each country in preventing further spread of HIV.[24]

A variety of techniques are available for reaching high-risk populations with the interventions needed to promote and distribute condoms and train people in their effective use. Unfortunately, few of these techniques have benefited from the rigorous impact evaluation focused on treatment interventions.[25] The great success of the 100 percent condom program in Thailand in the 1980s was predicated on the existence of brothels, which provided an easily identifiable focus for an effective prevention campaign.[26] A technique called the "PLACE Method" was developed in the past ten years to achieve the same objective in African epidemiological contexts.[27] The method uses interviewers' contacts with taxi drivers, market women, and other people in the street to identify the so-called hot spots in town where people gather to look for a date. Although the formative research to develop this technique and field-test it in a dozen African cities was funded by the U.S. Agency for International Development, neither that agency nor PEPFAR has attempted to evaluate the approach using rigorous methods or to scale up its implementation in order to saturate any region of any African country with prevention messages and condoms.

We recommend that PEPFAR support the initiation of government programs in the fifteen focus countries to map the hot spots in their major cities and towns, and to develop and launch plans to reach 90 percent of those locations with preventive behavioral interventions.

Mobilize AIDS patients for HIV prevention. It is easy to misunderstand the intent of this suggestion. Doctors could well argue that they are already counseling their patients in safe-sex methods and that involving AIDS patients in advocacy programs could put others at risk. However, we know from recent biological studies that patients who are effectively adhering to antiretroviral medication are at very low risk of transmitting the disease. The challenge lies elsewhere.

Patients who, thanks to their precise adherence to their medication regime, are in good health can be an important channel for reaching out to the larger population whose risk behavior can lead to infection. With proper training, motivation, and monitoring, patients can also work to ensure that AIDS treatment does not engender complacency and disinhibition, but instead encourages sharp reductions in risk behavior.

One way to encourage advocacy by patients is to build on the adherence support organizations mentioned above. When several such organizations exist in a community, they can be judged against one another not only on their success at maintaining adherence among their members but also on their efforts to reach out to nonmembers with HIV-prevention interventions. Organizations that do well only on adherence would not lose their funding (since reducing funds could disrupt the treatment of their members), but neither would they receive funding to enroll additional members. Organizations that excel at both adherence support and outreach prevention would, on the other hand, be rewarded with funding for additional members. In this way, through a process of muted "evolutionary" competition among treatment support organizations, treatment subsidies would also be leveraging prevention efforts.

Expand access to male circumcision. The evidence that male circumcision protects men from HIV infection has accumulated from both observational and experimental studies. The first observational study was a cross-country regression that showed a remarkable association between male circumcision prevalence and HIV prevalence.[28] Skeptics expressed doubt about the causal link because male circumcision prevalence was correlated with religious affiliation, which might be directly responsible for differences in sexual mores. For example, one cross-section study of HIV prevalence found that prevalence of male circumcision was statistically insignificant when percent-Muslim and seven other socioeconomic variables were controlled for.[29] However, in the past few years, randomized controlled trials in Kenya, South Africa, and Uganda have confirmed that the association between male circumcision and HIV is indeed causal.[30] In fact, the ethical review process actually halted the Kenyan trial after observing that only 22 of the 1,391 circumcised men became HIV infected, compared with 47 among the 1,393 in the uncircumcised group. Since the risk of becoming infected during the trial period was 53 percent smaller for the circumcised, the researchers concluded that male circumcision is comparable to a 50 percent-effective vaccination. Circumcision seemed to be equally protective in Uganda (a 51 percent reduction in risk) and perhaps even more so in South Africa (a 60 percent reduction in risk).[31] Furthermore, the studies found little evidence that circumcised men might be "disinhibited" and increase their risky behavior, which would offset some of the advantage of the circumcision.

As the encouraging results on male circumcision have accumulated, researchers have increasingly turned from the question of efficacy to that of feasibility. Small-scale nonrandom studies have generally supported the feasibility of scaling up access to male circumcision among the general population in Africa.[32] Building on these research results, PEPFAR should now allocate a substantial portion of its discretionary resources to making clean and safe circumcision at least as easily accessible to men as antiretroviral therapy in all the PEPFAR countries. Scale-up should be accompanied by monitoring to ensure that the extent of any resulting behavioral disinhibition does not approach the levels that would offset the benefits of the intervention.

Integrate family planning with AIDS treatment. Another key strategy to prevent infections that has not been sufficiently deployed is family planning. Although programs to prevent mother-to-child transmission of HIV are having increased success, they remain complex and uncertain. Every child who is infected despite such prevention efforts will be costly to treat for his or her entire life. Furthermore, these children stand a greater than average chance of becoming orphans, despite the efficacy and increased availability of AIDS treatment for their parents.

In view of the private and social cost incurred for each HIV-infected child, AIDS treatment programs and family planning programs should join forces to ensure that every HIV-positive woman has free and easy access to the birth control method of her choice, without fear of stigmatization. Unfortunately, because of the lack of integration of family planning and AIDS treatment, there appears to be substantial unmet need for contraception among HIV-positive women. As early as 1993, a study found that 60 percent of HIV-positive women would prefer not to have more children.[33] Several studies have found that family planning efforts are more cost-effective than, or equally as cost-effective as, interventions to prevent mother-to-child transmission once pregnancy has occurred.[34] Three of the authors of these studies have pointed out that the existing low levels of contraception in Sub-Saharan Africa have probably prevented only 173,000 HIV-infected births each recent year and that provision of family planning services to those with unmet need could avert an additional 160,000 HIV-positive births every year.[35] The version of PEPFAR authorization currently being proposed in Congress explicitly excludes support for family planning; the next president will have an opportunity to improve the U.S. AIDS program by simply proposing the removal of this exclusion.

Reorient HIV testing toward couples. As a supplement to health provider–initiated testing, PEPFAR should evaluate the feasibility and effectiveness of wide-scale couple counseling in the home. Such counseling has been found to be effective with discordant couples (where one party is HIV-positive),[36] and it has an even more promising role for concordant-negative couples (where neither person is yet infected). Furthermore, some studies suggest that people are more likely to accept couple counseling in the home than at health care facilities.[37] When couples learn each others' HIV status as well as their own, and receive counseling about the dangers of unprotected sex outside their partnership, such knowledge may increase condom use with other partners and reduce the frequency of such partners. Thus couple counseling, especially in the home, might be the intervention that would achieve Helen Epstein's elusive "invisible cure" by discouraging the practice of multiple concurrent partnerships, which are thought to be a major contributor to the epidemic.[38]

3. Ensuring the AIDS transition

Just as there have been demographic transitions and epidemiologic transitions in the past, the world can aspire to accomplish an "AIDS transition" in the next few decades.[39] What would such a transition encompass?

In the epidemiological dimension, an AIDS transition would see the growth of the number of people on treatment exceed the growth in the number of people infected with HIV. Even with the enormous progress of the past few years, the number of people placed on treatment worldwide in 2007 was only one-fourth to one-fifth the number of new HIV infections that year. Accomplishing the AIDS transition will require both accelerated treatment access and greatly reduced rates of new infections.

For PEPFAR, the AIDS transition can mean the program's gradual transformation from a predominately bilateral program to a more multilateral one. If the prevention part of the AIDS transition is to succeed in PEPFAR countries, the millions of people receiving AIDS treatment must be used as a force for the dramatic expansion and improved effectiveness of prevention programs.

More generally, the AIDS transition must mean refocusing the rhetoric, goal setting, and results orientation that is gaining force in AIDS treatment to also target AIDS prevention. The next U.S. president should ensure that the successor to two World Health Organization programs—the unsuccessful "3 by 5" program to expand treatment to 3 million by 2005, and the current "Towards Universal Access by 2010"—will be a program aimed at preventing 90 percent of current annual infections by 2012. Such a program should use all the means available, including schools, adherence support groups, and local governments. Measures of success must go beyond self-reporting and use biological markers of risk behavior, such as pregnancy, HIV infection, and infection with another sexually transmitted infection.

The most forward-looking part of the AIDS transition will be to broaden U.S. research funding on AIDS. Because the mandate of the National Institutes of Health is to focus on biomedical research, the critical operational questions of institutional mechanism design—how to efficiently scale up treatment programs and improve the effectiveness and reach of prevention programs—are under-researched.[40] The next U.S. president should ask Congress to channel 10 percent of all AIDS research funding through the National Science Foundation to examine how HIV/AIDS prevention and treatment services can best be delivered in a manner that complements, rather than undermines, other locally needed health care services.

President Bush's "emergency" AIDS assistance program to fifteen of the countries affected by the epidemic is in the best, generous traditions of American foreign assistance. PEPFAR has already prolonged the lives of more than a million people, provided care and support for orphans and other vulnerable children, and prevented many cases of HIV infection. Although the evidence is not yet in on the program's effects on the health care systems of all recipients, some countries' systems seem to have benefited from positive spillover effects from PEPFAR. Together with the Millennium Challenge Account (described in chapter 5 by de Tray and Moran), PEPFAR is arguably the Bush administration's most notable foreign policy success.

However, the research and analysis presented in this chapter suggest that the potential for several serious failures lies hidden within this apparent success. If the U.S. is seen to renege on its implied commitment to existing AIDS patients or if it is thought to have allowed treatment quality to degrade over time, failed to prevent new cases of HIV infection from swelling the ranks of those needing treatment, harmed the health care of patients who do not have AIDS, or facilitated the emergence and spread of drug-resistant forms of HIV, President Bush's initial success will metamorphose before our eyes into a deadly and shameful example of overreaching American incompetence—to be blamed inevitably on the new president. We argue that the next president can build on PEPFAR in such a way as to prevent these worst-case scenarios. If, in the existing fifteen PEPFAR focus countries, the next government can effectively manage the current AIDS treatment entitlement, prevent the future need for treatment, and help ensure the AIDS transition to the point that the disease becomes a manageable chronic condition, the next president will deserve a full measure of credit for the long-run benefits of PEPFAR, credit equal to or greater than that due to President Bush for launching the program. This chapter has suggested some of the specific ways that the new president can avoid the worst-case scenarios and assure this desirable outcome.

Notes

1. HIV is the acronym for the human immunodeficiency virus, which causes the acquired immune deficiency syndrome, or AIDS.
2. UNAIDS 2007.
3. For an opposing view on the economic benefits of AIDS treatment, see Ventelou and others 2008.
4. Hamoudi and Birdsall 2004.
5. Bell, Devarajan, and Gersbach 2004.
6. See Radelet 2003 for a discussion of the shifting politics of Bush's foreign aid policy.
7. For more detail, see Institute of Medicine 2007, p. 24.
8. Kates, Izazola, and Lief 2007, p. 10.
9. PEPFAR 2007.
10. The United States is estimated to have contributed about $25 million over the twelve years of the smallpox eradication campaign, or an average of about $2.5 million a year (Levine 2004). In current dollars this would be about $5 million a year, which is less than 1 percent of the U.S. expenditure on AIDS in 2006.
11. Of the 1.358 million individuals receiving treatment, PEPFAR provided treatment directly to about 1 million, and indirect support for the treatment of an additional 350,000 patients (OGAC 2008).
12. Although there is a growing literature on the investment benefits of programs to combat AIDS, there is only weak support for the proposition that subsidized AIDS treatment for poor patients will stimulate national growth—except in the health sector, where the policy is rumored to have substantially augmented the incomes of those who provide AIDS treatment.
13. The U.S. constituency for food aid is a coalition between supporters of altruistic aid to hungry people in developing countries and U.S. farmers who benefit when the United States buys food to be donated overseas. The U.S. constituency for the PEPFAR program has analogously consisted of a coalition between supporters of altruistic treatment for AIDS patients and U.S. multinational pharmaceutical manufacturers who benefit when the United States buys their products for donation overseas. The recent shift of U.S. policy toward approval of the purchase of generic drugs from non-U.S. sources weakens but does not completely vitiate this analogy.
14. Such organizations can include tuberculosis (TB) patients, because HIV-positive patients more easily contract TB and become carriers that can pass the disease to others. Adherence to TB medication is an important public health issue whether or not one has AIDS, and inclusion of TB patients in the group might reduce the stigma for AIDS patients. To the author's knowledge, no such group has been subjected to rigorous impact evaluation, which is urgently needed. The potential cost-effectiveness of such groups has been estimated for Thailand (Over and others 2007).

15. Because Congress has authorized an increase in the annual funding level of PEPFAR to $50 billion over the next five years, there is discussion of whether to expand the number of focus countries. Proponents of expansion argue that the absorptive capacity of the original fifteen countries is limited and may not accommodate such a large increase in funding, while substantial expansion of treatment coverage can be achieved more easily in other countries not currently included, such as Lesotho or Malawi. However, while the goals of universal treatment access and reduced incidence of new cases are far from met in the original fifteen countries, the United States will better manage its entitlements by channeling any funds not usable in those countries through the multilateral AIDS funding agencies—especially the Global Fund.
16. The two right panels of table 11.2 present the numerical projections under historical and rapid uptake, assuming incidence declines at 5 percent a year. Over the five-year period of the proposed PEPFAR reauthorization (2009–13), the table predicts that AIDS treatment expenditures will total $25.8 billion. As reported in box 11.1, Congress has recently authorized that 80 percent of $50 billion, or $40 billion, be spent on AIDS, of which more than 20 percent ($8 billion) should be spent on HIV prevention and another substantial portion on care and support for patients and their orphaned children. Furthermore a large, but unknown, proportion of the $40 billion would flow to the Global Fund for AIDS, Tuberculosis, and Malaria. Thus $25.8 billion represents up to 25 percent more AIDS treatment expenditure than has yet been authorized. These projections include estimates of the variable cost per patient in each country, but do not include any fixed cost per country or per treatment site. See Over 2008 for more details on the projections.
17. Center for Global Development 2007.
18. Piller and Smith 2007.
19. Price and others 2007.
20. This proverb suggests that the benefit-to-cost ratio of prevention might be 16 to 1, but the Thailand calculations cited earlier suggest a ratio of 43 to 1. In the AIDS epidemic, 1 ounce of prevention is thus worth more than 2.5 pounds of cure.
21. This goal is consistent with the president's call to avert 5 million new infections over the next five years. However, calculating averted infections requires estimating the number of infections there would be in the absence of U.S. effort—a tricky exercise. A preferable approach is to set a ceiling for the maximum absolute number of new infections at 90 percent lower than the estimated current level. Note that women, who now bear a disproportionate share of the burden of the epidemic, would reap most of the benefits of a vigorous prevention campaign. Thus there is no need to establish separate objectives regarding prevention among women.

22. This figure of $1.4 billion is the difference between $7.18 billion and $5.83 billion, the figures for 2020 "Total cost" in the top two panels of table 11.2. At rapid uptake, the saving in 2020 would be $4.34 billion, more than twice as large. This figure is the difference between the 2020 "Total cost" in the bottom two panels of table 11.2.
23. Wegbreit and others 2006.
24. Institute of Medicine 2007, p. 133.
25. Wegbreit and others 2006.
26. Ainsworth and Over 1997.
27. Weir and others 2002; Weir and others 2003, 2004.
28. Bongaarts and others 1989.
29. Over 1998. A more recent cross-section analysis found a statistically significant impact of male circumcision but did not control for socioeconomic variables (Drain and others 2006).
30. For the Uganda trials, see Gray and others 2007; for the South Africa trials, see Auvert and others 2005; and for the Kenya trials, see Bailey and others 2007.
31. However, the confidence intervals overlap.
32. Whether this would be true in South Asia, where the foreskin is a distinction of Muslim men, is a separate and potentially more difficult question.
33. Allen and others 1993.
34. Reynolds and others 2006; Stover and others 2003; Sweat and others 2004.
35. Reynolds and others 2005. This estimate rests on the assumption that the proportion of unwanted pregnancies is similar between HIV-positive and HIV-negative women. This assumption finds support in a recent working paper on Lesotho that found no statistically significant difference in desire for children with respect to known HIV status (Adair 2007).
36. Allen, Serufilira, and others 1992; Allen, Tice, and others 1992; Allen and others 1993; Padian 1993; Roth and others 2001.
37. Farquhar and others 2004; Matovu and others 2002; Were and others 2003.
38. Epstein 2007; Halperin and Epstein 2004; Morris and Kretzschmar 1997.
39. For a detailed discussion of the implications of an AIDS Transition, see Over 2004.
40. Institute of Medicine 2007; Klag 2007.

References

Adair, Tim. 2007. "Desire for Children and Unmet Need for Contraception among HIV-Positive Women in Lesotho." Demographic and Health Surveys Working Paper 32. Macro International, Inc., Calverton, Md.

Ainsworth, Martha, and Mead Over. 1997. *Confronting AIDS: Public Priorities in a Global Epidemic*. New York: Oxford University Press.

Allen, S., A. Serufilira, J. Bogaerts, P. Van de Perre, F. Nsengumuremyi, C. Lindan, M. Carael, W. Wolf, T. Coates, and S. Hulley. 1992. "Confidential HIV Testing and Condom Promotion in Africa. Impact on HIV and Gonorrhea Rates." *Journal of the American Medical Association* 268 (23): 3338–43.

Allen, S., J. Tice, P. Van de Perre, A. Serufilira, E. Hudes, F. Nsengumuremyi, J. Bogaerts, C. Lindan, and S. Hulley. 1992. "Effect of Serotesting with Counselling on Condom Use and Seroconversion among HIV Discordant Couples in Africa." *British Medical Journal* 304 (6842): 1605–9.

Allen, S., A. Serufilira, V. Gruber, S. Kegeles, P. Van de Perre, M. Carael, and T.J. Coates. 1993. "Pregnancy and Contraception Use among Urban Rwandan Women after HIV Testing and Counseling." *American Journal of Public Health* 83 (5): 705–10.

Auvert, B., D. Taljaard, E. Lagarde, J. Sobngwi-Tambekou, R. Sitta, and A. Puren. 2005. "Randomized, Controlled Intervention Trial of Male Circumcision for Reduction of HIV Infection Risk: The ANRS 1265 Trial." *PLoS Medicine* 2 (11): e298.

Bailey, Robert C., Stephen Moses, Corette B. Parker, Kawango Agot, Ian Maclean, John N. Krieger, Carolyn F. Williams, Richard T. Campbell, and Jeckoniah O. Ndinya-Achola. 2007. "Male Circumcision for HIV Prevention in Young Men in Kisumu, Kenya: A Randomised Controlled Trial." *Lancet* 369 (9562): 643–56.

Bell, Clive, Shantayanan Devarajan, and Hans Gersbach. 2004. "Thinking about the Long-Run Economic Costs of AIDS. In Markus Haacker, ed., *The Macroeconomics of HIV/AIDS*. Washington, D.C.: International Monetary Fund.

Bongaarts, John, P. Reining, P. Way, and F. Conant. 1989. "The Relationship between Male Circumcision and HIV Infection in African Populations." *AIDS* 3 (6): 373–77.

Center for Global Development. 2007. "HIV/AIDS Monitor: Tracking Aid Effectiveness." Washington, D.C. [www.cgdev.org/section/initiatives/_active/hivmonitor].

Drain, P.K., D.T. Halperin, J.P. Hughes, J.D. Klausner, and R.C. Bailey. 2006. "Male Circumcision, Religion, and Infectious Diseases: An Ecologic Analysis of 118 Developing Countries." *BioMed Central Infectious Diseases* 6:172.

Epstein, Helen. 2007. *The Invisible Cure: Africa, the West, and the Fight against AIDS*. New York: Farrar, Straus and Giroux.

Farquhar, Carey, James N. Kiarie, Barbara A. Richardson, Marjory N. Kabura, Francis N. John, Ruth W. Nduati, Dorothy A. Mbori-Ngacha, and Grace C. John-Stewart. 2004. "Antenatal Couple Counseling Increases Uptake of Interventions to Prevent HIV-1 Transmission." *Journal of Acquired Immune Deficiency Syndromes* 37 (5): 1620–26.

Gray, Ronald H., Godfrey Kigozi, David Serwadda, Frederick Makumbi, Stephen Watya, Fred Nalugoda, Noah Kiwanuka, Lawrence H. Moulton, Mohammad A. Chaudhary, Michael Z. Chen, Nelson K. Sewankambo, Fred Wabwire-Mangen, Melanie C. Bacon, Carolyn F. Williams, Pius Opendi, Steven J. Reynolds, Oliver Laeyendecker, Thomas C. Quinn, and Maria J. Wawer. 2007. "Male Circumcision for HIV Prevention in Men in Rakai, Uganda: A Randomised Trial." *Lancet* 369 (9562): 657–66.

Halperin, Daniel T., and Helen Epstein. 2004. "Concurrent Sexual Partnerships Help to Explain Africa's High HIV Prevalence: Implications for Prevention." *Lancet* 364 (9428): 4–6.

Hamoudi, Amar, and Nancy Birdsall. 2004. "AIDS and the Accumulation and Utilisation of Human Capital in Africa." *Journal of African Economies* 13 (July): i96–i136.

Institute of Medicine. 2007. *PEPFAR Implementation: Progress and Promise*. Washington, D.C.: National Academies Press.

Kates, Jennifer, Jose.-Aantonio Izazola, and Eric Lief. 2007. "Financing the Response to AIDS in Low- and Middle-Income Countries: International Assistance from the G8, European Commission and Other Donor Governments, 2006." Kaiser Family Foundation, Washington, D.C. [www.kff.org/hivaids/upload/7347_03.pdf].

Klag, Michael J. 2007. "Shift Tactics in AIDS Battle." *Baltimore Sun*. November 29.

Koshy, Rachel, Deborah Rhodes, Saraswathi Devi, and Stuart Grossman. 1998. "Cancer Pain Management in Developing Countries: A Mosaic of Complex Issues resulting in Inadequate Analgesia." *Support Care Cancer* 6:430–37.

Lesser, G., Stuart Grossman, K. Leong, H. Lo, and S. Eller. 1996. "In Vitro and In Vivo Studies of Subcutaneous Hydromorphone Implants Designed for the Treatment of Cancer Pain." *Pain* 65:265–72.

Levine, Ruth. 2004. *Millions Saved: Proven Successes in Global Health*. Washington, D.C: Center for Global Development.

Matovu, J.K., G. Kigozi, F. Nalugoda, F. Wabwire-Mangen, and R.H. Gray. 2002. "The Rakai Project Counseling Programme Experience." *Tropical Medicine and International Health* 7 (12): 1064–67.

Morris, Martine, and Mirjam Kretzschmar. 1997. "Concurrent Partnerships and the Spread of HIV." *AIDS* 11 (5): 641–48.

OGAC (Office of the United States Global AIDS Coordinator). 2004. *The President's Emergency Plan for AIDS Relief: U.S. Five-Year Global HIV/AIDS Strategy*. Washington, D.C.

———. 2007. *PEPFAR Third Annual Report to Congress*. Washington, D.C.

———. 2008. *The Power of Partnerships: Fourth Annual Report to Congress on PEPFAR*. Washington, D.C.

Over, Mead. 1998. "The Effects of Societal Variables on Urban Rates of HIV Infection in Developing Countries." In M. Ainsworth, L. Fransen, and M. Over, eds., *Confronting AIDS Evidence from the Developing World: Selected Background Papers for the World Bank Policy Research Report, Confronting AIDS: Public Priorities in a Global Epidemic*, 39–52. Brussels: European Commission.

———. 2004. "Impact of the HIV/AIDS Epidemic on the Health Sectors of Developing Countries." In Markus Haacker, ed., *The Macroeconomics of HIV/AIDS*, 311–44. Washington, D.C.: International Monetary Fund.

———. 2008. "Opportunities for Presidential Leadership on AIDS: Beyond Managing the Treatment Entitlement." Working Paper. Washington, D.C.: Center for Global Development.

Over, Mead, Ana Revenga, Emiko Masaki, Wiwat Peerapatanapokin, Julian Gold, Viroj Tangcharoensathien, and Sombat Thanprasertsuk. 2007. "The Economics of Effective AIDS Treatment in Thailand." *AIDS* 21 Suppl. 4 (July): S105–S116.

Padian, N.S., T.R. O'Brien, Y. Chang, S. Glass, and D.P. Francis. 1993. "Prevention of Heterosexual Transmission of Human Immunodeficiency Virus t hrough Couple Counseling." *Journal of Acquired Immune Deficiency Syndromes* 6 (9): 1043–48.

PEPFAR (President's Emergency Plan for AIDS Relief). 2007. "About PEPFAR." [www.pepfar.gov/about].

Piller, Charles, and Doug Smith. 2007. "Unintended Victims of Gates Foundation Generosity." *Los Angeles Times*. December 15.

Price, Jessica, Evode Micomyiza, Venuste Nyeimana, and Jean-Paul Tchupo. 2007. "Integrating HIV Clinical Services in Primary Health Centers in Rwanda." Presentation. [www.iom.edu/Object.File/Master/42/758/PEPFAR%20WSP%20 Price%205-1-07.pdf].

Radelet, Steven. 2003. "Bush and Foreign Aid." *Foreign Policy* 82 (5).

Reynolds, H.W., M.J. Steiner, and W. Cates. 2005. "Contraception's Proved Potential to Fight HIV." *Sexually Transmitted Infections* 81:184–85.

Reynolds, Heidi W., Barbara Janowitz, Rick Homan, and Laura Johnson. 2006. "The Value of Contraception to Prevent Perinatal HIV Transmission." *Sexually Transmitted Diseases* 33 (6): 350–56.

Rhodes, D., and Stuart Grossman. 1997. "Hydromorphone Polymer Implant: A Potential Alternative to Methadone Maintenance." *Journal of Substance Abuse Treatment* 14 (6): 535–42.

Roth, D.L., K.E. Stewart, O.J. Clay, A. van der Straten, E. Karita, and S. Allen. 2001. "Sexual Practices of HIV Discordant and Concordant Couples in Rwanda: Effects of a Testing and Counselling Programme for Men." *International Journal of STD & AIDS* 12 (3): 181–88.

Stover, John., N. Fuchs, D. Halperin, A. Gibbson, and D. Gillespie. 2003. "Adding Family Planning to PMTCT Sites Increases the Benefits of PMTCT." [www.fhi.org/NR/rdonlyres/earf7d7i4up5roh7hrpbxekmx55tprl5t5bcqq3tf4kfpprm3oprt3j4i6z-tqznwv5g3qthqjk7zfc/FPPMTCTissuebriefrev102203enrh.pdf].

Sweat, M.D., K.R. O'Reilly, G.P. Schmid, J. Denison, and I. de Zoysa. 2004. "Cost-Effectiveness of Nevirapine to Prevent Mother-to-Child HIV Transmission in Eight African Countries." *AIDS* 18: 1661–71.

UNAIDS (Joint United Nations Programme on HIV/AIDS). 2007. "Global HIV Prevalence Has Levelled Off; AIDS Is among the Leading Causes of Death Globally and Remains the Primary Cause of Death in Africa." Geneva.

U.S. Congress. 2003. *United States Leadership against HIV/AIDS, Tuberculosis, and Malaria Act of 2003*. Public Law 108-25, U.S. Statutes at Large 117 (2003): 711.

Ventelou, B., J.P. Moatti, Y. Videau, and M. Kazatchkine. 2008. "'Time Is Costly': Modelling the Macroeconomic Impact of Scaling-up Antiretroviral Treatment in Sub-Saharan Africa." *AIDS* 22 (1): 107–13.

Wegbreit, J., S. Bertozzi, L.M. DeMaria, and N.S. Padian. 2006. "Effectiveness of HIV Prevention Strategies in Resource-Poor Countries: Tailoring the Intervention to the Context." *AIDS* 20 (9): 1217–35.

Weir, S.S., C. Morroni, N. Coetzee, J. Spencer, and J.T. Boerma. 2002. "A Pilot Study of a Rapid Assessment Method to Identify Places for AIDS Prevention in Cape Town, South Africa." *Sexually Transmitted Infections* 78 Suppl. 1: i106–i113.

Weir, S.S., J.E. Tate, B. Zhusupov, and J.T. Boerma. 2004. "Where the Action Is: Monitoring Local Trends in Sexual Behaviour." *Sexually Transmitted Infections* 80 Suppl. 2: ii63–ii68.

Weir, Sharon S., Charmaine Pailman, Xoli Mahlalela, Nicol Coetzee, Farshid Meidany, and J. Ties Boerma. 2003. "From People to Places: Focusing AIDS Prevention Efforts Where It Matters Most." *AIDS* 17 (6): 895–903.

Were, Willy, Jonathan Mermin, Rebecca Bunnell, John P. Ekwaru, and Frank Kaharuza. 2003. "Home-based Model for HIV Voluntary Counselling and Testing." *Lancet* 361 (9368): 1569.

12 U.S. Policy toward Fragile States: An Integrated Approach to Security and Development

Stewart Patrick

For the United States, the experiences of the past several years have driven home a reality of international life in the twenty-first century: It is no longer possible for the world's richest and most powerful country to remain indifferent to the fate of the planet's impoverished, insecure, and misgoverned countries. On both moral and strategic grounds, the United States has a stake in promoting development—broadly conceived as effective institutions capable of delivering economic growth, human security, and good governance—in the world's most fragile countries.[1] One of the principal foreign policy priorities for the next U.S. administration must be to formulate a more balanced approach to addressing the inextricably linked security, governance, and development challenges in failing, failed, and war-torn states. This new strategy must place more emphasis on prevention than on reaction and rely at least as much on civilian as on military instruments.

Despite unprecedented rhetorical attention to fragile states since September 11, 2001, the American strategic

Stewart Patrick is a senior fellow and the director of the program on Institutions and Global Governance at the Council on Foreign Relations. This chapter was written while he was a research fellow at the Center for Global Development. He thanks Alexander Pascal and Kaysie Brown for invaluable substantive and editorial input to this chapter. He is grateful to Eric Schwartz, Christopher Blattmann, Masood Ahmed, Lant Pritchett, Nancy Birdsall, and Dennis De Tray for comments. And he is grateful to Stephen Del Rosso and the Carnegie Corporation of New York for their invaluable intellectual and financial support for the Center for Global Development's ongoing research and policy engagement on states at risk.

mindset has not fundamentally changed. U.S. policy has remained a set of fragmented half-measures. Spurred in part by the Iraq fiasco, the Bush administration took tentative steps to improve U.S. capabilities to help advance stability and reconstruction in post-conflict countries. However, the United States still lacks a preventive strategy to promote effective and legitimate institutions in fragile states and arrest their descent into instability and violence. Moreover, its policies remain remarkably self-contained, divorced from the actions of other governments and international institutions. The next administration will have a prime opportunity to lead a bold international effort to engage fragile states. A more successful U.S. approach to the challenge of fragile states will require five critical tasks:

1. Making a strategic commitment to preventing state failure.
2. Adapting U.S. development aid and policy to the fragile states' unique conditions.
3. Formulating a truly "whole of government" response.
4. Investing seriously in civilian capabilities needed to promote security and development in fragile states.
5. Embracing multilateralism to accomplish goals the United States cannot achieve on its own.

This chapter will deal with each of these tasks in turn but first examines the broader context.

What are fragile states and why do they matter?

Growing U.S. and international attention to the problems of fragile states reflects the confluence of national security concerns and the drive for poverty alleviation. During the 1990s, many in the U.S. foreign policy community regarded poorly governed, economically stagnant, often unstable states among developing countries primarily as humanitarian issues.[2] The 9/11 attacks stimulated a strategic reorientation. The 2002 National Security Strategy asserted that for the first time the United States faced a greater threat from weak and failing states than from conquering ones.[3] Development actors began to adopt this thinking as well. A 2003 report by the U.S. Agency for International Development, *Foreign Aid in the National Interest,* declared, "When development and governance fail in a country, the consequences engulf entire regions and leap across the world. Terrorism, political violence, civil wars, organized crime, drug trafficking, infectious diseases, environmental crises, refugee flows and mass migration cascade across the borders of weak states more destructively than ever before."[4] This view is also widely shared by other donor governments and multilateral institutions.[5]

Although the causal connections between state fragility and transnational threats are variable,[6] weak and badly governed states can incubate and transmit threats to global security.[7] Beyond bringing misery to their inhabitants, they can provide havens and operating bases for transnational terrorists, as al Qaeda found in Afghanistan and Sudan. From Burma to Colombia, Haiti to Sierra Leone, such states provide a haven for the production and transit of drugs, as well as trafficking in other illicit commodities. They can spawn violent conflicts and humanitarian catastrophes that spill over borders to destabilize regions, as in the multiple wars of Central and West Africa in the 1990s. Fragile states can also accelerate the spread of global pandemics, from HIV/AIDS to emerging diseases such as avian flu, and leave oil-importing countries like the United States vulnerable to disruption of foreign energy supplies with severe strategic and economic implications.[8]

Parallel with these growing security imperatives, the international development community is devoting new attention to the dilemmas posed by poorly performing countries,[9] which lack the capacity and often the will to pursue pro-poor policies, rendering traditional models of donor engagement ineffective. Over the past decade, these states have often been left behind, as donors direct a growing proportion of their aid to good performers, based on the belief that assistance is most effective in sound institutional and policy environments.[10] The Bush administration's Millennium Challenge Account embodies this selective approach, directing aid to countries that "rule justly, promote economic freedom, and invest in people."

The United States and other donors have struggled to develop strategies and instruments for the other end of the development spectrum, composed of some fifty-odd weak and failing or (in the current euphemism) "fragile" states, home to perhaps a billion of the world's inhabitants. Such countries suffer from deficits in one or all of four critical dimensions of state function: security provision, political institutions, economic management, and social welfare delivery. In the security realm, these states may strain to maintain a monopoly on the use of force, protect their populations from external and internal threats, control their borders and territory, provide public order, and ensure safety from crime. Politically, they may lack legitimate institutions of governance that can check political power, protect basic rights and freedoms, hold leaders accountable, deliver impartial justice and efficient administration, and permit broad citizen participation. In the economic sphere, they may struggle to design and implement basic macroeconomic and fiscal policies and to develop and enforce a legal and regulatory climate conducive to private enterprise and growth. Socially, they often fail to invest in and deliver basic services such as health and education.

There is no universal agreement on the number and identity of the world's fragile states, though most analysts suggest a number between forty and sixty.[11] In practice, state fragility is not an "either/or" condition but varies along a continuum of performance, as well as across areas of state function.

Some fail across the board, others only in certain areas. (A comparison of the Democratic Republic of the Congo with Colombia proves the point: The Democratic Republic of the Congo performs poorly in all categories of state function, whereas Colombia scores well on political, economic, and social welfare, but miserably on security, being unable to control 40 percent of its territory.)

All analysts agree that fragile states are highly concentrated in but not limited to Africa. Compared with other developing countries, such states are on balance more prone to suffer from low growth and to be farthest from the Millennium Development Goals.[12] Their inhabitants are more likely to be poor and malnourished; endure gender discrimination; lack access to education, basic health care, and modern technology; and suffer chronic illness and die young. They are also fifteen times more prone to civil war than member countries of the Organisation for Economic Co-operation and Development. Violence in fragile states is both more extreme and longer lasting than conflict in other developing countries.[13] Such countries are the overwhelming source of the world's refugees and internally displaced persons, and include some of the world's worst human rights abusers.[14] Clearly, advancing human development—as well as human security—requires dealing with the plight of the world's "bottom billion."[15] Success in this effort also demands that donors transcend traditional development assistance to address issues such as trade, investment, governance, and security.

And yet the world's fragile states are a heterogeneous lot. This diverse group encompasses countries in a wide variety of circumstances, including conflict-ridden countries (the Democratic Republic of the Congo and Sri Lanka), countries recovering from war (East Timor and Liberia), economically stagnant, aid-dependent countries (Zambia); politically inept countries (Bangladesh), resource-rich poor performers with autocratic regimes (Angola), brittle dictatorships (Burma and the Democratic Republic of Korea), collapsing countries (Zimbabwe), and tenuous transitions from authoritarian rule (Kenya).[16] Crucially, state fragility is not merely a question of inherent capacity, but also of will—namely, the willingness of the governing regime to engage with donors and to pursue constructive policies and reforms intended to provide its citizens with fundamental political goods. Distinguishing between a governing regime's ability to deliver the goods versus its commitment to do so enables us to identify four broad categories of these states:

- States with both the will and the way.
- Weak but willing states.
- States with means but not the commitment.
- States with neither the will nor the way.

These analytical distinctions should inform the mix of incentives that external actors deploy in engaging poor performers as disparate, for example, as

Mali and Zimbabwe. Given the diversity of fragile states, generalized one-size-fits-all international policy responses will not remedy their multitude of ills.

Recent U.S. policy

Like other Western countries, the United States continues to struggle with the challenges of engaging fragile states.[17] Since 9/11, the U.S. government has made tentative progress in designing new strategies and instruments to help restore security and promote recovery in war-torn contexts. The difficulties in stabilizing post-invasion Afghanistan and particularly Iraq prompted the Bush administration to belatedly recognize nation building as a mission the United States could not afford to ignore. In summer 2004, the State Department created a new Office of the Coordinator for Reconstruction and Stabilization. In late 2005, National Security Presidential Directive 44 gave that office lead responsibility within the U.S. government to plan and manage future U.S. government involvement in preventing and responding to state failure and post-conflict recovery.[18] Despite this ostensible authority, inadequate support from senior administration officials, vulnerability to bureaucratic turf wars, and a lack of resources have impeded the Office of the Coordinator for Reconstruction and Stabilization from fulfilling its ambitious mandate.[19] To date, the office has not developed a robust civilian capacity for post-conflict recovery that could make a tangible difference in the field.

More dramatic has been the shift at the Department of Defense. Stung by criticism of its failure to stabilize Iraq after deposing Saddam Hussein, the Pentagon approved Directive 3000.05 in November 2005. The directive, titled "Military Support for Security, Stability, Transition and Reconstruction (SSTR) Operations,"[20] established stability operations as a core military mission, on a par with war-fighting, and called for the uniformed services to alter their doctrine, organization, leadership, training, exercises, materiel, facilities, and planning accordingly. The document also emphasizes that given limited civilian U.S. government capabilities and the exigencies of insecure environments, the military must be prepared to carry out a wide range of security, stability, transition, and reconstruction activities, including retraining police, rebuilding physical infrastructure, reviving market economies, and developing institutions of representative government. Meanwhile, the U.S. Agency for International Development has created an Office of Conflict Management and Mitigation and, in 2005, released a Fragile States Strategy. It has also created a new Office of Military Affairs to serve as a liaison with the Department of Defense.

These post-conflict initiatives remain piecemeal and incomplete. Yet they far outpace any U.S. government efforts to help prevent weak and failing states from collapsing in the first place. Nearly seven years after 9/11, the United States still lacks a strategic, governmentwide approach that goes to the roots of institutional weakness, political instability, and violent conflict in fragile states. Instead, it has a loose collection of largely disconnected initiatives. At the State Department, the Office of the Coordinator for Reconstruction and Stabilization presides over a semiannual process with the National Intelligence Council to identify global hot spots for possible conflict prevention efforts and, along with the National Security Council, chairs a low-level interagency working group on conflict management and mitigation.[21] The Pentagon, for its part, coordinates an interagency effort on "ungoverned areas" or stateless zones that could be exploited by terrorists and other illicit actors to harm the United States and its allies,[22] while the regional Combatant Commands (including AFRICOM, the recently created Africa Command) are working to build the security capacities of friendly weak and failing states to control their borders and territories.[23]

Hopes that the Bush administration would develop a more rigorous approach to fragile states rose in early 2006, when Secretary of State Condoleezza Rice announced a sweeping "transformational diplomacy" initiative to promote the emergence of "democratic, well-governed states" in developing countries. Her plan included a significant reform of U.S. foreign assistance. Henceforth, U.S. foreign aid would be targeted toward five strategic objectives: promoting peace and security, investing in people, promoting economic freedom, supporting just and democratic rule, and providing humanitarian assistance. The new foreign aid framework proposed ways to meet these objectives in five categories of aid recipients: partnership, transforming, developing, rebuilding, and restrictive countries. Unfortunately, this new typology ignored fragile states and their unique development, governance, and security challenges.[24] Foreign aid reform also forced the U.S. Agency for International Development to abandon its promising Fragile States Strategy, which the agency had envisioned as the basis for a governmentwide approach to poor, conflict-prone countries with weak institutions. This hodgepodge of efforts left the United States without a systematic method for engaging fragile and post-conflict states, endangering U.S. national security and undercutting its development policy.

A new direction: reconceiving U.S. strategy toward fragile states

Because the sovereign state remains the building block of international society, the new president should announce, as a top foreign policy priority, the goal of helping to reform and strengthen weak and failing states among developing countries. To ensure a more effective U.S. approach to fragile states, the next administration should fill five current gaps in U.S. policy.

Task 1: Make prevention the priority

To start, the new administration must make preventing state failure a key objective of its foreign policy. Current U.S. engagement with fragile states remains almost entirely reactive, with the executive branch awaiting the outbreak of a major crisis to trigger a U.S. policy response. Adopting a more preventive stance will require winning over the American people to the imperative of state building, an enterprise that collides with a strong noninterventionist strain in U.S. political culture, to say nothing of a still-influential conservative ideology that favors shrinking the scope and size of government. The new president must persuade the public that there is no better bulwark against instability than strong, effective, and accountable states capable of providing their citizens with basic political goods.[25]

Persuading U.S. policymakers and legislators of the benefits of preventing state failure and violent conflict will be an uphill battle. Despite the intuitive awareness that prevention is cost-effective, it remains difficult to attract official attention, mobilize political will, or invest resources before a full-blown crisis. Moreover, the impact of preventive action is notoriously difficult to evaluate, and successful outcomes can seem banal: "nothing happens." To overcome inertia, the next administration should sell the prevention strategy to the American public as cost-effective in terms of U.S. dollars and lives, and initiate cost-benefit studies to assess the utility of prevention.

Draft an interagency fragile states strategy. In its first 100 days, the next administration should draft a comprehensive and authoritative U.S. strategy for weak and failing states in the form of a new National Security Presidential Directive. This document would not only establish preventing state failure as a U.S. national security priority but also offer a template for timely, integrated country planning for fragile states and a protocol to guide a U.S. government-wide response to a deteriorating situation in any particular country. It would provide a policy framework for executive branch agencies, requiring them to assess current conditions, explain U.S. national interests at stake, define the scale of U.S. ambitions and the objectives of U.S. policy, identify points of U.S. and international leverage, define the tasks for each phase of engagement and the tactics and instruments to achieve these ends, establish divisions of labor among U.S. agencies, identify international partners and their prospective roles, and create benchmarks to measure progress.

Empower a lead actor. The White House must designate a single, high-level focal point within the U.S. government for planning and implementing country-specific prevention, mitigation, and response efforts. Although National Security Presidential Directive 44 appears to assign this authority to the State

Department,[26] the question of leadership is far from settled.[27] The next president should designate the National Security Council—the sole entity to direct and coordinate all executive branch departments—as the U.S. lead in managing all conflict prevention and response activities. The White House should create a new National Security Council senior director for conflict prevention and response, with responsibility for developing civilian-military doctrine and U.S. capabilities for these tasks, leading contingency planning to head off state failure and internal conflict, and running country-specific task forces to prevent conflict and run post-conflict operations.[28] The precise strategy will vary according to the causes of weakness, particularly whether poor performance is rooted in inadequate capacity or weak political commitment.

Improve intelligence and early warning. The next administration should greatly expand U.S. human intelligence collection in fragile states—particularly in Africa—which atrophied during the 1990s and has only recently begun to recover. It should develop a more finely tuned system to measure and predict political and economic instability, based on a combination of structural indicators that change slowly (such as infant mortality and gross domestic product per capita), dynamic variables that reveal short-term trends, and analyses by respected country experts. In addition, the new administration should fund more open-source research and ease restrictions on sharing of unclassified information among U.S. agencies (including embassies, U.S. Agency for International Development missions, and Department of Defense operational units) and with other governments, U.N. agencies, nongovernmental organizations, development professionals, and private sector actors, who are sometimes better positioned to understand local dynamics.

Early warning, however, is rarely the issue; the true hurdle is early action. To help overcome bureaucratic resistance among risk-averse policymakers, the next administration should create an automatic triggering mechanism, whereby the National Security Council would direct relevant State Department bureaus and National Security Council regional directorates to formulate a "whole of government" strategy for any country integral to U.S. interests that enters a predefined danger zone.

Task 2: Tailor development aid and policy to fragile state realities

Realizing a more effective U.S. policy toward fragile states will require transforming the machinery, magnitude, design, and evaluation of U.S. development assistance.

Overhaul the structure of U.S. foreign aid and development policymaking. The first step is for the next president to transform a U.S. foreign aid system that experts on both sides of the political aisle agree is in need of modernization.[29] The ideal outcome would be the total overhaul of the Foreign Assistance Act and the creation of a cabinet-level Department for Global Development, empowered to formulate a national development strategy, control its own resources, and engage the Departments of Defense and State on an equal footing in shaping policy toward fragile states (see chapter 10 by Herrling and Radelet). To support this effort, the White House should also designate an interagency coordinator of U.S. foreign aid policy and assistance in the Executive Office of the President. This official (who would replace the current State Department director of foreign assistance) would lead interagency deliberations to determine overall country and sector allocations to meet the multiple objectives (including, but not limited to, development) of U.S. overseas aid.[30]

Expand the aid pool. Beyond improving the organization of U.S. foreign assistance, the next administration should devote a greater share of its official development assistance to fragile states and work with other donors to ensure that no countries are left behind. Today, the overwhelming allocation of bilateral U.S. aid to fragile states goes to a handful of countries, particularly Afghanistan, Iraq, and Pakistan—two battlegrounds and a key frontline state in the "global war on terrorism"—as well as several major recipients of HIV/AIDS spending (including Ethiopia and Kenya). Beyond these priority countries, bilateral U.S. aid per capita varies enormously among fragile states but tends to be much higher in post-conflict countries such as East Timor and Liberia than in teetering states such as Bangladesh and Yemen.[31] Although one would not expect the United States to be everywhere at the same level of funding, ad hoc selectivity can contribute to the phenomenon of "aid orphans," countries that are essentially abandoned by the donor community.[32]

Of course, providing aid to poor performers is a risky proposition, given frequently high corruption, low absorptive capacity, and repressive regimes. But if the risks of engaging fragile states are high, so are the costs of allowing them to "stew in their own juice."[33] Moreover, evidence suggests that fragile states' absorptive capacity often exceeds expectations and that carefully focused foreign assistance can raise growth, lower poverty, improve health and education, and reduce the risk of conflict even where states have weak policies and institutions.[34] In general, the United States should treat aid to fragile states like venture capital, liable to have a higher rate of failure than typical investments but with a potentially higher long-term return if it succeeds.

Focus on conflict prevention and state building. In addition to providing more aid, the next administration must ensure that this assistance is tailored to local political realities and designed to build local ownership and capacity.

The starting point for U.S. aid interventions must be a deep understanding of the political economy of fragility in each recipient country. In highly divided societies, the donor community must consider the likely impact of their assistance on underlying drivers of instability and be prepared to practice a form of "peace conditionality," by using aid to reward those constituencies working for peace and to marginalize those undermining it.[35] Beyond promoting peace, the emphasis of external action must be on state building, or improving the institutional capacity of the state to perform its basic functions. Where the governing regime has demonstrated a commitment to delivering goods to its citizens, the United States should put local officials in the driver's seat, with the goal of codifying the foreign assistance relationship in the form of a Millennium Challenge Account–like "contract," spelling out mutual obligations and establishing a common understanding of the process of institution building. In less promising contexts, where a regime's will or capacity is truly negligible, the United States and other donors should support those state structures capable of meeting basic human needs, while supporting service delivery through nonstate actors and working with local civil society to encourage political reform.[36] If the state needs to be bypassed altogether, the United States and other donors should build into the aid framework an eventual regulatory role for the state.[37]

A recurrent dilemma for external actors in fragile states is the tradeoff between delivering services rapidly to a needy population and building sustainable national systems to do so in the future. The donor community often exacerbates this predicament by channeling vast quantities of aid through their own service providers (rather than host-government ministries) and by poaching local talent. In doing so, donors undercut both the effectiveness and legitimacy of the state, in essence substituting for it.[38] The United States can help end this pattern by reducing the vast proportion of its aid that is currently "tied" to U.S.-sourced goods and service providers.[39] It should also work with other donors to overcome a common pathology in post-conflict assistance, namely, that the aid spigot varies inversely with the absorptive capacity of the recipient. The United States should help ensure that post-conflict aid tapers in, rather than being turned off just as it becomes effective.

Monitor and evaluate progress. The failure to take monitoring and evaluation seriously—a recurrent weakness of U.S. foreign aid—wastes valuable time and money. This failing is particularly common within the U.S. government. Current performance indicators to assess the effectiveness of its foreign assistance reforms are geared primarily to measure inputs (money spent) or outputs (programs implemented), rather than the impact of programs on conditions on the ground. Establishing appropriate benchmarks for progress is particularly tricky in fragile states, given the lack of baseline data and the multiple goals (including growth, security, and good governance) that donors pursue simultaneously. Beyond endorsing regular monitoring by the Government Accountability Office of the effectiveness of U.S. development assistance, the next president should commit the United States to joining the new International Initiative for Impact Evaluation.[40]

Task 3: Leverage all U.S. policy tools

As the Commission on Weak States and U.S. National Security underscored in 2004, fragile states pose interconnected security, governance, and development challenges that cannot be addressed with traditional development tools alone.[41] Accordingly, the next administration must adopt a "whole of government" approach, bringing the entire panoply of policy instruments at its disposal to promote state effectiveness in developing countries.[42] Beyond more effective development aid, the United States needs to promote balanced economic growth, encourage legitimate and accountable governance, and improve security and the rule of law.

Today, U.S. engagement with poorly performing states is often little more than a collection of independent, parallel, bilateral diplomatic, military, aid, trade, and financial relationships, each influenced by the institutional mandates, cultures, priorities, and time frames of respective U.S. agencies. A truly integrated approach would use coherent country plans outlining how the entire U.S. government, working with international partners, intends to integrate aid and other policy instruments to advance reform across the mutually dependent economic, political, and security spheres. Critical U.S. tools will include trade and investment policy, democracy promotion, rule of law assistance, security sector reform, and more balanced counterterrorism assistance.

Expand trade and investment, cushion shocks. For many of the world's most fragile states, such as Niger and Yemen, economic prospects are dismal. These countries will likely remain aid dependent for the foreseeable future. In other more functional states such as Mali and Pakistan, however, the United States and other donors can promote growth and poverty reduction by enhancing access to markets, providing political risk insurance to encourage foreign direct investment, and supporting new financial instruments to cushion them from external shocks. To expand trade opportunities for fragile states, the United States should lead a successful conclusion of the Doha Round of World Trade Organization negotiations that eliminates tariffs and nontariff barriers to trade in agriculture, upon which so many fragile states depend (see chapter 7 by Elliott). In addition, the United States should eliminate duties and quotas on imports from three categories of countries: heavily indebted poor countries, least-developed countries, and Sub-Saharan African countries.[43]

To overcome the risk barrier to private investment in fragile states, the next administration must work with Congress to reform the Overseas Private Investment Corporation to promote U.S. private sector investment in a greater range of labor-intensive manufacturing and assembly sectors (including textiles, apparel, and agribusiness) and broaden the capital loan guarantees and export credit insurance provided by the U.S. Export-Import Bank to U.S. businesses operating in risky transitional contexts.[44] Finally, many fragile states rely on a narrow range of commodities vulnerable to disruptions in the global market and local conditions. The International Monetary Fund and World Bank can help cushion the macroeconomic impact of such exogenous shocks by helping governments in developing countries hedge against volatility in foreign exchange, interest rates, commodity prices, natural disasters, and extraordinary drought. These initiatives would leverage private sector interests to improve the political economy and stability of some of the world's most beleaguered states.[45]

Pursue realistic democracy promotion. In recent years, U.S. democracy promotion has been discredited by the Bush administration's sweeping rhetoric and naïve expectations, by its association with military force, by the modest U.S. investment of resources, by the inconsistency (and in some eyes, hypocrisy) of U.S. policy, and by the erosion of U.S. commitment to the rule of law abroad and civil liberties at home. Nevertheless, it would be a mistake for the United States to abandon its support for democratic governance in fragile states. If the United States stands for anything globally, it is for the inalienable right of all people to choose their own government. Although democracy provides no guarantee of good policy choices, history shows that legitimate, transparent, and accountable institutions that protect individual liberties, allow freedom of speech, and provide checks against abusive power promote political stability, human security, and economic growth. Accordingly, the next president must reaffirm U.S. support for democracy assistance, while recognizing the limits of outside interventions.

The new administration should draft a governmentwide strategy for democracy promotion to improve coherence among the many U.S. agencies now involved in delivering assistance for public administration, political party development, legislative capacity building, public education, civil society, anticorruption campaigns, independent media, and other sectors. It should devote a greater share of the federal budget to democracy assistance (particularly for consolidating fragile democratic transitions), engage partners in the Community of Democracies and other forums to make democracy promotion efforts a multilateral undertaking, and reduce inconsistencies by holding friends as well as adversaries to account. At the same time, the accent must be on realism.

The next president should honestly acknowledge that democratic transitions take time and are often reversed; that elections can be divisive and unpredictable in highly divided (particularly post-conflict) societies; and that U.S. policy may appear hypocritical in some cases, given the scope of U.S. national interests.[46]

Expand U.S. rule of law capabilities. Five years after the fall of Saddam Hussein, the United States still lacks the capabilities to help fragile states grapple with a range of challenges related to public security and the rule of law that frequently arise in the aftermath of state failure or war. Unlike many Western donors, the United States does not possess constabulary forces that can perform critical missions falling between traditional peacekeeping and policing, including crowd control and the protection of high-value installations. Nor can it mobilize and deploy adequate numbers of civilian police, criminal investigators, judges, prosecutors, attorneys, court staff, and corrections officers essential to public security and justice. Particularly problematic has been the U.S. model of dispatching for international police service and training efforts personnel who are not part of a national police force, but are privately hired individual subcontractors. Such efforts, under the purview of the overstretched International Narcotics and Law Enforcement bureau of the State Department, have been plagued by poor performance, limited accountability, and occasional instances of gross misconduct. As Robert Perito bluntly states, "The provision of uniformed, armed police with executive powers and the authority to use deadly force is an inherent function of government." It is not one that can be left to the private sector. The next administration can begin to address these shortcomings by consolidating all U.S. efforts to advance the rule of law abroad—including International Narcotics and Law Enforcement–run civilian police programs, and the Department of Justice's International Criminal Investigative Training Assistance Program and the Overseas Prosecutorial Development, Assistance, and Training program—within a single office at the State Department. As proposed by the U.S. Institute of Peace, the office should also be charged with managing a new Rule of Law Reserves, a permanent cadre of qualified individuals drawn from the U.S. citizenry that can be deployed for service in crisis zones as temporary federal employees.[47]

Take an integrated approach to security sector reform. Beyond developing its own ability to deploy rule of law professionals, the United States must revamp its fragmented approach to security sector reform in weak and war-torn states. Currently, security sector reform authorities and programs are divided haphazardly among the Departments of Defense, Justice, and State and the U.S. Agency for International Development, with no clear interagency mechanism to determine programmatic or funding priorities. Moreover, security sector reform is rarely integrated into a broader agenda of good governance and development, but is instead pursued independently with an emphasis on generating large numbers of security forces and ensuring their operational effectiveness rather than institution building, professionalism, and democratic accountability. The shortcomings of this approach have been evident in both Afghanistan and Iraq.

Civilian control over professional security forces is one of the hallmarks of an effective, legitimate state. The rule of law and impartial justice must circumscribe the provision of order and security.[48] To help realize this goal in fragile states, the United States needs a governmentwide security sector reform doctrine. It would include protocols to govern cooperation among the Departments of Defense, Justice, and State and the U.S. Agency for International Development in training various security forces; designing and implementing disarmament, demobilization, and reintegration processes; and reforming the security-related ministries in fragile states. The administration should also launch a review of statutory restrictions that overly constrain the U.S. government's ability to provide assistance for security sector reform.[49]

Bolster the civilian dimensions of counterterrorism efforts. Since 9/11, the Bush administration has launched several interagency regional efforts to build the capacities and will of fragile states, particularly in Africa, to address the terrorist threat. These include the Trans-Saharan Counter Terrorism Partnership, the Combined Joint Task Force-Horn of Africa, and the East Africa Counter-Terrorism Initiative. The main drawback of all these programs to date is their overwhelmingly military nature. Although all U.S. players involved agree that the counterterrorism strategy should focus 80 percent on governance and development activities, and only 20 percent on the military effort, actual budgets have been closer to the reverse, making it difficult to address the underlying chronic sources of economic and political stagnation and instability.[50] The next administration should correct this imbalance by making greater investments in the governance and development components of state building.

Task 4: Invest in civilian capabilities

A better U.S. response to the security and developmental challenge of fragile states requires more than new strategies; it demands new resources, particularly investments in the civilian capabilities critical for effective preventive action and state building. Beyond channeling a greater share of federal spending to civilian U.S. agencies, particularly the State Department and the U.S. Agency for International Development, the next administration should create fast-disbursing contingency funds and constitute an expeditionary cadre of civilian personnel that can intervene early enough to make a difference in volatile environments, fragile states, and war-torn countries.[51]

Avoid overly militarized approaches. A key first step will be to restore some semblance of balance between the civilian and military components of U.S. engagement with fragile states. Despite a significant increase in total U.S. foreign aid during the past several years, the federal budget remains heavily skewed toward military expenditures.[52] This shortchanges investments in civilian components in America's national security apparatus best equipped to address the roots of weak governance, insecurity, and chronic poverty in developing countries. Since 9/11, the Pentagon has emerged as a direct provider of foreign assistance, particularly to states deemed to be of special concern in the global war on terrorism. Between 2002 and 2005 alone, the Department of Defense's share of total U.S. official development assistance nearly quadrupled from 5.6 percent to 21.7 percent, and the department now has special authority to conduct development work in Afghanistan, Iraq, and priority countries for counterterrorism. The Pentagon is actively seeking expanded and permanent authority for a larger range of pre-conflict settings as well, in order to build the capacities of partner countries to control their territories and borders. The creation of AFRICOM, the military's new interagency-oriented Combatant Command for Africa, reflects a growing aspiration to shape the trajectory of fragile states by alleviating the underlying sources of instability and conflict on the continent.[53]

There is much that is positive about the AFRICOM initiative, which promises to rationalize the Department of Defense's approach to the continent and provide a platform for more consistent engagement with African militaries. Likewise, the Pentagon's concern with state fragility and its desire to ensure a "whole of government" approach to the African continent are commendable. At the same time, unless carefully managed, the initiative carries some risk of militarizing (symbolically but also substantively) U.S. engagement on the continent, particularly given the tremendous disparity in resources available to the Department of Defense compared with those available to civilian agencies. The Pentagon exacerbated these perceived fears of militarization by its initial sweeping (and often clumsy) explanation of AFRICOM's mandate, which suggested that the new command would be the hub to integrate all U.S. policy on the continent. The next administration can alleviate these concerns by emphasizing that the command's activities will primarily focus on building professional and accountable militaries—and that these activities will be firmly embedded in a larger U.S. government strategy determined within civilian-led policymaking frameworks, notably within the National Security Council in Washington and under the authority of the U.S. ambassador in the countries concerned.[54] If AFRICOM places most of its energy and resources on security sector reform, it could make a significant impact in reducing state fragility.

More generally, the next president must work with Congress to bolster the capacities of civilian agencies to assume much of the burden in fragile states currently being shouldered by the Pentagon. The growing reliance on the Department of Defense to achieve U.S. foreign policy goals reflects an underlying structural mismatch between the authority ostensibly granted to the Secretary of State to lead the country's global engagement and the meager resources actually allocated to the State Department and the U.S. Agency for International Development to fulfill this mandate. The massive budget and capabilities of the Pentagon exert a constant gravitational pull, eroding civilian leadership of U.S. foreign policy. This leaves the United States well resourced to fight wars but not to address the causes of political instability and state failure, leading to an over-reliance on soldiers to conduct post-conflict activities, from policing to infrastructure, which should more appropriately be undertaken by civilian agencies and actors. The imbalance in funding deprives civilian agencies of resources to build up their own workforce and technical expertise to respond to unforeseen contingencies and provide critical aid to fragile and post-conflict states. Accordingly, the next president should submit to Congress a "smart power" budget[55] that promises to adequately fund the international affairs account,[56] which should be increased by 50 percent.

Create flexible resources for crisis response. The U.S. government does not possess a single nonhumanitarian contingency account to deliver aid in response to violent conflict or in support of a new democratically elected government.[57] Interagency meetings on crisis countries therefore quickly devolve into food fights over who will pay for any policy intervention. As a partial response to this dilemma, the Bush administration repeatedly sought $100 million from Congress for a revolving Conflict Response Fund to jump-start planning and early action in response to complex emergencies.[58] Denied these funds, it has had to use elaborate workarounds, including so-called Section 1207 funds that permit the Pentagon to transfer to the State Department up to $100 million for reconstruction activities.[59] The next administration must redouble efforts to secure a contingency fund for the State Department and scale it up significantly to $1 billion, as recommended by the bipartisan Commission on Weak States and U.S. National Security.[60]

Build surge capacity to deploy civilians rapidly. Afghanistan and Iraq have led to the recognition that the United States needs a standing cadre of qualified civilian personnel who could deploy rapidly to conflict and post-conflict settings in sufficient numbers to make a tangible difference on the ground. In this spirit, the bipartisan Stabilization and Reconstruction Management Act of 2004 called for the creation of a civilian reserve of several hundred staff, on call for service in global hot spots.[61] Spurred by this legislative initiative, the State Department's Office of the Coordinator for Reconstruction and Stabilization built a three-tiered model of civilian capabilities consisting of first responders within the State Department itself, an augmented core of technical experts across various sectors within the wider U.S. government, and expertise mobilized from outside the federal government. Unfortunately, progress in developing these human resources has been glacial. Under-resourcing has led to inadequate civilian capabilities, with serious consequences such as unfilled civilian slots in Provincial Reconstruction Teams in Afghanistan and Iraq. To help overcome this inertia, the next administration must transform the incentive structure within the State Department, the U.S. Agency for International Development, and other civilian agencies, and ensure that career advancement rewards service in hardship environments, as well as service across agencies.[62] The White House should also push harder on the Hill to ensure the emergence of a larger civilian reserve drawn from the wider citizenry, an objective that President Bush embraced (but provided no funding for) in his State of the Union Address in January 2007. Bush's fiscal year 2009 budget request sought $248 million from Congress for a Civilian Stabilization Initiative to begin developing the required civilian capabilities, but the legislative fate of this effort remained in doubt at the time of this writing. If Congress balks and the next administration fails to move this agenda forward, pressure will grow for the Pentagon to build up its own cadre of civilians capable of fulfilling this expeditionary mission, akin to a U.S. colonial service.

Task 5: Reach out to the world

Embrace multilateralism. Perhaps most importantly, U.S. efforts to bolster weak states cannot succeed if the United States goes it alone. To leverage the capabilities and investments of international partners, the next administration must make a renewed commitment to multilateralism by reaching out to major governments among developed and developing countries, engaging like-minded groupings such as the Group of Eight (G-8), and working through regional and international organizations to forge consensus on the challenges and requirements for effective state building, including equitable burden sharing.[63] The rationale for multilateral engagement is entirely practical: The United States is rarely the largest single donor in any one fragile state, making it unrealistic to assume that U.S. programs designed and implemented in isolation will achieve their goals. A new commitment to multilateralism will require greater U.S. sensitivity for the perspectives of fellow donors, who will sometimes have differing views about ways to balance the security, development, and governance components of external assistance.[64] The G-8—already a leading forum to tackle issues of global poverty, governance, conflict prevention, and peacekeeping—is one promising institutional vehicle for advancing the state-building agenda. But effective multilateral cooperation on state building must also engage major regional players and emerging donors in Africa, Asia, Latin America, and the Middle East, both on a bilateral basis and within forums like the still-nascent G-20. The United States will also need to offer strong support for parallel efforts within the United Nations, regional bodies, and the World Bank.

Expand support for U.N. and African Union peacekeeping. The United Nations is being called upon as never before to keep (and at times enforce) peace between warring parties, as well as to pick up the pieces when the shooting stops. Today, the United Nations is deploying more than 100,000 "blue helmets" in twenty-odd peacekeeping operations around the globe. The complexity and pace of these undertakings have stretched the modest capacities of the U.N. Department of Peacekeeping Operations. Given its modest budget and capabilities, the department has struggled to develop robust doctrines; procure logistical support from member states; ensure the quality and discipline of contributed troops; negotiate an effective division of labor with regional organizations; and integrate the humanitarian, development, governance, and security components of its interventions. The often fickle attitude of the United States toward U.N. peace operations has not made these tasks any easier. Since the end of the Cold War, Washington has repeatedly pressed the U.N. Security Council to authorize new operations with ambitious mandates, while sometimes withholding the political and financial support the United Nations needs to get the job done. The United States has also used the world body as a convenient scapegoat for failures that reflect shortcomings in its membership. The next administration must change this dysfunctional dynamic by persuading Congress that the best way to optimize U.N. performance and leverage America's 25 percent share of annual peacekeeping assessments is for the United States to serve as a reliable (if demanding) supporter of U.N. peace operations, rather than a fair-weather friend.[65] The United States should also fully support efforts by the U.N. Secretary-General to implement the new vision of U.N. "integrated missions" as a natural complement to its own "whole of government" effort.

It is equally important for the next administration to empower and equip regional organizations—particularly the African Union—to monitor and mediate brewing conflicts, launch preventive deployments, and undertake multidimensional peace operations. The African Union seeks a larger African role in addressing violent conflict on the continent. Meeting these aspirations will require greater U.S. investment in building the capacity and professionalism of African militaries, as well as providing logistical and material support for African Union troop deployments, whose shortcomings were revealed in the Assistance Mission in Sudan deployed to Darfur. With this in mind, the next president should endorse and expand support for the valuable Africa Contingency Training Assistance program and accelerate implementation of the G-8-sponsored Global Peace Operations Initiative to train at least 75,000 peacekeeping troops around the world, beginning with Africa.

Invest in post-conflict peace building. The U.N. Peacebuilding Commission, a promising creation of the 2005 U.N. High-Level Summit, deserves strong political and financial support from the next administration. Washington should contribute at least $50 million to the associated Peacebuilding Fund (which it has so far abstained from supporting) and mobilize support from other member states to expand the commission's mandate to include conflict prevention. Furthermore, Washington should increase its support for the World Bank's engagement with fragile states—notably the activities of the Fragile States and Conflict-Affected Countries Initiative. This should include backing an expansion of the World Bank's Low-Income Countries under Stress Trust Fund, as a multilateral model for delivering financial assistance quickly to weak and failing states that have limited access to other means of financial assistance.

Minimize negative externalities of globalization. Finally, beyond reinvigorating these partnerships, the next administration will need to catalyze multilateral cooperation to cut global taproots of state fragility. Although the concept of "weak and failed states" focuses attention on internal contributions to state fragility, the dynamics of the global economy—particularly its illicit components—can also undermine good governance and state capacity in the developing world. Priorities for multilateral action include shutting down international havens for ill-gotten gains by tracking and regulating financial transactions whereby political looters seek to stash their cash (see chapter 5 by de Tray and Moran),[66] by insisting on transparent revenue management in the exploitation of natural resources through the Extractive Industries Transparency Initiative and similar efforts,[67] by shutting down the illicit economies that fuel violence in many of the world's conflict zones, and by ending the sale of both heavy weapons systems and small arms to poorly governed countries.

Conclusion

The consequences of state fragility and failure for U.S. values and security are real—and potentially ominous. Yet the United States cannot improve its policy toward the world's fragile states by relying on traditional development aid alone. Rather, it must draw on a broad range of national instruments of power and influence, as well as international partnerships. Addressing the interconnected security, governance, and development challenges of fragile states will require significant integration among—and adaptations by—the historically distinct development, diplomatic, and defense communities within the U.S. government that constitute the so-called 3Ds. Achieving greater unity of purpose in building sustainable institutions of governance in some of the world's most precarious states will oblige individual agencies—not just the State Department, the U.S. Agency for International Development, and the Pentagon but also other relevant departments such as Commerce, Justice, and Treasury—to step out of their traditional lanes, mandates, and time frames. This agenda will also demand greater patience and a higher tolerance for political risk from the U.S. foreign policy and aid bureaucracies, as well as a larger, more flexible pool of resources from congressional paymasters.

The next administration can get off to a good start by formulating a comprehensive, governmentwide strategy that makes preventing state failure a foreign policy priority, designates clear leadership for interagency coordination, assigns roles and responsibilities to relevant departments, promotes better intelligence and analysis of states at risk, and creates mechanisms to link early warning to early action. It should simultaneously adapt U.S. development aid and policy to the unique conditions of weak and poorly governed developing countries, by (among other things) targeting more assistance to fragile states, tailoring aid to the political context, building local capacity rather than substituting for it, and monitoring and evaluating progress. To complement these reforms, the new administration should strengthen the nondevelopment dimensions of U.S. assistance by expanding trade and investment opportunities, embracing more realistic democracy promotion, and improving security and rule of law assistance in fragile states. Pursuing this ambitious agenda will require the United States to rebalance the military and civilian components of its engagement and to create new flexible U.S. aid windows and civilian surge capacities for rapid crisis response. Finally, the new president will need to embrace multilateral cooperation in order to alleviate global sources of instability and weakness and to share international burdens with like-minded governments and institutions.

Notes

1. Commission on Weak States and U.S. National Security 2004, p. 6.
2. Mandelbaum 1996. Condoleezza Rice adopted a similar position as an advisor to presidential candidate George W. Bush. See Rice 2000.
3. White House 2002.
4. USAID 2003, p. 1.
5. U.N. Secretary-General's High-Level Panel 2004, p. 9; Council of the European Union 2003; U.K. Prime Minister's Strategy Unit 2005.
6. Patrick 2006a.
7. Crocker 2003.
8. Patrick 2006b.
9. Torres and Anderson 2004.
10. See in particular Burnside and Dollar 2000.
11. For a useful survey of recent efforts to identify and, in some cases, rank fragile states, see Rice and Patrick 2008. Rice and Patrick use twenty well-established indicators to rank all 141 developing and transitional countries according to four core sets of state function (with each of the four weighted equally), identifying fifty-six weak states. Other lists can be found in DFID 2005 and in Fund for Peace 2007.
12. DFID 2005.
13. Collier and Hoeffler 2004.
14. Freedom House 2004.
15. Collier 2007.
16. For more detail, see Patrick 2008a.
17. For a survey of seven Western donor governments, see Patrick and Brown 2007a.
18. White House 2005.
19. For more detail, see Patrick 2007a.
20. DoD 2005.
21. Krasner and Pascual 2005.
22. Lamb 2007.
23. See CSIS 2007.
24. Most were lumped into the catch-all category of "developing" countries, although some are captured under the "rebuilding" and "restrictive" headings.
25. Fukuyama 2004, pp. 3–5.
26. Along with the National Security Council, the State Department's Office of the Coordinator for Reconstruction and Stabilization co-chairs a regular policy coordination committee on stabilization and reconstruction.
27. There is no formal linkage between Directive 3000.05 and National Security Presidential Directive 44. The Government Accountability Office has chided the Pentagon for failing to link its implementation of Directive 3000.05 to parallel civilian efforts (GAO 2007).

28. To empower the civilian side of the interagency, the senior director could be dual hatted as the head of the Office of the Coordinator for Reconstruction and Stabilization.
29. HELP Commission 2007.
30. The director of foreign assistance, a position created in January 2006 as part of Secretary of State Condoleezza Rice's "transformational diplomacy" initiative, serves simultaneously as administrator of the U.S. Agency for International Development. The director has control over all U.S. Agency for International Development and State Department foreign assistance accounts. Patrick 2007b.
31. In fiscal year 2007, the Bush administration's budget request to Congress sought $26 per capita for Liberia and $18 per capita for East Timor, but only $1.30 and $.35 per capita for Yemen and Bangladesh, respectively. Patrick and Brown 2006, p. 7.
32. OECD/DAC 2006a. Plausible aid orphans in recent years include Burundi, the Central African Republic, the Democratic Republic of the Congo, the Republic of Congo, and Niger. Levin and Dollar 2004; McGillivray 2006, pp. 11–12.
33. Chauvet and Collier 2004.
34. Chauvet and Collier 2006; Levin and Dollar 2004.
35. Boyce 2000.
36. OECD/DAC 2007a.
37. OECD/DAC 2007b.
38. Ghani, Lockhart, and Carnahan 2005.
39. "Tied" aid requires that the funds to procure goods and services be spent in the donor country itself.
40. Evaluation Gap Working Group, 2006.
41. Commission on Weak States and U.S. National Security 2004; Collier 2007.
42. OECD/DAC 2006b.
43. Cline 2003.
44. Moran 2003.
45. For one such proposal, see Miguel 2007.
46. Paris 2004.
47. See Perito 2004.
48. Ball 2005.
49. Candidates for review and potential amendment include Section 541 of the Foreign Assistance Act, which precludes the U.S. Agency for International Development from providing education and training to foreign militaries, and Section 660 of the act, which prevents the agency and the State Department from using security assistance funds to train, advise, or offer technical assistance to internal security forces (including police, corrections, and paramilitary forces) in many fragile states.
50. For more detail, see Patrick and Brown 2007b; CSIS 2007.

51. See remarks by Secretary of Defense Robert Gates (Gates 2007).
52. The Bush administration's proposed federal budget for fiscal year 2008 reflected this trend. Of the total $2.9 trillion requested, defense spending amounted to a whopping $623 billion, or 21.5 percent of the federal budget, outpacing investments in civilian aspects of global engagement ($39.49 billion) by a factor of some sixteen to one (the ratio rises even higher if the Bush administration's supplemental requests to fund the wars in Iraq and Afghanistan are included). Bazzi, Herrling, and Patrick 2007.
53. See CSIS 2007.
54. Patrick and Brown 2007b.
55. See Armitage and Nye 2007, pp. 63–67; Pemberton and Korb 2006.
56. The International Affairs (or "150") Account funds the operations and assistance streams of the State Department and the U.S. Agency for International Development.
57. Existing funding arrangements—including the International Disaster and Famine Assistance, Emergency Migration and Refugee Assistance, Transition Initiatives, and the U.N. Department of Peacekeeping Operations accounts—do not provide sufficient authority or resources to respond adequately to threats and opportunities in fragile states.
58. Such an account would be available, subject to presidential determination and justification to congressional committees, to be transferred to government agencies for implementation.
59. Section 1207 funds are named for a provision of the National Defense Authorization Act of 2006.
60. Commission on Weak States and U.S. National Security 2004.
61. Stabilization and Reconstruction Civilian Management Act of 2004 (S. 2127), February 25, 2004.
62. To further this objective, some have called on Congress to pass legislation akin to the landmark Goldwater-Nichols Department of Defense Reorganization Act of 1986, which—in addition to creating the Joint Chiefs of Staff—made "joint" service a precondition for career advancement.
63. Relevant organizations include the United Nations, the North Atlantic Treaty Organization, the European Union, the Association of Southeast Asian Nations, the African Union, the Organization of American States, the Organization for Security and Cooperation in Europe, the Organisation for Economic Co-operation and Development, the World Bank, and the International Monetary Fund.
64. Compared with most other Western governments, the United States continues to place heavy emphasis on the short-term security challenges posed by fragile states, as opposed to the long-term requirements of development, including the creation of strong indigenous institutions. For more detail, see Patrick and Brown 2007a.
65. This section draws on Patrick 2008b.

66. The World Bank estimates that some $40 billion a year is stolen by corrupt leaders around the world, including 25 percent of gross national product in some African countries. Hoge 2007, A7.
67. The U.K.-sponsored Extractive Industries Transparency Initiative insists that resource-rich countries demonstrate transparent and accountable public revenue management as a condition for bilateral and multilateral public sector financing of extractive industry projects. The next administration should also support the "Publish What You Pay" campaign championed by the nongovernmental organization Global Witness to discourage multinational corporations from subsidizing venal and autocratic governance, and the related "Publish What You Lend" campaign, which presses financial institutions to reveal how much they lend to resource-rich governments in anticipation of future revenues.

References

Armitage, Richard L., and Joseph S. Nye, Jr. 2007. *A Smarter, More Secure America: Report of the CSIS Commission on Smart Power*. Washington, D.C.: Center for Strategic and International Studies.

Ball, Nicole J. 2005. "Strengthening Democratic Governance of the Security Sector in Conflict Affected Countries." *Public Administration and Development* 25 (1): 25–38.

Bazzi, Samuel, Sheila Herrling, and Stewart Patrick. 2007. "Billions for War, Pennies for the Poor: Moving the President's FY2008 Budget from Hard Power to Smart Power." Center for Global Development, Washington, D.C. [www.cgdev.org/content/publications/detail/13232/].

Boyce, James K. 2000. "Beyond Good Intentions: External Assistance and Peace Building." In Shepard Forman and Stewart Patrick, eds., *Good Intentions: Pledges of Aid for Postconflict Recovery*. Boulder, Colo.: Lynne Rienner.

Burnside, Craig, and David Dollar. 2000. "Aid, Policies, and Growth." *American Economic Review* 90 (4): 847–68.

Chauvet, Lisa, and Paul Collier. 2004. "Development Effectiveness in Fragile States: Spillovers and Turnarounds." Oxford University Center for the Study of African Economics, Oxford, U.K. [www.oecd.org/dataoecd/55628.pdf].

———. 2006. "Helping Hand? Aid to Failing States." Oxford University Center for the Study of African Economics, Oxford, U.K. [http://users.ox.ac.uk/~econpco/research/pdfs/HelpingHand-AidtoFailingStates.pdf].

Cline, William R. 2003. "Trading Up: Trade Policy and Global Poverty." CGD Policy Brief 2 (4). Center for Global Development, Washington, D.C.

Collier, Paul. 2007. *The Bottom Billion: Why the Poorest Countries Are Failing and What Can Be Done About It*. Oxford, U.K.: Oxford University Press.

Collier, Paul, and Anke Hoeffler. 2004. "The Challenge of Reducing the Global Incidence of Civil War." Copenhagen Consensus Challenge Paper. Copenhagen Consensus Center.

Commission on Weak States and U.S. National Security. 2004. *On the Brink: Weak States and U.S. National Security*. Washington, D.C.: Center for Global Development. [www.cgdev.org/section/initiatives/_archive/weakstates].

Council of the European Union. 2003. *European Security Strategy: A Secure Europe in a Better World*. Brussels.

Crocker, Chester A. 2003. "Engaging Failing States." *Foreign Affairs* 82 (5): 32–44.

CSIS (Center for Strategic and International Studies). 2007. *Integrating 21st Century Development and Security Assistance*. Final Report of the Task Force on DoD Non-Traditional Security Assistance. Washington, D.C.

DFID (U.K. Department for International Development). 2005. *Why We Need to Work More Effectively in Fragile States*. London.

DoD (U.S. Department of Defense). 2005. "Military Support for Security, Stability, Transition and Reconstruction (SSTR) Operations." Directive 3000.05. November 28. [www.dtic.mil/whs/directives/corres/html/300005.htm].

Evaluation Gap Working Group. 2006. *When Will We Ever Learn? Improving Lives through Impact Evaluation*. Washington, D.C.: Center for Global Development. [www.cgdev.org/section/initiatives/_active/evalgap].

Freedom House. 2004. *The Worst of the Worst: The World's Most Repressive Societies*. Washington, D.C.

Fukuyama, Francis. 2004. *State-Building: Governance and World Order in the 21st Century*. Ithaca, N.Y.: Cornell University Press.

Fund for Peace. 2007. "Failed States Index." Washington, D.C. [www.fundforpeace.org/web/index.php?option=com_content&task=view&id=229&Itemid=366].

GAO (U.S. Government Accountability Office). 2007. *Military Operations: Actions Needed to Improve DoD's Stability Operations Approach and Enhance Interagency Planning*. Washington, D.C. [www.gao.gov/htext/d07549.html].

Gates, Robert. 2007. Landon Lecture. November 26. Kansas State University, Manhattan, Kansas. [www.defenselink.mil/speeches/speech.aspx?speechid=1199].

Ghani, Ashraf, Clare Lockhart, and Michael Carnahan. 2005. "Closing the Sovereignty Gap: An Approach to Statebuilding." Overseas Development Institute, London.

HELP Commission (U.S. Commission on Helping to Enhance the Livelihood of People around the Globe). 2007. *Beyond Assistance: The HELP Commission Reform on Foreign Assistance Reform*. Washington, D.C.

Hoge, Warren. 2007. "World Bank and UN to Help Poor Nations Recover Stolen Assets." *New York Times*. September 18.

Krasner, Stephen D., and Carlos Pascual. 2005. "Addressing State Failure." *Foreign Affairs* 84 (4): 153–63.

Lamb, Robert D. 2007. *Ungoverned Areas and Threats from Safe Havens*. Draft 1.0.0. Final Report of the Ungoverned Areas Project prepared for the U.S. Office of the Under Secretary of Defense for Policy. Washington, D.C.

Levin, V., and D. Dollar. 2004. "The Forgotten States: Aid Volumes and Volatility in Difficult Partnership Countries, 1992–2000." World Bank, Washington, D.C.

Mandelbaum, Michael. 1996. "Foreign Policy as Social Work." *Foreign Affairs* 75 (1): 16–32.

McGillivray, Mark. 2006. "Aid Allocation and Fragile States." Discussion Paper 2006/01. United Nations University, World Institute for Development Economics Research, Helsinki.

Miguel, Edward. 2007. "Poverty and Violence: An Overview of Recent Research and Implications for Foreign Aid." In Lael Brainard and Derek Chollet, eds., *Too Poor For Peace? Global Poverty, Conflict, and Security in the 21st Century*. Washington, D.C.: Brookings Institution.

Moran, Theodore. 2003. *Reforming OPIC for the 21st Century*. Policy Analyses in International Economics 69. Washington, D.C.: Institute for International Economics.

OECD–DAC (Organisation for Economic Co-operation and Development–Development Assistance Committee). "Ensuring Fragile States Are Not Left Behind." Paris. [www.oecd.org/dataoecd/36/56/38572891.pdf].

——. 2006b. *Whole of Government Approaches to Fragile States*. Paris. [www.oecd.org/dataoecd/15/24/37826256.pdf].

——. 2007a. *Principles for Good International Engagement in Fragile States*. Paris. [www.oecd.org/dataoecd/61/45/38368714.pdf].

——. 2007b. "Service Delivery in Fragile States: Advancing Donor Practice." Concept note prepared by United Nations Children's Fund and U.S. Agency for International Development. Paris. [www.oecd.org/dataoecd/45/28/35227311.pdf].

Paris, Roland. 2004. *At War's End: Building Peace after Civil Conflict*. Cambridge, U.K.: Cambridge University Press.

Patrick, Stewart. 2006a. "Weak States and Global Threats: Assessing Evidence of Spillovers." Working Paper 73. Center for Global Development, Washington, D.C.

——. 2006b. "Weak States and Global Threats: Fact or Fiction?" *The Washington Quarterly* 29 (2): 27–53.

——. 2007a. "The U.S. Response to Precarious States: Tentative Progress and Remaining Obstacles to Policy Coherence." CGD Essay. [www.cgdev.org/content/publications/detail/14093/].

——. 2007b. "Toolbox: Making Foreign Aid Reform Work." *The American Interest* 2 (5).

——. 2008a. "'Failed' States and Global Security: Empirical Questions and Policy Dilemmas." In Rafael Reuveny and William R. Thompson, eds., *North and South in the World Political Economy*. Oxford, U.K.: Blackwell.

——. 2008b. "A Return to Realism? The United States and Global Peace Operations since 9/11." *International Peacekeeping* 15 (1): 133–48.

Patrick, Stewart, and Brown, Kaysie. 2006. "Fragile States and U.S. Foreign Assistance: Show Me The Money." Working Paper 96. Center for Global Development, Washington, D.C.

——. 2007a. *Greater than the Sum of Its Parts: Assessing "Whole of Government" Approaches to Fragile States*. New York: International Peace Academy.

——. 2007b. "The Pentagon and Global Development. Making Sense of the DoD's Expanding Role." CGD Working Paper 131. Center for Global Development, Washington, D.C.

Pemberton, Miriam, and Lawrence Korb. 2006. "A Unified Security Budget for the United States." Institute for Policy Studies, Foreign Policy in Focus, Washington, D.C.

Perito, Robert. 2004. "Building Civilian Capacity for U.S. Stability Operations: The Rule of Law Component." Special Report 118. U.S. Institute of Peace, Washington, D.C. [http://usip.org/pubs/specialreports/sr118.pdf.].

Rice, Condoleezza. 2000. "Campaign 2000: Promoting the National Interest." *Foreign Affairs* 79 (1): 45–62.

Rice, Susan, and Stewart Patrick. 2008. *Index of State Weakness in the Developing World.* Washington, D.C.: Brookings Institution.

Torres, M. Moreno, and Michael Anderson. 2004 "Fragile States: Defining Difficult Environments for Poverty Reduction." U.K. Department for International Development, London. [www.gsdrc.org/go/display/document/legacyid/1343].

U.K. Prime Minister's Strategy Unit. 2005. *Investing in Prevention: An International Strategy to Manage Risks of Instability and Improve Crisis Response.* London.

U.N. Secretary-General's High-Level Panel. 2004. *A More Secure World: Our Shared Responsibility.* Report of the Secretary-General's High-Level Panel. New York. [www.un.org/secureworld/].

USAID (U.S. Agency for International Development). 2003. *Foreign Aid in the National Interest: Promoting Freedom, Security, and Opportunity.* Washington, D.C.

White House. 2002. *National Security Strategy of the United States of America.* Washington, D.C.

———. 2005. "Management of Interagency Efforts Concerning Reconstruction and Stabilization." National Security Presidential Directive 44. December 7. [www.fas.org/irp/offdocs/nspd/nspd-44.html].

13

Aid for Education: More Bang for the Buck

Kate Vyborny and Nancy Birdsall

Meera, age eight, lives with her family on a sidewalk in New Delhi, India. During the day she roams major intersections, her infant sister hanging from her hip, begging drivers for coins in the few words of English she knows. She does not go to school. In a few years she will be married off to a stranger. She will have six children, one of whom will go to school. Or she will die young, possibly immolated in a kitchen fire for having brought with her an insufficient dowry.[1]

* * *

Darweshi, age six, goes to primary school in his village in Tanzania. His teacher often shows up three hours late or doesn't come at all. When he does come, he is one of only two teachers in a school with seven grade levels, so the students spend most of their class time practicing on their own. With few books and many students, studying usually means copying notes from an outdated textbook—for those students who have notebooks—and then memorizing facts that the students don't understand. Darweshi hopes to go to secondary school but knows that only seven or eight of the twenty students in his class will do well enough on the exam to get in.

* * *

Robbinah, age sixteen, finished primary school—like two out of three girls in her native Zambia. But even though she

---

Kate Vyborny is a program coordinator and Nancy Birdsall is the president of the Center for Global Development. They gratefully acknowledge assistance from Ruth Levine, Michael Clemens, Barbara Bruns, Marlaine Lockheed, Luis Crouch, and others giving input to the Cash on Delivery Aid Project.

completed sixth grade, she, like two out of three of her former classmates, today cannot read a simple sentence out loud.[2]

* * *

Indrani, age ten, is the daughter of illiterate parents living in rural Bangladesh. She goes to school. Her older sister is finishing secondary school and plans to work in the garment factory in the market center. Her mother was betrothed at 12, but her parents have decided that their daughters must finish school before marrying.

* * *

Dejen went to a village school in rural Ethiopia. He was one of two students who passed the test at the end of primary school. The whole village laughed at his parents for sending him to town to attend secondary school, because they will miss his help on the farm while he attends secondary school. If he fails the secondary exit exam, as the few other students from his village who have left for secondary school have done, he will likely return to his village to farm, unable to find a job in the city.

* * *

We need to add little to the stories of these children to make the case that education in poor countries is important and that improving it should be a part of the global development agenda of the next president. Education is important both instrumentally, with significant benefits for the health and productivity of those who have access to education and for their whole societies, and intrinsically, as a right and a commitment made by the international community.

Primary education has always been an area of U.S. aid appealing to policymakers and the public, consistent with U.S. values of expanding opportunity for all. But aid for education has been neglected in U.S. aid programs in the past two decades: While health aid has sextupled in real terms since the early 1990s, education aid has increased by only a third.[4]

Meanwhile, poor countries themselves have made education a priority and are achieving amazing progress. With the help of a new international framework, the Education for All Fast Track Initiative, other donors have been expanding and improving their education aid. The next president should consider announcing U.S. support for a big international push to expand quality primary schooling in low-income countries, so that poor, minority, and disabled children everywhere have the chance to learn. And he or she should take the lead in committing to improve the effectiveness of U.S. aid, collaborating with other donors through the Fast Track Initiative to promote local innovation and learning through rigorous evaluation, and manage aid programs that reward progress against clear, measurable objectives.

This is the only chapter that focuses solely on how the United States could better manage its aid in a specific sector; education is a good example of where the United States could be more ambitious and more effective in its foreign assistance. While this chapter concentrates on making quality primary education universal, the United States should also take a leadership role at the university and graduate levels, which have also been rejected.[3]

The state of education

Steady increases have been made in primary schooling, but minorities lag, quality is low, and few continue to secondary school. Poor countries have made steady progress in expanding primary schooling in recent years. The primary completion rate in low-income countries increased from 66 percent to 74 percent between 1991 and 2004, with growth in all the poorer regions.[5] In fact, even many of the countries sometimes characterized as "off-track" for reaching the Millennium Development Goal for primary completion on a country level have actually accelerated primary education faster than today's rich countries did at similar levels of development: Burkina Faso, for example, is ahead of where the United States and other rich countries were when they were at a similar level of income.[6]

And more of the children entering primary school for the first time are girls: the gender gap seems to be closing, at least for primary school. Girls have caught up to boys in school enrollment in much of the world. Worldwide, eight girls are enrolled in primary school for every ten boys, with steep increases since the 1960s in every region.[7]

The unprecedented pace of progress in getting children to school is happening in most poor countries. But three major challenges remain worldwide: expanding access to the poorest and most marginalized groups, improving quality, and ensuring that students continue to higher levels of education, so that schooling can deliver on its promise of increasing productivity and income, well-being, and social mobility for the poor.

The children who still do not receive a primary education are the hardest to reach. Almost three-quarters of girls who remain out of school worldwide are "doubly disadvantaged" by their ethnicity, language barriers, or rural isolation.[8] And two children out of five who are out of school suffer from disabilities.[9] Expanding access to these populations will be more challenging and costly than the initial broad expansion of enrollment.

Of course, getting children to school is only the first step. Making sure they learn something while there is harder. Forty-six percent of third through fifth graders surveyed in several districts of Andhra Pradesh, India, could not count the kites in a picture of six balls and three kites.[10] And various competency tests show very low levels of learning in many poor countries in every region. High dropout rates and low primary completion rates, even where initial enrollment is universal, are also associated with low quality.[11]

Why are children enrolling in school yet learning so little? A whole host of reasons: poorly trained teachers with high rates of absenteeism and moonlighting, particularly in rural areas where teachers are unlikely to want to be posted; curricula that focus on memorization of facts; lack of materials; poor attendance or failure to do homework because of house or field work at home; and hunger or health problems that go unaddressed, keeping children home or impeding their concentration.[12]

Yet some countries do much better than others when it comes to education quality. For instance, 20 percent of young Zambian women who finished fifth grade can read a simple sentence; that number is 80 percent in Malawi and 90 percent in Ethiopia and Rwanda.[13] It does seem possible to improve learning outcomes even in countries with very low average income levels.

What works, what's needed

What is needed to get children into school? On the supply side: building schools, buying textbooks, and training teachers—subsidizing the supply of education. Significant external funding for the supply of education will be needed to reach the remaining children who are out of school.[14]

But spending on supply is only one piece of the puzzle. On the demand side: providing conditional cash transfers, such as Bangladesh's Food for Education, Brazil's Bolsa Escola, or Mexico's Oportunidades programs, to compensate parents and children for other costs associated with sending their children to school, such as uniforms and supplies, and, most important, the cost of sending children to school instead of having them work or help with domestic or agricultural labor. School breakfast or lunch programs, such as those in Jamaica and Tamil Nadu, India, have also been a widely successful demand subsidy because giving students a nutritious meal helps improve concentration and learning.[15] These programs have increased enrollment, in addition to transferring income directly to the poor.[16]

What can be done to ensure that once children make it to school, they learn something? Improving quality can be not only costly but also often politically difficult, with powerful teachers' unions in many countries sometimes opposing initiatives to improve quality, which increase the burden on their often under-prepared and under-resourced members to improve student achievement.[17] Political challenges may arise not only with high-profile initiatives such as teacher testing (met with major strikes and political opposition in Peru and elsewhere) but even with seemingly technocratic objectives such as making test scores comparable over time because the need to equate test results with those from previous years can conflict with political pressure to release scores as soon as possible.

Lack of information about what works to improve quality is also a factor. For example, teacher literacy and attendance are strongly related to students' scores on competency tests, but this information does not indicate whether increasing teacher salaries and introducing a particular teacher training or attendance monitoring program will improve these learning outcomes.[18] Programs using community and parent participation in El Salvador, student- and teacher-driven participatory schooling in Guatemala, performance-based teacher bonuses in Chile, flexible rural extension schools in Bangladesh, and training and radio programs for interactive math teaching in Venezuela have demonstrably improved students' completion rates, promotion to secondary schooling, and tested learning. Many more such studies are urgently needed to test the effect on learning outcomes of interventions, including teacher training and community participation. The right set of tools to improve learning will differ by country; the longer-term goal must be to support countries' systems for evaluating their own attempts at improving quality. And that means improving data. Education data, particularly on learning outcomes, are still patchy in low-income countries: for one thing, most do not have tests that are comparable over time.[19] This limits not only the ability of governments and outside researchers to evaluate quality efforts but also the ability of civil society, communities, and parents to push for improvements.

The availability of good, comparable, and detailed information on learning outcomes is limited in poor countries for several reasons. Although most countries test children at the end of primary school, in many countries the tests are designed to pass the number of children equivalent to the number of spots available in secondary schools. So rather than giving feedback to parents and communities, they may just report whether the child passed—which can imply different standards, depending on how many other students were taking the test, and is little help as feedback if the student fails at the end of primary school and has no opportunity to continue schooling. Information may also be available only in complex formats that are difficult for parents with limited education to access or understand. With little information on the performance of their children and their schools, parents cannot demand better service from teachers and governments and cannot be confident that keeping their children in school is a worthwhile investment.[20]

There is another issue, generally ignored in U.S. and other aid programs. As one government official from a low-income African country said in exasperation, "donors will support building a school but not the road to the school. They will fund a health clinic but not the power plant to power the clinic." The reality is that many factors entirely outside the control of education officials and institutions matter for delivering good education. In rural areas, improving roads might increase access more than building more schools. Students who are hungry or suffering from worms cannot concentrate; a study in Kenyan schools showed that worm treatments dramatically reduced absenteeism.[21]

The United States could better recognize the limitations of narrowly directing funds to building schools, training teachers, and buying textbooks. In Millennium Challenge Corporation countries, for example, U.S. aid programs for education could provide leadership in focusing on data systems, management information, and evaluation. That in turn might allow for more credible measures of progress on quantity and quality, and for more discretion in the allocation of aid funds to country policy leaders. This issue is addressed below.

Overcoming unpredictability, red tape, and the lack of evaluation

Aid for education is expanding, but it is still unpredictable, wrapped in red tape, and under-evaluated. U.S. aid for education totaled just under $800 million in 2005; if a new presidential fund announced in September 2007 is added to existing funds, the total is closer to a billion.[22] This is about a tenth of the world total, and about a quarter of these funds go to Afghanistan and Iraq. So, in terms of spending, the United States is one player among many in aid for education. But we can help improve the lives of poor children worldwide by spending the money wisely, multiplying the effects not only of U.S. funds but those of other donors as well.

And there is clearly political will to support education in poor countries provided the funds are well spent. Two of the three leading presidential candidates at the time of this writing have proposed significant expansions of aid for education. In May 2007, Senators Hillary Clinton and Gordon Smith and Representatives Nita Lowey and Spencer Bachus introduced the Education for All Act, which, if passed, would more than double U.S. aid for education in the first year and continue to scale up funding to the sector, reaching $3 billion in 2012.[23] This expansion would present a window of opportunity to direct substantial new funds to good uses without the need to reallocate funding from existing programs. Democratic presidential candidate Senator Barack Obama has also committed to a significant increase in funding: $2 billion in a new Global Education Fund.[24]

But beyond the aggregate funds, the United States needs to ensure that it delivers financing in ways it can best be used. The bulk of the costs that countries incur to expand primary schooling to all children—as much as 90 percent by some estimates—are recurrent costs, such as teacher salaries.[25] However, countries have had a difficult time securing aid to support this spending because donors have been reluctant to finance recurring costs and because even general support funds that could be used for these purposes are too short-term and unpredictable to allow countries to take on those expenses. Hiring thousands of new teachers when funds might dry up after three years is a risky proposition. Aid needs to be made more predictable to be more useful for education.

Funds also come wrapped in red tape in the form of congressional earmarks that restrict how funds can be spent and in which countries. A former head of mission for the U.S. Agency for International Development described despairing at being offered a big lump sum of funding for education on short notice—he knew he had to spend the one-time funds in the single year they were allocated or risk losing them altogether, but he could not find a useful way to spend the funds all at once. Why such a sudden mixed blessing? The agency was trying to shift funds among countries and sectors to meet all the earmarks, and the only way to do so was to put specific funds in places that did not make sense in the field. This problem occurs in areas other than education as well, and it requires a big solution: an overhaul of foreign assistance legislation (see chapter 10 by Herrling and Radelet).

Beyond the earmarking issue, other issues make aid funds harder to use and less effective at building the ability of countries to provide education. There is a tendency to micromanage the inputs that countries must purchase with funding—the U.S. Agency for International Development might promote a particular curriculum reform program or give countries funds specifically to purchase books or build schools. One result is that countries typically have to use a lot of their human resources at a very high level to secure aid funding and negotiate how it can be used: education ministers and even presidents must meet regularly with aid officials from not only the United States but, in many cases, dozens of donor countries and agencies, to say nothing of the time the technocrats spend writing reports on how aid is used instead of actually managing the education system. It also means that countries have little flexibility to determine the most important needs and fund them. And in most U.S. aid—even in the innovative and flexible Millennium Challenge Accounts—aid is spent outside the country budgetary and procurement systems. This may increase short-term convenience, but it also creates more coordination problems for recipient governments. In the long term, it seriously hinders the development of recipient-country institutions and capacity to deliver education and other services.[26]

These problems are not unique to U.S. aid. The United States and other rich countries have recognized these problems publicly in a number of major declarations in previous years.[27] But U.S. leadership is urgently needed to help energize these discussions and put the commitment into action to make aid, for education and all other sectors, more effective.

Recommendations for the next U.S. president

The next U.S. president should take three practical steps to maximize every dollar of U.S. aid for education: collaborate for predictable, manageable funding; innovate, evaluate, and scale up what works; and manage aid for outcomes and long-term systems, rather than micromanaging inputs for quick fixes.

Collaborate for predictable, manageable funding

As is emphasized throughout this volume, the challenges of global poverty—as well as the increase in the number of rich countries and institutions playing a role—mean that collaboration is needed to be effective. Aid for education is an area in which this is particularly important. Working with other donors through joint mechanisms such as the Education for All Fast Track Initiative, the United States can provide funding that works better together, cutting through red tape and making the money predictable enough to be useful.

One joint initiative in particular, the Fast Track Initiative, is helping to unwrap education aid from red tape, but it needs more commitment from the United States. Under the Fast Track Initiative, donors are committed to working together to fund education in countries that have developed credible education plans and meet other eligibility requirements (such as responsible budget management). The partner donors of the Fast Track Initiative have committed to providing long-term, predictable funding for the education needs that countries themselves identify. It also means donors go through the process of vetting country plans jointly instead of through costly duplication. This coordinated approach to supporting eligible countries' own plans is more advanced than in most other sectors (with the important exception of health). This makes it all the more important that the U.S. support, as well as benefit and learn from, this process, which could become a model for other sectors.

In addition to the joint vetting of country plans, the Fast Track Initiative has a joint "catalytic fund" to help countries get started with implementing their plans and a small technical assistance fund (the United States currently does not support either of these).[28] But the approach is not to pool all education funding, rather to coordinate it—so while the Fast Track Initiative has helped to address the problems of unpredictability and red tape in education aid to some extent, a lot of work still remains to be done by the United States, in addressing these problems in our own system, as well as by the other bilateral donors.

In September 2007, the Bush administration announced a new presidential initiative for basic education, to support six countries that have qualified through the Fast Track Initiative process: Ethiopia, Ghana, Honduras, Liberia, Mali, and Yemen.[29] The initiative was announced with a commitment to seek congressional authorization of $525 million over five years in addition to other aid for this initiative, although it is less clear whether this will be achieved in the final months of the Bush administration. The choice to support Fast Track Initiative countries (implicitly using the joint vetting process), the appointment of the initiative's director as one of the U.S. representatives at Fast Track Initiative partnership meetings, and the symbolic support for the initiative arc positive steps.[30] However, there is still a real need to reduce the red tape involved for countries: Although there is some flexibility in how the money earmarked for each country is spent, each of the six countries now negotiates how the money will be spent directly with the initiative's director, in addition to their ongoing work with the U.S. Agency for International Development and, in some cases, the Millennium Challenge Corporation, not to mention the other donors.[31] The Education for All legislation in Congress also highlights the Fast Track Initiative, but it is not yet clear to what extent this new funding would be used to take advantage of the initiative's collaborative vetting process.

The president should take the lead in supporting this international effort to make aid for education work better, contribute to the FTI's dedicated funds, and work more effectively with the FTI through U.S. bilateral aid. To do so, the president should exercise leadership with Congress to streamline the aid system, make more long-term agreements with recipient countries like the contracts used by the Millennium Challenge Corporation or the ten-year partnership agreements of the U.K's Department for International Development, and provide more flexible financing that addresses the needs of each country once its plan has been approved.[32]

Innovate and evaluate to scale up what works

A crucial shortage of careful, rigorous evaluations pervades development assistance.[33] Aid agencies frequently assess whether an intervention—such as a teacher training program—made any difference and what aspects of it could be improved or changed on the basis of data collected after the intervention, often without comparable baseline data from before the intervention started or without the ability to take into account changes that might have occurred anyway, such as those brought about by changes in demographics, income, or even other aid programs happening at the same time and place. Careful evaluation to ensure more solid evidence of what works means collecting baseline data first for more accurate measurement and, where appropriate, can include techniques like randomized evaluation, in which individuals or communities are chosen randomly to receive an extra intervention, such as a conditional cash transfer or early childhood education, or to receive standard service as part of a "control" group. The results are then tested statistically to check whether the extra intervention made a difference. With some forethought, these methods can be applied in ways that still give additional services to anyone involved in the evaluation, by providing a basic package of services to the control group or by using a phased rollout of an intervention to compare those who received services earlier and later. When well designed, impact evaluation can not only tell us whether a school feeding program or teacher training course worked; it can also give feedback to program managers at the local level on which aspects of it are working well and what could be improved.[34]

One of the greatest benefits of investing in impact evaluation is that it not only improves how U.S. aid dollars are spent but also generates knowledge that can be used by any aid donor, multiplying the effects of the United Kingdom's pounds and Japan's yen. Most important of all, it can inform how the poor-country government itself makes policy and chooses to spend its money, which in most poor countries is more of the spending on education and health than all the donors' money put together. And that is the long-term prize on which the United States should focus: not how to spend its money on bits and pieces of what is needed in the short term, but the long-term task of building the institutions for poor countries to provide education to all.

The public and policymakers want to see stories of how aid money succeeded and to spend as much money on program activities as possible. As a side effect, incentives are created for the agencies not to invest the (sometimes substantial) resources needed for careful, independent evaluation that could show that a program did not work. And so, paradoxically, donors seldom really test whether they are getting their money's worth in aid. When interventions are evaluated, there is also a strong tendency to publish disproportionately those that show success. In part because of the resulting lack of hard evidence, aid is notoriously driven by fads.[35]

This does not mean donors and developing countries should not take unproven approaches. Rather, innovation is needed, but its benefits can be multiplied by accompanying it with efforts to learn while doing. And the education sector is particularly amenable to rigorous evaluation. Governments, including those of Kenya and Mexico, as well as nongovernmental organizations such as Pratham in India, have conducted rigorous evaluations establishing the impact of programs—including conditional cash transfers, remedial education, grants to schools, and many other types of interventions—and helping to ensure the political sustainability of and funding to scale up these programs.[36] For example, the innovative idea of paying parents to send their children to school—through conditional cash transfers—was originally seen with some skepticism by many. The rigorous evaluation of the PROGRESA (now called Oportunidades) program strongly addressed these concerns, and partly as a result of this, similar mechanisms have been adopted in many other developing countries, and even in New York City.

More such studies are needed to answer enduring questions about what works in education and other public services, such as how to improve the productivity of employees in the education ministry. Evaluation is also needed to establish which types of interventions work best in different types of settings, and to give feedback on how well a given project is working and how it could be improved.

The president should provide leadership in ensuring that more and higher quality evaluations of education interventions are conducted and that their results are used. He or she could take an easy but powerful first step by joining the governments of Canada, Mexico, the Netherlands, Uganda, and the United Kingdom in becoming a member of the International Initiative for Impact Evaluation, a new organization that will fund independent evaluations of development interventions. By funding evaluations conducted by individuals and institutions based in developing countries, and by ensuring the independence of the funding for evaluations from their results, the initiative will help develop country capacity and combat the bias toward positive evaluations. The president should also work with Congress to establish a requirement that 1 percent of all U.S. aid funds be used for evaluation and push for similar requirements in the multilateral institutions in which the United States is a stakeholder. Unlike country or sector earmarks, such a requirement would enhance the use of funds rather than restricting how they can be useful. The president could also catalyze learning about what works in education by promoting the improvement of education data, particularly data on learning outcomes. Some of the data could be collected or improved quite simply through existing mechanisms, such as increasing the number of countries in which the Demographic and Health Survey includes a simple test of retained literacy, rather than a self-assessment.[37] "Cash on delivery" aid for education, discussed in detail below, would also present an approach to giving incentives to countries to improve the quality of their education data systems.

The president could also kill several birds with one stone by taking a leadership role to establish an "innovation fund" in the Fast Track Initiative, in which a set percentage of the funds would be earmarked for evaluation and learning from innovations. This would not only promote learning from innovations but also support the collaborative approach of the Fast Track Initiative and cut down on the administrative costs of this funding, all with a single commitment.

Manage aid for outcomes and long-term systems

To address the problem of red tape and micromanagement of inputs such as books and schools, the president should push the aid bureaucracy to manage for and measure successes by outcomes, such as increasing literacy rates, rather than inputs, such as building schools or buying textbooks. Education and aid experts Deon Filmer and Lant Pritchett have proposed a "Millennium Learning Goal" to focus international attention on the outcome of quality primary education.[38] For the next president to recognize such a goal would send a signal of U.S. commitment to quality education. Better still, the president should demand that aid administrators report their progress to the executive in terms of this and other outcome indicators. This would help orient the U.S. aid system toward real outcomes, and it might also help give Congress the confidence needed to let go of controlling the details through earmarks.

One way to help achieve such a learning goal would be to link new education aid to incremental progress in the simple mechanism of "cash on delivery": the United States would promise to pay poor countries $100 per additional child completing a quality primary education.[39] Countries would agree to make detailed data on school completion and reading and math test results available to their citizens and to allow a third-party auditor to double-check those results with random field visits or retests of a sample of children. The countries would then be allowed to choose how to spend the money: education supply, such as building schools or training teachers; education demand, such as school feeding programs or conditional cash transfers; or spending outside the education sector, such as on roads that promote economic development and also make transportation to school easier. This flexibility is particularly important because, as already emphasized, there are limitations on how much additional supply-side spending can do to increase access. It would also streamline administrative costs of joint donor-recipient planning of inputs, and of coordination between multiple donors all deciding on different or overlapping inputs to purchase with aid, particularly if the funding were provided through the existing framework of the Fast Track Initiative. Most important, it would build the long-term systems in recipient countries to allow them to provide education to their own citizens, instead of the status quo of building up systems to provide and regulate aid.

Because of the limitations of a big financial push on the supply side of education, and because the constraints differ by country, measures of progress should be as close as possible to outcomes such as the number of children completing school or improvements in the average or bottom quintile test score, rather than inputs such as the number of schools built or the number of teachers trained. In countries where linking funding to test scores would present a significant logistical and audit challenge, one way to help promote quality as well as access would be to reward countries for additional children completing primary school, while requiring the countries to implement and publish the results of a competency test with results that would be comparable over time.

This "cash on delivery" approach would provide fodder for civil society to pressure national or state governments for improved quality, or create "school report cards" for parents and communities to do so at a local level. At the same time, it would create demand for improved data quality at the national level, and transparently link funding that countries could choose to use for quality interventions to the implementation and publication of testing, so that citizens would receive information but also know that the funding is available for their governments to make improvements. The argument that funds are short would thus become less credible.

At the same time, the clear link to results could make it easier to command congressional and public support for increased funding for education—there is no waste in this form of aid because funds are not disbursed until progress happens.

These recommendations provide a recipe for the next U.S. president to make U.S. education aid better support learning in developing countries. More broadly, they provide an example of how the principles for better spending could be applied in each sector. Supporting education in poor countries is not about finding all the answers for each country and programming them into U.S. aid; it is about finding ways to support countries in developing, implementing, and evaluating solutions. That is a lesson that, applied to U.S. aid for education, health, or any other purpose, will help get more bang for the buck.

Notes

1. Selected anecdotes used with permission from authors. Lewis and Lockheed 2006.
2. Lloyd 2005, p. 90.
3. Higher education is needed to increase productivity, allow countries to compete on the global labor market, and provide public services such as health and education. Of course, expanding primary and secondary education requires expanding higher education, to increase the supply and improve the training of teachers. The recently passed House bill reauthorizing the President's Emergency Plan for AIDS Relief includes a component requiring some funds to be used to help expand tertiary education for new health care providers, including the use of U.S. universities in assisting universities in developing countries. See

the Web site of the National Association of State Universities and Land Grant Colleges for more information (www.nasulgc.org). See also Kapur and Crowley 2008.

4. OECD–DAC Creditor Reporting System.
5. Filmer, Hasan, and Pritchett 2006.
6. Clemens 2004. Whether the Millennium Development Goals were intended to be achieved on a country level is debated; they are certainly far more realistic on a global level.
7. Lewis and Lockheed 2006.
8. Lewis and Lockheed 2006.
9. UN Millennium Project 2005.
10. Filmer, Hasan, and Pritchett 2006.
11. Competency tests measure only some of the benefits education provides—even if little formal learning takes place, the evidence demonstrates that participating in schooling has important benefits, particularly for girls, who grow up to have fewer and healthier children and more frequently send their own children to school. These effects are present even for those who barely retain literacy to adulthood. But learning these basic skills is unquestionably a key part of the missing link between schooling and education. There is also much evidence that rote learning of knowledge is a large component of class time in many low-income countries, suggesting that other skills not tested by competency assessments, such as critical thinking, are also not emphasized.
12. Boissiere 2004; UN Millennium Project 2005. Closely related to the learning gap is the abrupt dropoff in school enrollment after primary school. In Senegal, for example, nine out of ten children enroll in primary school, and five of the nine complete primary school, but only two or three continue to secondary school. The low numbers of children who continue to secondary school reflect low achievement in primary school as well as access to secondary school, which is limited by the number of schools and teachers, farther distances to travel, and higher fees, as well as issues like concern for the safety of teenage girls, who in some places may be subject to sexual assault on the way to school or in school—even by the teacher. Limited access to secondary schooling gives parents little reason to keep their children in primary school.
13. Lloyd 2005.
14. Bruns, Mingat, and Rakotomalala 2003; UN Millennium Project 2005. Making education accessible is only a piece of the puzzle. Countries that have recently eliminated school fees, such as Kenya and Uganda, have had huge increases in enrollment—Uganda nearly doubled enrollment within two years of eliminating fees. But it is clear that making schools available and free is not enough for the poorest families in some countries. Distance to school has an effect on enrollment but not large enough to ensure that all children get to school simply

by building enough schools. After school fees were eliminated, Uganda's gross enrollment stayed above 100 percent for years (indicating many students starting school late as well as grade repetition), but primary completion has hovered around 60 percent. This suggests that while children can get to school, they or their families decide it is not worth it for them to finish because the lost income from their work or help around the house outweighs the prospect of improved skills and higher income. Clemens 2004; Filmer 2004; World Bank World Development Indicators database.

15. UN Millennium Project 2005.
16. UN Millennium Project 2005; Morley and Coady 2003.
17. Corrales 1999.
18. See Lewis and Lockheed 2006, p. 65.
19. Lockheed (forthcoming).
20. There are several international tests that can provide comparable and more detailed feedback, but few low-income countries participate in international tests, in part because it is extremely difficult politically for national leaders to push against teachers' unions and other entrenched interests to implement a test that may then reflect poorly on their educational systems. These tests are also less useful for countries starting at a low level in learning outcomes because the tests provide little useful feedback at the lower end of the spectrum. Attempts to make existing national tests comparable over time have had limited success, for a combination of technical and political reasons. But there are a number of regional and international testing initiatives funded by the World Bank and the U.S. Agency for International Development, as well as civil society "school report cards" that give parents and communities clear, usable information about how their students and schools are performing compared with other schools. The "cash on delivery" approach we propose later in this chapter would help allow civil society and communities greater access to the data required for this and other quality accountability initiatives.
21. Miguel and Kremer 2004.
22. OECD–DAC Creditor Reporting System; White House 2007.
23. S. 1259 and H.R. 2092, May 2007. Library of Congress THOMAS database (http://thomas.loc.gov/).
24. See the candidate comparisons on the Web site of One Vote 08. (http://onevote08.org/candidatesvideos/compare.html?c=2&c=13).
25. UN Millennium Project 2005.
26. See Moss, Pettersson, and van de Walle 2006.
27. See High Level Forum on Aid Effectiveness 2005; International Conference on Financing for Development 2002.
28. FTI 2007.
29. White House 2007.

30. Participants' list, FTI partnership meetings, Dakar, Senegal, December 2007.
31. Conversation with Dr. Thomas Corts, director of the President's International Education Initiative, March 2008.
32. DFID, Foreign and Commonwealth Office, and Her Majesty's Treasury 2005.
33. Evaluation Gap Working Group 2006.
34. See remarks by Chris Blattman to the U.K. Department for International Development, on February 14, 2008 (www.chrisblattman.org/DFID.talk.Feb2008.pdf).
35. See, for example, Rodrik 2007.
36. Duflo and Kremer 2003.
37. Lloyd 2005.
38. Filmer, Hasan, and Pritchett 2006.
39. Barder and Birdsall 2006; Birdsall, Savedoff, and Vyborny 2007. For more information, see "'Cash on Delivery': Progress-Based Aid for Education" (www.cgdev.org/section/initiatives/_active/pbaedu).

References

Barder, Owen, and Nancy Birdsall. 2006. "Payments for Progress: A Hands-Off Approach to Foreign Aid." Working Paper 102. Center for Global Development, Washington, D.C. [www.cgdev.org/content/publications/detail/11550].

Birdsall, Nancy, William D. Savedoff, and Katherine Vyborny. 2007. "Cash on Delivery Aid for Education: A Proposal for a Hands-Off Approach." Center for Global Development, Washington, D.C. [www.cgdev.org/doc/Cash%20on%20Delivery%20AID/PBAfulldoc.pdf].

Boissiere, Maurice. 2004. "Determinants of Primary Education Outcomes in Developing Countries: Background Paper for the Evaluation of the World Bank's Support to Primary Education." World Bank, Washington, D.C.

Bruns, Barbara, Alain Mingat, and Ramahatra Rakotomalala. 2003. *Achieving Universal Primary Education by 2015: A Chance for Every Child.* Washington, D.C.: World Bank.

Clemens, Michael. 2004. "The Long Walk to School: International Education Goals in Historical Perspective." Working Paper 37. Center for Global Development, Washington, D.C. [www.cgdev.org/content/publications/detail/2754].

Corrales, Javier. 1999. "The Politics of Education Reform: Bolstering the Supply and Demand; Overcoming Institutional Blocks." *Education Reform and Management Series* 2:1. Washington, D.C.: World Bank.

DFID (U.K. Department for International Development), Foreign and Commonwealth Office, and Her Majesty's Treasury. 2005. "Partnerships for Poverty Reduction: Rethinking Conditionality." London. [www.dfid.gov.uk/pubs/files/conditionality.pdf].

Duflo, Esther, and Michael Kremer. 2003. "Use of Randomization in the Evaluation of Development Effectiveness." Paper prepared for the World Bank Operations Evaluation Department Conference on Evaluation and Development Effectiveness, July 15–16, Washington D.C. [http://econ-www.mit.edu/files/765].

Evaluation Gap Working Group. 2006. *When Will We Ever Learn? Improving Lives through Impact Evaluation*. Washington, D.C.: Center for Global Development. [www.cgdev.org/section/initiatives/_active/evalgap].

Filmer, Deon. 2004. "If You Build It, Will They Come? School Availability and School Enrollment in 21 Poor Countries." Policy Research Working Paper 3340. World Bank, Washington, D.C.

Filmer, Deon, Amer Hasan, and Lant Pritchett. 2006. "A Millennium Learning Goal: Measuring Real Progress in Education." Working Paper 97. Center for Global Development, Washington, D.C. [www.cgdev.org/content/publications/detail/9815].

FTI (Fast Track Initiative). 2007. *Quality Education for All Children: Meeting the Challenge*. Washington, D.C.: World Bank.

High Level Forum on Aid Effectiveness. 2005. "Paris Declaration on Aid Effectiveness." [www.oecd.org/document/18/0,2340,en_2649_3236398_35401554_1_1_1_1,00.html].

International Conference on Financing for Development. 2002. "Monterrey Consensus on Financing for Development." [www.un.org/esa/sustdev/documents/Monterrey_Consensus.htm].

Kapur, Devesh, and Megan Crowley. 2008. "Beyond the ABCs: Higher Education and Developing Countries." Working Paper 139. Center for Global Development, Washington, D.C. [www.cgdev.org/content/publications/detail/15310].

Lewis, Maureen, and Marlaine Lockheed. 2006. *Inexcusable Absence: Why 60 Million Girls Still Aren't in School and What to Do About It*. Washington, D.C.: Center for Global Development. [www.cgdev.org/content/publications/detail/15310].

Lloyd, Cynthia B., ed. 2005. *Growing Up Global: The Changing Transitions to Adulthood in Developing Countries*. Washington, D.C.: National Academies Press.

Lockheed, Marlaine. 2004. "The Purpose of Good Quality Education." Paper commissioned for the *EFA Global Monitoring Report 2005, The Quality Imperative*. [http://portal.unesco.org/education/en/files/36496/11005356383Lockheed.doc/Lockheed.doc].

———. Forthcoming. "Measuring Progress with Tests of Learning." Center for Global Development, Washington, D.C.

Miguel, Edward, and Michael Kremer. 2004. "Worms: Identifying Impacts on Education and Health in the Presence of Treatment Externalities." *Econometrica* 72 (1): 159–217.

Morley, Samuel, and David Coady. 2003. *From Social Assistance to Social Development: Targeted Education Subsidies in Developing Countries*. Washington, D.C.: Center for Global Development. [www.cgdev.org/content/publications/detail/2913].

Moss, Todd, Gunilla Pettersson, and Nic van de Walle. 2006. "An Aid-Institutions Paradox? A Review Essay on Aid Dependency and State Building in Sub-Saharan Africa." Working Paper 74. Center for Global Development, Washington, D.C. [www.cgdev.org/content/publications/detail/5646].

OECD–DAC (Organisation for Economic Co-operation and Development–Development Assistance Committee). Creditor Reporting System database. [www.oecd.org/dataoecd/50/17/5037721.htm].

Rodrik, Dani. 2007. *One Economics, Many Recipes*. Princeton, N.J.: Princeton University Press.

UN Millennium Project. 2005. *Toward Universal Primary Education: Investments, Incentives, and Institutions*. Task Force on Education and Gender Equality. New York: Earthscan.

White House. 2007. "Fact Sheet: Today's Education Announcement." Press Release. September 24. [www.whitehouse.gov/news/releases/2007/09/20070924-3.html].